Advanced Praise

In my opinion trading education is delivered in two styles: quantitative and qualitative. The vast majority of information in the trading universe is quantitative—"hard-coded" information that can be replicated by the majority. However, successful trading only comes about by an understanding of qualitative learning—how you can readily teach someone to learn to lose when it goes against everything we're brought up to believe. Brent's "Just One Piece of Advice" section is one of the best attempts to get this qualitative message across. Take it. Read it. Then read it again and again.

Nick Radge
Trader and Adviser (AFSL 288200)
Author of Adaptive Analysis
www.thechartist.com.au

This book cries out to be placed in any trader's library. Brent does a superb job of outlining, exploring and evaluating the current state of position sizing algorithms. As successful traders know, money management is one of the three pillars of trading success. He also provides a unique trading plan. A great book!

Ray Barros
Professional Trader and Fund Manager
Author of The Nature of Trends

This book is a "must-read" for anybody approaching the world of trading but also for skilled traders. I've read many books but this is the one I wished I had found when I was starting this adventure. Brent addresses exactly what a trader should really focus on.

Andrea Unger
Winner of the World Cup Championship of Futures Trading®️ 2008 & 2009

Normally when asked to review a book, I will skim through it and make a few comments. With this book, I just kept reading—I couldn't stop! Brent has an amazing ability to tell it like it is. His "Just One Piece of Advice" section is brilliant, and worth the price of the book many times over. If you have a genuine deep desire to be a consistently profitable trader and want to learn what traders really need to know as opposed to what most think they need to know, do yourself a favor and read this—please!

Stuart McPhee
Trader
Author of Trading in a Nut Shell

In my 25 years in the market I have read and seen just about every trading book there is. Very few get to the crux of trading like Brent has. Get it. Read it. This is not your typical trading book, this is a comprehensive book written by a real trader for traders, everyday people who are serious about becoming successful traders.

John (JR) Robertson
Director, I-Deal Financial Group

Crawling in the right direction beats running in the wrong direction every time and *Universal Principles of Successful Trading* will definitely get you heading in the right direction. Straight forward language, simple concepts and emphasis given where emphasis is needed. I wish this book was around when I started out because to master the markets now all you have to do is master this book.

Alan Hull
MPM 070917 *Trader and Fund Manager*
Printed in Singapore *Author of* Active Investing

When Brent asked me to review his new book *The Universal Principles of Successful Trading* I was both excited and curious. Having read his first book and recommended it to many of my clients I knew to expect something big. Brent is one of the very few authors who actually puts into practice the strategies he espouses, which lends great credibility to his words. He provides the most comprehensive approach to the various strategies of money management I've ever seen. A must read for anyone serious about trading.

David Montuoro
Futures Broker
Director, Bellmont Securities

Concise, to the point, and relevant for gaining the trading skills and strategies needed to maneuver in today's marketplace, Brent provides a clear road map on how to emulate the elite traders who consistently win over the long-term. Forget the hype you hear about trading and get this book. Read it, read it and read it again. And then study it until your eyeballs drop out. Brent keeps it real and if you can too then you may just find yourself in the exclusive 10 percent winner's circle! This book is destined to become a trading classic.

Steve Mater
CFD Business Development, MF Global

In his first book Brent hits the nail on the head with a down to earth, no nonsense explanation of what you need to be a successful active trader. I haven't seen a more practical guidebook for traders in over 20 years in the financial markets. If you want to stop being in the 90 percent of traders who lose and join the elite 10 percent who win, then I suggest you throw out all your other textbooks and read this book from cover to cover. This is a book written for traders by a trader and is the obvious starting point for a successful trading career.

Tony Makowiak
Head of Dealing, Aliom Pty Ltd

The Universal Principles of Successful Trading

Essential Knowledge for All Traders in All Markets

The Universal Principles of Successful Trading

Essential Knowledge for All Traders in All Markets

BRENT PENFOLD

WILEY

John Wiley & Sons (Asia) Pte. Ltd.

Other Wiley Editorial Offices

John Wiley & Sons, 111 River Street, Hoboken, NJ 07030, USA

John Wiley & Sons, The Atrium, Southern Gate, Chichester, West Sussex, P019 8SQ, United Kingdom

John Wiley & Sons (Canada) Ltd., 5353 Dundas Street West, Suite 400, Toronto, Ontario, M9B 6HB, Canada

John Wiley & Sons Australia Ltd, 42 McDougall Street, Milton, Queensland 4064, Australia

Wiley-VCH, Boschstrasse 12, D-69469 Weinheim, Germany

Library of Congress Cataloging-in-Publication Data

ISBN 978-0-470-82580-8

Typeset in 10/12pt New-Baskerville by Thomson Digital
Printed and bound by CPI Group (UK) Ltd, Croydon, CR0 4YY

C9780470825808_021024

To my beautiful wife Katia, who has given me the two greatest gifts a husband could hope for, two beautiful little boys, Beau and Boston.

CONTENTS

ACKNOWLEDGMENTS

Although this is my book, and mine alone, its contents and richness of information are not mine alone. Within these pages, you will meet a number of elite traders, whom I call the Market Masters. They are successful traders who have generously agreed to share their experiences and success with you. Their experiences and their advice are their content, not mine, and I'd like to thank them for agreeing to participate in the book.

Some of these Market Masters I personally know, many I don't. I'd just like to take this opportunity to acknowledge my gratitude to a number of these Market Masters who generously introduced me to some of the other traders.

First to Daryl Guppy, who introduced me to Greg Morris. In addition, Daryl nearly helped me to share with you both John Bollinger and Martin Pring's thoughts. But unfortunately John was on a tight schedule at the time of writing, and was unable to participate, but he did say he thought the outline of this book was excellent. And Martin Pring was too committed due to him finalizing a new book and preparing for an imminent workshop. So a big thank you to Daryl for not only his own participation but also for introducing my book project to Greg Morris and for his warm and complimentary foreword.

I'd just like to also acknowledge my thanks to Larry Williams, who generously introduced me to Tom DeMark, Lee Gettess, Brian Schad, and Andrea Unger. Without Larry, you and I would not have had the opportunity to hear from these successful traders, so a big thank you to Larry for both his introductions and his contribution.

In turn, I'd like to give a big thank you to Andrea Unger for both his contribution and introducing me to both Kevin Davey and Michael Cook.

And I'd also like to take this opportunity to thank the rest of my Market Masters: Ray Barros, Mark D. Cook, Michael Cook, Tom Demark, Lee Gettess, Richard Melki, Geoff Morgan, Greg Morris, Nick Rage, Brian Schad, and Dar Wong for generously accepting my invitation to participate and help make this a better book.

PREFACE

Generally everyone loses in trading.

And I mean everyone.

Regardless of whether people trade forex, shares, commodities, options, warrants, futures, or contracts for difference, everyone loses. Even the elite traders who do win lose on plenty of their trades. There is no such thing as 100 percent accuracy.

And here is the sobering truth about active trading: fewer (and possibly many fewer) than 10 percent of active traders are consistently profitable over the long run. This may surprise you given the marketing hype that surrounds trading.

Despite the perceived glamor, it's a disappointing truth that very few traders are consistently profitable over the longer term. And this goes for all active traders, regardless of which markets, time frames, or instruments they choose to trade. Very few traders are consistently profitable over the longer term.

You can ignore all those dinner party conversations where you have sat in envy listening to others recount the killings they've made in the markets. You can ignore the sound of their triumphant voices as they retell their trading victories. These market warriors are more often trading chumps than trading champs. They're spinners of half truths. They're masters of deflection. They're hollow people who will only recount their victories and not their disasters. They will not share their misfortunes. They will not remember their follies. They will not talk about their big losses. And believe me most of them do have big losses, because everyone does. They are people to be ignored.

That's the bad news.

The good news is that the elite traders who do win don't necessary know any trading secrets. Certainly, some will have very interesting trade setups and entry, stop, and exit techniques. However, there are other elite traders who use surprisingly simple ideas. Very simple ideas. Nonetheless, regardless of the individual trading techniques the elite traders use, their overall success can be traced back to the universal principles of successful trading. Principles that are universal to all consistently profitable traders—the few 10 percent of traders who win. These principles are common among the winners. They distinguish the few winners from the majority who lose.

Their profitability is not dependent upon a single magic indicator or secretive trading technique. Their profitability is not dependent upon the market or markets they choose to trade, nor is it dependent upon the time frame or time frames they choose to monitor. Nor is their profitability dependent upon the financial instrument they choose to trade. No, their success can be traced directly back to the universal principles of successful trading. Principles that most losing traders don't know.

If you are serious about becoming a consistently profitable trader, then you will need to learn, understand, embrace, and implement the universal principles that every consistently profitable trader understands and follows. To ignore them is to guarantee your trading demise.

Regardless of what or how you trade, to be consistently profitable you need to adhere to some basic first principles of trading. You need to remember that a market is a market is a market and that a chart is a chart is a chart. So regardless which individual markets you may choose to trade, or which time frame you choose to follow, or which security you choose to trade, what comes first in profitable trading is adopting and embracing a good process of trading. The selection of which markets to monitor and which instruments to trade is secondary to the adoption and implementation of a good process of trading, and those are what the universal principles of successful trading are all about.

So if you wish to succeed in trading, you will need to understand and accept the simple truth that what distinguishes a group of successful traders from the majority who lose is not their individual entry and exit techniques but their adoption of the universal principles.

Losing traders don't know this. They are unaware of the universal principles. They continue to trade and lose in total ignorance. They continue to focus on looking for that perfect risk-free 100 percent accurate entry technique. They're unaware that there are key principles to adhere to when trading.

In my opinion, regardless whether you choose to trade the currency, equity, interest rate, energy, metals, grains, or meat markets, the universal principles of successful trading are essential to your success. And this goes for everyone regardless of whether you are a day trader, or a short-term, medium-term, or longer-term positional trader. The universal principles of successful trading are essential to your success. There is no escaping them. Regardless of whether you choose to trade options, CFDs, futures, shares, margin forex, or warrants, the universal principles of successful trading are essential to your success. I cannot say this enough. And regardless of whether you choose to base your trades upon either traditional technical analysis, fundamental analysis, Elliott wave, W.D. Gann, candlesticks, Fibonacci, indicators, mechanical systems, seasonals, geometry, pattern recognition, or astrology, the universal principles of successful trading are essential to your success.

In a nutshell, if you trade, regardless of where, how, or why you do it, the universal principles of successful trading are essential to your success. To ignore them is to ignore the truth. To ignore them is the same as ignoring the losses in your trading account.

In my opinion there is only one universal truth in trading. And it's this. If you can get the basic first principles of trading right, then the profits will follow. They must. Period. Full stop. However, if you ignore the universal basic principles of trading, then you will continue to lose. Period. No negotiation. No arguments. No ifs or buts. You will continue to lose. Period.

And wouldn't you like to stop losing in such a consistent and miserable manner? Wouldn't you like to learn what actually makes a trader consistently profitable? Wouldn't you like to start making money in a consistent and reliable fashion? Wouldn't you like to stop jumping between failed trading methodologies and actually learn what makes a trading methodology robust and reliable? If so, then this book is for you.

If you wish to make money trading, then I am going to show you how by getting you back to the basics by teaching you the universal principles of successful trading.

But first a number of warnings. If you're here looking for a new entry, stop, or exit technique then this book is not for you. If you're here looking for a new technique to analyze market structure, then this book is not for you. And if you're here looking for a simple solution to get you profitable, then this book is not for you and nor can I help you. Although trading and the universal principles, once you know them, are relatively simple, they are not easy. There are no easy shortcuts to achieving consistent long-term profitable trading.

If you are looking for certainty in your trading, then this book is not for you and nor can I help you. There is no certainty in the markets and there is certainly no certainty in trading. There is only 100 percent probability. If you're a person who can only function in an environment that offers a high level of certainty and security, like being in a secure relationship or secure job, then trading is not for you.

If you are an intellectual who rarely admits to being wrong, then trading is not for you, because the markets have a regular tendency to belittle you and make you wrong. Intellectuals struggle with not knowing the correct answer, not being in control, and being regularly proved wrong.

However, if you are prepared to do the work, trading can offer you unlimited possibilities. Today, trading is as egalitarian as it can be. It lets everyone compete equally. There are no barriers to entry. Today, institutions no longer have a competitive advantage over the private trader. There are no limits to foolishness when institutional traders can be just as ignorant and clueless about what works in the market as the private trader. There are no ceilings to success when private traders can achieve profitability comparable to or better than some of the best institutional traders. Trading today is the ubiquitous level playing field.

If you are patient, if you are prepared to do the work, and if you have an open mind, then I believe the universal principles will transform your trading. But it will be up to you, you alone, and no one else. Take responsibility for your actions and your actions will transform your trading account.

Good luck, good studying, and sensible trading.

Brent Penfold
Sydney, Australia

FOREWORD

It took me more than 30 years to get enough spare savings together to become involved in the market. In that 30 years, I had lots of enjoyment and adventure, including mining underground, operating heavy machinery while building roads in very remote parts of the Northern Territory in Australia, working in the Torres Strait Islands, and administering Aboriginal communities in the desert. My parents regarded this as largely a waste of a good university humanities education. Unfortunately, money slipped through my fingers like water into the sand after a desert rainstorm. It was not helped by my expensive addiction to reading new books.

The traditional road to wealth in Australia is to buy a house—and then another. With a miserable $2,000 and a variegated work history, no bank manger regarded me as a good risk for a housing loan. I needed to make money work for me, rather than me working for money. Around this time, Warren Buffett was becoming a better-known name, and I fondly imagined I could turn $2,000 into a reasonable sum within a reasonable time if I bought shares in a business I knew something about.

So while living in the middle of the Australian desert I bought a blue-chip mining company. I watched its share price go up and down, delivering 30 percent returns and then taking them away. I collected one of those 30 percent returns and reinvested some of the money in another blue-chip mining company at its all-time high price, never to be achieved again in the 12 years before it was finally delisted. The amount was small, so I kept the stock to remind me why I was not an investor.

The desert is a hard environment, and you survive only by learning from the experience of others. I found the market was a similar harsh environment, and survival depended on learning from the experience of others who had taken the time to write.

Books about trading were difficult to come by, and in the vast expanse of the Australian desert, there were no other traders to talk to and learn from. I fed my long standing addiction to new books with mail-order books written by other traders, mainly from the U.S. (Most of them unfortunately were lost when my office was destroyed by flood in 1998. It's not just the market that gives and takes away.) With a spreadsheet on an Apple computer, I created rudimentary charts of price activity and learned how to understand what they were saying about the market and the activities of other traders and investors in the market.

Along the way I discovered, or learned, some of the universal principles that apply to trading. I wish I had had this book then, because it would have accelerated my market education. These principles are the core of every successful trader, although the mix and proportions are as diverse as the opportunities in the market. They are united by perhaps one common factor. It's not mentioned in this excellent coverage of the universal principles of trading, perhaps because it's so obvious that Brent Penfold, and the other traders he interviews, just assume it's natural and not worthy of note. Or perhaps it's ignored because it's not unique to trading success.

The common factor is a passion for the activity of trading. By common reckoning, it takes a minimum of 10,000 hours to become an expert in your chosen field. Brent Penfold and the traders in this book have multiples of tens of thousands of hours behind them, and these hours are further augmented by a passion for what they do. Successful traders have an aptitude and a passion. Mine started in the remote deserts of Australia, sparked initially by need. Brent found his in the dealing rooms. Others discover theirs in different locations and situations. This book is one of the results of Brent's passion for trading, for markets, and for helping others along the road to success in the market. If you aspire to the same passion, then this book will help you to identify the universal principles of trading no matter what your background.

Daryl Guppy
Trend Trading:
The 36 Strategies of The Chinese for Financial Traders
Shanghai, 2010

INTRODUCTION

This book came about for a number of reasons.

First, the success of my first book *Trading the SPI*[1] came as a surprise to me. The book was about trading the Australian "SPI" or Share Price Index futures contract. I knew for a fact that there weren't enough private SPI index futures traders to warrant the number of book sales. Although the local index futures contract was the single largest equity instrument in Australia, it was a contract dominated by institutions, not the small private trader. So my book's success was initially a mystery to me until I figured out why. And the why became the first reason for considering this book. You see, my first book was divided into three parts, and I believe the second part, which discussed the preparation necessary to become a successful trader, was the reason for the book's success. Traders had come to hear about its message and bought my book even though they weren't interested in trading the SPI index futures contract. They wanted to learn more about how to prepare themselves to become successful traders, because trading is trading and the principles discussed in part 2 were universal to all markets and all traders. I always thought part 2 was the book's best section and I believe it was responsible for the book's success. So the first reason for doing this book was to get its universal message on trader preparation, which I call the universal principles of successful trading, out to a wider audience.

As a sidebar to those of you who have read my first book *Trading the SPI*, much of what you're about to read you will have seen before, so I hope you will accept my apologies for going over familiar ground. However, I hope you can understand my desire to share my ideas with a wider audience. It's also not in my nature to make up content for the sake of content. I can only write about what I believe and what I do and what I know that works. And that is what I'm doing. So I hope this book, although parts will seem repetitive, will be an opportunity for me to reinforce to you the universal principles of successful trading.

The second reason came to me while I was in Singapore presenting at the Asian Traders and Investors Conference (ATIC). I was chatting with Stuart McPhee, an Australian share trader, educator, and author, who was sharing a story with me about how difficult it was for him to encourage people to purchase his book *Trading in a Nutshell*.[2] This surprised me because I rate Stuart's book highly, and said as much when I reviewed his second edition in the *Your Trader's Edge* magazine. Stuart shared with me the Singaporeans reluctance to purchase a book that had "Australian Shares" written on the front. They told Stuart they couldn't see the value in purchasing an "Australian" book since they lived in Singapore. Now although Stuart and I knew that a security is irrelevant to learning how to trade, since a chart is a chart and good trading habits take precedence over any particular market, for those new to trading, a reference to a foreign market on a book's cover can be a stumbling block. This became my second reason for doing this book. I wanted people who attended a presentation of mine, regardless of which country I presented in, to be able to purchase a book to learn more about how I approach trading.

Over the years I have been fortunate enough to be invited to present to traders in China, India, Singapore, Malaysia, Vietnam, Thailand, New Zealand, and of course Australia. And during my many presentations and workshops throughout Asia–Pacific, I have come to the clear realization that the markets do not discriminate between traders and their passports. All traders from all countries suffer equally in the tumultuous world of active trading. So I wanted a book that any trader, regardless of their geographic location, could purchase and learn what I thought was important to become a sustainable and consistently successful trader. I wanted to write a book that would transcend borders. I wanted a "borderless" book that anyone would find relevant. This became the second motivation behind this book.

The third reason was the challenge to write an outstanding "one-stop" book on how to become a successful trader. To give people a valuable resource guide for their trading, regardless of the market, time frame, instrument, or technique they preferred to trade.

By the end of this book, I will have given you a blueprint on how to become a consistently profitable trader that I wished I had been when I started out over 27 years ago. I would have certainly avoided many years of disappointment. When I joined Bank America as a trainee dealer back in 1983, I knew absolutely nothing about trading and the markets. And even after a few years of institutional trading experience, I was still ignorant about what actually worked, and it would take me many more years before I would realise it.

Since my first trade in 1983, I've probably tried just about every technique there is to trading. If there was a book, a seminar, a workshop, or a software program that could help my trading, I either bought it, attended it, or installed it. During the 1990s, in my quest to find an edge, I felt like I was walking through a revolving seminar door. I attended many well-regarded seminars. I attended the Turtles seminar with Russell Sands, learned PPS with Curtis Arnold, studied geometry with Bryce Gilmore, and attended Larry Williams' Million Dollar Challenge (MDC) seminar. I picked up useful bites here and there, and it was Larry Williams' MDC seminar that reinforced my work with short-term mechanical price patterns.

As a trader, I trade the global index and currency futures over multiple time frames with simple mechanical models. I trade possibly the two most liquid and volatile market segments on the planet: indices and currencies. I trade a portfolio of 14 markets. For index futures, I trade the SPI, Nikkei, Taiwan, Hang Seng, Dax, Stoxx50, FTSE, Mini-Nasdaq, and E-Mini S&P500 index futures contract. For the currency futures, I trade the five main currency pairs against the US dollar, which includes the euro, British pound, Japanese yen, Swiss franc, and Australian dollar. I trade my portfolio on an almost 24/7 basis, where a day doesn't go by without me placing an order for either an index or currency future somewhere in the world.

I'm principally a pattern trader. Apart from a 200-day moving average, which I use to determine the dominant trend, I focus purely on price. And please do not read too much into my use of a 200-day moving average. There is nothing magical about me using 200 days. It's just a length I have always used. I don't even know whether it is the optimal length to determine the dominant trend, nor do I care. The last thing I would want to do in my trading is start using "optimised" variables because that's one of the quickest routes to the poorhouse.

And please understand that I don't use the 200-day moving average for finding my trade setups. I don't use it to find entry, stop, or exit levels. I just use it to determine the dominant trend because I prefer not to place trend trades against it.

From the outset, I want to make it clear that I do not consider myself a trading expert or an expert on the markets. Neither do I believe such a person exists (except possibly Larry Williams, the world-renowned trader and educator, who will trade live in front of his students while teaching). However, there is one area in which I will rate myself against most people, and that is my experience in losing money. If you want to learn the common mistakes people make in trading, I'm your man. I have more cuts, bruises, and bumps than any other trader, so I feel comfortable in claiming to be an expert in them. However, although I've hit many speed humps, I have also managed to survive and navigate my way through the confusing world of technical analysis. Hopefully, I'll help you to survive as well.

Now, although I trade 14 global index and currency futures on an almost 24/7 basis, I don't really commit a lot of time actually to "trade" these markets. I'm not a slave to my computer, where I have to watch the markets tick by tick. I trade off daily bars and it only takes me an hour a day to collect all my data, run my models and forward my orders to my broker. Remember I'm a mechanical trader, trading simple mechanical solutions. I have programmed my trading models into Visual Basic for Applications (VBA) for Excel to produce my orders automatically. I email my orders to my broker. Once my broker confirms receipt of all my orders (by return email), I relax for the next 24 hours. My broker operates a 24-hour trading desk, where my orders are well looked after.

As a mechanical trader, I trade with a positive expectancy. I use a trading strategy that delivers me clear buy and sell signals, which I consistently follow. I trust my methodologies to return long-term gains despite any short-term losses. Apart from running my website and trading, I spend most of my time researching and programming up new ideas.

As I've said, I'm no expert; however, over the years I've discovered what really counts for being successful in trading and what has really allowed me to succeed. And it's my hope that by the end of this book you will know what I know, and you will really understand that what separates the winners from the losers are the universal principles of successful trading.

As I've mentioned, it's my objective to make this a one-stop trading book, which will become a valuable resource for your trading. If you're really serious about making money from the markets, then I don't think you'll be disappointed.

From my experience, one of the reasons so many people lose in trading is that they believe what they read in trading books and magazines and what they see on charting programs. It's an unfortunate truth that most of what is written about trading or incorporated into trading programs does not work. It only makes money for the author, publisher, and software developer.

My point is, if you aren't already, please become a skeptic when you read trading books, including this one. Just because I or another author writes something, it does not necessarily make it true. I'm a big believer that all traders should welcome all opinions and ideas they hear, see, or read about trading. Every trader should embrace the choices out there in trading. However, I believe all traders, including you, should also reserve the right to determine whether an idea you have heard, seen, or read has value for you in your hands. What may work for me or another author may not necessarily work for you. After welcoming all ideas on trading you will need to first independently validate the idea for yourself before you can pass judgment. Please do not rely on another's opinion about trading, including mine. Please remain a skeptic at all times when reading trading books, like this one, and please learn how to validate ideas first before you accept the belief has value. It pays to be a skeptic in this business of trading.

Since the introduction of CFDs and margin FX, active trading has exploded among small private traders. People can now trade just about any domestic or international share, index, currency, or commodity of their choosing from the comfort of their home PC. Between CFDs, traditional futures, and the globalization of financial markets you can now access any market you choose to. And with the knowledge you will gain from learning the universal principles of successful trading contained in this book, I believe you will do so with purpose and confidence.

And please remember that what I write is only my opinion and should not be accepted as the truth. If you like what you read then please first independently validate the ideas yourself. I hope this book will be of benefit to you and help you discover what really makes a trader successful over the longer term. If you have any questions, please do not hesitate to contact me through my website, www.IndexTrader.com.au.

THE UNIVERSAL PRINCIPLES

In this book, you will learn the foundations to successful trading. In time, you will discover that these principles are universal to all traders and all markets. Regardless what markets you trade—whether it be equities, indices, currencies, bonds, or commodities, regardless what time frame you monitor, whether it be day trading, short-term, medium-term, or long-term trading, and regardless which security you trade to gain an exposure to your preferred market—shares, CFDs, futures, forex, options, or warrants, trading is trading. Full stop. Which market, time frame, or instrument you choose is secondary to the process of good trading, which this book explores in depth through the universal principles of successful trading.

These principles will outline the essential steps I believe all successful traders must navigate before they place their first order. The principles will outline the importance of being process oriented in trading regardless whether one has a preference for discretionary or mechanical trading (in discretionary trading, a trader will make the final decision whether to trade; in mechanical trading, a trader must follow his or her trade plan's exact entry, stop, and exit rules without fear or favor, without hesitation or discretion). The principles will take you through the nuts and bolts of practical trading covering key concepts such as risk of ruin, (my) Holy Grail, expectancy, opportunities, validation, TEST, money management, methodology, and psychology.

Chapter 8 on money management alone is worth the price of this book. Once you learn where I place the importance of money management, you'll understand why it's one of the largest chapters. I don't believe you'll find another book so accessible to the average reader (who isn't armed with a Ph.D. in mathematics) that has such a breadth of examination and depth of practical investigation into various money management strategies.

Regardless of your trading experience, I believe all traders will benefit from the universal principles. They explore what is necessary to be prepared and well positioned to succeed.

Following the universal principles, you'll meet a group of successful traders. I refer to them as the Market Masters, successful traders who are prepared to give you one piece of advice based upon their years of experience and success. Some of them you will recognize, while others you will not have heard of. Some are recent and current trading champions, the new young guns of trading. Some are market legends, the wise heads who have had a significant impact on the world of technical analysis and who have been trading the markets since the 1960s. One Market Master is possibly one of the largest individual E-Mini S&P500 traders in the world. Some are prolific authors and are the biggest names in trader education. Some trade investment funds. Some are private traders. They represent a diverse group of traders from around the world, from Singapore, Hong Kong, Italy, the U.K., America, and Australia. All of them are successful. All of them have survived the Global Financial Crisis. And all of them have generously agreed to offer you one singularly powerful piece of advice to help you toward your trading success.

By the end of this book, I hope you'll have acquired the knowledge and confidence to consider whether you're prepared to be involved in active trading. For many of you who are honest with yourselves, you will decide not to trade. You will determine that you don't have the heart to put in the hard work necessary to prepare yourself for trading. If you are one of those, then congratulations because you will be saving yourself a lot of money and heartache.

For those of you who think you can skip the universal principles, then I cannot help you. If you're not prepared actually to listen to what I'm saying, then you deserve the results you get. All I can suggest is to remember this book and write yourself a diary note to revisit it in, say, 12 months. Possibly, you'll be in a better position then to begin listening with both ears.

For those of you who realise there are no free lunches and no shortcuts along the road to successful trading, then I wish you all the best. You know it's all hard work ahead of you. And please remember there is no rush to get involved in active trading. There is no gold medal for being the first one in. Take your time. Work carefully through all the steps. Be thorough to the point of obsession in validating your ideas and remember to take a break from time to time because it does get exhausting, believe me. Once you reach the summit, you'll remember where you started, and you'll be pleased you took the long route. Your reward for effort will be entrance into the winners' circle, a rare membership most never attain.

Let's get started.

NOTES

1. Penfold, Brent, *Trading the SPI* (Wrightbooks, John Wiley, 2005).
2. McPhee, Stuart, *Trading in a Nutshell* (Wrightbooks, John Wiley, 2001).

CHAPTER 1

A Reality Check

Trading's only real secret is . . .

The best loser is the long-term winner.

—Phantom of the Pits

Believe it or not, this is probably the only real secret behind successful trading. Although it may seem to you to be a cliché, I hope by the end of this book you'll understand why it's a core truth behind a sustainable career in trading.

In my opinion, Phantom of the Pits' quote encapsulates what is required to succeed. Most traders are bad losers. They hate taking losses, moving stops and looking for any excuse to keep a trade alive, finding all sorts of reasons to rationalize their actions. While they have money left in their accounts, poor traders will ignore a losing position until it becomes so large they can no longer ignore it and are forced to stop themselves out at a catastrophic loss. They delay the inevitable while there is still hope that the trade will turn around. While the trade remains open, there is still a chance they can be proved right. While the trade remains open they do not have to acknowledge they're wrong because they haven't taken the loss. People hate to acknowledge they're wrong. Most people are only bad traders because they are bad losers. Learn to take losses as an integral part of trading and you will have taken your first concrete step towards success. Continue as a bad loser and you'll be off to the poor house. Successful long-term trading will require you to be a good loser.

In my own trading, losing seems to be what I spend most of my time doing. In my short-term trading I only average about 50 percent winners, while my medium-term trend trading sits about 30 percent. So since I don't win very often, I have to be a good loser to survive in trading, otherwise my account would be empty and I wouldn't be able to trade. I hope you can become a good loser.

1

As an exercise, it's certainly worth going back over all your trades and seeing what your results would have been if you had followed a simple stop rule. A simple stop rule for long trades (and the reverse for short trades) could be to exit on a break of the lowest low within the last three bars. Alternatively, you could use a break of the previous week's low to stop yourself out. It doesn't matter which stop you use as long as it's consistent with the time frame you trade. Now, you may find that it doesn't turn your losses into profits, but I'm sure it will show that your account would have looked healthier than what it was. Believe me, it pays to be a good loser.

If you're currently profitable in your trading, you can skip this little discussion. If you're not, heads up, pens down, and eyes off the market! This discussion is for your immediate benefit. Please cease all trading.

If you're currently trading without profits and are attempting to battle your way out of a drawdown—that is, attempting to come back from a loss in your trading capital—the best thing you can do right now is to walk away from your trading account. I know it's hard—especially when walking away feels like an admission of failure. Don't worry about it. It's not failure. You'll only be suspending your trading until you can introduce positive expectancy. Don't be despondent. Be thrilled that real help is here. There is no shame in losing—it happens to everyone. I've been there many times and pride myself on being good at it (remember, the best loser is the long-term winner!).

If you're a loser I'd like you to listen carefully to what I'm about to say. A huge reason you're losing is that your trading methodology doesn't work. It's not what's in your head that is holding you back. Despite the overwhelming message many trading educators would have you believe, its not psychology that is your nemesis. It can certainly be a challenge, but it's not your nemesis.

It's your methodology. It doesn't work. Although your trading account is telling you it's poor, you're ignoring its message. And I can understand why. You've no doubt read numerous books and attended many trading seminars that say your method or ideas can be used for trading but unfortunately they can't. Take it from your trading account—your method is letting you down. The reason may not be that it's totally without merit; however, as a whole, the reason your method doesn't work is that it doesn't have an edge and its expectancy has not been validated.

You need to validate your methodology's expectancy. I'm sure what you will find will mirror your trading account. You will find it's negative. Furthermore, if you had independently validated your methodology before placing a trade, you would have never traded with it. You would have thrown it out and recommenced your search for a trading methodology with an edge that can be correctly validated to offer a positive expectancy.

So take a deep breath and walk away from trading for the time being. You're about to embark on a quest for real trading knowledge, which, among other things, will show you how to validate a trading idea correctly.

And I should have said not to worry if you are currently losing, because you're actually in good company. Let me share an unfortunate truth with you. *Over 90 percent of all traders lose!* Let me share with you my understanding on why this is.

WHY DO 90 PERCENT OF TRADERS LOSE?

The simple answer to why 90 percent of traders lose is ignorance.

While many analysts argue that psychology is the main reason, I maintain that the deeper answers are gullibility and laziness. It's human laziness that causes traders to look for the line of least resistance. Why work harder when you can work smarter, right? Unfortunately, this can make traders gullible, and they start to believe what they read, what they hear, and what they install on their computers. This is because traders desperately want to believe there is a simple path to trading riches. And it's this line of least resistance that prevents them from correctly validating what they think may work in the markets.

Even though traders may have read a great many books and attended a lot of seminars, they're still ignorant. It may come as a surprise, but not many books or seminars reveal what actually works in trading. This is because many authors and educators are ignorant themselves about what actually works; they're usually failed traders. If you look at the vast bulk of financial literature and various products, most rely on the "greater fool" theory. That is, the customers or purchasers are the "greater fools" but they don't know it! Remember, just because a trading idea is either written down, or delivered by a PowerPoint presentation, does not make it true.

However, if you have the correct knowledge, and the patience to validate a trading idea, you will not be ignorant—I intend to provide you with this knowledge. While you may not be making money in the early stages, at least you'll be knowledgeable enough to realize that it's because you don't yet know enough to succeed.

Psychology

Psychology is often provided as an excuse for the traders' failure to succeed. However, while it can be a contributing factor, psychology is not the sole reason, as many commentators suggest. To succeed in trading, you need to cover three important areas:

- methodology
- money management
- psychology.

They're (almost) equally important and I'll cover each in greater depth later. At this point, you just need to be aware there are three components to successful trading.

Whenever I make presentations I usually ask the audience which part of trading they believe is the most important:

- methodology—the analysis and trading plan behind why you buy and sell
- money management—the amount of money you commit to trades
- psychology—having the discipline to follow your trading plan.

Interestingly, most people raise their hands at psychology. I'm not surprised by this response because the overriding message from most trading material available is that psychology is the hardest part of trading and the key to success.

The usual message is along the lines of "the only thing that separates the winners from the losers is psychology, nothing else" . . . "the winners have no special trading skills, no special trading secrets, no secret formulas to win in trading" . . . "what sets winners apart from losers is their psychology" . . . "winners think differently than losers."

I disagree with this. What holds the losers back is their ignorance of knowing and validating what works in their hands. Although psychology is important, I believe money management and methodology rank higher.

I mentioned earlier that ignorance, gullibility, and laziness are the main reasons 90 percent of traders lose. To show you how these three evils manifest themselves in trading behavior, I'll explore in some depth the common mistakes many traders make during their first three years of trading. I'll group the common mistakes under the three main building blocks of successful trading: methodology, money management, and trader's psychology.

As an aside, you already know I don't claim to be an expert on trading, but I'm certainly well qualified to discuss these common mistakes because I've been guilty of making all of them at some point!

COMMON MISTAKES—YEAR ONE

Welcome to your first year of trading. If you ever had any doubt at all about your level of ignorance then rest assured that during your first year of trading you are "King Ignorant!"

Methodology

- Listening to others and following tips
- Reacting to the nightly news

- Asking others for their opinions
- Averaging entry levels
- Failing to use stops
- Failing to have a trade plan

Money management
- What is money management?

Psychology
- Trading for excitement
- Trading for revenge or to get even

Methodology
Listening to others and following tips

When most people start trading, they will invariably listen to others and follow tips. This is a recipe for disappointment. Sometimes the tip may be successful, but over the longer term, it's a loser's game. You should only ever trade because of what you think, not because of what others say in the corridor or over a dinner table.

Reacting to the nightly news

Often, inexperienced traders will hear some news, such as that most companies are reporting good earnings or the quarterly GDP growth numbers were ahead of forecast, and the next day they'll go long only to be stopped out at a loss. It takes a long time to understand that once the news arrives in our living rooms in the evening, the information is already old. The market has already anticipated and reacted to the news and new traders don't realize this.

Asking others for their opinions

New traders often seek out the opinions of others. If they have no idea where the market is heading, they'll usually ask their brokers, friends and family for their opinion. Unfortunately, unless they're full-time traders, the views of others on the market may not be much better than those of new traders.

Averaging entry levels

New traders are usually the world's worst losers. They hate losing and will try to avoid it at all costs. The usual response is to "average" out their entry levels. For example, say you buy a share at $6.60, and straight away it falls to $6.00. New traders often convince themselves there were good reasons the share went down to $6.00. They also convince themselves there are even better reasons it should rebound. They then purchase additional shares at $6.00, averaging down their entry level to $6.30, and hoping to benefit from the expected rebound. But in this circumstance, it's unlikely the share will rebound, and all those traders have done is compounded their losses. While being long at $6.30 may sound better than being long at $6.60, it doesn't when you've laid out twice as much money. "Averaging" entry levels goes against being the "'best loser''—it makes the new trader the "worst loser."

Failing to use stops

Unless they've had the benefit of some trading experience, new traders rarely trade with stops or preplanned exit points. It doesn't occur to them that they could lose until it's too late and too costly.

Failing to have a trade plan

All of that can be summarized under this most common mistake. Listening to tips, reacting to the nightly news, asking others for their opinions, averaging entry levels and failing to use stops are clear signs that traders are trading without a trade plan. Remember, trading without a trade plan will catch up with you sooner or later.

Money Management
What is money management?

Usually, the only concern for first-time traders is that they have enough money to initiate a trade. The idea of money management is given little thought. New traders usually have no concept of their "risk of ruin" (which I will explain later) brought about by risking too large a slice of their account balance on any one trade.

Recalling where I place the importance of money management, you can understand how making this common mistake can be, and usually is, fatal for new traders.

Psychology
Trading for excitement

One of the reasons many people trade is that it provides an exciting distraction from what may be a relatively orderly and conservative life.

Trading gets the heart racing and adrenalin flowing. Even if they're losing, traders often keep at it because the next trade is always an exciting mystery—will they win or will they lose?

Trading for revenge or to get even

When they lose, traders often get angry and want to get "even" with the market. Losing is like receiving two blows: one to your pride and one to your wallet. And when new traders get pushed they want to push right back! Revenge rather than logic motivates their trading. Being emotional is a common behavior for new traders; however, it's also a shortcut to the poorhouse!

COMMON MISTAKES—YEAR TWO

If traders manage to survive their first year of trading without losing all their money, most will enter their second year with ignorant resolve and unwarranted optimism. During the first year, most were no more than accidental traders; however, it's during the second year that they become a genuine danger to themselves. As they start to gain a little knowledge, or so they think, second-year traders embark upon a determined campaign of self-destruction.

Methodology
- Believing what is read and heard
- Believing technical analysis is the only answer
- Falling into the prediction trap
- Believing more is best
- Picking tops and bottoms
- Believing "paper trading" will help
- Failing to see the trend or respect stops
- Taking profits too early
- Failing to use a trade plan
- "Coat tailing" other traders
- Switching methodologies
- Switching gurus
- Switching markets
- Switching time frames
- Switching client advisers

Money management
- Overtrading

Psychology

- Becoming addicted to the market
- Being impatient
- Having unrealistic expectations
- Being a rationalist

Methodology
Believing what is read and heard

A common mistake traders make is to believe what they read or hear about trading. If it's written or said, most traders believe it must be true, only to find out later, when they lose money, that it's not. Traders want to believe it's true because it offers the line of least resistance to easy money. Remember—the only thing that makes any trading idea true is your own validation, no one else's.

Believing technical analysis is the only answer

Technical analysis broadly refers to the study of past prices to gain insight into future price movements. During the second year of trading, however, many people make the common mistake of believing technical analysis is all they need to make money, ignoring money management and psychology.

Believing more is best

As relatively new traders embrace technical analysis, they fall into the common mistake of believing complexity will provide the answers. Instead of realizing technical analysis is not enough by itself, they believe adding more technical indicators is the answer.

When purchasing charting software, traders invariably fall into the trap of lighting up their screens with as many indicators as possible. However, attempting to explain every move in the market is a recipe for disaster. The story is familiar—if the indicator didn't predict a strong gap up, they'll search for one that would have. This is known as the first stage of "curve fitting," in which novice traders will attempt to mould their collection of indicators to fit past data.

Believing "paper trading" will help

Many inexperienced traders make the common mistake of believing "paper trading" will help. Paper trading is the process of recording trades (on paper) according to your own trading rules. Once you're happy with the "paper" results, you can start with real cash. However, although the intention is good, I believe it is a foolhardy exercise.

The problem with paper trading is that it does not reflect the real world of trading. It doesn't provide an arm's length, neutral but fair "policing" element to observe and independently check your paper trades. It's open to fiddling. When paper trading, you can always erase a losing trade and revise your past actions because you suddenly notice some filter you hadn't seen before. It's amazing what people will do to protect their sensitive egos, and I can tell you that in my 27 years of trading experience I have never met a losing "paper" trader!

Falling into the prediction trap

My first influence in trading was Elliott wave and then geometry. This lasted for 15 years until I changed to simple pattern trading. However, during my 15-year preoccupation with Elliott wave and geometry, I reckon I'm almost at the head of this class based on this fault! What do I mean by "prediction trap"? Simply, trying to determine where the market is heading, or having a view of where it's going, how far it's going, and when it's going. Any theory on market behavior that suggests markets move to a preordained pattern is a predictive theory. Two of the highest-profile predictive theories are Elliott wave and W.D. Gann.

Predictive theories maintain that traders can predetermine market direction and turning points. Novice traders are seduced into believing it's possible to consistently know where the markets will head. This is appealing because it holds out the possibility of certainty in trading by knowing when to buy low and when to sell high. Once again it provides a line of least resistance to easy trading success, which is very appealing to new traders.

Unfortunately, many traders don't realize these predictive theories may not be the most effective way to trade until it's too late. It's not until they're poorer for the experience that they begin to question the ideas presented by these theories. Once they do, and begin validating the theories according to their own interpretation, they soon discover that the theories, in their own hands, have a negative expectancy.

Picking tops and bottoms

Most traders make the common mistake of looking to sell tops and buy bottoms. When a market makes a new all-time high, inexperienced traders generally look to sell it. Selling what are perceived to be over-valued prices (picking tops) seems logical and smart, and to consider the opposite is unthinkable. Unfortunately, traders can't help themselves and commonly make the mistake of buying extreme weakness and selling extreme strength.

Failing to see the trend

Failing to see the trend is usually compounded by the previous common mistake. The end result is the same as traders attempt to swim against the tide by trading against the underlying market trend. However, it's not that easy to define the trend, because it can vary depending on the time frames used to identify setups (such as monthly, weekly, or daily) and trade plans (such as weekly, daily, or hourly).

Failing to respect stops

If traders are lucky enough to trade with stops during the second year, a common mistake many make is occasionally to move stops to avoid being taken out of trades. This tendency is part of the fear of being proved wrong. The consequence is that traders end up losing more money than if they had left the stop in its original position. Moving your stops makes you a bad loser and, therefore, a long-term loser!

Taking profits too early

On the one hand, traders can fail to respect their stops by moving them further away. On the other hand, traders are also fearful that what profit they do have will be snatched away. This anxiety makes traders take their profits too early. Traders are not only bad losers, but they are also bad winners! Is it any wonder that most people fail at trading when they are so bad at executing the two key engagement points with the markets, their stops and exits?

Being slow to takes losses and quick to take profits is a recipe for disaster. It takes many years of failure before traders come to realise successful and profitable trading lies in being quick to take losses and slow to bank profits!

Failing to use a trade plan

Many traders make the common mistake of not trading with a clearly defined trade plan. They rarely trade with clearly defined and unambiguous rules to determine their entry level, stop level, and exit level.

"Coat tailing" other traders

Even though most traders have the resolve and determination to continue trading into their second year, there comes a time when continual losing will wear them down. This insistent chipping away at their confidence leads them toward another common mistake of "coat tailing"—that is, blindly following—other traders.

Switching methodologies

I'm reluctant to call this a common mistake because, on occasion, it can be the right thing to do—how else can you find out what works in trading if you don't go searching? However, I've included it here because many prematurely switch methodologies before they've given a particular one enough investigation. Traders can become too impatient during their search and don't take the time to delve deep enough to determine correctly whether a methodology has value.

Switching gurus

I define gurus as those people who are placed upon the pedestal of trading wisdom by the popular press, various institutions or internet chat sites. Typically, if traders fail by following one guru, they'll replace him or her with another, rather than working out what works for themselves.

Switching markets

If traders have failed to make money by switching methodologies and gurus, many then conclude that it is the market that is holding them back, rather than their approach to it.

Switching time frames

Many traders believe a switch in time frames will improve their results. They feel trading a lower time frame will reduce their risk and hence their losses. This usually leads them to try their hand at day trading. However, reducing the time frame does not reduce the risk. What traders usually do when they switch to a lower time frame like day trading, is inadvertently to improve their risk and money management by closing losing positions at the close of business. Once again, it's not the time frame that is holding them back but their money management and methodology.

Switching client advisers

Many traders have been known to blame poor results on client advisers, blaming them for bad fills, even if these were created by the market. By fills I mean the execution of orders into and out of the market. If they're losing, further bad fills will lead them to change client advisers, believing that their client adviser, not their trading, is responsible for their poor results.

Money Management
Overtrading

By the second year of trading, most traders will have come across the concept of money management. Although many might believe they understand money management, the reality is that they don't really. Novice traders will still overtrade, given their account size. That is, they'll risk too much of their trading account on any individual trade.

Psychology
Becoming addicted to the market

The excitement of trading gives traders a natural high. The adrenalin rush produces an unhealthy addiction to trading. Craving the next trade can cause traders to push marginal trades that don't exist, and they suffer the usual poor results.

Being impatient

Most traders lose patience with the market. If this happens, when patience is required, they'll instead ignore their previous conviction to trade only validated setups. In a rush, traders will start executing any marginal opportunity and continue to lose.

Having unrealistic expectations

New traders make the common mistake of believing the marketing hype surrounding trading, which creates unrealistic expectations. Expecting to earn a 100 percent or more return places traders under enormous pressure and feeds their downward spiral into financial (and emotional) self-destruction.

Being a rationalist

Often, traders seek to explain away their losses. They always find a reason the market took their money—"If the Dow Jones hadn't fallen last night I would have been able to take my profits this morning!" or "Oh no, I miscounted my waves. How did I do that?" or "The 20-bar cycle must have inverted!'

In the minds of novice traders, it's never their fault.

COMMON MISTAKES—YEAR THREE

Having muddled through the first year of trading and survived the second year, those who get to the third year should be applauded for making it through! These traders usually step into their third year of trading with a determined resolve and battle-weary cautiousness.

Although adopting the posturing of a veteran campaigner, traders in their third year still have the potential to be dangerous. They have more knowledge, or so they think, and believe that the markets owe them big time—both financially for the money it has "borrowed" and for their time "invested" in unraveling its mystery. To cap it off, their egos have taken a huge battering. This is an explosive cocktail to carry around. Welcome to the third year of trading!

Methodology
- Failing to let go of what has been learned
- Forgetting it's all about simple support and resistance
- Confusing technical analysis with trading and failing to separate trade plans from setups
- Failing to develop trade plans that support setups
- Failing to understand positive expectancy
- Failing to validate methodologies

Money management
- Continuing to overtrade

Psychology
- Focusing on the profits and not the process
- Having poor discipline
- Believing markets are impossible
- Believing there are trading secrets
- Believing the greatest risk is losing money
- Believing the hardest thing is psychology

Methodology
Failing to let go of what has been learned

Failing to let go of what has been learned is a major mistake that nearly every trader makes and there is almost no way to avoid it. This is due to that important ingredient to success—determination. On the one hand, it's the only way to succeed, because trading throws so many obstacles in your path that without it you'll never progress. Yet determination can make you so pigheaded that you won't walk away from a losing methodology, even though your trading account, your partner, and your accountant are telling you to. Believe me, I know—it took me 15 years to walk away from Elliott wave!

Forgetting it's all about simple support and resistance

In the pursuit of the ultimate trading strategy, many traders will be seduced into believing that complexity is the trick to win in the markets. They believe that if everyone loses in the market, trading can't be simple—if it were, wouldn't everyone be winning? They begin studying intricate and esoteric methodologies, looking to the stars and peeking under pyramids to find the "secret key" to unlock the markets. They lose sight of the simple truth that trading is all about identifying potential support and resistance levels.

Why would traders buy unless they believed the market may have found support? Why would traders sell unless they believed the market may have hit resistance? Unfortunately, in pursuit of "clever" trading, traders lose sight of the fact that trading is all about simple support and resistance levels.

Confusing technical analysis with trading and failing to separate trade plans from setups

In the initial part of their trading career, many traders confuse technical analysis with trading. They make the common mistake of not having a separate setup and trade plan. They're so focused on working out where the market is heading that once they believe they've worked it out, they immediately enter the market.

Say for example your setup may use a 40-day moving average to identify the trend. It may use a sentiment indicator to tell you when the market is oversold, identifying a safe place to buy on a pullback in an uptrend. It may even use a key reversal pattern to confirm a price reversal and resumption of a trend. What will happen is that you'll see three green lights (trend up, retracement down with sentiment oversold, trend continuation up with reversal pattern) and get excited. Off you'll go to buy the market either on the day's close or the next day's open, because your analysis or methodology had identified a possible resumption of the uptrend.

In this case, you've made the common mistake of failing to develop a separate trade plan from your setup. Automatically entering the market based on the setup alone is wrong. Successful traders know it should be a two-step process.

The first step is to complete your analysis and identify a setup. The second step is to work out how to take advantage of the setup correctly by following a separate trade plan.

Failing to develop trade plans that support setups

If you have developed a separate setup and trade plan, you would complete your analysis and find your setups the night before to establish a preference to either buy or sell the next day. During the next day, your only focus would be your trade plan, not your setup. You would trade according to it, not your setup. What many traders fail to do is design their trade plans to support and confirm their setups. Instead, their trade plans only incorporate an entry, stop, and exit technique.

A good trade plan will require the setup to deliver positive market action before committing a trader to a position. For a sell setup, a good trade plan will demand lower prices before committing to a trade. For a buy setup, a good trade plan will demand higher prices before committing to a trade. Unfortunately, most fail to incorporate this "supporting" role into their trade plans.

Failing to understand positive expectancy

Another common mistake is being ignorant of "positive expectancy." Although people trade to make money—and subconsciously want to make a great deal of it—they have no practical knowledge of their actual "expectancy." They don't know what they are likely to earn over the longer term for every dollar they risk in trading. I will talk much more about expectancy later.

Failing to validate methodologies

Most traders, whether new or experienced, make the mistake of not correctly validating their methodologies. Some believe that a simulated equity curve and calculated expectancy, combined with paper trading, will validate their system. Unfortunately, this is not the case.

Most traders will only validate their methodologies by trading real money in the markets. If they make money, their methodologies are validated; if they lose, their systems are no good. However, the only way to validate your methodology correctly without risking money is to trade the market according to your rules, at arm's length from your ego, by following my TEST procedure. You will hear more about TEST later.

Money Management
Continuing to overtrade

This is one area that most people struggle with early on in their trading career. Although many traders believe they understand money management, they still risk too much of their risk capital on each trade. They're not patient enough to take smaller bets to reduce their risk of ruin and sensibly build their account balance over time. Trading conservatively is just not exciting enough!

Psychology
Focusing on the profits and not the process

Focusing on profits does not make money. Traders should be focusing on the process of trading, not the profits—that is, focus on money management, identifying setups, and executing trade plans. If you learn to focus on the process of trading, the profits will follow.

Having poor discipline

Poor discipline is another common mistake. Traders can get easily distracted when they play with their setups and trade plans, entering and placing stops in an almost random fashion.

Believing that markets are impossible

If you're lucky enough to still be trading by the third year and you're still losing, you'll be close to the end of your tether. If so, you'll probably make the common mistake of believing that markets are impossible to trade.

Believing there are "trading secrets"

Once you start thinking that markets are impossible to trade, you remember that a small group of traders do succeed. This leads traders to believe this select group of winning traders must know "trading secrets." It can be the only way they win. It's the only logical conclusion inexperienced traders can come to.

Believing the greatest risk is losing money

Another common mistake traders make is to believe the greatest risk in trading is losing money. However, the greatest risk you're exposed to in trading is tampering with a methodology that works! When faced with boredom, you'll need to ignore the temptation to modify your system to squeeze out extra profits.

Believing the hardest thing is psychology

By the end of their third year, struggling traders make the common mistake of believing that psychology is the hardest part of trading. After purchasing so many books and software programs and attending so many seminars and workshops, they believe they must have the knowledge to trade successfully. They know they are not stupid so they believe it mustn't be their trading "knowledge" that is letting them down but the "application" of it. They believe their psychology is their biggest hurdle. And this belief is reinforced when most trading books support the notion that psychology is a person's single greatest challenge to becoming a successful trader.

Now, although psychology is important, I personally believe it isn't the greatest challenge to successful trading.

HOW TO JOIN THE 10 PERCENT WINNERS' CIRCLE

The simple answer is to avoid the common mistakes made by private traders and learn from the winners—the professional commodity trading advisers (CTAs), who manage billions of dollars through active trading. They can teach you to become process oriented in your trading.

Adopting a process orientation toward your trading, like that of the CTAs, will define boundaries within which you can explore and experience trading. If done properly, you may never trade, and by not trading you won't lose, which will put you ahead of 90 percent of all traders. While you may not join the 10 percent winners' circle, at least you won't be contributing to their pockets!

Let's look at a new trader's typical journey, as shown in figure 1.1.

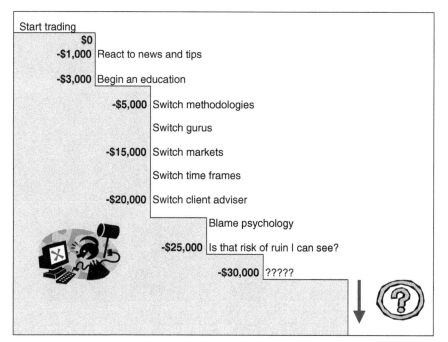

FIGURE 1.1   A trader's typical journey

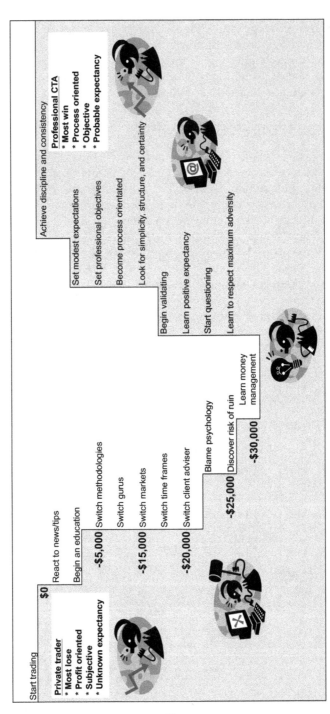

Start trading

$0

Private trader
* Most lose
* Profit oriented
* Subjective
* Unknown expectancy

React to news/tips

Begin an education

−$5,000 Switch methodologies

Switch gurus

−$15,000 Switch markets

Switch time frames

−$20,000 Switch client adviser

Blame psychology

−$25,000 Discover risk of ruin

−$30,000 Learn money management

Learn to respect maximum adversity

Start questioning

Learn positive expectancy

Begin validating

Look for simplicity, structure, and certainty

Become process orientated

Set professional objectives

Set modest expectations

Achieve discipline and consistency

Professional CTA
* Most win
* Process oriented
* Objective
* Probable expectancy

FIGURE 1.2 A winner's climb

18

As you know from the common mistakes traders make, there is a high probability you'll have an unhappy experience when you begin trading. As you search for what works, you'll get beaten from pillar to post, completely clueless in your endeavors to make money.

For those traders who are fortunate enough to pick themselves off the floor, there is usually a clear pattern of behavior.

For the few traders who win, not only do they learn about money management, they also come to the realization that its correct application is required for their financial survival, as shown in figure 1.2.

Most long-term winning traders have learned:

- the market's number one rule of maximum adversity
- to give the market the respect it deserves
- to question everything they read and hear
- that just because an author writes it, or a presenter says it, it isn't necessarily true
- about positive expectancy
- to validate all ideas
- to look for simplicity, structure, and certainty
- to be process-orientated in their research, design, and validation
- to establish professional objectives and modest expectations
- to achieve discipline and consistency in their trading.

Most of these few winners are the professional CTAs. Most losers are you and me, the small private trader.

IN SUMMARY

When people begin their trading experience, they usually do so with little structure and little certainty. During the process, they damage both their wallets and souls. If they're lucky enough, they will begin moving toward simplicity, structure, and certainty. They'll begin adopting a process-oriented focus. The glue that builds the structure is discovering the importance of positive expectancy and correct validation. If you do this, you'll begin to think and behave like a professional CTA.

By the end of this book, through teaching you the universal principles of successful trading, I hope to have you thinking and behaving like the professional traders, regardless whether your preference is for discretionary or mechanical trading.

CHAPTER 2

The Process of Trading

In this chapter I'll introduce the six universal principles of successful trading. In the following chapters, I'll expand on the individual principles.

Figure 2.1 highlights the daunting array of choice facing the average trader.

So who is confused about where to start trading? It seems there are so many decisions traders have to make! Rather than describing all of these techniques, my intention is to get you thinking about the process involved in becoming successful traders. The process will follow the universal principles of successful trading.

THE PROCESS OF TRADING

The universal principles of successful trading outline the process of trading. There are six essential principles of successful trading:

- preparation
- enlightenment
- development of a trading style
- selecting markets to trade
- the three pillars
- commencement of trading.

Let's take a quick look at each.

Preparation explains what traders can expect from the markets and trading. It also shows traders what they can do before they even start trading to ensure they don't go too far. Good preparation will provide you with a strong foundation to your trading.

Enlightenment discusses what is necessary to succeed. It points out where traders should be directing their energy. Enlightenment will guide you down the correct path to survive in trading.

FIGURE 2.1   The confusing world of technical analysis

Development of a trading style brings into focus what you need to know when selecting a method to trade.

Knowing how to select the best markets to trade is crucial. Trading is hard enough without having to trade small markets that are susceptible to manipulation.

The three pillars address the three tangible ingredients of successful trading—money management, methodology, and psychology.

The commencement of trading puts it all together.

As you can see, trading is the last principle of the six. I hope you can understand why so many traders lose—they start trading almost immediately, when it should be the last thing they do.

Figure 2.2 provides an outline of what is involved in each essential principle.

As you can see, there is a tremendous amount of work involved in becoming a successful trader. For many people it would represent too much hard work. For those willing to put in the effort, it presents a clearly defined path toward success.

In the next chapter I'll commence the process of trading by beginning with the first essential universal principle of successful trading—preparation.

1. Preparation	2. Enlightenment	3. Developing a trading style	4. Selecting markets	5. The three pillars	6. Trading

Maximum adversity
Emotional orientation
Losing game
Random markets
Personal boundary
Best loser wins
Risk management
Trading partner
	Avoid risk of ruin
	- Best loser wins
	- Money management
	Holy grail = E x O
	Simplicity
	- Support/resistance
	Tread where majority fear
	Validation - TEST
		Style
		- Trend trading
		- Swing trading
		Time frame
		- Intraday
		- Short-term
		- Medium-term
		- Long-term
			Characteristics
			Single markets
			Multiple markets
				Trading's three pillars
				1. Money management
				2. Methodology
				3. Psychology
				
				1. *Money management*
				  - Fixed risk
				  - Fixed capital
				  - Fixed ratio
				  - Fixed units
				  - Williams fixed risk
				  - Fixed percentage
				  - Fixed volatility
				
				2. *Methodology*
				Approach - Discretionary
				          - Mechanical
				
				Method
				= Setup + Trade plan + Validation
				Setup
				Analysis - which market theory?
				Trading's pandora's box
				  - Astrology
				  - Cycles
				  - Dow theory
				  - Elliott wave
				  - Fibonacci
				  - Fractal
				  - Geometry
				  - Indicators
				  - Market profile
				  - Patterns
				  - Seasonals
				  - Statistical
				  - W.D. Gann
				Trade plan
				Entry + Stop + Exit
				
				Validation - E(R)
				TEST (Thirty emailed simulated trades)
				3. *Psychology*
				Managing hope, greed, fear, and pain
					Putting it all together
					Monitor performance
					Positive reinforcement
					Equity momentum

Yep, just like school
it's a lot of hard work!

FIGURE 2.2 The universal principles of successful trading

Principle One: Preparation

Everyone get comfortable. Why not make yourself a cup of coffee or tea (and if your other half isn't looking, why not pinch a couple of biscuits?) and sit back and enjoy what possibly may, and hopefully will, be the beginning of your new process-oriented trading career.

We'll begin with the first universal principle of successful trading—preparation. Preparation will help you to measure your determination to trade. If you aren't prepared to accept the ideas in this chapter, you shouldn't really be trading. If you don't think you're up for it, you should quit while you're ahead; it will be a lot cheaper and far less disappointing.

Preparation demands that before any consideration can be given to trading you must consider the following ideas and accept the ramifications of each:

- maximum adversity
- emotional orientation
- losing game
- random markets
- best loser wins
- risk management
- trading partner
- financial boundaries.

Let's have a look at each.

MAXIMUM ADVERSITY

Maximum adversity is the market's number one rule and it is this: *The market will do what it has to do to disappoint most traders.* And you should never forget this.

Let me repeat myself. The market will do what it has to do to disappoint most traders. It will throw every possible obstacle in your path. Although trading is relatively simple, it's not easy. And maximum adversity will do its best to make it as hard as possible, making you doubt your every move, your every trade.

Maximum adversity refers to the discipline the market imposes on all participants. Through maximum adversity, the market will ensure money is always transferred from the majority, who are the weak hands, into the minority, who are the strong hands. Hey, if trading was easy, everyone would be doing it and winning!

Unfortunately, most traders don't learn this rule until it's too late. However, to survive in trading, you have to acknowledge it, comprehend it, and respect it. To do otherwise will ensure your trading demise.

Remember the old cliché—if something sounds too good to be true, it probably is? Well this goes for trading as well. If a particular trading idea sounds too good to be true, or a simulated equity curve appears too smooth to be true, or a charting program makes trading look too easy to be true, it probably is. However, most traders who are not aware of maximum adversity will believe what they have heard, they will believe what they have read, and they will believe what they have seen. It is only through experience and gaining a healthy level of skepticism that people start to independently investigate these too-good-to-be-true trading ideas, these too-good-to-believe extra-smooth equity curves and these too-good-to-be-true charting programs. It is only through experience and doing the work that they uncover maximum adversity at work and finally realize these ideas, extra-smooth equity curves, and brilliant charting programs are too good to be true.

Maximum adversity is also at work in the markets. If a chart throws up what looks like to be an obvious trade, don't be surprised if it fails!

Maximum adversity makes it clear to new traders that the market will not make it easy for them to succeed. You should always keep this in the back of your mind when reading and researching new trading ideas. You should keep it in the back of your mind when considering purchasing a new charting program or a new trading system or attending a seminar or workshop on trading. You should keep maximum adversity in the back of your mind when researching, back testing, and correctly validating a trading methodology. You should keep it in the back of your mind when studying charts looking for your next trading opportunity.

Maximum adversity demands that you stay vigilant against all ideas or suggestions that successful trading is easy and that plentiful profits are available for everyone. Maximum adversity demands that you stay vigilant when looking at charts for your next trading opportunity. Maximum adversity demands that you stay vigilant when reading advertisements for trading new markets or for opening trading accounts to take advantage of new trading platforms. Maximum adversity demands that you stay vigilant when reading reports in which the analyst appears to have a strong view and strong opinion. Beware of the analyst who seems to have all the answers.

Maximum adversity will ensure your life as a trader is not how it's advertised to be. Life as a trader does not resemble those sunny images you have seen of carefree traders sunning themselves beneath palm trees trading away on their laptops. Maximum adversity will do its best to discourage you from being a trader by making your trading world as uncomfortable as possible. Maximum adversity will ensure your trading world is full of constant pain. It will make your trading hard, harder and harder still. It will make trading feel like it's 100 percent boot camp. It will make it feel like it's 100 percent disappointment. Maximum adversity will make your trading full of 100 percent hurt on so many levels. Maximum adversity will ensure you occupy a world of pain. When you lose money, it will hurt. When you make money, you will think about how much more money you could have made if you had stayed in the market longer. When you think about the amount of money you left on the table, it will hurt. When you spend considerable time and energy studying a plausible theory on trading and it doesn't work, maximum adversity will ensure it hurts. When you spend considerable money on what you think are reputable seminars and workshops and you lose money implementing the ideas learned, it will hurt. When you spend considerable time and energy researching, developing, programming, testing, and validating a new idea and it doesn't work, it will hurt. When you spend considerable time and energy over many years working to improve on the edge you have and fail to improve on it, despite all the time and energy spent, it will disappoint and it will hurt. And when you're out of the market looking and waiting for that next trading opportunity, maximum adversity will ensure the anxiety you feel about not being in the market and potentially missing out on the next big move will hurt. As I said, maximum adversity will ensure your trading world will be full of pain and hurt.

Maximum adversity demands that you take 100 percent responsibility for all your actions. Maximum adversity demands that you should expect to be ambushed at every turn. Maximum adversity demands that you should learn to expect the unexpected! Maximum adversity demands that right now you should determine whether you have the fortitude and stomach to accept the miserable existence of a trader's life despite the potential financial rewards.

EMOTIONAL ORIENTATION

Emotional orientation is particularly important for success. It refers to two fundamental areas of trading—objectives and expectations.

If your objective in trading is to win, or always to be right when you trade, it's an almost guaranteed outcome that you'll fail. If your expectation is to earn a great deal of money from trading, that's another guarantee you won't succeed.

Although some traders may be able to achieve those objectives occasionally, they are difficult to sustain over the longer term without increasing your risk to a dangerous level. Remember, you can never escape the old risk/return trade-off—the more return you want, the more risk you'll have to accept. Unless you're able to achieve what I refer to as "emotional orientation," you'll find it difficult to succeed.

You become emotionally disoriented when you begin dreaming of being the perfect trader and pocketing unrealistic returns. Not only do you expose yourself to an impossible goal and unacceptable risk, you also place too much expectation and pressure on your trading.

Objectives

Believe it or not, winning, or being right, isn't that important. This is something most traders fail to learn until it's too late! To succeed, traders need to reprogram their thinking. You come to trading with a focused and single-minded determination to win that sees you pour your resources and energy into figuring out how to beat the market. These blinkers prevent you from seeing any other objective in trading, except to win.

Most people, especially traders, love to compete, and even more, they love to win. However, to win also means you need to be right. Instinctively, people want to buy the right car, the right house, the right insurance policy. They want to select the right school for their kids, the right share investment, the right lotto numbers, and the winning horse.

Unfortunately, the desire to win, to be right, works against making money from trading. What you'll learn later, when I discuss positive expectancy, is that winning is only one half of the equation. Wanting to win is wrong. By focusing solely on winning, traders are looking in the wrong direction—they're emotionally disoriented.

Obviously, winning is nice, but to have it as your primary objective is inappropriate and disorienting. If you wish to succeed, your objective in trading should be to manage your risk capital. Managing your risk capital will broaden your objectives and responsibilities. It will lift your objective from a myopic focus on winning to one that is conservative and professional. Managing your risk capital steers you away from the goal of making a pile of money by winning, to one of consistent, sensible, and sustainable trading. Once you can set yourself this goal, you'll be halfway to establishing your emotional orientation. The other half of the equation has to do with your expectations.

Expectations

Unrealistic expectations are the twin evil to the obsession with winning. These combine to create havoc with your emotional orientation. For example, if your expectation is to make a fistful of dollars you'll almost certainly guarantee your trading demise. What is paramount for sustainable success is the adoption of modest expectations. Looking to make a 20–30 percent return is far more achievable, and far less challenging, than a return of 50 percent or more. Most people lose because they want more. It's a case of good old-fashioned greed, or unrealistic expectations.

People usually associate trading with making money—more trading will result in more money. I maintain that this "more trading = more money" phenomenon is created (or at least reinforced) by most rainbow merchants and trading promoters who spin the wealth dream. So many traders come to trading with an "activity" prejudice—more trading and more activity means more money. I call this a "top down" approach. This activity bias will condition traders to want more, and wanting more creates unrealistic expectations.

This "more is best" philosophy keeps lifting the bar, and creates a self-perpetuating greed effect. This is where greed brings traders unstuck. Even if you have a robust trading plan that makes you real money in real time, the "more is best" prejudice will lead traders to quickly become bored with what they have, or assume they could be doing more. At this stage, traders place higher expectations on their trading and winning methodology, leading them to fiddle with their winning approach, ultimately resulting in self-destruction.

It took a long time for me to develop a modest expectation, which I still struggle with from time to time. With my models, I can see how easily I could double or triple my returns if I just cranked up the risk a little. What is surprising is that when my expectations are under control, my trading actually becomes easier. I'm content with my methodology's performance, and I continue to trade it through the good and the bad times.

To complete your emotional orientation, you need to develop a modest expectation toward your trading. To do this, you need to have what I call a "bottom up" approach and throw away the "top down" fantasy.

A "bottom up" approach is to view the risk capital you have allocated to trading and ask yourself, "What return would I be happy to earn on my risk capital over the next 12 months?" or "If I could look back over the past year, what return would I have been satisfied to achieve?"

It seems the returns on global sharemarkets have averaged between 8 and 12 percent per annum over the past couple of decades. So it's safe to say you would prefer to earn more than this on your risk capital. So if you could turn the calendar forward 12 months and look back at what you had achieved, what percentage return on your risk capital would make you happy? Would it be a 20 or 30 percent return? In light of this, I personally only want to make a 20 percent plus return per annum on my risk capital. To me, that's reasonably achievable—the hardest part is achieving it consistently.

If you seriously want to succeed in trading, you should develop a robust trading methodology that you'll be able to apply over the years consistently to earn a modest, but healthy, return year in and year out. If your methodology's performance suggests your target is achievable, you should be content with your methodology and not fiddle with it. You shouldn't think you have to trade every day to produce a good return on your risk capital. If you adopt a "bottom up" approach to trading, you'll develop a modest expectation and complete your emotional orientation.

If you can emotionally orient yourself by setting a professional objective with modest expectations, you'll find your task of developing a robust methodology much easier. In addition, once you've achieved this, you'll be content with its performance and continue to trade it through both the good and bad times. If you can achieve this objective, your task of becoming a successful trader will be a lot easier!

LOSING GAME

Your preparation continues when you accept the truth that trading is a losers' game. Don't try to convince your friends that you're going to trade and succeed, because the odds are heavily stacked against you. You should also be aware of my "90 × 90" rule: *90 percent of traders will lose their risk capital within 90 days.*

Not only can you tell friends and colleagues that your pursuit is difficult, you can also put a time factor on it. Preparation requires that you have a clear understanding that in choosing to trade actively you're about to enter a losers' game.

RANDOM MARKETS

Preparation also requires traders to accept the truth that markets are essentially random. You should ignore all the marketing hype out there that suggests otherwise.

You can easily be forgiven for thinking it's possible to predict markets given that there are so many predictive theories on market behavior, such as cycles, Elliott wave, market profile, seasonals, and W.D. Gann, to mention just a few. However, the reality is that it's impossible, on a consistent statistical basis, to predict market direction. Please be aware that successful traders know this, and that they make their money from knowing how to react to market direction; they don't try to predict it.

At the end of the day, you should accept that markets are essentially, although not totally, random, and you should not take on the task of trading believing you are going to find the key that unlocks the market's universal secrets.

BEST LOSER WINS

Your preparation continues when you learn that the only real secret to successful trading is to manage your losses. If you can keep your losses small and manageable, and your wins larger than your losses, you'll stay ahead of the losers' game. You can almost ignore your winners because they generally look after themselves—they just take off and rarely look back. However, to succeed you need to focus all your energy and determination on managing the losses.

When I was reading Arthur L. Simpson's e-book *Phantom of the Pits*, I came across a great expression used by the anonymous subject of the book, Phantom: *The best loser is the long-term winner.* I thought his expression best described the importance of focusing your efforts on managing your losses.

The book is essentially an interview with a 30-year veteran trader from Chicago in the US. The trader wanted to provide his insights into trading without revealing his identity, hence he was known only as "Phantom."

If you're a mechanical trader like myself, this truth demands you never, ever move your stops. You respect your strict trade plan. In addition, when designing your trading plan you should try to implement a dual-stop trigger, one based on price and one on time.

It all comes back to managing your losses. If you've placed a discretionary trade and it doesn't get a move on, you should listen to the market and jump out. You should become the best loser. Don't let losing trades hang around, chipping away at your confidence and slowly grinding you down tick by tick as it eventually hits your original stop level. Being the best loser means exiting a losing position as quickly as possible.

The only real secret to successful trading is being the best loser, so this should be your goal. To become the best loser, you should always be looking to improve your losing. You should be asking yourself whether there is a better way to lose faster, without short-changing your setup.

RISK MANAGEMENT

By now, you should realize trading is a very risky business. This must mean successful trading is really all about successful risk management. To survive as traders, you will need to look at your business of trading as a business of risk management.

If you ever have the opportunity to chat with a successful trader, you will probably find that his or her thoughts are dominated by how to improve his or her risk management. A central part of good risk management is money management (more about this later); however, risk has to be respected first and foremost before you can honestly apply proper money management principles.

Good traders are good risk managers. This is the difference between the winners and the losers. They respect what the market can do to them, they understand that it's a losers' game, they strive to be the best loser, and their objective is to manage their risk capital with modest expectations. Their whole focus is survival, and that depends on their success at being good risk managers.

If you want to trade, you'll need to approach your task from a risk manager's perspective; leave the trading profit bias to the punters.

TRADING PARTNER

Your preparation continues when you realize the importance and value of having a trading partner. This is the business end of preparation. Before you proceed any further, you need to take an audit of your determination to trade—if you have accepted the previous points I've made, it's time to move forward; if you haven't, you probably shouldn't trade.

Preparation requires you to find a trading partner. This is an important part of preparing to trade. Your trading partner does not necessarily have to be a trader, but he or she must be someone you respect. He or she must be at arm's length from you, meaning he or she can't live under your roof. He or she must be a person who'll take an interest in what you're doing and agree to help.

The purpose of a trading partner is to prevent traders from lying to themselves. It's amazing what the market will do to people, most of whom arrive at trading as rational, objective, and honest human beings. They begin trading and before they know it, they're transformed into a state of irrationality and delusion. They become confused about their abilities and begin telling themselves little white lies.

A trading partner will help you remain rational and honest. He or she will play two important roles—one during pretrading and the other during actual trading.

First, a trading partner will help you correctly validate your trading methodology using the TEST procedure (more about that later). He or she will discourage you from trading until you can demonstrate your methodology has a probable positive expectancy. Second, when you begin trading, your trading partner will act as your conscience—he or she will keep you honest.

He or she will know your financial benchmarks, which should include, as a minimum, your financial boundary, your modest expectations, and your money management rules.

Each month, you should make a report and ask your trading partner to measure your performance against your financial benchmarks. He or she will act as your trading confessor. This will help your discipline and consistency. You'll find it harder to stray from your trade plan when you know your trading partner is watching. This will also help you to remain rational.

The question is where you can find a trading partner. If you can't find a suitable and willing candidate among your friends, you should consider joining an association of like-minded people, such as the Technical Analysts Associations that exist in many countries.

FINANCIAL BOUNDARIES

This is the final step to complete your preparation. Just like using stops when you trade, you should place a financial boundary around your trading careers. You should establish your personal financial commitment to learning how to trade successfully. This is the risk capital you're prepared to invest in your education—or the total amount you're prepared to lose. Let your trading partner know your limit and make a personal commitment that if you lose the total, you'll accept that trading is not for you and you'll walk away.

Just like trading, where you should always use a contingency stop, you should know what you're prepared to lose before you embark on a trading career. I'm sure a lot of traders in the past had wished they had made a similar commitment to someone they respected and walked away when they hit their limit. They'd be a lot happier and have fuller pockets than they have today!

IN SUMMARY

I hope the first universal principle of successful trading has prepared you to accept that trading is hard work. You need to respect the market and accept that trading successfully will probably be one of the hardest challenges you'll ever attempt. Basically, trading is boot camp.

If you decide to walk down this path, you have to accept that it's all against you. The market will place roadblocks at every turn. Due to human nature, you will find it difficult to establish professional objectives and modest expectations. Most of your fellow traders will be losers, making it difficult to find positive role models. The market will not leave too many clues about its likely direction, cherishing its random nature. Intuition is turned on its head—it's not the winner who gets the prize but the best loser. The primary driver behind making money is not so much trading well but being good risk managers. A trading partner will help you stay on the right track, and establishing a personal financial boundary will (hopefully) limit your potential total loss.

If you can accept all of this, then you would have learned, comprehended, and accepted the first essential universal principle of successful trading—preparation. You will be well prepared to expect the unexpected, and you'll be in good shape to continue.

Now that you're prepared, the next essential universal principle of successful trading is to become enlightened.

CHAPTER 4

Principle Two: Enlightenment

In this chapter, I take a look at the second essential universal principle of successful trading—enlightenment.

Enlightenment will help you avoid getting caught up in the confusing world of technical analysis and help you to focus on what is necessary to survive in trading. You will have noticed the emphasis is now on "survival." From this point on you should switch perspectives from wanting to succeed in trading, to wanting to "survive" in trading.

As I have mentioned, trading is risky. To succeed you have to become a successful risk manager. Accordingly, your focus now in trading should be on survival. If you're able to survive in trading, you will have succeeded.

Enlightenment will guide you to where you should focus your energy and resources. Enlightenment occurs when you realize your survival in trading is dependent upon the following:

- avoiding risk of ruin
- embracing trading's Holy Grail
- pursuing simplicity
- treading where most fear
- validating your expectancy with TEST.

If you want to survive, you must learn to stay within the boundaries these rules create, as shown in figure 4.1.

AVOIDING RISK OF RUIN

What you are about to learn, in my humble opinion, is probably the most important concept in trading. Yet most traders are ignorant of it. Very few authors write about it. Very few seminars mention it. Very few workshops teach it. Is it any wonder so many traders lose when they don't know their own personal risk of ruin?

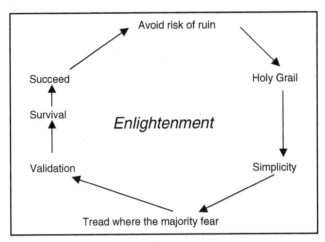

FIGURE 4.1   The enlightenment circle

When you calculate your own risk of ruin you'll start to properly under-stand why you have failed in trading. Yes, you know that you've lost money, however you're probably not really sure why. Understanding risk of ruin will give you the "why." The "why" will be your aha! moment.

So what is risk of ruin? Well let's have a look. Risk of ruin refers to the chance you'll lose so much money that you'll stop trading. Simple. So avoiding risk of ruin must now become your number one priority as risk managers. If you can avoid ruin, you will have survived, and thus succeeded in trading.

Risk of ruin is a statistical concept that tells traders the probability of them being ruined—that is, the likelihood that they'll incur such a large accumulative loss that they'll stop trading. This accumulative loss is referred to as the "point of ruin."

Risk of ruin doesn't necessarily mean losing your entire account balance. It could be a 50 percent, 75 percent, or 100 percent loss of your account, depending on your individual risk tolerance. Your point of ruin is the financial boundary, or risk capital, you established during your preparation.

The first step in avoiding your point of ruin is to calculate the probability of your chances of reaching it. If the probability is too high, you must look to lower it. If you can lower your probability of ruin to an acceptable level, you will have taken a significant step toward survival in trading. In essence, the larger the percentage of your trading capital you risk on any one trade, the higher your probability of being wiped out, or your risk of ruin, will be.

Let me use an example to help explain risk of ruin. Let's look at two traders: Trader Bob and Trader Sally. Trader Bob and Trader Sally have been to the same seminar, where they have learned a simple currency

$$\text{Risk of ruin} = \left[\frac{[1 - (W - L)]}{[1 + (W - L)]} \right]^{U}$$

where

    W = Probability of winning

    L = Probability of losing

    U = Number of units of money in the account

FIGURE 4.2   The risk of ruin formula

trading system called System_One. System_One's average win is equal to its average loss and it has an accuracy rate of 56 percent. Both Trader Bob and Trader Sally have established their financial boundary at $10,000 each, and have defined their point of ruin as a 100 percent loss of their risk capital ($10,000). Trader Bob, being the adventurous type, decides to risk $2,000 per signal (or in other words his trade setup). Trader Sally is more conservative and decides to risk only $1,000 per signal (or trade setup).

Accordingly, Trader Bob has five units of money to trade with ($10,000/$2,000) and Trader Sally has 10 units of money ($10,000/$1,000). If Trader Bob commences trading and has five losing trades in a row, he'll be ruined (5 × $2,000). Trader Sally would need 10 consecutive losing trades to be ruined (10 × $1,000).

The question Trader Bob and Trader Sally have to ask themselves is—what is their respective risk of ruin? That is, when will they lose $10,000?

To answer the question you can use the risk of ruin formula summarized in figure 4.2.

This formula assumes a trader's average win is equal to his or her average loss. Figure 4.3 shows how to calculate Trader Bob's risk of ruin.

Figure 4.4 shows Trader Bob's and Trader Sally's respective probability of being ruined.

As you can see, although Trader Bob and Trader Sally are trading the same currency system, they have varying probabilities of ruin. Trader Bob has a 30 percent probability of losing his risk capital, while Trader Sally has only a 9 percent probability of being wiped out. Clearly, Trader Sally's risk is preferable to Trader Bob's.

Although System_One has an accuracy rate of 56 percent, it doesn't mean that it can't have a long streak of losing signals. Consequently, if both traders start with $10,000, it would only take five consecutive losing signals to ruin Trader Bob, while for Trader Sally it would take a losing sequence of 10 signals.

However, is Trader Sally's probability of being ruined (9 percent) low enough to survive in trading? The answer is no. As traders, you need to approach trading *with a 0 percent risk of ruin.* Any statistical probability of

% wins	W	56%
% losses	L	44%
Number of units of money	U	5

$$\text{Risk of Ruin} = \left[\frac{[1 - (0.56 - 0.44)]}{[1 + (0.56 - 0.44)]}\right]^5$$

$$= \left[\frac{[1 - (0.12)]}{[1 + (0.12)]}\right]^5$$

$$= \left[\frac{0.88}{1.12}\right]^5$$

$$= [0.785714286]^5$$

$$= 0.299449262$$

$$= 30\%$$

FIGURE 4.3   Trader Bob's risk of ruin

financial ruin above 0 percent is too high. It is a gold-plated guarantee you will eventually go bust; it's just a matter of time. However, even if you do approach trading with a 0 percent risk of ruin, you must understand that it's no guarantee that you will avoid being ruined. This is because a 0 percent risk of ruin cannot guarantee that your trading methodology's accuracy and average win and average loss will not change overtime into the future. If they remain constant, or even improve, your 0 percent risk of ruin will ensure you will avoid ruining your account. However, a 0 percent risk of ruin cannot guarantee that your trading methodology will not deteriorate

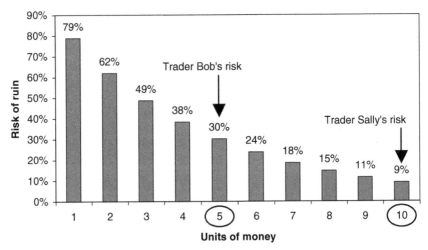

FIGURE 4.4   How risk of ruin declines with additional units of money

and stop working in the future. You need to understand risk of ruin is a statistical measure that relies on its inputs. If they remain constant or improve, then a 0 percent risk of ruin will prevent you from reaching your point of ruin. However, if they suffer then so will your risk of ruin as it rises above 0 percent. You need to remember risk of ruin is only statistical measure, not a miracle worker!

The next question is how you can reduce a methodology's risk of ruin. The previous example has provided the first clue—risk less money per trade. This comment highlights the importance of money management and why you as risk managers have to get your money management strategy right if you are to survive and succeed in trading. To bring your risk of ruin into acceptable limits, logic demands you risk a smaller amount of your trading account on any individual trade. If it's too high, you'll be knocked out.

This is the biggest mistake I made when I began trading. I had no idea of the concept of risk of ruin and how money management is used to reduce and manage it. My only thought was "How much money can I make from trading futures?" Please don't repeat my mistake!

Let's introduce another trader—Trader Tom—and compare his risk of ruin to Trader Bob's and Trader Sally's. Trader Tom also trades currencies with System_One and has the same $10,000 financial boundary and definition of ruin. He has a little more experience than the others, and is aware of the concept of risk of ruin and how to reduce it. Trader Tom knows that by risking less money per trade he will reduce his probability of ruin. Trader Tom would like to trade with a lower risk of ruin, so he decides to risk only $500 per signal (or trade setup). As such, Trader Tom will have 20 units of money to trade with ($10,000/ $500). That is, at a minimum, if he never has a winning signal, he will have enough money to place 20 trades before being ruined. Using the same formula, Trader Tom's probability of ruin can be calculated. Figure 4.5 shows each trader's respective risk of ruin.

As you can see, Trader Tom, by reducing his risk to $500 per signal— which provides him with 20 trading opportunities compared to Trader Bob's five and Trader Sally's 10—has lowered his risk of ruin to 1 percent! A 1 percent risk of ruin is far more acceptable then Trader Sally's 9 percent. Certainly, he won't make as much money as Trader Bob would if Trader Bob won; however, there is a much higher probability (30 percent) that Trader Bob will not be around to enjoy many $2,000 wins.

Remember, successful trading is all about survival and good risk management. This is the first lesson in how to reduce your risk of ruin—reduce the dollar risk per trade or, in other words, learn to apply sensible money management principles. As a minimum, you should divide your risk capital by 20 so you'll have at least 20 units of money, and reduce

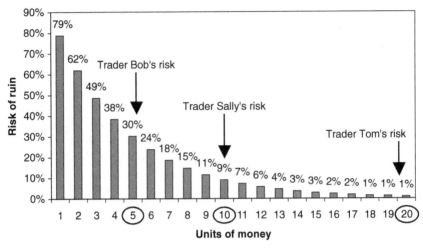

FIGURE 4.5 Comparison of risk of ruin

your probability of ruin to 1 percent (assuming your methodology has a 56 percent accuracy and 1:1 average win to average loss). Although this will not guarantee your survival, it will at least help you lower your probability of ruin and improve your chances of survival.

The second lesson in how to reduce your risk of ruin is to improve the accuracy of your methodology. Assume that System_One is upgraded to System_One_MkII. System_One_MkII's improvement is seen in its accuracy, lifting from 56 percent winners to 63 percent winners. The average win to average loss payoff remains equal. Using the previous formula, let's recalculate each trader's risk of ruin with the higher accuracy system, assuming they keep their respective dollar risk per signal ($2,000, $1,000, and $500). Figure 4.6 summarizes their respective individual risk of ruin.

Trading a higher-accuracy system (when the average win to average loss remains equal) reduces the risk of ruin across the various levels of dollar risk—that is, number of units of money—per trade. Trader Bob's risk of ruin has fallen from 30 percent to 7 percent, Trader Sally's from 9 percent to 0.5 percent and Trader Tom's from 1 percent to *0 percent*. This is not surprising because a higher-accuracy system by definition should have a lower probability of failure because it wins more often than it loses (assuming the average win to average loss remains equal).

Now before I continue I just need to mention that it is mathematically impossible for the risk of ruin formula to reach 0 percent (0.0 percent). However, it is certainly possible to get it to below half of one percent (0.5 percent), which when rounded does become 0 percent (0.0 percent).

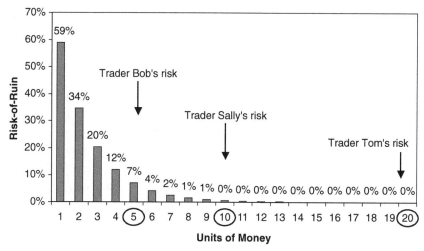

FIGURE 4.6   The value of higher-accuracy strategies

The third way to reduce your risk of ruin is to improve your methodology's average win-to-average loss payoff. Unfortunately, there isn't a simple formula you can use to calculate risk of ruin where the average win is greater than the average loss. What literature there is attempts simulation exercises to demonstrate how a higher payoff will reduce your risk of ruin. With the help of good friend and fellow trader Geoff Morgan, I wrote a similar model (a risk of ruin simulator) that duplicates the logic shown in appendix B of Nauzer Balsara's *Money Management Strategies for Futures Traders.*[1] See appendix A for an explanation of the logic of my risk-of-ruin simulator, and appendix B for a full disclosure of the programming code.

The results from my simulation are shown in table 4.1. For each simulation, I've assumed the methodology had a 50 percent accuracy rate and the trader 20 units of money. I defined ruin as being a 50 percent drawdown on the account. For each payoff ratio I ran 30 simulations and then took an average to produce a risk of ruin (see appendix C for a summary of the 30 simulations). Apart from the 1.1:1 payoff ratio, this simple simulation demonstrates how a higher payoff ratio can reduce your risk of ruin. From this example you can see that the only payoff you would

TABLE 4.1   Risk of ruin simulations with various win-to-loss ratios

	Average win-to-loss ratio					
	1.0	1.1	1.2	1.3	1.4	1.5
Risk of ruin	64%	20%	32%	21%	5%	0%

want to trade with is 1.5:1, as its simulated risk of ruin is 0 percent. All the others are above 0 and are therefore a guarantee that you will go bust; it will just be a matter of time.

You now know your objective as good risk managers is to pursue a trading methodology with a 0 percent risk of ruin.

In summary, there are three key tools to reduce risk of ruin:

• reducing the amount of money risked per trade
• increasing your accuracy (or win) rate
• increasing your average win to average loss payoff ratio.

The three key tools in the fight against risk of ruin can be summarized into two key weapons:

• money management
• expectancy.

The first line of defense against risk of ruin is the awareness, knowledge, and application of good money management. The second line of defense is the awareness, knowledge, and pursuit of expectancy over accuracy. I will be discussing more about expectancy later in the chapter and money management strategies will be discussed in depth in chapter 8.

Be aware that risk of ruin is always present, and as good risk managers, you should battle to avoid it. If you do, you'll survive, and if you survive, you'll succeed in trading.

However, before I move on, I want to note that determining risk of ruin does have a number of limitations. You need to understand that the figure:

• is only a statistical measure—it doesn't guarantee you'll avoid risk of ruin because it's dependent on its inputs. If they suffer, so will you
• is not static and changes from trade to trade
• has no practical value for actual trading.

After you start trading, you won't base any decisions like position size or cessation of trading on your risk of ruin. As you'll learn later, you need to use different ideas such as equity momentum and system stops to tell you when you should stop trading a particular methodology—you won't base your decision on your risk of ruin calculation.

Despite these limitations, the concept of risk of ruin is paramount—it's the gateway to survival. In my opinion . . . *Risk of ruin is the key that opens the doorway to real trading knowledge.* As I mentioned earlier, in my opinion risk of ruin is the most important concept in trading.

It demands that you shouldn't consider trading unless your risk of ruin is at 0 percent. Every trader has a statistical risk of ruin yet most don't know it. Most are ignorant. Most lose. Traders who don't know their own risk of ruin should calculate it immediately, and if it's above 0 percent, they should cease all trading. They have no business engaging with the market because they're guaranteed to go bust; it's just that they don't know when. Once traders become aware of the significance of risk of ruin, they become more knowledgeable traders, and if they're honest with themselves, they'll walk away from trading until they can reduce their risk of ruin to 0 percent. Remember, any risk of ruin above 0 percent is a guarantee of going bust; it'll just be a matter of time.

As I said, I believe risk of ruin is the most important concept in trading. It cuts to the truth about trading and says that if you're not sensitive to the perils of trading, you won't last.

If you can risk less money per trade, you will lower your risk of ruin, and you will have a better chance at enjoying a long-term trading career. If you can improve your methodology's accuracy, you will lower your risk of ruin. If you can improve your payoff ratio, you will lower your risk of ruin and improve your odds of survival. I suppose at the end of the day it doesn't matter how you lower your risk of ruin, as long as you do it. What is important is that you have no business trading the markets unless your statistical risk of ruin is 0 percent. Please do not trade if it isn't! Please!

EMBRACING TRADING'S HOLY GRAIL

Enlightenment continues when you discover the real Holy Grail of trading. You may have heard of people chasing (or pursuing like I have in the past) the perfect trading system. One with a very high accuracy rate with minimal drawdown—the Holy Grail. I'm sure it won't come as a surprise to learn that the Holy Grail of trading systems does not exist.

However, in my mind there is a Holy Grail of trading—the pursuit of a methodology that yields a positive expectancy that can be traded across multiple opportunities, as shown in figure 4.7.

$$\$\$ = E \times O$$

E = Positive expectancy
O = Opportunities

FIGURE 4.7   My Holy Grail of trading

$$\begin{array}{c}\text{Expected} \\ \text{return per} = \\ \$\$\end{array} \left(\begin{array}{c}\text{Probability} \\ \text{of} \\ \text{winning}\end{array} \times \dfrac{\text{Average win}}{\text{Average loss}}\right) - \left(\begin{array}{c}\text{Probability} \\ \text{of} \\ \text{losing}\end{array} \times \dfrac{\text{Average loss}}{\text{Average loss}}\right)$$

FIGURE 4.8   The expectancy formula

Your aim, assuming you've survived by avoiding risk of ruin, is to apply a validated edge to multiple trading opportunities. It's the only way you'll be able to add to your trading accounts. So what does all this mean?

EXPECTANCY

From my experience, expectancy is the idea that is the least understood by most people who are either planning to or who are trading. Expectancy refers to what you can expect to earn, on average, for every dollar you risk in a trade. To calculate your methodology's expectancy, you need to know how often you win, how often you lose, and the size of your average winning and average losing trades. Once you have the information, you can use the formula in figure 4.8 to calculate your probable expectancy.

Let's calculate Trader Bob's expectancy from System_One. System_One has an accuracy rate of 56 percent; however, for the ease of explanation I'll increase it to 60 percent. System_One has an average win equal to its average loss and it generates 10 signals per year. Trader Bob risks $2,000 per trade. Table 4.2 shows Trader Bob's trading performance (assuming he manages to avoid risk of ruin).

As you can see, Trader Bob was able to earn $4,000 after a year of trading. He placed 10 trades, winning six and losing four, risking in total $20,000. Trader Bob's expectancy for the following year, based on his historical performance, would be 20 percent ($4,000/$20,000). In other words, Trader Bob should expect to earn, on average, assuming his methodology continues to perform as well into the future as it has in the past, 20 cents for every dollar he risks.

Alternatively, you can use the expectancy formula to calculate Trader Bob's expectancy, as shown in figure 4.9.

Let's calculate Trader Sally's expectancy from System_One, shown in figure 4.10.

The only difference between Trader Sally and Trader Bob is that Trader Sally's average win and average loss is $1,000. She will also expect, assuming she avoids risk of ruin, to earn on average 20 cents for every dollar risked. When she risks $1,000 she'll expect to earn on average $200, and if she takes the 10 trades during the year she'll expect to earn $2,000. Trader Sally also has a probable positive expectancy.

Finally, let's calculate Trader Tom's expectancy of System_One, shown in figure 4.11.

TABLE 4.2   Trader Bob's performance trading System _One

System_One		
Accuracy		60%
Average win		$2,000
Average loss		$2,000
Yearly trade result		
		Trades
6 Wins	1	$2,000
	2	$2,000
	3	$2,000
	4	$2,000
	5	$2,000
	6	$2,000
4 Losses	7	−$2,000
	8	−$2,000
	9	−$2,000
	10	−$2,000
Profit		$4,000

System_One

Accuracy   60%

Average win $2,000

Average loss $2,000

Expectancy per dollar risked

$E(R) = [60\% \times (\$2,000/\$2,000)] - [40\% \times (\$2,000/\$2,000)]$

   $= 20\%$

Expectancy per trade

   $= 20\% \times \$2,000$

   $= \$400$

Expectancy per trading year (assuming avoidance of risk of ruin)

Trade no.   10

$$ risked $20,000

   $= 10 \times 20\% \times \$2,000$

   $= \$4,000$

FIGURE 4.9   Trader Bob's expectancy trading System_One

System_One

Accuracy	60%
Average win	$1,000
Average loss	$1,000

Expectancy per dollar risked

$$E(R) = [60\% \times (\$1,000/\$1,000)] - [40\% \times (\$1,000/\$1,000)]$$
$$= 20\%$$

Expectancy per trade

$$= 20\% \times \$1,000$$
$$= \$200$$

Expectancy per trading year (assuming avoidance of risk of ruin)

Trade no.	10
$$ risked	$10,000

$$= 10 \times 20\% \times \$1,000$$
$$= \$2,000$$

FIGURE 4.10   Trader Sally's expectancy trading System_One

System_One

Accuracy	60%
Average win	$500
Average loss	$500

Expectancy per dollar risked

$$E(R) = [60\% \times (\$500/\$500)] - [40\% \times (\$500/\$500)]$$
$$= 20\%$$

Expectancy per trade

$$= 20\% \times \$500$$
$$= \$100$$

Expectancy per trading year (assuming avoidance of risk of ruin)

Trade no.	10
$$ risked	$5,000

$$= 10 \times 20\% \times \$500$$
$$= \$1,000$$

FIGURE 4.11   Trader Tom's expectancy trading System_One

Once again, the only difference between the traders is the amount of money risked per trade, which is $500 in Trader Tom's case. Trader Tom will also expect, assuming he avoids risk of ruin, to earn on average 20 cents for every dollar he risks. When he risks $500 he'll expect to earn on average $100 and if he takes the 10 trades during the year he'll expect to earn $1,000. Trader Tom also has a probable positive expectancy.

Interesting. So who do you think has the superior results? The correct answer is no one. They all earnt 20 percent on the money they risked. The only difference was their risk of ruin, which was 30 percent for Trader Bob, 9 percent for Trader Sally and 1 percent for Trader Tom, suggesting Trader Tom had a much higher probability of surviving the trading year than either Trader Bob or Trader Sally.

As you now know, expectancy refers to the amount of money you can expect your methodology to earn for every dollar you risk. As you can see from the previous examples, a methodology's expectancy is the accumulation of all the wins and all the losses. This involves four variables:

- how often it wins
- how often it loses
- the average win
- the average loss.

Expectancy doesn't favor either variable, although you may do so as you might psychologically prefer a methodology with a higher accuracy rate.

Let's look at the performance of the following four methodologies shown in table 4.3 and see whether further insight into expectancy can be gained.

For each methodology, I assumed a constant $500 was risked per trade, which represented a total of $5,000 risked for the 10 signals. The differences between these methodologies are their accuracy and average win. These differences will help you to appreciate the significance of expectancy.

System_One, continuing the preceding roundup, has a 60 percent accuracy and an average win of $500. Jobber has extraordinary accuracy of 90 percent and the lowest average win of $300. Swinger has high accuracy with 70 percent and a higher average win of $614. Trendy has a low 30 percent accuracy rate but has the highest average win of $2,267.

Which is the superior methodology? The answer is Trendy. It made the highest profit of $3,300, and had the highest expectancy of 66 percent. It did this despite its low 30 percent accuracy.

Strange, isn't it? The methodology with the lowest accuracy had the highest profit and highest expectancy. However, this doesn't suggest that all low-accuracy methodologies will have the highest expectancy. I'm simply

TABLE 4.3   Comparing expectancy between methodologies

Dollar risk per trade	500			
Yearly trade result	System_One	Jobber	Swinger	Trendy
1	500	400	650	2,100
2	500	100	700	2,500
3	500	300	350	2,200
4	500	350	400	−500
5	500	200	900	−500
6	500	150	800	−500
7	−500	400	500	−500
8	−500	350	−500	−500
9	−500	450	−500	−500
10	−500	−500	−500	−500
Profit	1,000	2,200	2,800	3,300
Total money risked	5,000	5,000	5,000	5,000
Expectancy	0.2	0.44	0.56	0.66
Performance				
Wins	6	9	7	3
Loses	4	1	3	7
Accuracy	60%	90%	70%	30%
Average win	500	300	614	2,266
Average loss	−500	−500	−500	−500
Average win:loss	1	0.6	1.2	4.5
Expectancy	20%	44%	56%	66%

trying to illustrate the importance of expectancy, and that it can be good with a low accuracy system if the system's average win is significantly larger than its average loss.

Clearly, accuracy is not that important when developing a methodology. What is important is developing a methodology with a probable positive expectancy. Expectancy is made up of accuracy and payoff.

As risk managers, you should develop methodologies for expectancy, not accuracy. And once you enter the market you should trade for expectancy, not accuracy.

It's all about expectancy. Don't be too concerned about either your accuracy or average win-to-average loss payoff. Focus instead on your expectancy. Improving the accuracy and the average win-to-average loss payoff are important tools to reduce your risk of ruin. When you combine accuracy with the average win-to-average loss payoff you arrive at expectancy—a key weapon against risk of ruin.

Developing a methodology with a probable positive expectancy will take you a step closer to survival. This is a trading plan that over the longer term will produce enough winners to not only pay for the losses, but also produce a profit. My trading strategies give me a positive expectancy when I trade.

Expectancy is mandatory for survival in trading. Expectancy is your edge. Trading without expectancy would be like taking a knife to a gunfight—not very smart. However expectancy is only one-half of my Holy Grail; the other half is opportunities.

OPPORTUNITIES

Opportunities simply refer to the number of times you can apply your expectancy. You can have a methodology with the highest expectancy, but unless you get opportunities to trade it, there will be little reward. Take a look at the following examples shown in table 4.4.

If you were to focus purely on expectancy you would prefer to trade currencies with High octane. Its expectancy of 100 percent is clearly superior to Swinger and Busy bee. Or is it? Although it has the highest expectancy, it only produced a profit of $1,500 due to the small number of trading opportunities presented during the year. Therefore, High octane is the least effective methodology in this example.

Swinger and Busy bee seem identical in most of the key areas. Both have the same accuracy (70 percent), similar average win ($614 and $604), and similar expectancy (56 percent and 55 percent). So the question is— how do you choose between the two? You need to look at the opportunities they present. For the same period, Busy bee had 20 trading opportunities compared to Swinger's 10. Consequently, Busy bee produced a higher profit of $5,450 compared to Swinger's $2,800. Busy bee had the opportunity to apply its 56 percent expectancy across 10 additional trades. Therefore, Busy bee is superior to Swinger.

The message here is that you must take into account the number of opportunities your methodology will present to you. Even if you discovered the mythical Holy Grail, it would be no good if it only produced one trading opportunity per year. Trading once a year is not enough. By combining opportunities with expectancy you have the only Holy Grail in trading.

Your enlightenment continues when you understand:

- As risk managers, you must develop methodologies for expectancy and opportunities.
- As traders, you trade for expectancy and opportunities, not accuracy.

TABLE 4.4   Trading opportunities for three methodologies

Dollar risk per trade	500		
Yearly trade result	High octane	Swinger	Busy bee
1	1,000	650	400
2	1,000	700	650
3	−500	350	700
4		400	400
5		900	800
6		800	900
7		500	700
8		−500	500
9		−500	600
10		−500	500
11			550
12			400
13			700
14			650
15			−500
16			−500
17			−500
18			−500
19			−500
20			−500
Profit	1,500	2,800	5,450
Total money risked	1,500	5,000	10,000
Expectancy	100%	56%	55%
Performance			
Wins	2	7	14
Loses	1	3	6
Accuracy	67%	70%	70%
Average win	1,000	614	604
Average loss	−500	−500	−500
Average win:loss	2	1.2	1.2
Expectancy	100%	56%	55%

Expectancy and opportunities, if you survive, will be responsible for putting the dollars in your trading accounts, not trend lines, not indicators, not gurus.

Wanting to make a profit is not enough for you to survive and succeed. You have to know what your expectancy is, and then seek to maximize it, which is more than just improving your accuracy. You now know you can sacrifice accuracy for improved payoff if you gain expectancy. In addition, you should not focus on developing the highest-expectancy methodology to the exclusion of opportunities.

If you develop a good-expectancy methodology and find it doesn't present you with enough opportunities, you have to find a way to increase your opportunities.

The easiest way to do this is to trade extra markets. If you add one market, you'll double your opportunities, add a third and you'll triple them, and so forth. Assuming your account can afford the extra margin requirements and you're comfortable with the potential extra drawdowns, trading a portfolio of markets is a sensible way of presenting your methodology with additional opportunities.

PURSUING SIMPLICITY

Enlightenment continues when you understand that simplicity is the key to developing methodologies with robust expectancy. Simplicity works on two levels—simplicity of design and simplicity of support and resistance levels.

Simplicity of Design

A trading methodology must be able to pass the McDonald's test—that is, can a teenager understand and trade your methodology? If not, your methodology may just be too complex. You need to keep it simple.

Less is best in designing methodologies. If you have too many components with adjustable variables, then logically more can go wrong. And you need to avoid the intellectual trap trading presents. Many people who fail in trading believe the answer must lie in complexity—because surely the market wouldn't give up its secrets so easily? They start to see the market as a Rubik's cube that needs to be solved. So any theory that offers a clever and deep-thinking perspective will attract their attention. They enjoy the intellectual challenge and stimulation it takes to learn and understand the intricacy of the theory and its application to analyze the market.

My suggestion is to resist the intellectual attraction you may feel toward these theories. And if you do capitulate, please remember to keep in the back of your mind that there are numerous clever theories, as well more sensible middle-of-the-road ones, all with persuasive, logical, and seductive arguments. As you listen to these attractive voices, please just keep reminding yourself that they all can't be right, they just can't be, and you better be able to pick the one which is right. Are you feeling lucky?

You better hope so if you entertain their offerings. However, as I've said, it's best to keep it simple.

Simplicity of Support and Resistance Levels

At its core, trading is simply the identification of potential support and resistance levels. Traders enter a trade because they believe the potential support or resistance level will hold and provide them with profit. Stops are placed where traders think the market will prove the potential support or resistance level has failed. Successful trading is nothing more, nothing less. You buy because your methodology believes the market has found potential support and it will move higher. You place your stop at a level you believe your methodology's analysis will be proven wrong. You sell because your methodology believes the market has hit potential resistance and it will move lower. Again, you place your stop at a level you believe your methodology's analysis will be proven wrong.

Don't get caught up in the latest software or intricate market analysis. Never lose sight of the basic objective of your analytical endeavors—to find potential support and resistance levels.

Why would you buy unless you believed the market had found support, or sell unless the market had found resistance? Sounds straightforward, doesn't it? Yet many traders get so caught up in their particular field of analysis (Elliott wave, Gann, geometry, candlestick, computer systems, astrology, seasonal, divergences, and so on) that they lose sight of their objective—to find where the market is likely to find support or resistance.

Make sure you regularly lift your head from your analysis and keep an eye on the bigger picture—is the market looking at potential support or resistance? It's so simple. In chapter 9, I'll return to simplicity in depth and provide a few examples.

TREADING WHERE MOST FEAR

Enlightenment continues when you learn to tread where most fear. If most active traders lose, you should be treading where they fear to walk, rather than following them. You must learn to move away from the pack; fight the instinct to mingle with the crowd where you enjoy the safety of numbers.

This means thinking outside the square. Essentially, the idea is that if most are looking west, you should look east. Only 10 percent or fewer of traders are in the winners' circle, so for your own survival you need to be in the minority. Not only will you be trading where most fear, you'll also be where the minority cheer.

Some areas where most fear to walk include:

- *Being the best loser:* Most hate to lose and regularly move their stops to give their trades a little bit more room. You should strive to be the best loser. I do.
- *Being the best winner:* Most are so anxious they'll lose what little profit they have, they ignore their trade plans and prematurely exit winning positions. You should strive to be the best winner you can be, you should strive to hold on to winning trades for as long as your trade plan says. I do.
- *Being a trend trader:* Unfortunately, markets do not trend all the time. As a result, trend trading usually has a low accuracy rate, where traders will only win around a third of their trades. Now, the majority cannot stomach only winning a one-third of their trades, even though it has been proven beyond doubt that trend trading works! So you should strive to learn how to trade successfully with the trend. You should learn how to survive on winning only a third of your trades. You should strive to be successful at what most cannot achieve. You should strive to enjoy what the misery trend traders suffer when they generally lose on 67 percent of their trades. Pride yourself on being able to do what most traders can't—lose on most your trades. I do.
- *Embracing simplicity:* Most mistrust the obvious and simple solutions, seeking clues and advantages in complexity. You should strive to investigate, research, and develop simple trading solutions with few moving parts, which if proved worthwhile, will have a better chance of remaining robust and profitable due to the lack of moving parts. I do.
- *Being skeptical of commercially available charting programs:* Most have charting programs with the usual array of indicators. Ensure you independently validate any indicator before adding it to your methodology. I do.
- *Being skeptical of commercially available trading systems:* Most believe the marketing hype surrounding commercially available trading systems. Most are susceptible to clever advertising and marketing campaigns. You should strive to remain objective and at arms length to the promises of easy riches and strive to ask the tough questions. I do.
- *Doing the work: Most are lazy:* You should strive to research, investigate and validate every trading idea you think is worthwhile. You should strive to do the work independently. I do.

VALIDATION

Validation refers to validating your expectancy with the TEST procedure. TEST is my acronym for Thirty Emailed Simulated Trades. Validating your expectancy with TEST will complete your enlightenment.

Having designed a simple methodology with good expectancy and opportunities, your final step before you commit real money to trading is to validate your expectancy. The only way to validate your expectancy correctly is to use out-of-sample data under simulated real-time trading conditions. Out-of-sample data is data that has not been used. The best out-of-sample data to use is real-time "live" data.

Paper trading your methodology will not validate its expectancy because it does not involve an independent observer. Paper trading with yourself is pointless because it does not simulate the uncompromising nature of the market. The market will not allow you to change or fudge your trading rules midstream. It will not allow you to remove a trade when you incur another paper loss. Paper trading does not place you and your soul under an enormous spotlight, as the market does. There is no final judgment, just giggle and fun times as you play with yourself making imaginary paper profits.

The only way to correctly validate your expectancy is to TEST your methodology. For 30 simulated trades you need to email your complete orders to your trading partner before the markets open. Your trading partner will need to print a hardcopy of your simulated orders and he or she should be under instructions only to accept orders sent before the market in question opens. Your trading partner will become your virtual client adviser, recording your results. Once 30 simulated trades are completed, your trading partner will return the hardcopy emails to you so you can calculate your expectancy, using the formula provided earlier in the chapter.

If your expectancy is positive, you should overlay your equity curve on the underlying market. You should be hoping for a smooth equity curve. Examining your equity curve will tell you whether your methodology's results are dependent on one or two "lucky" trades. Obviously, you would prefer your methodology's results to be evenly spread and not reliant on a couple of key trades, because then you wouldn't know whether your results were just "lucky" or well deserved.

Thirty emailed simulated trades are necessary to ensure your simulation sample size is large enough to be statistically valid. The use of email is all about simulating the real market. This is why it's important to have a trading partner who doesn't live with you. As with a real trade, once you email your simulated order, there is no going back. You can't pull back the email (unless it's before the market opens or the market hasn't triggered your order level). Just like real trading, your simulated trade's fate will be left in the hands of the trading gods.

You will find it difficult to bare your trading soul to your trading partner. However, trading "naked" is about as close to real-time trading as you will get. Although it may inflict some embarrassment and humiliation upon you, it will be a lot more preferable to losing hard-earned dollars in the real market.

When you follow the TEST procedure, you must remember to only trade single lots when you email your simulated trades. Your objective should be to validate your methodology's expectancy. If it is positive, and not reliant on a single extraordinary trade, you'll know your methodology is validated.

If your expectancy is not positive, it's back to the drawing board, where you must repeat the TEST procedure until you have validated your expectancy.

The TEST procedure applies to both discretionary and mechanical traders. If you're a mechanical trader, you should not mistake a smooth historical equity curve as validation for your system. It only shows that you have been successful in managing to fit your methodology to historical data. Looking backward is cheating; going forward is what counts.

Some discretionary traders may believe it's impossible to email a complete order to their trading partner. They may say they don't know what they're going to do before the market opens because they want to watch it first. They may argue that although they're in a position, they're not yet sure when or how they'll take their profits. If this is the case, those traders do not have a clearly defined trade plan. Although you may prefer to wait for the market's opening, you should already know what to look for before you enter. If you know what you're looking for, you should be able to articulate it in your order to your trading partner.

This also applies to those discretionary traders who want to let their profits run. You can still write your exit instructions for your trading partner because you should have clearly defined rules for exiting winning positions, even those that you want to let run. If you use a trailing stop, you must communicate it to your trading partner so he or she can trail it.

Even discretionary traders should have a clear and unambiguous trade plan for triggering entries, placing stops, and exiting winners. The rules should not change from trade to trade. Even if you operate a different trade plan per setup, for the same setup the trade plan should not change.

If you can think of your trade plan, you can write your trade plan. If you can write your trade plan, you can email your trade plan. If you can email your trade plan, you can email your trade plan before the market opens. Apart from validating your expectancy, you also need to believe in your methodology.

Even if you developed a good-expectancy system by chance, you may still find it hard to trade it due to your subconscious mind not believing in it. This is why you may find it difficult to trade commercially available systems (assuming they're robust). Your belief system has not been "tuned into" the system's expectancy. It's only when your internal belief system unconditionally embraces a methodology that you're able to trade it. This is where your "head" comes into it and why psychology is a hurdle you have to jump (not conqueror to the exclusion of all else) to survive and prosper in trading.

The best way to develop a strong belief system in your methodology is to simulate real-time trading conditions as best you can, which the TEST procedure allows you to do. If your methodology holds up with a positive expectancy, your belief system will know it and embrace it and make it easier for you to follow in real-time trading.

Electronic Trading Simulators

Many electronic brokers allow you to open dummy accounts to try your skills at trading. You can use these dummy accounts as trading simulators to test your methodology. Before using the TEST procedure, you may find it useful to first road-test your methodology on one of these dummy accounts. I would not use them as a substitute for the TEST procedure because I believe you can't replace the benefits gained from having a trading partner monitor your trading performance. There is nothing like having another person peek over your shoulder to really focus the mind, just like when you risk real dollars in a real market. So following the TEST procedure to validate your expectancy is nonnegotiable. It is a must-do step in your trading journey. However, I can see the benefit in using a dummy account as a "pre" TEST run.

IN SUMMARY

Enlightenment is the second essential universal principle of successful trading and I believe the most important. Enlightenment has drawn clearly defined boundaries for you to operate within. If you stay within them, you'll have a greater chance of survival and, as a consequence, trading success. The objective of enlightenment is to help you avoid risk of ruin. Avoid it and you will become a successful trader.

Enlightenment has shown that you can reduce your risk of ruin by:

- applying sensible money management rules to reduce your dollar risk per trade
- improving your methodology's accuracy
- improving your methodology's average win to average loss payoff
- designing your methodology for expectancy, not accuracy
- designing your methodology for opportunities
- designing a simple methodology
- designing a methodology that identifies potential support and resistance levels

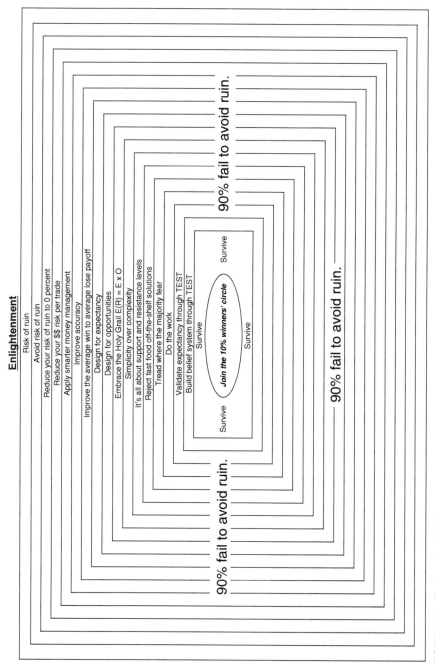

Enlightenment

- Risk of ruin
- Avoid risk of ruin
- Reduce your risk of ruin to 0 percent
- Reduce your $$ risk per trade
- Apply smarter money management
- Improve accuracy
- Improve the average win to average lose payoff
- Design for expectancy
- Design for opportunities
- Embrace the Holy Grail E(R) = E x O
- Simplicity over complexity
- It's all about support and resistance levels
- Reject fast food off-the-shelf solutions
- Tread where the majority fear
- Do the work
- Validate expectancy through TEST
- Build belief system through TEST

Survive   Survive

Join the 10% winners' circle

Survive   Survive

90% fail to avoid ruin.

90% fail to avoid ruin.

90% fail to avoid ruin.

FIGURE 4.12 The Pyramid of Enlightenment

57

- treading where most fear and the minority cheer
- validating your expectancy with the TEST procedure and
- building up your belief system through validating your expectancy.

Hopefully, enlightenment has shown you the way to survive. If you survive, you will succeed in trading! See "The Pyramid of Enlightenment" in figure 4.12.

In the next chapter I will discuss the third universal principle of successful trading—developing a trading style.

NOTE

1. Balsara, Nauzer, *Money Management Strategies for Futures Traders* (John Wiley, 1992).

5

Principle Three: Trading Style

In this chapter, I'll be exploring how to select an appropriate trading style, the third essential universal principle of successful trading. Selecting an appropriate trading style requires two decisions to be made concerning:

• trading mode
• trading time frame.

TRADING MODE

Trading mode refers to the type of trading you would like to use. There are two types of mode:

• trend trading
• countertrend trading.

You either trade with the trend, or against the trend. That's the easy part. The hard part is working out the trend! Countertrend trading is usually referred to as swing trading. So I'll use ''swing'' rather than ''countertrend'' in this discussion.

A simple explanation of trend and swing trading can be seen in figure 5.1.

Markets rarely trend consistently, spending roughly 85 percent of the time being range bound, chopping around, and frustrating trend traders. Trend traders trade when they recognize a distinct trend, and will trade in the direction they believe the trend is heading. Swing traders trade against the market's trend direction. They believe the market trend will reverse, or offer a quick opportunity to trade a pullback against the trend.

Trend traders usually have low accuracy and lose often, but when they win, they win big, and their average length of trade is usually weeks, if not months. Swing traders usually have higher accuracy with lower average wins. They're out of their positions within a few days or weeks at the latest. The difficult part for either type of trader is to determine the trend's direction.

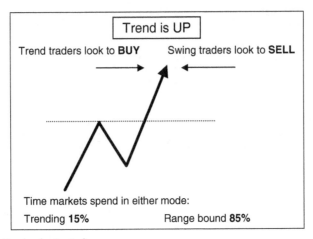

FIGURE 5.1   Trend and swing trading

As traders, you will need to select a mode—either trend trading, swing trading, or a combination of both. Many successful traders will usually incorporate both trend trading and swing trading into their trade plans. Another important factor will be your time frame.

TIME FRAMES

You have to decide on a time frame to trade—day, short-term, medium-term, or long-term trading. Day trading refers to being "square," or out of the market, by the end of day.

Day traders never hold a position overnight and may trade a number of times during the day. Traders using the other three time frames do hold positions overnight—although for varying lengths of time. Short-term traders may hold positions for up to one week. Medium-term traders may hold positions up to a couple of weeks, while long-term traders can hold positions for more than a month. However, there are no hard or fast time-line delineations between these types of traders.

CHOOSING YOUR TRADING STYLE

Between trading mode and time frame, there are plenty of combinations you can choose as an appropriate trading style. Now the general consensus in the average trading books is that when deciding upon your preferred trading style you should look to use, select, or develop a trading style that suits your personality and temperament. You need to feel comfortable, to be as one with your trading style. If you don't, you'll find it difficult to follow and execute.

You've probably read or heard this advice plenty of times. And it does make intuitive sense since we are all different, with varying levels of temperaments and personalities. It makes sense to find a trading methodology that will fit your personality. However, there are a couple of small problems with this general guideline. Although it is well intended, it generally ignores the reality of the markets and trading..

First, if everything ever written or said about the markets worked, you could cherrypick a trading approach that made you feel comfortable, warm, and secure. Unfortunately, most of what is written about trading and the markets doesn't work, and is rarely supported with proof that it does. Usually, readers will only see a couple of well-chosen chart examples to support the idea. There is no objective evidence the idea can consistently make money, and I'm not surprised because most of what is written about trading doesn't work. Fact. If it did then you wouldn't see 90 percent of traders lose. It would be the other away around: 90 percent would be winning. So unfortunately maximum adversity won't allow you to cherry-pick a trading idea or approach to suit your personality because most trading ideas aren't worth a cracker.

Second, what feels "comfortable" in trading generally does not work. If trading was comfortable, everyone would be doing it and doing it with extraordinary profits. Remember, maximum adversity rarely hands out "comfortable" profits. For example those trades that feel the most comfortable usually occur when the average trader feels they are in good company where the majority thinks the same. The trader feels comfortable in committing to a long trade because all the analysis they have read and all the chat sites they have visited have all expressed the same view as them. The trader feels comfortable in the safety of numbers. Yet generally when an idea has reached the masses, it is already priced into the trade. Those traders joining the trade when most are in agreement are usually the last ones in. Being the last means there is an absence of buyers left to join the trade to help push prices higher. Once everyone is in a "comfortable" trade, markets tend to have an irritating habit of reversing—stopping everyone out. From my experience, it's usually best to trade with the minority, and being in a minority or holding a minority view is not comfortable because you're an outsider to the crowd. Generally, "comfortable" can kill a trader. Consequently, although the general advice to develop a trading style to suit your personality is well intended, it does ignore a market reality that "comfortable" trades are rarely profitable.

Third, not all trading styles require the same financial commitment from traders. Generally, short-term swing trading requires a smaller financial commitment than longer-term trend trading. If you have unlimited financial resources, this consideration isn't a stumbling block. However, if you, like most private traders, have limited risk capital for trading, then this is an important consideration. Generally, the longer your trading horizon is, the larger your trading account has to be.

For example, say you look to buy when your 20-day moving average crosses over your slower 60-day moving average, and the reverse for sells. I don't know the results of this long-term approach; however, I'd be surprised if you didn't make money if you traded it correctly over a portfolio of markets and applied sensible money management. The results of this strategy would possibly show that even if you only won 30 percent of the time, but were able to have generated an average win-to-average loss ratio of, say, 3:1, you would be making money. Using the expectancy formula from the previous chapter, you should expect to earn at least 20 cents for every dollar risked, or a 20 percent return. However, to trade this dual moving average crossover system successfully you would have to trade a portfolio of 20 to 30 markets, which is usually beyond the financial means of most private traders.

The problem for small private traders arrives when you look at the size of the portfolio you would have to trade to be successful. The reason long-term trend trading works is that a trader's net is thrown as wide as possible, for as long as possible, to cover as many markets as possible. By doing this, the trend trader will increase their chance of snagging one or two runaway markets. Long-term trend traders need to monitor and trade between 20 and 30 markets to be successful.

Let's take the Turtle Trading system for example. It's a famous long-term trend trading program that needs to trade between 20 and 30 markets. Figure 5.2 shows the results for 2007 assuming a million-dollar account was trading it. For 2007 it had an outstanding year. The only problem was that it suffered a 60 percent drawdown when the account went from $1,250,000 in February 2007 to $500,000 in late March 2007. A $750,000 drawdown! Now, not many private traders would have been able to stand such a loss.

Some promoters may say that long-term trend traders could trade fewer than 20 markets. However, what they're doing is curve fitting the markets into a portfolio to help promote their course or product. What would happen if none of the selected 15 markets showed a big winner for some years? I imagine the poor long-term trend trader would be doing it tough! If you can afford to fund the initial and variation margins for between 20 and 30 futures contracts plus their respective possible drawdowns per market, you could consider long-term trend trading as your preferred trading style. If not, you cannot afford to consider it even though it may suit your personality. Usually, short-term swing trading, which allows you to focus on only one or two markets, is more achievable for private traders. Traders with slightly larger accounts, who can monitor and trade about 10 markets, can consider a medium-term trend trading style.

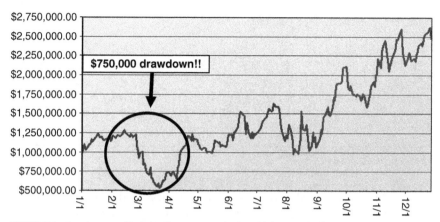

FIGURE 5.2   Actual contract Turtle Trading system results from 1/1/07 to 12/28/07 using a $1 million model portfolio

Source: www.turtletrading.com

Russell Sands and Larry Williams each present useful seminars on ways to trade. Sands teaches the legendary long-term trend trading turtle system, while Williams teaches his own short-term pattern-based trading style. Both presenters and seminars are excellent, particularly as Larry Williams would trade live while presenting his Million Dollar Challenge (MDC) Workshop. As an aside, Larry called his seminar the "Million Dollar Challenge" because he wanted to challenge himself to make a million dollars trading live while teaching his students: hence the "Million Dollar Challenge," And he achieved his challenge by making more than $1.2 million trading during his MDC workshops. I have summarized the results in table 5.1.

And I can attest to having witnessed Larry trade live on two occasions because I have personally attended two MDC workshops. But this is only an aside. Now back to comparing Russell Sands' and Larry Williams' seminars. As I've said, they're both excellent. However, Williams' approach to trading is more suited to private traders than Sands' long-term trend trading Turtle seminar. Using Williams' approach, you can focus on one or two markets, which is achievable for most small private traders. However, Sands' Turtle seminar requires a trading account large enough to fund up to between 20 and 30 markets. If I had known the financial commitment required to trade the Turtle system before committing to the seminar, I would never have attended. Not because I didn't think the methodology was worthwhile, but because my account wasn't large enough to trade it.

As an aside, I was chatting with a trader who called me for my opinion about the Turtle system. I gave him the same view, that it was not appropriate for small private traders. Well, just recently he called me again. He was despondent about his trading. Ignoring the advice I gave him, this

TABLE 5.1   Larry Williams' live trading results

Oct 1999	$250,000	Nov 2000	$46,481	Oct 2001	$48,225	Apr 2003	$12,046	Sep 2004	$26,023
May 2000	$302,000	Mar 2001	−$9,640	May 2002	$32,850	May 2003	−$750	Oct 2004	$92,075
May 2000	$35,000	Apr 2001	$149,000	Oct 2002	$79,825	Oct 2003	$34,600	Jun 2005	$6,000
Oct 2000	$22,637	May 2001	$23,300	Mar 2003	$35,034	Jun 2004	$34,000	Nov 2005	$34,000
								Jun 2006	$3,800
									$1,256,506

Source: Larry Williams

trader did undertake the weekend Turtle seminar with Russell Sands and the inevitable happened; the normal drawdowns long-term trend traders experience occurred and knocked out his small account. It wasn't the system, because he told me it had recently traded out of its drawdown, but it was the financial commitment to fund so many open positions along with the inevitably large drawdown. Please let this be a lesson to you.

I'll now take a closer look at long-term trend trading and short-term swing trading.

LONG-TERM TREND TRADING

As you know, long-term trend trading should only be considered by those who can afford to trade with a large account. Looking at table 5.2, you can see the key characteristics and their impact on long-term trend trading. I have

TABLE 5.2   The key characteristics of long-term trend trading

Component	Key metrics	Impact	
Money Mgt	Portfolio	Large	20 to 30 markets
	Drawdowns	Large	
		Long	
	Financial commitment	High	20 to 30 × initial margins
Method	Time frame	Long	1+ months
	Accuracy	Low	25% to 35%
	Avg. win: avg. loss	High	3.0+
	Expectancy	Good	
	Opportunities per market	Low	
	Brokerage and slippage	Low	
Psychology	Emotional hurdles	High	Frequent losses. Long drawdowns. Difficult to take breaks.

grouped each characteristic under one of the three key components required to survive in trading—money management, method, and psychology.

Money Management
Portfolio

A long-term trend-trading approach requires a large portfolio to succeed. Since markets only trend 15 percent of the time, trend traders need to monitor and trade between 20 and 30 markets to ensure they capture one or two of each year's best trending markets.

Drawdowns

Long-term trend trading approaches have a few big winners and many small losers. If you were trading 20 to 30 markets and were losing frequently, the drawdowns would accumulate in size and accumulate often. Since you would spend more time losing than winning, this approach would, and does, spend a long time in drawdown.

Financial commitment

As I have mentioned, the financial commitment for long-term trend trading is quite high. Monitoring and trading between 20 and 30 markets requires trend traders to be able to fund all of those positions fully simultaneously. It's unlikely a long-term trend-trading system would simultaneously trigger 20–30 entry signals across all markets; however, trend traders would have to be prepared for such an occurrence, and couldn't afford to pick and choose their signals. Trend traders have no idea which market or signal is going to make their trading year, so they have to trade all markets and all opportunities, regardless of their timing.

Method
Time frame

Trend traders could expect to hold positions that are not stopped out for more than a month. They'd need to learn really to ride their winners, which would have to pay for the losses incurred along the way.

Accuracy

The accuracy of long-term trend trading is low and can vary between 25 and 35 percent. This is not surprising because markets only spend 15 percent of their time trending.

Average win-to-average loss payoff ratio

The average win-to-average loss payoff ratio is high. A good long-term trend-trading methodology should deliver an average win that is at least three times above the average losing trade. Trend traders would need the high average winning trades to more than make up for all the small losses to generate a return on their risk capital. Invariably, successful long-term trend traders bag a couple of huge wins that make their whole year.

Expectancy

The expectancy for long-term trend trading is good. A trend trading approach that averages 30 percent winners with a 3:1 average win-to-average loss payoff will deliver a 20 percent expectancy ([30 percent × 3.0] – [70 percent × 1.0]).

Opportunities

The opportunities per single market are poor. Trend-following approaches are slow to trigger entry setups and therefore do not present enough trading opportunities per market during the year. Where trend trading makes up for lack of opportunities per market is by trading a large portfolio of markets. Trading a portfolio of 20–30 markets would present enough opportunities to succeed.

However, for traders looking to trade a single market, even if you had a large enough account to consider using a long-term trend-trading approach, it still would not be appropriate for you to do so. This is because a long-term trend trading approach requires, like any methodology, plenty of opportunities to apply its expectancy. Trading a single market would not present a long-term trend-trading approach with enough opportunities. The only way to do so would be to trade a portfolio of markets.

Transaction costs—brokerage and slippage

Transaction costs of brokerage and slippage are low in long-term trend trading. Because this is a slower trading approach, there are usually fewer trades than in swing trading. Fewer trades mean less brokerage. When brokerage and slippage are incurred, they usually represent a low percentage of the profits since the average wins are so high.

Psychology
Emotional hurdles

Long-term trend trading is emotionally hard. Frequent losses do not provide the positive feedback our body and soul require. Like anything in life, it's easier to continue along a chosen path when you receive constant positive feedback. When the frequent feedback is negative, it does make it more difficult to keep trading. Your finger will want to push the trade button but your mind would be screaming, "No, not again, not another losing trade!"

Frequent losses lead to long drawdowns. Once again, it makes it emotionally difficult to keep taking the trades when you're constantly in a drawdown.

In addition, long-term trend trading can be emotionally and physically tiring. This is because long-term trend traders cannot afford to miss one signal, ever. The reason for this is because they don't know from where or when the next big winner will come. This makes long-term trend trading exhausting. It can become almost impossible to take a holiday unless you have someone who can place your orders for you.

SHORT-TERM SWING TRADING

Table 5.3 summarizes the key characteristics of short-term swing trading.

Money Management
Portfolio

Short-term swing trading can work with a single market portfolio. This is good for small private traders who want to trade just a single market. Naturally, you can trade more than one market; however, short-term swing trading doesn't require multiple markets to make money.

TABLE 5.3   The key characteristics of short-term swing trading

Component	Key metrics	Impact	
Money Management	Portfolio	Small	1+ markets
	Drawdowns	Small	
		Short	
	Financial commitment	Low	1 × initial margins
Method	Time frame	Short	1-5 days
	Accuracy	High	50%+
	Avg. win: avg. loss	Low	1.0+
	Expectancy	Good	
	Opportunities per market	High	
	Brokerage and slippage	High	
Psychology	Emotional hurdles	Low	Frequent wins. Short drawdowns. Easy to take breaks.

Drawdowns

Since short-term swing trading can operate on a single market, the draw-downs are manageable. Trading one market can still be uncomfortable, but at least it's not going to be magnified by multiple markets.

In addition, drawdowns are usually shorter in duration. Short-term swing trading usually produces a relatively smooth equity curve because the results are not dependent on a few huge winners each year. This smoothness of the equity curve implies that drawdowns, when they occur, are over relatively quickly.

Financial commitment

The financial commitment for short-term swing trading is low. It takes less money to trade a single market than it does to trade multiple markets.

Method
Time frame

Short-term swing traders are usually out of the market within one to five days. They are just looking to capture short "swings" in the market and not ride a new trend into the sunset.

Accuracy

Short-term swing trading usually has an accuracy rate of more than 50 percent. It requires higher accuracy than trend trading because it usually has a lower average win-to-average loss payoff ratio.

Average win-to-average loss payoff ratio

Due to the short time swing traders are in the market, their average win-to-average loss payoff ratio is low—usually between 1.0 and 2.0.

Expectancy

Expectancy for short-term swing trading is good if the combination of accuracy and payoff is enough. For a short-term swing trading approach with an accuracy of 55 percent and an average win-to-average loss payoff ratio of 1.3, traders could expect to earn 26.5 cents ([55 percent × 1.3] − [45 percent × 1.0]) for every dollar risked in a trade. Naturally, expectancy can be improved through improving either the accuracy or payoff ratio.

Opportunities

Opportunities are good for short-term swing traders because markets are range bound or choppy for 85 percent of the time. Short-term swing traders find plenty of support and resistance levels to trade from, which provides plenty of trading opportunities.

Transaction costs—brokerage and slippage

Transaction costs of brokerage and slippage are high in short-term swing trading and have to be taken into account when validating a methodology's expectancy. Trading frequency is high because there are plenty of opportunities to trade and each win is relatively small. This results in high brokerage. In addition, due to the average win being relatively small when compared to long-term trend trading, the percentage cost of brokerage and slippage is high. This is why it is so difficult for day traders to make money. They have less of the market's movement to trade, and have to pay for their transaction costs, in comparison to a long-term trend traders, who can use a whole month of price movement to pay for their brokerage and slippage.

Psychology
Emotional hurdles

Short-term swing trading is emotionally easier to trade compared to a longer-term system. This is because frequent winners provide frequent positive feedback that what you're doing is right. Frequent winners re-inforce good trading behavior, and make it easier for short-term swing traders to keep taking their signals. They keep drawdowns manageable and short in duration. This minimizes the emotional hurdles traders have to navigate to continue following their trade plan. In addition, short-term swing traders are able to take a break from trading, since missing the next one-to-10 signals isn't performance threatening to their trading year.

LONG-TERM TREND TRADING VERSUS SHORT-TERM SWING TRADING

Examining the key characteristics of long-term trend trading and short-term swing trading has shown that the trading style of the latter is preferable for small private traders. The financial and emotional characteristics of short-term swing trading:

- portfolio
- drawdowns
- financial commitment
- emotional hurdles

TABLE 5.4   The key characteristics of various trading styles

General trading style screen analysis		Short-term swing trading	Medium-term swing trading	Short-term trend trading	Medium-term trend trading	No good! Long-term trend trading
Component money management	Key metrics					
	Portfolio	Small	Small	Small	Small	Large
	Drawdowns	Small	Medium	Small	Medium	Large
		Short	Medium	Short-term	Medium	Long
	Financial commitment	Low	Low	Low	Low	High
Method	Time frame	Short	Medium	Short	Medium	Long
	Accuracy	High	High	Low	High	Low
	Avg. win: avg. loss	Low	Good	Low	Good	High
	Expectancy	Good	Good	Good	Good	Good
	Opportunities per market	High	Medium	Good	Medium	Low
	Brokerage and slippage	High	Medium	High	Medium	Low
Psychology	Emotional hurdles	Low	Medium	Low	Medium	High

are smaller and easier to cope with than in long-term trend trading.

The expectancy can be the same between the trading styles, so that should not be a deciding factor. However, you should take into account the number of opportunities you'll receive if your preference is to swing trade a single market.

I have compared the two extremes of trading styles to provide you with an insight into the intricacies of both approaches. Traders can trade with the trend across all time frames, whether intraday, short or medium term. Now that I have examined the two extremes, it would be worthwhile to have a look at the strategies in between. Table 5.4 compares the various trading styles.

The purpose of table 5.4 is to provide you with a rough guide of what you are likely to experience if you adopt a certain trading style. You should spend some time looking at it to determine where your "personality" type sits. I personally trade short-term and medium-term swing and trend continuation patterns.

Unfortunately, there is some bad news. As mentioned, the rule of maximum adversity means that traders are not going to be able simply to choose a trading style that suits their personality.

What will influence your eventual trading style will be expectancy, opportunity and validation, not your personality; in other words, what makes the hard dollars.

IN SUMMARY

This third principle of successful trading says that when you come to select an appropriate trading style you will need to factor in the following:

- the financial commitment required to trade the particular style
- the trading style's expectancy, opportunities and its validation
- possibly whether the trading style feels comfortable and fits your personality (if you're lucky).

Whether you look to the stars, use indicators, identify chart patterns, or follow an Italian mathematician to find trading signals, it doesn't matter how you feel as long as your methodology has a probable positive expectancy of making money. Business comes before feelings. Trading deals with reality, not niceties. In the next chapter I'll discuss how to select an appropriate market to trade.

C H A P T E R

Principle Four: Markets

In this chapter, I'll be looking at the fourth essential universal principle of successful trading—how to select appropriate markets to trade. I'll examine what makes a market good for trading and explain why the index and currency markets are some of the best. These are my preferred markets to trade for the reasons you're about to read. However, you may prefer other markets, so with this chapter you'll learn what makes an appropriate market to trade to help you in your selection.

I believe an appropriate market to trade should have most of the attributes listed in table 6.1.

If a market has most of these attributes, it is worth considering. It should not come as a surprise to learn that the first hurdle any market needs to jump concerns operational risk management attributes. As I have mentioned, survival is the number one objective in trading, so I will first examine the operational risk management characteristics.

GOOD OPERATIONAL RISK MANAGEMENT ATTRIBUTES
Price and Volume Transparency

Price and volume transparency refers to a market's ability to show all participants all price and volume activity. There are several important questions to ask about a market—can you see all the trading activity going on and receive all the price and volume information? Will you be able to rely on the information to make an informed decision about your trading? Operational risk—are you seeing everything?

The best securities to trade are those that can only be traded in one marketplace. A single marketplace ensures you receive the best price for your supply or demand, at any given moment. You should determine whether only one marketplace exists for your security. It's important to avoid trading securities with competing marketplaces where other traders can execute significant business and hide important market volume.

TABLE 6.1   Superior trading attributes

Good operational risk management attributes
Price and volume transparency
Liquidity
24-hour coverage
Zero counterparty risk
Honest and efficient marketplace
Low transaction costs
Good trading attributes
Volatility
Research
Simplicity
Ease of short selling
Specialization
Opportunities
Growth
Leverage

Liquidity

Once you have established that there are no competing marketplaces for your preferred trading security, you need to determine whether the security has enough liquidity. Operational risk—can you exit your position quickly? Is there enough liquidity to do so?

Although it is usually easy to enter a market, being the best loser means you need to be able to exit a position when you want to, not when the volume picks up enough to let you out. To ensure this, you need to trade highly liquid securities.

24-Hour Coverage

An excellent trading market will have 24-hour coverage. The only market to do this correctly (a full 24 hours of continuous trading) is the foreign exchange market through the wholesale interbank over-the-counter (OTC) market. The OTC market never closes, as banks around the globe will always quote a price. However, the Chicago Mercantile Exchange's (CME) electronic futures contracts do close for one hour as it only trades 23 hours a day on its Globex platform. CME's currency futures close at 4.00p.m. and reopen an hour later at 5:00pm Chicago, U.S. time.

Operational risk—can you exit your position overnight when it all goes pear shaped?

The operational benefit of 24-hour trading is that you can have your stop working 24 hours a day. This is a significant operational risk management hurdle.

Zero Counterparty Risk

Another risk traders face is their counterparties' ability to honor their side of the trade. It's no good executing a winning trade if you can't collect the money. Operational risk—will you be able to collect your money?

Due to novation, the clearinghouse guarantees the performance of all futures contracts. You can enter into positions and not worry about the counterparty risk. However, other securities are not so creditworthy. For example, when you purchase a share there is no guarantee the company will not go into liquidation. When you trade either margin FX, CFDs, or spread bets, there is no guarantee the providers themselves will not get into financial difficulty. With those securities, a trader does face counterparty risk and must weigh the risks against any potential gain in trading them.

Honest and Efficient Marketplace

It's hard enough surviving in trading without having to deal with questionable operational practices and inefficiencies. Operational risk—are there clearly defined rules to play by?

When you trade futures, you are dealing in an honest and efficient marketplace. This is due to the exchanges being regulated. Regulation requires the exchange and its service providers (futures brokers and advisers) to follow legislative procedures that are designed purely for the protection of market participants—you and me.

You can trade with confidence knowing the exchange and its participants are operating with the highest level of integrity, and that they cannot change the rules to suit themselves. This is not the case with sharemarkets. During the 2008 Global Financial Crisis many sharemarket exchanges around the world banned short selling. If you were a share trader at the time you would have lost half of your trading opportunities! In my mind, a sharemarket may not be as efficient for trading as many people would have us believe (particularly from the exchanges themselves).

Low Transaction Costs

The final operational risk is the cost of doing business—that is, brokerage and slippage. Operational risk—is the cost of trading competitive?

Traders trade for expectancy, and slippage and brokerage reduce this. The more you minimize your transaction costs, the more expectancy you'll have and the greater your chance of survival. So you should be looking at markets that allow you to minimize your costs of execution.

Let's compare the brokerage cost between a futures contract and a portfolio of shares. In this example, I'll use the Australian SPI index futures contract. You can use whichever index contract you trade and the results will still be the same. The SPI's point value is $25. So for every point it moves, the SPI's value changes by $25. At an index value of 6,250 a SPI contract's face value is $156,250 ($25 × 6,250). To buy and sell one SPI contract you should not have to pay more than $50. To buy an equivalent portfolio of shares valued at $156,250, I'll assume an active equity trader has a very competitive brokerage rate of only 0.15 of 1 per cent. For the equity trader to buy and sell $156,250 worth of shares they would have to pay $468.75 (2 × 0.0015 × $91,400) in brokerage. If both traders execute one trade per week, the SPI trader would have paid $2,600 in brokerage, while the share trader would have paid $24,375! I know which brokerage bill I'd prefer! As you can see, the cost of trading index futures compared to physical shares is very competitive.

In summary, any security you trade should be able to satisfy the majority of these operational risk management benchmarks.

Let's now take a look at what gives a market good trading attributes.

GOOD TRADING ATTRIBUTES
Volatility

Without price movement traders can't make money. Trading attribute—is there enough price movement to trade?

In my opinion the two most volatile market segments in the world are the indices and currencies markets.

Research

To trade without research and investigation is to gamble. Trading attribute—are there sufficient historical data for research?

It's best to research and back test a methodology's expectancy over the largest data sample possible. Even better is to have a large enough data sample so that you can split it in half for back testing. This would allow you to develop your methodology on the first half of data, and once satisfied, run it across the other half of out-of-sample data to see how it would have gone in forward testing. Doing so is nearly as good as following my TEST procedure to validate your system's expectancy.

Simplicity

At one extreme, it's easier to focus on a single market portfolio as compared to focusing on a long-term trend trader's 20-to-30-market portfolio. Trading attribute—is the market simple to monitor?

Here you would need to determine how easy it would be to collect and monitor the daily data for the markets you wish to trade. Today, this is quite easy given the existence of the internet and so many electronic data providers. With one click of a button you can download data from more than 100 markets within a few minutes or less!

Ease of Short Selling

Traders want to be able to buy and sell when they choose to. Trading attribute—is it possible to sell short without conditions?

For futures and options traded on regulated exchanges and for margin FX, there are no conditions preventing traders from short selling (unless a particular exchange does have price limits in place and a market does reach that limit intraday).

Unfortunately, you cannot say the same for shares, as we witnessed during the 2008 Global Financial Crisis sharemarket meltdown, when many exchanges banned the short selling of shares, and in particular financial shares.

Specialization

For the small private trader, it pays to specialize. It's financially easier to narrow your focus on fewer similar markets than to trade a larger portfolio containing varying markets. Trading attribute—is it possible to specialize in the market and use your trading knowledge?

Monitoring and trading a portfolio consisting of a single market segment such as the indices, currencies, interest rates, energies, metals, grains or meats definitely allow you to both specialize and use your knowledge.

Opportunities

It's not enough to have a methodology with a positive expectancy. Unless you can find opportunities to trade, you'll fail to build your trading account. Trading attribute—will the market provide enough trading opportunities?

You will find that markets that exhibit both good liquidity and price volatility will provide you with plenty of trading opportunities. But you must remember to take into account your trading style, as well as that long-term trend trading methodologies will produce fewer trading opportunities compared to short-term swing trading.

Growth

Traders require markets large enough to allow them to enter and exit easily when they choose to. In addition, they require markets large enough to allow them to grow their position size as their trading accounts grow. Trading attribute—is the market's daily volume large enough to allow traders to increase their position size?

This is another reason markets with good liquidity are so important.

Leverage

Leverage allows traders access to markets they would not normally be able to afford. Trading attribute—can the market be traded at a fraction of its face value?

Futures, options, warrants, margin FX, CFDs, and spread betting all allow traders to access their markets at a fraction of the respective contract face value.

IN SUMMARY

I hope this universal principle has shown you how important it is to select the right markets to trade. In my opinion, you will need to select markets that satisfy most of these attributes because your trading survival may depend on it. I personally trade the index and currency futures because I believe they satisfy all of the attributes, which make them some of the best markets to trade for the active private trader.

In the next chapter, I'll take a look at the next essential universal principle of successful trading—the Three Pillars.

CHAPTER

7

Principle Five: The Three Pillars

The universal principles continue in this chapter as I look at the fifth and largest principle of successful trading—the Three Pillars of trading. The Three Pillars of trading consist of:

• money management
• methodology
• psychology

and are the nuts and bolts of practical trading. If you want to achieve your objective of becoming successful traders, where success is measured by dollars in the bank, you must comprehend, develop and execute a plan for each component of trading's Three Pillars.

As I have mentioned, I consider money management to be the most important element, followed by methodology, and then psychology. Although many people argue that psychology is the most important element of trading, I believe it's not more important than money management or methodology. I believe the difference between winners and losers is ignorance, gullibility, and laziness, not the six inches between their ears.

As you may remember, figure 2.2 in chapter 2 showed the *process of trading* and indicated that the Three Pillars form the biggest step on your path toward successful trading. Rather than trying to cover the Three Pillars in a single chapter I'll discuss each key component in its own chapter, but first I'll provide an overview of each component.

MONEY MANAGEMENT

Money management is numero uno. It is the secret behind survival and prosperity. Survival will keep you from ruin while prosperity will keep a smile on your face. I will discuss the following seven money management strategies in chapter 8:

- fixed risk
- fixed capital
- fixed ratio
- fixed units
- Williams fixed risk
- fixed percentage
- fixed volatility.

METHODOLOGY

Methodology is your day-to-day combat instructions. It articulates how you'll trade for expectancy. Your methodology will consist of two parts:

- a setup
- a trade plan.

A setup will identify an area of possible future support or resistance—that is, when you should be looking to enter the market and whether you should be looking to buy or sell.

Your trade plan should tell you how to take advantage of your setup. It should have clear and unambiguous instructions on how to enter, place stops, and exit.

Your methodology should be simple and logical. If it is, you'll have a good chance of trading a robust methodology, where the real-time results will match the validated TEST results.

In chapter 9, I will explore the architecture of methodology. Knowing the building blocks will help you in either creating your own methodology or accepting or modifying someone else's methodology.

PSYCHOLOGY

Even with the best money management strategy and methodology, you still need a plan to deal with your emotions. Psychology is the glue that keeps the Three Pillars together. From time to time hope, greed, fear and pain will distract you from your path to success. The constant emotional pain the market's maximum adversity inflicts will challenge your resolve to stay the course.

Chapter 10 will take a look at psychology and explore what you can do to keep those emotions under control. What you'll learn in time is that practical trading is much like cooking—there is a recipe to follow. Follow it and just as cooking sustains the body, your trading will sustain your financial goals. Deviate from the recipe and you'll derail your goals!

Once you have a plan in place for each component of the Three Pillars, you'll be in a position to consider trading, but not before!

CHAPTER

Money Management

In this chapter, I'll examine the most important element of practical trading—money management. This is the first leg of trading's Three Pillars, and is a key weapon against risk of ruin. Since your objective in trading is survival, you need to understand and implement proper money management. If you don't do this, you'll almost certainly be guaranteed permanent membership of the 90 percent losers' club. There'll be no invitations to join the 10 percent winners' circle.

Money management is the secret behind survival and big profits. The essence of proper money management is very simple—when you lose money from trading, you should reduce your trading exposure or position size, and when you make money from trading, you should increase your trading exposure or position size.

Just a quick sidebar: since I personally trade futures, I will refer to them when discussing position sizing in this chapter. If your preference is to trade shares, options, CFDs, margin FX, forex, warrants, or whatever, then please bear with me when I use a foreign reference such as "futures contracts." If I refer to increasing the number of futures contracts to trade, I'm simply referring to increasing the "position size." Similarly, if I refer to decreasing the number of futures contracts, I'm referring to cutting back the "position size." I just find it easier to refer to what I actually do each day as a futures trader. So please accept my apologies if futures contracts are foreign to you and you have no interest in trading them. I just hope you can understand it's easier for me to refer to what I trade with each day. Thanks for your understanding and patience in this. Now back to money management.

Proper money management has two objectives:

• survival—avoiding risk of ruin
• big profits—generating geometric profits.

Proper money management will allow you to achieve these objectives if you can trade less (reduce your position size) when you lose and trade more (increase your position size) when you win. Proper money management is the real secret behind your survival and big profits, not your methodology. While your methodology's positive expectancy will provide the edge, good money management will magnify it.

There are two schools of money management:

- Martingale
- anti-Martingale.

MARTINGALE MONEY MANAGEMENT

Martingale money management looks to trade more contracts when you lose and fewer when you win. It appeals to the gambler's instinct to "double up" after a loss. Martingale money management follows the theory that there is a higher probability a winning trade will follow a losing trade, and therefore one should take advantage of it by trading more contracts following a loss.

This strategy is an invitation to disaster. Increasing the number of contracts (i.e. increasing the position size) you trade after a loss accelerates you toward risk of ruin. There is no guarantee a winning trade will follow a losing trade. There is no higher probability that a win will follow a loss. It will always be a 50 percent probability of either experiencing a win or a loss. In addition, there is no guarantee that you won't experience your longest losing sequence of trades and hit your ruin point before your time.

Martingale money management will accelerate your probability of ruin. It's best to leave this strategy to the gamblers.

ANTI-MARTINGALE MONEY MANAGEMENT

Anti-Martingale is the correct strategy for money management. Anti-Martingale money management will help you to survive because it directs you to trade less when you lose and more when you win. The money management strategies I'll discuss later are all anti-Martingale.

Anti-Martingale money management has two key characteristics:

- geometric profits
- asymmetrical leverage.

Anti-Martingale strategies create a geometric growth in profits during a series of winning trades, but suffer from what is called asymmetrical leverage during a series of losing trades, or drawdown.

$$\text{Required \% gain} = \left(\frac{1}{(1 - \% \text{ loss})}\right) - 1$$

FIGURE 8.1   The asymmetrical formula

$$
\begin{aligned}
\text{Required \% gain} \ &= \left(\frac{1}{1 - \% \text{ loss}}\right) - 1 \\
&= \left(\frac{1}{1 - 0.30}\right) - 1 \\
&= \left(\frac{1}{0.70}\right) - 1 \\
&= 1.4286 - 1 \\
&= 0.4286 \\
&= 0.43 \\
&= 43\%
\end{aligned}
$$

FIGURE 8.2   A 30 percent loss requires a 43 percent gain to break even

Geometric profits means earning profits far greater than what could be earned trading a single contract where money management is not applied. Asymmetrical leverage means that when you suffer a loss, your ability to regain the loss diminishes. That is, if you suffer a 10 percent loss, you'll need more than a 10 percent gain to recover (see figure 8.1). If you suffer a 50 percent loss of your account balance, you'll need to earn a 100 percent return to recover.

You can use the following formula in figure 8.1 to calculate the percentage gain you would need to earn to recover from a percentage loss.

Take a 30 percent loss, for example, as shown in figure 8.2.

Table 8.1 illustrates the percentage gains required to regain certain percentage losses.

TABLE 8.1   Various gains required to recover losses

Loss incurred	Gain required
10%	11%
20%	25%
30%	43%
40%	67%
50%	100%

The problem is not so much that only anti-Martingale strategies suffer from asymmetrical leverage, because Martingale strategies do as well. Rather, the problem is that anti-Martingale strategies take longer to recover the higher percentage gain because they have to do so with fewer contracts, or from a smaller position size, because an anti-Martingale strategy requires you to trade fewer contracts (smaller position size) after a loss. This takes more effort and time than if the original number of contracts (or position size) were still being traded.

KEY CONCEPTS

The first underlying concept is about risk management. Even with the most robust and validated methodology, you can't predict your own performance. Also, you can't influence how a market will behave. One element that you can exercise some control over is the amount of capital you're prepared to risk on any one trade. Money management will tell you how much money you should risk.

The second underlying concept is about expected performance. In general terms, the more stable your equity curve is, the more aggressive you can be in selecting and applying your money management strategy.

A stable equity curve indicates your methodology is performing as well today as it has in the past—that is, it's robust. If you're confident your validated expectancy will continue, you would select the money management strategy that generated the greatest geometric profit. If you're cautious about your methodology's future performance, you should select the money management strategy that preserves capital— that is, account balance—over profit and minimizes your risk of ruin. If you're mildly confident but also mildly cautious, you can select a money management strategy that balances geometric profits with capital preservation. There is no right or wrong money management strategy: each has its supporters and critics. The only right decision in money management is to ensure that it's an anti-Martingale strategy. This chapter will provide various anti-Martingale strategies.

When you do look at these strategies, keep in mind their application is not black and white. With a little imagination you could adjust and refine the strategies or combine two that you like. Don't accept the following descriptions and application as the only way they can be applied. You can make your own adjustments as long as you ensure you trade less when you lose and more when you win.

In addition, even though you may get excited about the results you're about to see, and start believing money management is the only secret behind big profits, you must not believe it's more important than your methodology's expectancy. This may sound contradictory, but even if you have the world's best money management strategy, without a methodology that produces a validated positive expectancy with a stable equity curve, you have nothing.

Good money management can turn a low-expectancy system into a rewarding experience, and a good-expectancy system into a thrilling, life-changing experience. But the point here is that positive expectancy must first exist. In addition, good money management results are dependent on a methodology's expectancy continuing, or in other words the equity curve remaining "stable." A good money management strategy may preserve your capital and help you avoid ruin during a prolonged drawdown, but it certainly won't make money when the expectancy has turned negative. The more stable your equity curve, the better.

HISTORY

Before I discuss the various anti-Martingale money management strategies, I want to first share with you an extract from Larry Williams' book *Long-term Secrets to Short-term Trading*.[1] You see, Larry was the first to discuss money management strategies with the public—many traders are unaware of this and the contribution Larry has made to this topic. So I thought it would be beneficial for you to share an extract from his book that retells Larry's personal experience, discovery and journey into the realm of money management.

Now, Larry Williams has been trading full time since 1966 but it wasn't until the 1980s that Larry incorporated money management into his personal trading with extraordinary effect. So effective that it helped him win trading championships.

Although today money management is common practice and widely written about, back then it was only used by professional money managers such as Richard Dennis, who used fixed-volatility money management during the 1970s. He later taught it to his famous Turtle students in 1984 and 1985. However, in the realm of private traders it was unknown. It wasn't on the radar. It wasn't in the vocabulary. It didn't exist. That is until Larry Williams nutted it out for himself with Ralph Vince, who later went on to bring it to the public's attention through three books on money management.

I believe the following extract will not only give you an insight into the history and development of money management but it will also illustrate to you both the power and importance of it. The following extract is from chapter 13 of his book *Long-term Secrets to Short-term Trading* (John Wiley, 1999) tilted "*Money Management—The Keys to the Kingdom*."[2]

Here it is, the most important chapter in this book, the most important chapter in my life, the most valuable thoughts I can transfer from me to you. I have nothing of more value that I could possibly give you than what you are about to learn. This is not an overstatement.

What I am going to explain, is the formula I have used to take small amounts of money like $2,000 to over $40,000, $10,000 to $110,000 and $10,000 to $1,100,000. These were not hypothetical victories . . . we are talking real time, real money, real profits . . . .

The truly shocking thing about money management is how few people want to hear about it or learn the correct formulas.

The public . . . . thinks there is magic to trading . . . nothing could be further from the truth. Money is made in this business by getting an advantage in the game, working that advantage on a consistent basis, and coupling this with a consistent approach to how much of your bankroll (capital) you have behind each trade (i.e. money management).

In 1986, I ran across a money management formula for playing blackjack originally developed in a 1956 paper, "A New Interpretation of Information Rate", regarding the flow of information and now called the Kelly formula by commodity traders.

 . . . I began trading commodities using the Kelly formula. Here it is;

$$F = ((R + 1) * P - 1)/R$$

$$P = \text{Percentage Accuracy of the System Winning}$$

$$R = \text{Ratio of Winning Trade to Losing Trade}$$

Let's look at an example using a system that is 65 percent accurate with wins 1.3 times the size of losses. The math is done as follows using P as 0.65 and R as 1.3:

$$F = ((1.3 + 1) * 0.65 - 1)/1.3$$

$$F = 38\%$$

In this example, you would use 38 percent of your money behind every trade; if you had a $100,000 account you would use $38,000 and divide that by (the) margin to arrive at the number of contracts. If the margin was $2,000, you would be trading 19 contracts.

What this formula did for my trading results was phenomenal. In a very short time, I became a real-life legend, as very small amounts of money sky-rocketed. Using a percentage of the money in the account, based on the Kelly divided by the margin, was my approach. It was so good that I was kicked out of one trading contest because the promoter could not believe the results were accomplished without cheating.

Let me just jump in here to give you some context for the next extract. In 1987 Larry won the Robbins World Cup Championship of Futures Trading® by trading a $10,000 account into more than $1,100,000 within 12 months, an achievement that no other trader has come close to achieving. His percentage gain still remains the record to this day. Now let's go back to the extract:

> To this day, people on the Internet claim I used two accounts, one for winning trades and one for losers! They seem to forget, or not know, that in addition to being highly illegal, all trades must have an account number on them before the trade is entered, so how could the broker, or myself, know which trade should have the winning account number on it?
>
> But, what would you expect, when no one to my knowledge, had turned in that type of performance ever before in the history of trading. To make matters "worse," I did it more than once. If it wasn't a fluke or luck, the losers lament is that it must have been done by pinching some numbers or trades along the way!
>
> What I was doing was revolutionary. And, as with any good revolution, some blood flowed in the streets. The blood of disbelief was that first the National Futures Association and then the Commodity Futures Trading Commission (CFTC) commandeered all my account records, looking for fraud!
>
> The CFTC went though the brokerage firm's records with a fine-tooth comb, then took all my records and kept them for over a year before giving them back. About a year after getting them back, guess what, they wanted them back again! Success kills.
>
> All this was due to market performance that was unheard of. One of the accounts I managed went from $60,000 to close to $500,000 in about 18 months using the new form of money management. Then the client sued me, her lawyer saying she should have made $54 million instead of half a million.
>
> . . . What a story, huh?
>
> But there are two sides to the edge of this money management sword.
>
> My extraordinary performance attracted lots of money for me to manage. Lots of money, and then it began to happen: the other side of the sword flashed in the sun. Amidst trying to now be a business manager (i.e. running a money management firm) . . . my market system or approach hit the skids,

with a cold streak that saw equally spectacular erosions of equity. Whereas I had been making money hand over fist, I was now losing money, hand over fist!

Brokers and clients screamed . . . my own account had started the first year at $10,000 (yes, that is $10,000) and reached $2,100,000 . . . . Got hit along with everyone else's . . . it too was caught in the whirlpool, spiraling down to $700,000.

About then, everyone jumped ship but me. Hey, I am a commodity trader. I like roller coasters, is there another form of life? Not that I knew, so I stayed on, trading the account back to $1,100,000 by the end of 1987.

What a year!

Watching all this over my shoulder every day was Ralph Vince . . . long before I could see it, he saw it . . . we were using the wrong formula! This may seem pretty basic . . . but back then we were in the midst of a revolution in money management and this stuff was not easy to see. We were tracking and trading where, to the best of my knowledge no one had gone before. What we saw were some phenomenal trading results, so we did not want to wander too far from whatever it was we were doing.

. . . My trading stumbled along with spectacular up-and-down swings, while we continued looking for improvement, something, anything that would tame the beast . . . . to avoid the blowup phenomenon inherent in the Kelly Formula.

In talks with Ralph . . . I became aware that what was causing the wild gyrations was not the percent accuracy of the system, nor was it the win/ loss ratio or drawdown. The hitch and glitch came from the largest losing trade and represents a critical concept . . . what ate us alive was that large losing trade. That is the demon we need to protect against and incorporate into our money management scheme.

The way (I solved this) was to first determine how much of my money I want to risk on any one trade . . . generally speaking, you will want to take 10 percent to 15 percent of your account balance, divide that by the largest loss . . . to arrive at the number of contracts you will trade.

So there it is, my money management formula:

(account balance * risk percent)/largest loss = Contracts or shares to trade

There are probably better and more sophisticated approaches, but for run-of-the-mill traders like us, not blessed with a deep understanding of math, this is the best I know of. The beauty of it is that you can tailor it to your risk/reward personality. If you are Tommy Timid, use 5 percent of your bank;

should you think you are Normal Norma, use 10 percent to 12 percent; if you are Leverage Larry, use 15 percent to 18 percent.

I have made millions of dollars with this approach. What more can I tell you— you have been handed the keys to the kingdom of speculative wealth.

I'm giving you the history here to put into context how effective and how important money management is – and how pioneering and revolutionary Larry Williams was! Larry refers to his money management strategy as Williams fixed risk, and I will be giving you a further insight into it later on.

Let me now summarize a number of anti-Martingale money strategies (including Williams fixed risk) that you can consider for your own trading.

ANTI-MARTINGALE MONEY MANAGEMENT STRATEGIES

I'll be examining the following anti-Martingale money management strategies:

- fixed risk
- fixed capital
- fixed ratio
- fixed units
- Williams fixed risk
- fixed percentage
- fixed volatility.

To help you understand and compare the seven strategies, I'll apply them over a currency trading methodology I'll call Forex_Trader. The methodology trades currency futures so position sizing will refer to the number of contracts being traded. Over the sample period the methodology has produced more than 362 hypothetical trades, which will be enough data to apply the various money management strategies. Using the same methodology will help you compare the various strategies and help you to develop a thorough understanding of each strategy's individual characteristics. In addition I've limited the maximum number of futures contracts a strategy can reach to 100. I've done this to make the results more realistic. As you become more familiar with money management you'll soon come to the realization that particular strategies can have you hypothetically trading an extraordinary number of futures contracts, or position size—which in the hard cold light of day would not necessarily reflect actual trading. So to keep it "real" so to speak I've limited the maximum number of contracts each strategy can possibly trade to 100.

Before I begin I'll look at Forex_Trader's results trading a single contract for each signal where no money management has been applied.

TRADING FOREX_TRADER USING A SINGLE CONTRACT WITH NO MONEY MANAGEMENT

All the following results and figures are in dollars. Over the test period, Forex_Trader produced a hypothetical net profit of $255,100 trading one JPY/$ currency futures contract per signal with $50 deducted for brokerage and slippage. The account began with $20,000, there were no margin calls and the model produced a 2.3 percent standard deviation between trades. Every signal was traded regardless of the individual risk, market volatility, or current drawdown. During that time, the worst dollar drawdown was $13,638, while the worst percentage drawdown was 9 percent. With a high net profit-to-drawdown ratio, the single-contract approach provided very good value, making $19 for every $1 lost during the worst dollar drawdown. Figure 8.3 shows the equity curve trading a constant position size or a single futures contract without any money management strategy being applied.

The question is whether higher profits could have been achieved by using an anti-Martingale money management strategy.

To answer this, I'll initially examine each of the seven strategies. I'll apply their respective money management strategies to Forex_Trader's trading results. Once I've explored how each strategy works and performs on the data sample, I'll compare and analyze the strategies to see whether further insight can be gained into their respective methodologies.

FOREX_TRADER USING FIXED-RISK MONEY MANAGEMENT

Figure 8.4 shows Forex_Trader's equity curve using fixed-risk money management. I'll discuss fixed-risk money management before examining its impact on Forex_Trader's performance.

Fixed risk money management limits each trade to a predefined, or fixed, dollar risk. The fixed dollar risk per trade can be calculated by dividing the starting account by the number of units of money you wish to begin trading with. It's a simple calculation, as follows:

$$\text{Fixed dollar risk} = \frac{\text{Account balance}}{\text{Number of units of money}}$$

The key variables here are your account balance and the number of units of money, or trades, you would like.

In this example, the starting $20,000 account balance is divided into 40 units of money, which will make the fixed dollar risk $500. Accordingly,

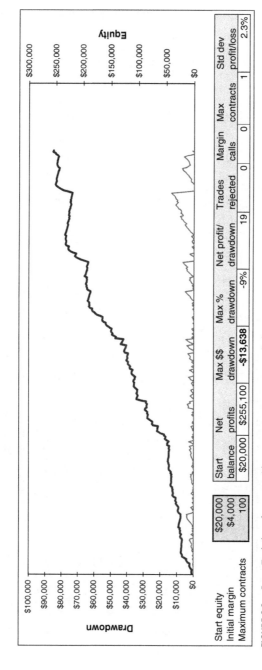

FIGURE 8.3 Forex_Trader's performance with no money management applied

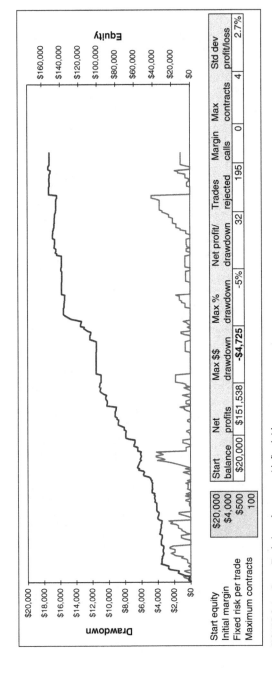

FIGURE 8.4 Forex_Trader's performance with fixed-risk money management

TABLE 8.2   Number of contracts to trade

Fixed risk	Trade risk	Contracts traded	
		Actual	Rounddown
$500	$650	0.8	0
$500	$350	1.4	1
$500	$265	1.9	1
$500	$200	2.5	2

you would only take those trades that present a dollar risk equal to, or lower than, $500. To calculate the number of contracts you would trade, divide the fixed dollar risk by the individual trade risk (i.e. the dollar amount between the entry and stop price plus brokerage), ensuring you round down to the nearest whole integer. Use the following simple formula:

$$\text{Number of contracts} = \frac{\text{Fixed risk}}{\text{Trade risk}}$$

If the individual trade risk was $200, according to the money management rules, you would trade two contracts ($500/$200). Table 8.2 shows the number of contracts you would trade, assuming a fixed risk of $500.

The first question to ask when applying the fixed risk money management strategy to Forex_Trader's results is whether fixed risk achieved the objectives of money management—that is, trading fewer contracts when losing and trading more contracts when winning. Unfortunately, fixed risk fails on both fronts. When you're losing, fixed risk still expects you to risk a constant $500; there is no opportunity to trade fewer contracts when you're in a drawdown. By risking a larger percentage of your account with each trade when you're losing, you're actually increasing your risk of ruin while in a drawdown. When you're winning, you're not allowed to trade more contracts. The maximum number of contracts that could be traded was only two. To add insult to injury, because the trades had to be limited to $500, 195 signals had to be rejected. As a result, only $151,538 was made. This is considerably less than the single contract's $255,100 in net profits.

One adjustment that could be made is to increase the fixed dollar risk upon the completion of 40 trades. You could again divide your account balance into 40 units of money and increase your dollar risk. In addition, you may even increase the number of units of money to reduce your risk of ruin further. On both counts you would benefit. You could trade more contracts since you're risking more money, and you could do so with a lower risk of ruin since you have more units of money to trade with, making it harder to reach your ruin point. Later on I'll be discussing fixed units, which builds on fixed risk.

Although fixed risk fails to achieve correct money management using a constant fixed $500 per trade, it does have some benefits. It allows traders with small accounts to begin trading. As long as your methodology has a validated and stable expectancy, it would be highly unlikely you would suffer financial ruin within any particular streak of 40 consecutive trades.

Another benefit of fixed risk is that it does manage to distinguish risk between individual trades. If a trade's risk is too high, it will not allow you to trade it, thereby reducing your exposure. Although fixed risk fails in its money management objectives, it does help in managing your risk, which is a positive.

FOREX_TRADER USING FIXED-CAPITAL MONEY MANAGEMENT

Figure 8.5 shows that after applying fixed-capital money management, Forex_Trader's single contract profit has soared from $255,100 to more than $18,000,000. Although the geometric profits are outstanding, higher returns don't come without higher risk.

Fixed capital will trade one contract for a fixed unit of capital. If the fixed unit of capital is $15,000 and your account balance is $20,000, you would trade one contract. If your account balance was $30,000, you would trade two contracts. You would use the following formula to calculate the number of contracts to trade according to the fixed-capital money management strategy:

$$\text{Number of contracts} = \frac{\text{Account balance}}{\text{Fixed unit of capital per contract}}$$

You should round down to the nearest whole integer to calculate the number of contracts to trade. Using the example above, if your account was $32,000 you would be trading two contracts ($32,000/$15,000 = 2.1 or 2.0 after rounding down). If you suffered a loss and your account fell to $29,000, fixed capital would only allow you to trade one contract ($29,000/$15,000 = 1.9 or 1.0 after rounding down). You would not be able to trade two contracts until your account moved above $30,000. Table 8.3 illustrates how fixed capital rounds fractions down to the nearest whole integer.

Fixed capital does permit you to trade a minimum of one contract even if your account falls below your fixed unit of capital, otherwise you would have to stop trading. You could use a "fall below your minimum fixed unit of capital" as a trigger to top up your account if you wanted to continue trading.

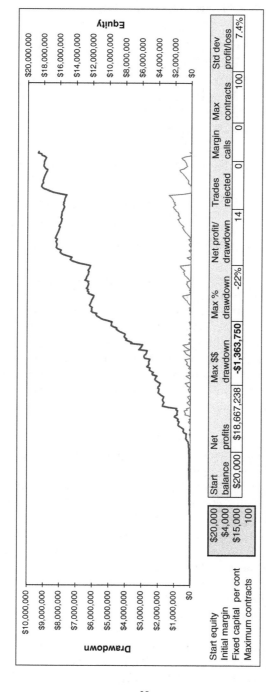

FIGURE 8.5 Forex_Trader's performance with fixed-capital money management

TABLE 8.3   Number of contracts to trade

Fixed capital	Account balance	Contracts traded	
		Actual	Rounddown
$15,000	$8,000	0.5	1
$15,000	$29,000	1.9	1
$15,000	$32,000	2.1	2
$15,000	$48,000	3.2	3
$15,000	$51,000	3.4	3

To calculate the fixed unit of capital you would use the following formula:

$$\text{Fixed unit of capital} = \frac{\text{Largest drawdown(actual or expected)}}{\text{Percentage blowtorch risk}}$$

In this example I've arbitrarily selected $15,000 as the fixed capital's "unit" of capital.

According to the single contract example, Forex_Trader's worst drawdown was $13,638. Working with this figure will help you understand how to calculate a fixed unit of capital. You could either use this historical drawdown or use a larger one. I believe your worst drawdowns are always in front of you. Remember, trading is all about survival. Being in a defensive position, expecting the market to do its worst, will maintain your respect for what the market's maximum adversity is capable of doing and what it can do to disappoint you at the most inappropriate time.

I'll take Forex_Trader's largest historical drawdown and increase it to $14,000.

The percentage blowtorch risk needs a little explanation. It refers to how much pain you can bear, or how much of your account balance you are comfortable losing in percentage terms.

Using the previous formula, if you're comfortable about losing 30 percent of your account you would, according to fixed capital, trade one contract for every $46,667 ($14,000/0.30) in your account. You wouldn't begin trading two contracts until the account balance moved to $93,334 ($46,667 × 2).

More conservative traders could lower their percentage blowtorch risk, while more aggressive traders could increase it. Fixed capital provides plenty of flexibility.

Table 8.4 shows how the fixed unit of capital can change depending on your individual risk levels.

If you use the expected $14,000 drawdown and combine it with a very aggressive (most would say suicidal) 93.3 percent blowtorch risk, you would trade one contract for every $15,000 in your account ($14,000/0.933).

TABLE 8.4   How individual risk tolerance changes fixed units of capital

Blowtorch risk	Expected drawdown	Fixed "unit" of capital
20.0%	$14,000	$70,000
30.0%	$14,000	$46,667
40.0%	$14,000	$35,000
50.0%	$14,000	$28,000
93.3%	$14,000	$15,000

If you had done just this (like I have in the example), Forex_Trader would have earned an amazing profit of more than $18,000,000, as shown in figure 8.5.

Let's take a closer look at how fixed capital allows you to increase the number of contracts you trade.

Fixed capital is one of the fastest strategies to accumulate contracts. It does this by requiring a smaller contribution of profit from each contract at the new contract level before moving to the next contract level.

As you can see in figure 8.6, you commence trading one contract with a $20,000 starting account balance. As the single contract makes a profit of $10,001, it will take the account balance to more than $30,000, at which point you'll be allowed to trade two contracts. You can only trade three contracts once the account is above $45,000, which is only $15,000 away,

Number of contracts	Account balance level	Total profit by contract							
		1st Cont $33,893	2nd Cont $23,893	3rd Cont $16,393	4th Cont $11,393	5th Cont $7,643	6th Cont $4,643	7th Cont $2,143	8th Cont $0
8									
7	$120,000	$2,143	$2,143	$2,143	$2,143	$2,143	$2,143	$2,143	
6	$105,000	$2,500	$2,500	$2,500	$2,500	$2,500	$2,500		
5	$90,000	$3,000	$3,000	$3,000	$3,000	$3,000			
4	$75,000	$3,750	$3,750	$3,750	$3,750				
3	$60,000	$5,000	$5,000	$5,000					
2	$45,000	$7,500	$7,500						
1	$30,000	$10,000							
Fixed cap.	$15,000	$20,000 Start							

Contracts increase with unequal effort.

Contracts are increased by requiring a smaller contribution to profits from each additional contract.

FIGURE 8.6   Account levels at which the number of contracts increases

and there are two contracts now to help achieve this. So, rather than having to make $10,000 for a single contract, a $7,500 profit has to be made from each contract to reach the next level. Once the account has moved above $45,000, three contracts can be traded. To reach a $60,000 account balance and begin trading four contracts, each of the three contracts only has to make $5,000 each. As each contract level increases you can see how less profit is required. Contracts are increased by requiring a smaller contribution to profits from each additional contract.

This explains why fixed-capital produces such high geometric profits of more than $18,000,000. It requires less profit for each individual contract at each successively higher contract level.

Due to fixed capital's ability to accumulate contracts quickly, I've limited the maximum number of contracts to 100 in the Forex_Trader example. I did so because it's easy to get carried away and trade 1,200 contracts ($18,000,000/$15,000), which may not be realistic.

If you believed your strategy had a robust and stable equity curve, or guaranteed future expectancy, you would consider trading with fixed capital because it produces astronomical profits. However, because there are no guarantees in trading, fixed capital may not be appropriate.

Let's take a closer look at fixed capital's performance. Does fixed capital achieve proper money management objectives—that is, does it trade fewer contracts when losing and more contracts when winning? The answer for both is yes.

Fixed capital provides a simple calculation to tell you how many contracts to trade depending on your account balance and fixed unit of capital. As you lose and your account balance falls below a certain level, fixed capital requires you to trade one less contract, or possibly more if your account falls below two or more levels of contracts. When you're winning and your account balance is growing, you can use the same calculation to trade more contracts. As a consequence, fixed capital achieves both money management objectives—survival and generating big profits. Indeed, it produces very high geometric profits.

Fixed capital, like fixed risk, is an approach that can be used by traders who have a small account. It provides a simple mechanism to build accounts quickly and back off when trouble hits. However, unlike fixed risk it does not manage the risk of individual trades, treating them all the same by taking all signals.

Although fixed capital's greatest advantage is that it allows small accounts to build quickly, its disadvantage is that it does so with increased risk. It usually produces a large drawdown, like it has in our example (22 percent, as shown in figure 8.5). Losing $1,363,750 may not look so bad when you're making more than $18,000,000; however, I can assure you that it won't feel too comfortable when it occurs!

FOREX_TRADER USING FIXED-RATIO MONEY MANAGEMENT

Figure 8.7 shows Forex_Trader's results when fixed-ratio money management is applied. Before I take a closer look at this figure, I'll examine fixed-ratio money management.

Fixed ratio was developed by Ryan Jones and introduced in his book *The Trading Game*.[3] Fixed ratio requires traders to adjust the number of contracts they trade by a "fixed ratio." The "fixed ratio" is called the delta, and is related to a methodology's drawdown. You can use the following formula to calculate the next level in your account at which you can trade an extra contract:

Next account level = Current account level
+ (Current number of contracts × Delta)

While there is no hard and fast rule on how to calculate delta, it's important to realize it is the most important variable in fixed-ratio money management. Changes in the delta will affect fixed ratio's performance— the higher the delta, the more conservative the return and drawdown will be, while a more aggressive, or smaller, delta will produce more profits, but at the expense of suffering higher drawdowns. The delta should be linked to a methodology's drawdown on a single contract basis.

To be conservative you should look to make your delta large enough for a single contract to experience its greatest drawdown while still having enough money for an initial margin to continue trading. In this instance, delta would be calculated by using the following formula:

Delta = Drawdown + Initial margin

In the following example, I have used a maximum drawdown of $14,000 and assumed an initial margin requirement of $4,000 making the delta $18,000. Using an $18,000 delta value, fixed-ratio money management says you should not increase to your next contract level until every current contract you're trading has been able to contribute $18,000 in profit. Once they have, you can trade an extra contract, at which level the previous contracts plus the new contract together must all make another $18,000 each before adding an additional contract. More aggressive traders could use a smaller delta, while more conservative traders could use a larger delta. Fixed ratio provides enough flexibility to suit all traders with varying risk profiles.

Figure 8.8 shows how the fixed-ratio formula calculates the levels at which you're able to increase your contract size.

This example begins with a $20,000 account balance and uses an $18,000 delta. One delta, or an $18,000 profit per contract, is required before stepping up to two contracts. Once $18,000 in profit has been made

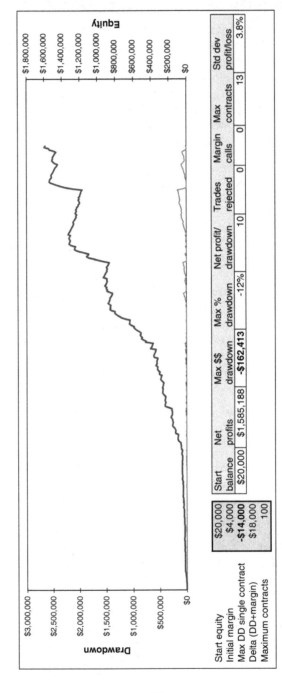

FIGURE 8.7 Forex_Trader's performance with fixed-ratio money management

Number of contracts	Account balance level	Total profit by contract							
		1st Cont $126,000	2nd Cont $108,000	3rd Cont $90,000	4th Cont $72,000	5th Cont $54,000	6th Cont $36,000	7th Cont $18,000	8th Cont $0
8									
7	$524,000	$18,000	$18,000	$18,000	$18,000	$18,000	$18,000	$18,000	
6	$398,000	$18,000	$18,000	$18,000	$18,000	$18,000	$18,000		
5	$290,000	$18,000	$18,000	$18,000	$18,000	$18,000			
4	$200,000	$18,000	$18,000	$18,000	$18,000				
3	$128,000	$18,000	$18,000	$18,000					
2	$74,000	$18,000	$18,000						
1	$38,000	$18,000							
Delta	$18,000	$20,000 Start							

Contracts increase with equal effort.

Contracts are increased by requiring an equal contribution to profits from each additional contract.

FIGURE 8.8   Account levels at which the number of contracts increases

and $38,001 reached, two contracts can then be traded. With two contracts, fixed ratio requires an additional $18,000 in profit to be made for each contract being traded. Once $36,000 in additional profits has been made and $74,001 reached, three contracts can then be traded, and so on.

This is the key to fixed ratio—you cannot increase your contract size until your existing contracts have each made an additional delta in profits.

Naturally, if you suffer a loss and fall below a previous account level you'll have to reduce your contract size until your account balance recovers. When decreasing your contract size you can simply use the previous account levels or you can increase the rate at which you decrease. So, rather than waiting to lose a whole delta in profits before decreasing your contract size, you can do it sooner. You could use a fraction of delta as being the trigger at which you'll reduce your contract size faster. However, the downside to this is the time and effort it would take to recover from the asymmetrical leverage. Not only would you have to earn a greater percentage gain compared to your percentage loss, but you would have to make the gain on fewer contracts, thereby taking longer to recover.

There is always a tradeoff. If you decrease the number of contracts faster than the delta at which you increased them, you'll be reducing your risk while protecting profits, but at the expense of magnifying asymmetrical leverage over a smaller number of contracts. Alternatively, if you decrease the number of contracts at the same delta rate at which you increase them, you'll maintain your geometric profit potential by maintaining the same number of contracts for longer. The downside is you'll be maintaining your geometric profit potential at the expense of higher risk and potentially lower profits as the drawdown continues.

Does fixed ratio achieve the objectives of money management—trading fewer contracts when losing and more when winning? The answer is yes. Once you have made enough delta for each contract you're trading, you're allowed to increase the number of contracts. If you suffer a loss and fall below a previous level, you must reduce the number of contracts.

Figure 8.7 shows that fixed ratio was able to deliver geometric profit growth by producing more than $1,500,000 in net profit with an $18,000 delta. Although not as much as fixed capital, it was far greater than the single contract's $255,100 net profit. In addition fixed ratio produced a net profit-to-drawdown payoff of 10:1. It delivered $10 of gain for every $1 of drawdown pain.

Apart from achieving its money management objectives, fixed ratio has other attractive features. Like fixed risk and fixed capital, fixed ratio also provides a money management strategy for traders with a small account. With a suitable delta you can begin trading and over time steadily increase your number of contracts (or position size). Delta also provides enough flexibility, depending on your level of conservatism or aggressiveness. A smaller delta will allow you to grow your account at a faster rate while maintaining your drawdown at a constant percentage level.

Figure 8.9 shows potential profits when the delta is reduced to $11,000.

By using half the maximum drawdown and reducing the delta to $11,000, you can see how the net profit would have increased by more than 60 percent! In addition, not only is the percentage drawdown consistent with a higher delta, but the net profit-to-drawdown payoff is also consistent, delivering the same $10 of gain for every $1 of pain inflicted by the drawdown.

However, like fixed capital, fixed ratio does not distinguish between individual trade risk. It expects traders to take all signals, regardless of their individual risk.

TO CHASE $18,000,000 IN PROFITS OR TO CHASE $1,500,000 IN PROFITS, THAT IS THE QUESTION

So far, fixed capital seems to be the best money management strategy, delivering $18,000,000 in hypothetical profits compared to fixed ratio's $1,500,000 net profit.

However, fixed capital's $18,000,000 in profits comes with a great deal of risk. This risk becomes clear when examining what would happen if both fixed capital and fixed ratio suffered a catastrophic loss.

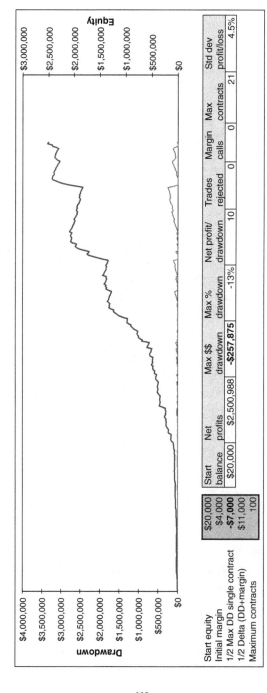

Start balance	Net profits	Max $$ drawdown	Max % drawdown	Net profit/ drawdown	Trades rejected	Margin calls	Max contracts	Std dev profit/loss
$20,000	$2,500,988	-$257,875	-13%	10	0	0	21	4.5%

Start equity	$20,000
Initial margin	$4,000
1/2 Max DD single contract	**-$7,000**
1/2 Delta (DD+margin)	$11,000
Maximum contracts	100

FIGURE 8.9 Forex_Trader's performance using a smaller delta

In these examples, I have commenced with small $20,000 accounts and have assumed an arbitrary $14,000 drawdown for fixed capital and fixed ratio. I'll define a catastrophic loss as a single trade loss that accounts for just more than 70 percent of the historical drawdown—a single $10,000 loss per contract. This will make it conservative, while being realistic in relation to the discussions so far.

I'll assume the catastrophic $10,000 loss per contract will occur at the same level of seven contracts. This implies it would happen at different times in the data set because fixed capital accumulates its contracts at a much faster rate than fixed ratio. However, for the purpose of this exercise, it doesn't matter because the issue here is linked to the number of contracts being traded. You need to be aware of the impact of such a loss on each strategy at the same accumulated contract level (or position size). In addition, it's also relative to their respective main variables—the fixed unit of capital and the fixed delta. The following example would still be instructive regardless of the contract level at which you believed the catastrophic loss would occur.

What would happen if this $10,000 catastrophic loss occurred out of the blue at the seven-contract level? Figure 8.10 shows the effect on a trader using fixed-capital money management and figure 8.11 shows the effect on a trader using fixed-ratio money management.

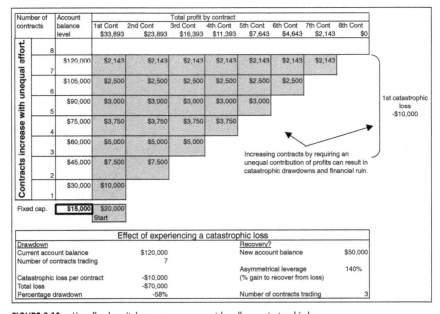

FIGURE 8.10   How fixed-capital money management handles a catastrophic loss

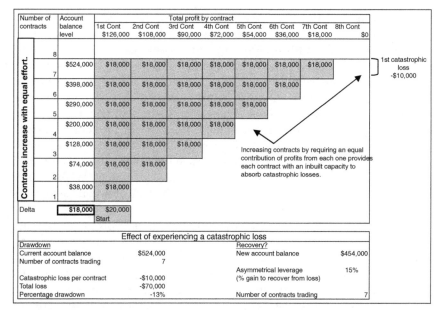

Number of contracts	Account balance level	Total profit by contract								
		1st Cont $126,000	2nd Cont $108,000	3rd Cont $90,000	4th Cont $72,000	5th Cont $54,000	6th Cont $36,000	7th Cont $18,000	8th Cont $0	
8	$524,000	$18,000	$18,000	$18,000	$18,000	$18,000	$18,000	$18,000		1st catastrophic loss -$10,000
7	$398,000	$18,000	$18,000	$18,000	$18,000	$18,000	$18,000			
6	$290,000	$18,000	$18,000	$18,000	$18,000	$18,000				
5	$200,000	$18,000	$18,000	$18,000	$18,000					
4	$128,000	$18,000	$18,000	$18,000						
3	$74,000	$18,000	$18,000							
2	$38,000	$18,000								
1										
Delta		$18,000	$20,000 Start							

Contracts increase with equal effort.

Increasing contracts by requiring an equal contribution of profits from each one provides each contract with an inbuilt capacity to absorb catastrophic losses.

Effect of experiencing a catastrophic loss			
Drawdown		Recovery?	
Current account balance	$524,000	New account balance	$454,000
Number of contracts trading	7		
		Asymmetrical leverage	15%
Catastrophic loss per contract	-$10,000	(% gain to recover from loss)	
Total loss	-$70,000		
Percentage drawdown	-13%	Number of contracts trading	7

FIGURE 8.11   How fixed-ratio money management handles a catastrophic loss

The fixed-capital trader would suffer a $70,000 loss and 58 percent drawdown! The fixed-ratio trader would suffer a $70,000 loss and 13 percent drawdown. For the fixed-capital trader, this is almost financial ruin! Although it's unlikely a catastrophic loss of this magnitude would occur, if it did, you may possibly be saying bye bye to the fixed-capital trader. For the fixed ratio trader, you'd be saying bad luck, but well done for surviving and staying in the game.

Let's take a closer look at each money management strategy and see where and why fixed capital fell apart and fixed ratio stayed standing.

As mentioned, fixed capital accumulates contracts faster because it requires less profit to be made by each contract at each higher contract level. The first contract is required to make $10,000 in profit before a second contract can be traded. When you're trading seven contracts you only need to make $2,143 in profit for each contract before you can begin trading eight contracts. Fixed capital requires an unequal effort to increase contracts.

This unequal effort creates a "house of cards." It makes geometric profits look impressive without revealing the fragility underneath. Experiencing a catastrophic $10,000 loss per contract would see an $120,000 account experience an 58 percent drawdown. If that is not enough to reach your point of ruin, the 140 percent asymmetrical leverage would certainly bring a tear to your eye, particularly when the 140 percent gain necessary to recover would begin with trading only three contracts.

Let's look at fixed ratio. Figure 8.11 outlines fixed ratio's money management strategy and the effect a catastrophic loss would have on it.

Fixed ratio requires an equal profit contribution for every contract traded before the number of contracts can be increased. You have to make an $18,000 profit with one contract before you can step up a contract level. At the next level, fixed ratio leaves fixed capital. Once your account reaches $38,001 and you can trade two contracts, each one still has to make $18,000 in profit before you can consider trading three contracts. When you're trading seven contracts you still need to make $18,000 per contract before you can consider stepping up to eight contracts.

Fixed ratio requires an equal delta contribution in profits to increase contracts. This equal effort creates a solid foundation in your trading account.

Although the geometric profits don't look as impressive as with fixed capital, they do have a feeling of real substance. Experiencing a catastrophic $10,000 loss per contract would see a $524,000 account experience only a 13 percent drawdown. This manageable drawdown would only require a 15 percent asymmetrical leverage gain to recover. Not only is the 15 percent asymmetrical leverage less than fixed capital's 140 percent but fixed ratio, even after a $10,000 loss per contract, would not even slip down one contract level, allowing you to continue trading with seven contracts as you make 15 percent to regain the lost 13 percent. Consequently, fixed ratio is preferable to fixed capital.

FOREX_TRADER USING FIXED-UNITS MONEY MANAGEMENT

Figure 8.12 shows Forex_Trader's performance when fixed units is applied. Before I discuss the implications of this I'll first explore fixed-units money management.

The fixed-units strategy builds upon fixed risk. Fixed-units money management will limit each trade to a predefined dollar risk that is a function of a predefined number of units. You will define the fixed number of units that you would like to trade with. The dollar risk per trade is calculated the same was as with fixed risk, by dividing the starting account by the number of fixed units of money you wish to begin trading with. It's the same simple calculation, as follows:

$$\text{Dollar risk per trade} = \frac{\text{Account balance}}{\text{Fixed number of units of money}}$$

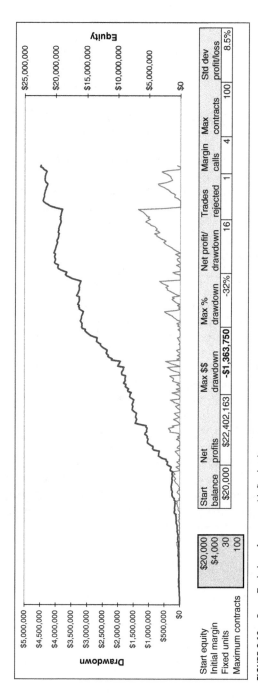

The chart contains the following data tables:

Start equity	$20,000
Initial margin	$4,000
Fixed units	30
Maximum contracts	100

Start balance	Net profits	Max $$ drawdown	Max % drawdown	Net profit/ drawdown	Trades rejected	Margin calls	Max contracts	Std dev profit/loss
$20,000	$22,402,163	-$1,363,750	-32%	16	1	4	100	8.5%

FIGURE 8.12 Forex_Trader's performance with fixed-units money management

The key variables here are your account balance and the number of units of money, or trades, you would like. Where fixed units departs fixed risk is when your account balance increases. As your account balance makes new equity highs, fixed units will demand that you recalculate your dollar risk per trade. The fixed dollar risk calculation now becomes:

$$\text{Dollar risk per trade} = \frac{\text{New higher account balance}}{\text{Fixed number of units of money}}$$

As you are making money and your account balance grows fixed units will require you to risk more money per trade. Although your number of trading units (the number of trades you'd like to make before your account diminishes to zero) will remain fixed, your actual dollar risk per trade will increase.

Now this change in the dollar risk per unit only occurs when your account balance is increasing. It does not decrease when you are losing. If you are in a drawdown, fixed units will still require you to risk the same dollar risk per trade. The key variable here for the trader is the number of fixed "units" of money they would like to trade with.

You know from chapter 4's discussion on risk of ruin that the minimum number of units a trader should consider having as a minimum is 20. In fixed risk, we used 40 units of money, so for this example I will assume the trader's preference is to have a fixed 30 units of money.

If a trader has a starting $20,000 account balance and wishes to trade with a fixed 30 units of money, he or she would simply divided his or her account balance by 30 to calculate the dollar risk per trade. This would be the amount of money they would be prepared to risk on each trade, which in this example would be $667. Accordingly, you would only take those trades that present a dollar risk equal to, or lower than, $667. To calculate the number of contracts you would trade, you simply divide the fixed dollar risk by the individual trade risk (i.e. the dollar amount between the entry and stop price plus brokerage), ensuring you round down to the nearest whole integer. You would use the following formula:

$$\text{Number of contracts} = \frac{\text{Dollar risk}}{\text{Trade risk}}$$

If the individual trade risk was $200, according to this calculation, you would trade three contracts ($667/$200). Table 8.5 shows the number of contracts you would trade, assuming a fixed risk of $667.

Now where fixed units differs from fixed risk is that the dollar risk doesn't remain constant. It will increase as your account balance grows. Table 8.6 shows how the dollar risk will increase as an account balance grows and the number of units remains fixed.

TABLE 8.5   Number of contracts to trade

Dollar	Trade	Contracts traded	
risk	risk	Actual	Rounddown
$667	$800	0.8	0
$667	$350	1.9	1
$667	$265	2.5	2
$667	$200	3.335	3

TABLE 8.6   Number of contracts to trade with various account balances

Account	Fixed	Dollar	Trade	Contracts traded	
balance	units	risk	risk	Actual	Rounddown
$20,000	30	$667	$800	0.8	0
$30,000	30	$1,000	$350	2.9	2
$40,000	30	$1,333	$265	5.0	5
$50,000	30	$1,667	$200	8.333	8

Figure 8.13 shows how a trader can quickly accumulate contracts using fixed units.

For the purposes of illustration, I have assumed a constant individual trade risk of $667. Naturally, individual trade risk will fluctuate depending on individual trade setups. However, for the purpose of this example, a

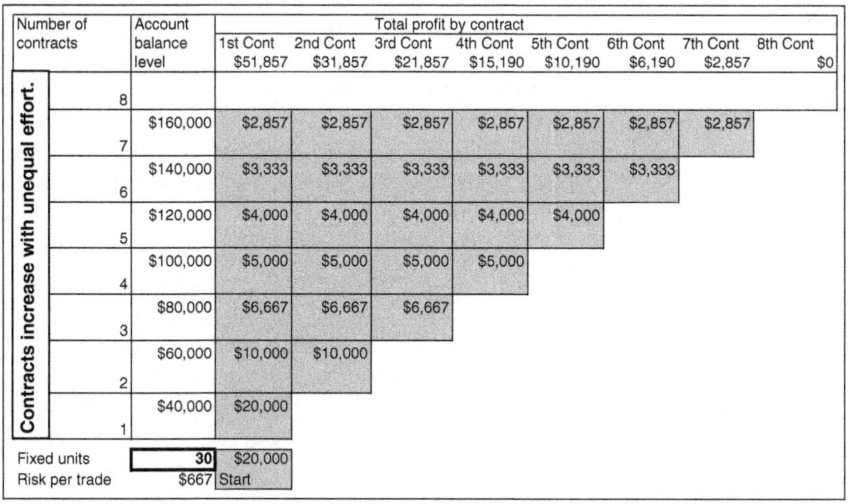

FIGURE 8.13   Account levels at which the number of contracts increase

constant trade risk will adequately demonstrate how fixed units can quickly accumulate contracts.

Starting with a $20,000 account and a fixed 30 units of money, a trader is able to risk $667 per trade. Once the account reaches $40,001, a trader is able to trade two contracts assuming the trade risk per contract remains at $667 ($40,000/30 = $1,333).

$$2 = \$1,333/\$667$$

Once the account reaches $60,001 and trader is able to trade 3 contracts ($60,000/30 = $2,000).

$$3 = \$2,000/\$667$$

As you can see in figure 8.13 less profit is required to be made by each additional contract, allowing the trader to accumulate contracts quickly. This enables the trader to earn geometric profits (assuming the strategy remains stable).

The first question to ask when applying the fixed units money management strategy to Forex_Trader's results, is whether fixed units achieved the objectives of money management—that is, trading fewer contracts when losing and trading more contracts when winning.

Well, the answer is both no and yes.

No, because when you're losing, fixed units still expects you to risk a constant dollar risk, there is no opportunity to trade fewer contracts or risk less money when you're in a drawdown. By risking a larger percentage of your account balance with each trade when you're losing, you're actually increasing your risk of ruin while in a drawdown.

And yes, because when you're winning and your account balance is growing, your dollar risk is increasing allowing you to trade more contracts. As a result, the maximum number of contracts was reached allowing fixed units to earn more than $22,000,000! That is significantly more then the single contract's $255,100 in net profits. Fixed units does allow a trader to enjoy geometric profits.

As I've mentioned before, due to the strategy's ability to accumulate contracts quickly, I've limited the maximum number of contracts it can trade to 100. I did so because it's very easy to get carried away and trade 1,100 contracts (($22,000,000/30)/$667), which may not be realistic.

In summary, fixed units achieved impressive results. More than $22,000,000 in net profits with a maximum dollar and percentage drawdown of $1,363,750 and 32 percent respectively. Fixed units achieved a high net profit-to-drawdown ratio, generating $16 in profit for every $1 of drawdown pain, and experienced a 8.5 percent standard deviation between trades.

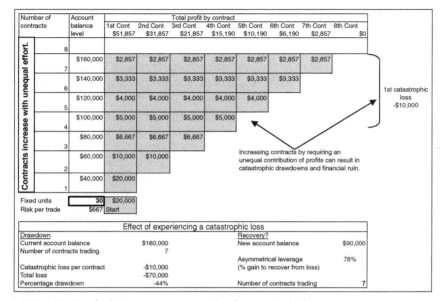

Number of contracts	Account balance level	Total profit by contract								
		1st Cont $51,857	2nd Cont $31,857	3rd Cont $21,857	4th Cont $15,190	5th Cont $10,190	6th Cont $6,190	7th Cont $2,857	8th Cont $0	
8										
7	$160,000	$2,857	$2,857	$2,857	$2,857	$2,857	$2,857	$2,857		
6	$140,000	$3,333	$3,333	$3,333	$3,333	$3,333	$3,333			1st catastrophic loss -$10,000
5	$120,000	$4,000	$4,000	$4,000	$4,000	$4,000				
4	$100,000	$5,000	$5,000	$5,000	$5,000					
3	$80,000	$6,667	$6,667	$6,667						
2	$60,000	$10,000	$10,000							
1	$40,000	$20,000								
Fixed units 30	$20,000									
Risk per trade $667	Start									

Increasing contracts by requiring an unequal contribution of profits can result in catastrophic drawdowns and financial ruin.

Contracts increase with unequal effort.

Effect of experiencing a catastrophic loss			
Drawdown		Recovery?	
Current account balance	$160,000	New account balance	$90,000
Number of contracts trading	7		
		Asymmetrical leverage	78%
Catastrophic loss per contract	-$10,000	(% gain to recover from loss)	
Total loss	-$70,000		
Percentage drawdown	-44%	Number of contracts trading	7

FIGURE 8.14   How fixed units money management handles a catastrophic loss

Now although impressive, fixed units, like fixed capital, is vulnerable during a drawdown. Figure 8.14 shows how fixed units would cope with a catastrophic loss.

So although the geometric profits look impressive, they do come with substantial risk.

Experiencing a catastrophic $10,000 loss per contract when trading seven contracts would see a $160,000 account balance experience a 44 percent drawdown. This drawdown would require a healthy 78 percent gain to recover.

Now although the climb back up is significant, unlike fixed capital, where a trader could only recommence trading with three contracts after a catastrophic loss, the fixed units trader has retained his gun power by still retaining seven contracts to trade. This is a huge benefit for a fixed-unit trader in that they maintain their ability to earn good profits following a catastrophic loss. The downside is that they are substantially increasing their risk of ruin by doing so.

If you believed your strategy had a stable equity curve, then you would consider trading with fixed units because it produces extraordinary profits. However, the downside is that it doesn't allow you to risk less when in a drawdown, increasing the risk you will reach your point of ruin. However, as I said, if you believe your strategy is robust and stable, it is an aggressive strategy worth considering, since it would be very unlikely that you would reach your ruin point during any particular streak of 30 consecutive trades (assuming your equity curve remains stable over the long term). In addition if you wish to be more conservative you could even begin with 40 units of money. Another idea worth considering is to use a variable "fixed" number of units, say, increasing your number of units at certain account levels.

Although fixed units fails to reduce a trader's risk during a drawdown, it does have some benefits. It allows traders with small accounts to begin trading. It allows traders to accumulate contracts quickly. It has enough flexibility to allow traders to increase the number of fixed units they trade to reduce the risk they'll reach their point of ruin further during any particular streak of consecutive trades and pursing drawdowns. Although it does produce large drawdowns, it does allow a trader to retain the ability to trade out of drawdowns quickly by maintaining contract levels.

Another benefit of fixed units is that it does manage to distinguish risk between individual trades. If a trade's risk is too high, it will not allow you to trade it, so reducing your exposure. Although fixed units fails in its money management objective to reduce risk during a drawdown, it does help in managing individual risk and it does earn geometric profits.

FOREX_TRADER USING WILLIAMS FIXED-RISK MONEY MANAGEMENT

Figure 8.15 shows Forex_Trader's performance when Williams fixed risk is applied. Before I discuss the implications of this I'll first explore Williams fixed-risk money management.

You have already seen this strategy in the extract I shared with you from Larry Williams' book *Long-term Secrets to Short-term Trading.*[4]

$$\text{Number of contracts} = \frac{\text{Dollar risk}}{\text{Largest loss}}$$

$$\text{Dollar risk} = \text{Account balance} \times \text{Percentage risk}$$

Percentage risk represents the amount of your trading account you are prepared to lose if you experience your largest loss.

Let's assume you have a $30,000 account balance. Let's also assume that you are prepared to lose 10 percent of your account balance if you incur your largest loss. If this was the case then you would be prepared to lose $3,000 per trade ($30,000 × 10 percent). This would become your dollar risk per trade. If the largest loss (or expected largest loss) from your strategy was $2,563, then you would only be able to trade one contract.

$$1.0 = \frac{\$3,000 (\text{dollar risk})}{\$2,563 (\text{largest loss})}$$

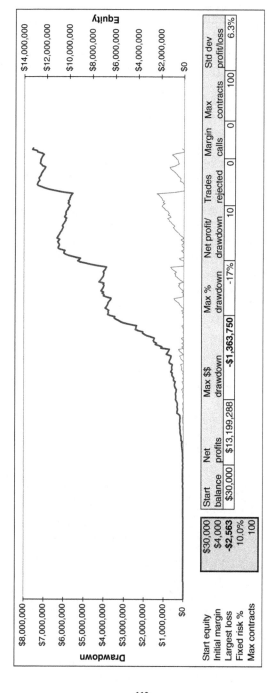

FIGURE 8.15 Forex_Trader's performance with Williams fixed-risk money management

TABLE 8.7   Number of contracts to trade

Account balance	Fixed risk	Dollar risk	Largest loss	Contracts traded	
				Actual	Rounddown
$30,000	10%	$3,000	$2,563	1.17	1
$50,000	10%	$5,000	$2,563	1.95	1
$70,000	10%	$7,000	$2,563	2.73	2
$90,000	10%	$9,000	$2,563	3.51	3

Like all the other strategies, for conservatism, you round down when calculating the number of contracts to trade.

Table 8.7 shows the number of contracts you would trade, assuming a fixed risk of 10 percent and a largest loss of $2,563.

The key variables here are the fixed percentage risk and largest loss.

As your account balance grows, Williams fixed risk will require you to recalculate your dollar risk per trade. You will then divide the dollar risk by the largest loss to calculate the number of contracts you can trade (remembering to round down).

Figure 8.16 shows how a trader can accumulate contracts with Williams fixed risk.

For this example, I have used a higher $30,000 starting account. This is because the strategy can't really be used on a small account unless the largest loss is relatively small or the percentage risked is relatively high.

Starting with a $30,000 account and a fixed 10 percent risk, a trader is only able to trade one contract while the account is under $51,250. Once

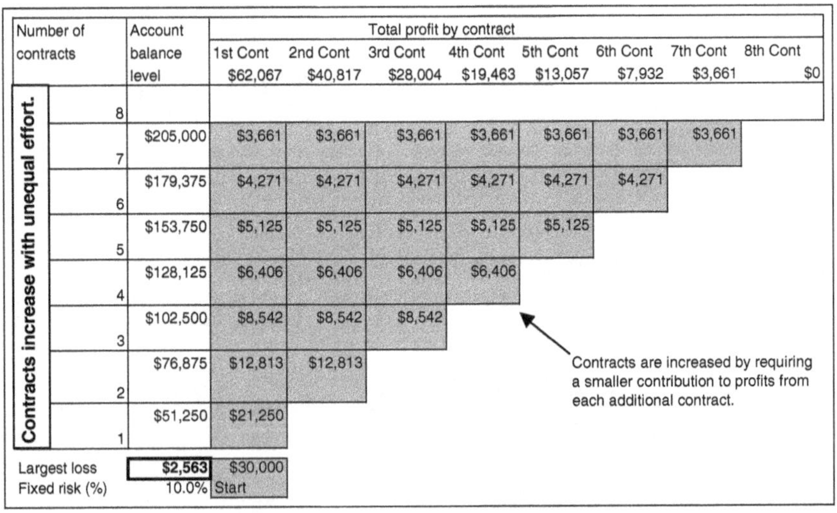

FIGURE 8.16   Account levels at which the number of contracts increases

the account trades above $51,250 the trader is able to trade two contracts (($51,250 × 10 percent)/$2,563). When the account trades above $76,875 the trader is able to trade three contracts (($76,875 × 10 percent)/$2,563). When it dips below $76,875 and remains above $51,250, the trader will only be able to trade two contracts.

As you can see in figure 8.16, less profit is required to be made by each additional contract, allowing the trader to accumulate contracts relatively quickly. This enables the trader to earn geometric profits.

The first question to ask when applying Williams fixed-risk money management strategy to Forex_Trader's results, is whether it achieves the objectives of money management—that is, trading fewer contracts when losing and trading more contracts when winning. The answer is yes to both.

When you're losing, your dollar risk will reduce. With a lower dollar risk, you will be expected to trade fewer contracts or trade with a smaller position size. And when you're winning your dollar risk will increase. With a higher dollar risk you will be able to trade more contracts or trade with a larger position size. As a result, the maximum number of contracts was reached, allowing Williams fixed risk to earn more than $13,000,000, significantly more then the single contract's $255,100 in net profits. Williams fixed risk does allow a trader to enjoy geometric profits.

As with the other strategies, I have limited the maximum number of contracts to 100. In summary, Williams fixed risk generated more than $13,000,000 in net profits, with a maximum dollar and percentage drawdown of $1,363,750 and 17 percent respectively. It generated $10 of profit for every $1 of drawdown pain, and the strategy experienced a 6.3 percent standard deviation between trades.

Now although impressive, it is still worth while considering how the strategy would have handled a $10,000 catastrophic loss. Figure 8.17 tells you the story.

Although the geometric profits look impressive they do come with risk. Experiencing a catastrophic $10,000 loss per contract when trading seven contracts would see a $205,000 account balance experience a 34 percent drawdown. This drawdown would require a gain of 52 percent to recover. In my opinion, this is rather reasonable given the trader was hit with a catastrophic loss. In addition, what is nice with Williams fixed risk is that a trader would only have slipped down two contract levels. A trader could continue trading with five contracts and would have a reasonable expectation of trading out of his or her drawdown relatively quickly. One criticism of the strategy is that it doesn't allow traders with small accounts to begin trading.

However, all up Williams fixed risk not only achieves its money management objectives of trading less when losing and trading more when winning, but it also comfortably handles a catastrophic loss.

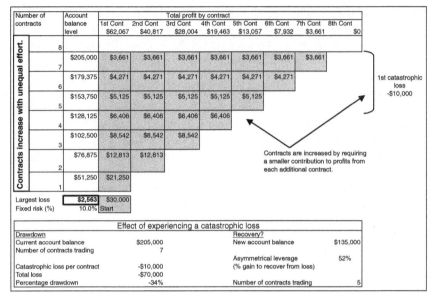

FIGURE 8.17   How Williams fixed-risk money management handles a catastrophic loss

FOREX_TRADER USING FIXED-PERCENTAGE MONEY MANAGEMENT

Figure 8.18 shows Forex_Trader's performance when fixed percentage is applied. Before I discuss the implications of this I'll first explore fixed-percentage money management.

Fixed percentage is perhaps the most common money management strategy used among professional traders. If you're finding it difficult to understand all these money management strategies, you could do far worse than deciding to simply "follow the winners" and implement what they use—fixed percentage.

Fixed percentage requires you to limit your losses to a fixed percentage of your account balance. To calculate the number of contracts to trade according to fixed percentage you would use the following formula:

$$\text{Number of contracts} = \frac{\text{Fixed percentage} \times \text{Account balance}}{\text{Individual trade risk}}$$

If you had a $30,000 account balance and wanted to limit your risk to 2 percent of your account, and you were faced with a $500 trade risk, you would trade one contract ([$30,000 × 0.02]/$500 = 1.2 or 1.0).

Table 8.8 shows how the number of contracts you can trade changes with your account balance and the individual risk of each trade.

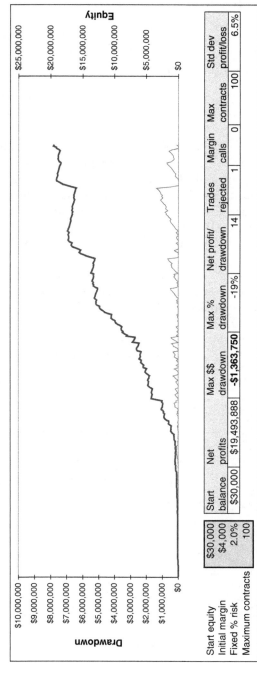

FIGURE 8.18 Forex_Trader's performance with fixed-percentage money management

TABLE 8.8   Number of contracts to trade

Account balance	Fixed percent	Fixed % dollars	Trade risk	Contracts traded	
				Actual	Rounddown
$30,000	2%	$600	$200	3.0	3
$40,000	2%	$800	$650	1.2	1
$50,000	2%	$1,000	$350	2.9	2
$60,000	2%	$1,200	$265	4.5	4

For conservatism, the figures in this table have been rounded down to the nearest integer. You will need to determine what percentage of your account balance you would like to risk on each trade. As your account balance grows, you'll be able to risk more money and trade more contracts. Similarly, if your account balance falls, you'll be restricted to risking less money and trading fewer contracts.

Figure 8.19 illustrates how fixed percentage allows contracts to be accumulated.

Figure 8.19 has a $30,000 starting account balance and only risks 2 percent of the account on any one trade. For ease of explanation I'll assume every trade has a fixed risk of $500. As figure 8.19 shows, once the account balance reaches $50,000 two contracts can be traded ([$50,000 × 0.02]/ $500 = 2.0). Once a total profit of $25,000 has been made between two contracts and $75,000 reached, three contracts can be traded, and so on.

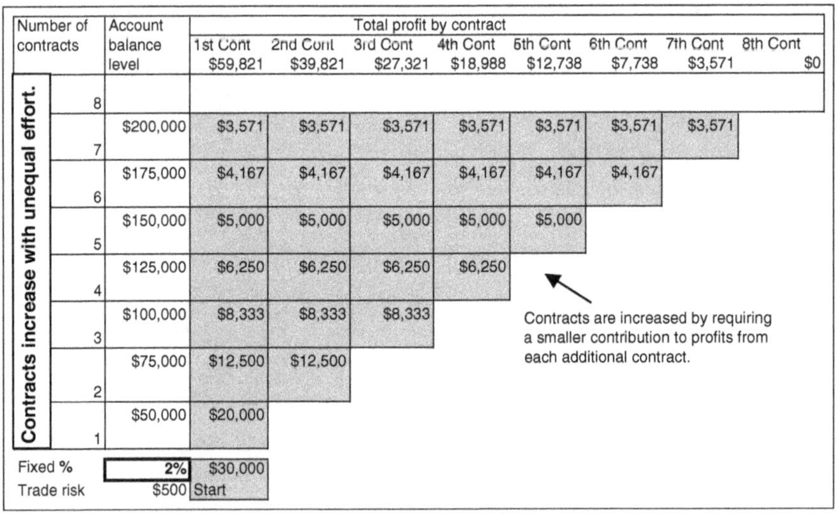

FIGURE 8.19   Account levels at which the number of contracts increase

As you can see, fixed percentage requires a smaller contribution in profit from each contract at the next contract level. This unequal contribution in profits between contract levels allows fixed percentage to accumulate contracts at a steady pace.

Figure 8.18 shows Forex_Trader's performance using fixed percentage. Starting with a $30,000 account, limiting the risk to 2 percent of the account balance, rounding down to the nearest integer, and trading a maximum of 100 contracts would have seen Forex_Trader achieve profits of more than $19,000,000, while incurring a maximum dollar and percentage drawdown of $1,363,759 and 19 percent respectively. Fixed percentage made $14 of profit for every $1 of drawdown pain, and it generated a 6.5 percent standard deviation between trades.

Does fixed percentage achieve the objectives of money management—trading fewer contracts when losing and more when winning? The answer is yes. When you're losing money, fixed percentage requires you to risk less money and therefore trade fewer contracts. When you're winning and your account balance grows, fixed percentage requires you to risk more money and therefore trade more contracts.

Like fixed risk, fixed units, and Williams fixed risk, fixed percentage can also help to manage individual trade risk. Since you are limited to exposing your account to a maximum fixed percentage, you will be restricted in the trades you can take. In Forex_Trader's example, fixed percentage rejected one trade because its dollar risk was too high for the account. So apart from providing a good money management strategy, fixed percentage also helps manage individual trade risk.

One criticism of fixed percentage is that it makes it difficult for traders with small accounts to begin trading. If your risk capital was limited to $10,000, you would find it difficult to find a trade with a small enough risk to trade. If you wanted to limit your risk to 2 percent of your $10,000 account, you could only trade those signals with a dollar risk of $200 or less, and you may not find many of them.

The main reason professional traders prefer fixed percentage is because it's very effective at lowering a trader's risk of ruin. Remember, professional traders aren't focused on how much money they can make, but whether they're managing their risk as well as they can, and fixed percentage is very effective at managing risk. Table 8.9 clearly demonstrates this.

What table 8.9 shows is the number of consecutive losing trades it will take, where each loss is limited to a fixed percentage of the account's outstanding balance, to reach a zero account balance. For example, if a zero account balance is defined as the ruin point, and a fixed 5 percent of the account balance is risked on each trade, it will take 104 consecutive losing trades before the account balance reaches zero, or ruin. If only 1 percent was risked, it would take 528 consecutive losing trades to be ruined. Most

TABLE 8.9   Number of losing trades before ruin

Fixed % risk of account	Number of losing trades before ruin
5%	104
4%	130
3%	174
2%	263
1%	528
0.5%	1,058

professional traders look to risk less than 1 percent. If only 0.5 percent of the account balance was risked, it would take 1,058 consecutive losing trades before the account reached a zero balance.

Let me put it another way. With fixed risk, dividing a small account into 20 units of money was the minimum traders should attempt if they want to trade with a low risk of ruin. Using fixed percentage and limiting the risk to 1 percent would provide 528 (diminishing) units of money. Having the opportunity to trade 508 additional signals while experiencing a losing streak helps to increase the odds of survival for fixed percentage traders.

Figure 8.20 illustrates how fixed percentage would handle a catastrophic loss.

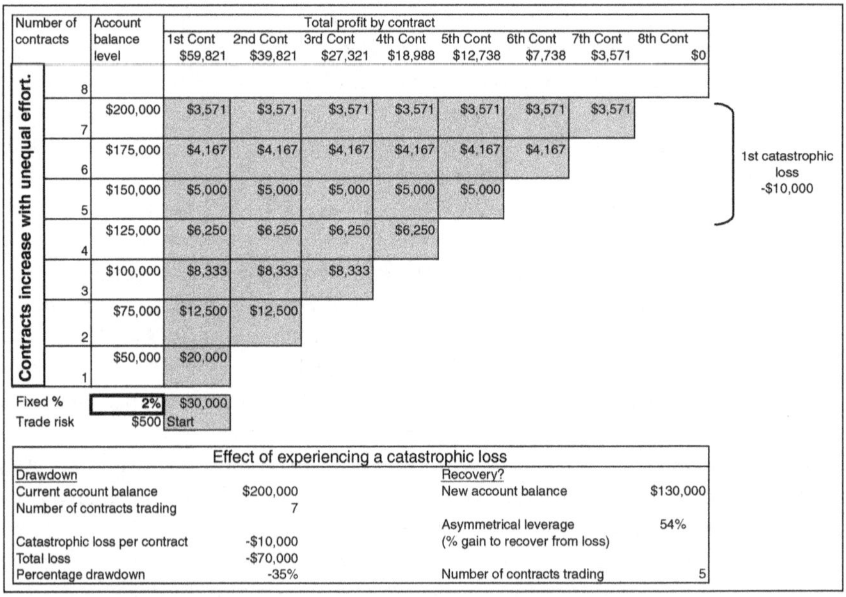

FIGURE 8.20   How fixed-percentage money management handles a catastrophic loss

Using the same example as before, it seems that fixed percentage handles a catastrophic loss quite well. Assuming the $10,000 loss occurs at the same seven-contract level with the account at $200,000, you would expect to suffer a $70,000, or 35 percent, drawdown. If this happened, although nasty and painful, you would still be able to continue trading. Your asymmetrical leverage would require a 54 percent gain to recover, and you could begin doing so with five contracts because you would have only slipped down two contract levels. This is not a bad position to be in if such a catastrophic loss occurred.

FOREX_TRADER USING FIXED-VOLATILITY MONEY MANAGEMENT

Figure 8.21 shows Forex_Trader's performance when fixed volatility is applied. Before I discuss the implications of this I'll first explore fixed-volatility money management.

Fixed volatility could also be called fixed-percentage volatility, as it looks to limit the market's volatility to a fixed percentage of your account balance.

You would use the following formula to calculate the number of contracts to trade:

$$\text{Number of contracts} = \frac{\text{Fixed percentage} \times \text{Account balance}}{\text{Market volatility}}$$

Market volatility refers to market movement over a defined period. One measure of market volatility could be a 10-, 20-, or 30-day average of the daily range. You could use a weekly or a monthly time frame to measure volatility. It's best to align your volatility measure with your trading time frame. Short-term traders could use a daily measure, while long-term trend traders (with large accounts) could use a monthly measure. For this discussion, the time frame and volatility measure will be daily.

To measure a market's volatility, or the distance it travels between the high and low, you can either use the actual daily range or its true range. The true range will take into account any gaps between the previous day's close and the day's actual high or low.

Essentially, the previous day's close is used to measure the true range (or true distance traveled) if it is either lower than the current day's low, or higher than the current day's high. Once the preferred range is defined, a period of time can be selected to calculate an average. For this example I'll assume a 10-day average true range (ATR) to measure the market's volatility.

Fixed volatility does not take into account a trade's individual risk. If the market's volatility measure is within the fixed-percentage account limit, a trade is taken, regardless of its individual risk. Similarly, if the market's

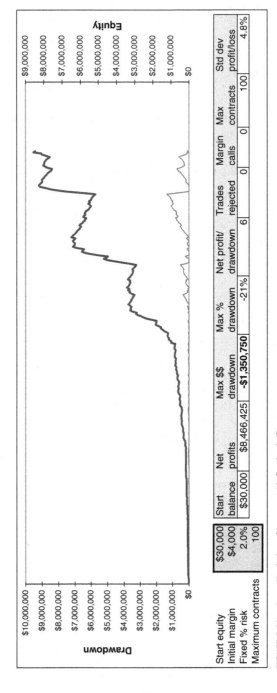

FIGURE 8.21 Forex_Trader's performance with fixed-volatility money management

TABLE 8.10   Number of contracts to trade with various levels of market volatility

Account balance	Fixed percent	Fixed % dollars	Trade risk (ignored)	Market's 10-day ATR			Contracts traded	
				Points	Pt value	$$ vol	Actual	Rounddown
$50,000	2%	$1,000	$200	0.0031	$125,000	$388	2.6	2
$50,000	2%	$1,000	$1,650	0.0045	$125,000	$563	1.8	1
$50,000	2%	$1,000	$150	0.0075	$125,000	$938	1.1	1
$50,000	2%	$1,000	$265	0.0125	$125,000	$1,563	0.6	0

volatility expands and exceeds the fixed percent account limit, a trade will not be selected, regardless of its individual trade risk, even if it's only risking, say, $100.

This is the money management strategy Richard Dennis taught his famous Turtle traders.

Let's take a look at an example. Starting with a $50,000 account balance and limiting the market's volatility to a fixed 2 percent of the account balance, I'll assume the currency market's current 10-day ATR is 0.0031 points. Multiplying the points by the value of a whole points of $125,000 would calculate the markets volatility at $388 (0.0031 × $125,000). That is, over the last 10 days the currency market has, on average, had a daily true movement of $388. If I want to limit the market's volatility to a fixed 2 percent of the account balance ($50,000 × 0.02 = $1,000), I'll only be able to trade two contracts ($1,000/$388 = 2.6 or 2.0).

Similar to the other strategies, for conservatism, I have rounded down to the nearest integer.

Table 8.10 illustrates how the number of contracts traded changes with the market's volatility.

As you can see, the number of contracts traded fluctuates with the market's volatility, as measured by the 10-day ATR. In addition as the account grows, and/or the market's daily volatility falls, the trader will be expected to trade more contracts. Similarly, if the account falls, or the market's daily volatility expands, the trader will be expected to trade fewer contracts (i.e. reduce their position size).

Figure 8.22 illustrates how fixed volatility allows contracts to be accumulated. In this example, the market's 10-day ATR, or volatility, remains constant at 0.0060 points, or $750 (0.0060 × $125,000). Naturally, this is unrealistic as the market, like all markets, constantly changes—volatility continually expands and contracts depending on market conditions.

Nevertheless, for the purpose of this explanation, two variables (fixed percentage and volatility) have to be fixed to see how the number of contracts increases as the account balance grows.

Like fixed capital, fixed units, Williams fixed risk, and fixed percentage, fixed volatility requires a lower contribution of profit from each additional

Number of contracts	Account balance level	Total profit by contract							
		1st cont 104732.14	2nd cont 59732.14	3rd cont 40982.143	4th cont 28482.14	5th cont 19107.14	6th cont 11607.14	7th cont 5357.143	8th cont 0
8	$300,000	$5,357	$5,357	$5,357	$5,357	$5,357	$5,357	$5,357	
7	$262,500	$6,250	$6,250	$6,250	$6,250	$6,250	$6,250		
6	$225,000	$7,500	$7,500	$7,500	$7,500	$7,500			
5	$187,500	$9,375	$9,375	$9,375	$9,375				
4	$150,000	$12,500	$12,500	$12,500					
3	$112,500	$18,750	$18,750						
2	$75,000	$45,000							
1 Fixed % 10ATR	2% $30,000 $750 Start								

Contracts increase with unequal effort.

Contracts are increased by requiring a smaller contribution to profits from each additional contract.

FIGURE 8.22 Account levels at which the number of contracts increase

contract at the next contract level. This smaller contribution allows contracts to be accumulated at a steady pace.

It should be noted that if your trading methodology uses a 10-day ATR range for its stop, then fixed percentage and fixed volatility would produce the same money management results.

Figure 8.21 summarizes Forex_Trader's performance using fixed volatility. Starting with a $30,000 account, limiting 2 percent of the account balance to a market's 10-day ATR, rounding down to the nearest integer and trading a maximum of 100 contracts would have resulted in Forex_Trader achieving profits of more than $8,400,000 while incurring a maximum dollar and percentage drawdown of only $1,350,750 and 21 percent respectively. Fixed volatility achieved $6 in profit per $1 of drawdown pain, and generated a 4.8 percent standard deviation between trades.

Fixed volatility clearly achieves money management's objectives, surpassing the single contract's profits of $255,100. Not only are fewer contracts traded as either the account balance falls or the market's volatility expands, but geometric profits are able to be earned by trading more contracts when either the account balance grows or the market's volatility contracts.

What fixed volatility achieves that none of the previous strategies have is the ability to manage your account's exposure to market volatility. When market volatility is high, fixed volatility tells you to trade less because the market is wild and dangerous. When the market settles down, fixed volatility tells you to trade more because the market is behaving itself.

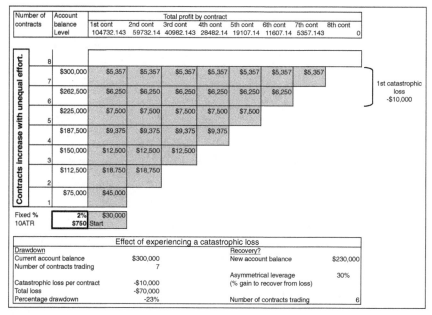

FIGURE 8.23 How fixed-volatility money management handles a catastrophic loss

What fixed volatility does not help with is managing your trades' individual risk. Regardless of a trade's risk, you are expected to take all signals if the market's volatility is within your fixed percentage account limit. Another criticism of fixed volatility is that, just like Williams fixed risk and fixed percentage, it doesn't allow traders with small accounts to begin trading.

Figure 8.23 illustrates how fixed volatility would handle a catastrophic loss.

Keep in mind the limitation with testing fixed volatility and a catastrophic loss—a fixed 10-day ATR of 0.0060 points, or $750, is being used, which is not realistic. A market's volatility cannot remain constant due to daily information continually influencing market forces. With that limitation in mind, fixed volatility does quite well at handling a catastrophic loss. Assuming the $10,000 loss occurs at the same seven-contract level with the account at $300,000, you would expect to suffer a $70,000 loss, or a 23 percent drawdown. If this happened, you would still be able to continue trading. Your asymmetrical leverage would require a 30 percent gain to recover and could begin doing so with six contracts because you would have only fallen one contract level.

This brings us to the end of the discussion on the seven anti-Martingale money management strategies—fixed risk, fixed capital, fixed ratio, fixed

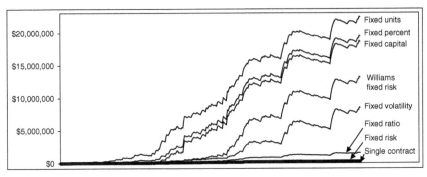

FIGURE 8.24   Money management strategies

units, Williams fixed risk, fixed percentage, and fixed volatility. Next I want to take a closer look at each strategy to see whether you can gain further insight into the individual strategies.

WHICH MONEY MANAGEMENT STRATEGY TO CHOOSE?

Figure 8.24 and table 8.11 summarize Forex_Trader's performance with each money management strategy.

First up, I want to talk about the equal drawdowns among fixed capital, fixed units, Williams fixed risk, fixed percentage, and fixed volatility. At first glance, this seems to be an anomaly and possibly an error. It isn't. It's just a quirk of the trade sample and the maximum number of contracts each strategy was limited to. What happened with Forex_Trader was that it hit its worst drawdown when all the strategies had reached their 100-contract

TABLE 8.11   Summary of money management strategies

	Start balance	Net profits	Max $$ drawdown	Max % drawdown	Net profit/ drawdown	Trades rejected	Margin calls	Max contracts	Std. dev. profit/loss
Single contract	$20,000	$255,100	−$13,638	−9%	19	0	0	1	2.3%
Fixed risk	$20,000	$151,538	−$4,725	−5%	32	195	0	4	2.7%
Fixed capital	$20,000	$18,667,238	−$1,363,750	−22%	14	0	0	100	7.4%
Fixed ratio	$20,000	$1,585,188	−$162,413	−12%	10	0	0	13	3.8%
Fixed units	$20,000	$22,402,163	−$1,363,750	−32%	16	1	4	100	8.5%
Williams fixed risk	$30,000	$13,199,288	−$1,363,750	−17%	10	10	0	100	6.3%
Fixed percentage	$30,000	$19,493,888	−$1,363,750	−19%	14	1	0	100	6.5%
Fixed volatility	$30,000	$8,466,425	−$1,350,750	−21%	6	0	0	100	4.8%

limit. They all hit the worst drawdown at the same time they were all trading 100 contracts. Consequently, they all experienced similar drawdowns.

Now back to making some observations about these competing strategies. One fact that you have to accept is that there is no hard or fast characteristic that can be used to select a superior money management strategy quantitatively and unambiguously. You have to look at each separately and consider all the parts. For example, if you were confident that your equity curve will remain stable into the future, then the more aggressive you can be in your strategy selection. However, you then have to remember that the primary objective in trading is survival, so if you're feeling confident, keep in mind that the market's maximum adversity is still out there, hiding away waiting patiently to ambush you when you least expect it.

However, I think you could safely do away with fixed risk because it failed to generate good profits, even though it produced the lowest drawdown, lowest standard deviation, and highest net profit-to-drawdown ratio. With this in mind, your selection would now come down to six strategies.

One approach could be to select a strategy that produced the lowest percentage drawdown. If this was the case, you would look to trade fixed ratio with its paltry 12 percent drawdown. However, since Williams fixed risk had only a slightly higher 17 percent drawdown, and was accompanied by eight times the profit, most would probably prefer Williams fixed risk over fixed ratio.

Yet Williams fixed risk's higher profits arrived with greater volatility because its individual trade results generated a 6.3 percent standard deviation, which was almost twice that of fixed ratio. Fixed volatility earned significantly more than the single contract result, it achieved this with both a reasonable 21 percent drawdown and 4.8 percent standard deviation. All up very attractive. As you can see, there is no standard rule you can apply—your own individual risk tolerances and needs have to be considered.

Another characteristic you could use is one that would ignore the percentage drawdown. Although important, the percentage drawdown only considers one side of the decision equation—risk. It doesn't provide any feedback on the other half—reward. This is important to remember. When you do select an appropriate strategy that satisfies your personal risk tolerance, it must also be weighed up against the probable reward.

An alternative to looking at the percentage drawdown would be to measure the actual dollar drawdown against the dollar reward generated. This is a simple risk versus reward question—which strategy will produce the best value, or reward, per dollar drawdown, or risk, incurred?

To help answer this question, look at the net profit to dollar drawdown ratio, or what I call the value payoff, calculated using the following formula:

$$\text{Value payoff} = \frac{\text{Net profit}}{\text{Dollar drawdown}}$$

The idea is to select a strategy that produces the highest reward dollar for the grief and pain you're guaranteed to suffer when you experience a drawdown. That is, how many dollars have been contributed for every dollar removed during a maximum drawdown? Rather than focusing on the risk side alone, you should keep one eye on the reward side. Table 8.12 shows which strategy provides the highest reward dollar for each risk dollar incurred.

As you can see, fixed risk provides the highest reward dollar for each risk dollar removed during the worst drawdown. However, since fixed risk produces the lowest profits, I'd suggest not many traders would consider it. If you also ignore the single-contract result, then fixed units would be the preferred money management strategy based on this criterion, earning $16 dollars in profit for every $1 of pain incurred during the worst drawdown. The only drawback in using this criterion is that fixed units also generated the highest standard deviation, producing the most volatility in its results (and not to mention having a higher risk of ruin during the drawdown).

Although the risk versus reward value payoff is a reasonable characteristic to help in strategy selection, there are additional issues that need to be taken into account. Table 8.13 provides a summary of each strategy's key features. This will help to identify the issues that need to be considered.

The most important features are the first two—money management's objectives. Only fixed risk fails both to cut back your trading when you're losing and increase your contracts when you're winning. Fixed units also fails to cut back when losing, but then it does trade more when you're winning.

An important feature of the remaining strategies concerns contract profit contribution. This has a direct impact on each strategy's ability to handle a catastrophic loss. Although unlikely, the market's maximum

TABLE 8.12   The value payoff table

	Net profits	Max $$ drawdown	Net profit/ drawdown	Std. dev. profit/loss
Fixed risk	$151,538	−$4,725	32	2.7%
Single contract	$255,100	−$13,638	19	2.3%
Fixed units	$22,402,163	−$1,363,750	16	8.5%
Fixed capital	$18,667,238	−$1,363,750	14	7.4%
Fixed percentage	$19,493,888	−$1,363,750	14	6.5%
Fixed ratio	$1,585,188	−$162,413	10	3.8%
Williams fixed risk	$13,199,288	−$1,363,750	10	6.3%
Fixed volatility	$8,466,425	−$1,350,750	6	4.8%

TABLE 8.13   Summary of key features of strategies

Key Feature	Single contract	Fixed risk	Fixed capital	Fixed ratio	Fixed units	Williams fixed risk	Fixed percent	Fixed volatility
Achieve money management's key objectives?								
Trade less when losing to preserve capital and minimise ruin?	x	x	√	√	x	√	√	√
Trade more when winning for geometric profits?	x	x	√	√	√	√	√	√
Require equal contribution from each contract?	x	x	x	√	x	x	x	x
Manage a catastrophic loss?	√	√	x	√	√	√	√	√
Manage small accounts?	√	√	√	√	√	x	x	x
Manage individual trade risk?	x	√	x	x	√	x	√	√
Manage market volatility?	x	x	x	x	x	x	x	√
Lowest probability of ruin?	x	x	x	x	x	x	√	√

adversity should be respected. You need to believe that the market can and will cause "unexpected" catastrophic losses.

The trick for a strategy's ability to earn geometric profits is the speed at which it can accumulate contracts. Strategies that accumulate contracts the fastest are those that require a smaller profit contribution from each additional contract. They begin trading more contracts sooner and earning higher profits. This unequal effort makes those strategies (fixed capital, fixed units, Williams fixed risk, fixed percentage, and fixed volatility) seem obvious stars. However, when the pressure is applied, like a $10,000 catastrophic loss, the stars lose their shine. The reason for this is that their accumulated contracts are based on increasingly smaller profit contributions— when a catastrophic loss occurs at a higher contract level they do not have the accumulated profits to fall back on.

Table 8.14 illustrates how each strategy handled the catastrophic loss.

TABLE 8.14   Summary of strategies' catastrophic losses

	Account balance	No. of cont.	Catastrophic loss per cont.	Total loss	Percent drawdown	Asymmet. leverage	Conts. to recover
Single contract	$255,100	1	−$10,000	−$10,000	−4%	4%	1
Fixed risk	$151,538	1	−$10,000	−$10,000	−7%	7%	1
Fixed capital	$120,000	7	−$10,000	−$70,000	−58%	140%	3
Fixed ratio	$524,000	7	−$10,000	−$70,000	−13%	15%	7
Fixed units	$160,000	7	−$10,000	−$70,000	−44%	78%	7
Williams fixed risk	$205,000	7	−$10,000	−$70,000	−34%	52%	5
Fixed percentage	$200,000	7	−$10,000	−$70,000	−35%	54%	5
Fixed volatility	$300,000	7	−$10,000	−$70,000	−23%	30%	6

Although fixed capital seemed to be a profit star due to its ability to accumulate contracts the fastest, it did so on the basis of requiring the smallest contribution in profit from each additional contract. As a result, fixed capital was a complete disaster when the catastrophic loss occurred, incurring an 58 percent drawdown and requiring a 140 percent gain, beginning with one contract, to recover from the asymmetrical leverage. So fixed capital should probably be crossed off your list.

At this stage, the strategy selection has been narrowed down to fixed ratio, fixed units, Williams fixed risk, fixed percentage, and fixed volatility.

Fixed units also suffered from the catastrophic loss, although it still retained its whole seven contracts and ability to trade out of the drawdown within a reasonable time.

The remaining strategies all survived the catastrophic loss, although fixed ratio and fixed volatility survived in better shape. They only required a respective 15 percent and 30 percent gain to recover from their asymmetrical leverage, compared to fixed percentage's 54 percent and William's fixed risk's 52 percent required gains.

If you're a small trader with only a $10,000 account, you'd find it difficult to trade employing either Williams fixed-risk, fixed-percentage, or fixed-volatility money management strategies. It would be near impossible to find either single trades small enough, or a time when the market's volatility was low enough, to allow you to trade. Accordingly, fixed ratio and fixed units seem more appropriate as strategies to follow if you're a small trader. And if your preference is to focus on risk control, then fixed ratio would be preferred over fixed units since it suffered a smaller drawdown from a catastrophic loss and produced less volatility in its individual trade results. The only drawback is that fixed ratio only produced $1.5 million compared to fixed units' $22.0 million. Ah, it's never an easy decision. However, the correct conservative choice would be to select fixed ratio over fixed units. Remember, as a professional risk manager, your objective is survival, not making gigantic profits. And as your account grew, you could then consider switching to either Williams fixed risk, fixed percentage, or fixed volatility.

It's also important to understand why fixed ratio was able to handle its catastrophic loss so well. Unlike the other strategies, it required an equal profit contribution from every contract. Fixed ratio creates a solid foundation for its multiple contracts. Although it will lose money when a losing streak occurs, it will have earned more profit per contract than any other strategy, allowing it to handle a catastrophic loss better.

However, fixed ratio is not the best strategy to handle a long streak of losing trades. Unlike fixed percentage, it won't help manage a trade's individual risk, expecting you to take all signals. In addition, it won't allow you to reduce your dollar risk as you trade through a long sequence of losing trades. You're only able to cut back on the number of contracts when you slip to a lower contract level. Unless you increase the rate at which you decrease your number of contracts, fixed ratio can be slow to cut back and reduce your dollar risk per trade.

Although examining how each strategy would survive a catastrophic loss was a useful exercise, it does not really reflect the normal market conditions traders and their money management strategy would usually be exposed to. Most likely, you'll experience a long sequence of losing trades, rather than a catastrophic loss. If this was the case, Williams fixed risk, fixed percentage, and fixed volatility would be preferable to fixed ratio. This is because they provide the best strategies for minimizing risk of ruin, which is why fixed percentage is the preferred choice of professional traders, because it does it best.

Maximum Contract Limit

As you know, I limited the maximum contracts each strategy could trade. I did this to make the analysis a little more realistic. The disadvantage of this is that I limited the full potential of each strategy. As a consequence, my decision had a significant impact on the results of each strategy. For example, most of the dollar drawdowns were of a similar size since they occurred when most of the strategies had reached, and were trading, the 100-contract limit. Consequently, my decision removed any differentiation among most of the strategies on their dollar drawdowns, masking any real information you could learn. As a result, I thought it would be best to look at the performance figures from a number of different angles.

Speed to Reach the Contract Limit

Table 8.15 shows how fast each strategy was able to reach the 100 maximum contract limit.

TABLE 8.15   Speed to reach 100 contracts

	Total trades	Max contracts allowed	Max contracts reached	Trade position when reach max conts.	
				Trade number	Trade %
Fixed risk	362	100	1	NA	
Single contract	167	100	4	NA	
Fixed units	362	100	100	121	33%
Fixed capital	362	100	13	NA	
Fixed percentage	361	100	100	93	26%
Fixed ratio	362	100	100	207	57%
Williams fixed risk	361	100	100	153	42%
Fixed volatility	362	100	100	275	76%

As table 8.15 shows, fixed units was first to reach its 100-contract limit, doing so within 26 percent of the data sample set. If you were looking for the most aggressive strategy, to accumulate contracts the fastest, then you would consider fixed units. If you were extra conservative and prefered to delay stepping up your position size, then you could consider fixed volatility, because it was the slowest to reach its contract limit, taking 76 percent of the data sample set. If you preferred to go faster than fixed volatility but slower than fixed units, you could possibly choose to use either Williams fixed risk or fixed percentage as your preferred money management strategy.

Full Potential Without Contract Limit

Table 8.16 summarizes each of the strategies' full results without my arbitrary 100-contract limit.

Well, how about that. And the winner is fixed units with a super duper hypothetical, and totally ridiculous, result of $436 billion! But at what cost. An 83 percent drawdown, 23.8 percent standard deviation, and having to find 68 million contracts to trade toward the end of the data sample set. I told you these money management strategies can get out of hand!

What is interesting is that these full results do give you probably a better insight into the strategies regarding their drawdown and volatility. Although fixed units was the winner, it came with a suicidal 83 percent drawdown and huge volatility in its profit and loss. And it also came with an unrealistic contract quantity of 68 million. There is not an exchange in the world today that would do 68 million contracts a day on its own across its liquid futures contracts.

TABLE 8.16   Full strategy potential without the 100-contract limit

	Start balance	Net profits	Max $$ drawdown	Max % drawdown	Net profit/ drawdown	Trades rejected	Margin calls	Max contracts	Std. dev. profit/loss
Single contract	$20,000	$255,100	−$13,638	−9%	19	0	0	1	2.3%
Fixed risk	$20,000	$151,538	−$4,725	−5%	32	195	0	4	2.7%
Fixed capital	$20,000	$12,144,227,375	−$4,194,172,650	−61%	3	0	0	866,672	13.8%
Fixed ratio	$20,000	$1,585,188	−$162,413	−12%	10	0	0	13	3.8%
Fixed units	$20,000	$436,291,722,113	−$186,714,403,862	−83%	2	1	12	68,602,176	23.8%
Williams fixed risk	$30,000	$100,591,275	−$22,762,050	−42%	4	4	0	4,084	7.9%
Fixed percentage	$30,000	$699,003,363	−$198,115,237	−40%	4	1	0	62,588	8.8%
Fixed volatility	$30,000	$12,188,113	−$2,332,475	−29%	5	0	0	607	5.2%

Fixed capital suffered the same, with a high 61 percent drawdown, high volatility and trading an unrealistic number of contracts.

A good risk manager instead would prefer Williams fixed risk, fixed percentage, and fixed volatility, because they provided a good mix of profits and drawdown, with fixed volatility producing the highest net profit-to-drawdown ratio.

If you were looking at trading as a marathon, I suppose you would choose between fixed percentage and fixed volatility because they produced the highest profits with manageable drawdowns.

However, there is no need to look at trading as a marathon, nor is it necessary for you to look at these strategies in isolation—choosing one above all the others. There is no reason you can't create a hybrid solution to satisfy your needs, that is, being more aggressive earlier in your trading to build your account up, and then becoming more conservative, risking less when you have more to lose.

Let's now look at the strategies from a profit objective perspective.

Profit Objective: $100k

Let's say a trader's first profit objective is to make $100,000. Table 8.17 shows the speed at which each strategy achieved the target.

As you would expect, fixed units was first to the post making $100,000 in profit within 4 percent of the data sample set. Table 8.18 summarizes each strategies performance at the $100,000 profit mark.

Now this is interesting. This hypothetical data set shows fixed units had the second-lowest percentage drawdown of 6 percent, but it did so with the

TABLE 8.17   Speed to reach $100,000

	Total trades	Trade position when profit = $100k	
		Trade number	Trade %
Account balance starts at $20,000			
Single contract	362	150	41%
Fixed risk	362	176	49%
Fixed capital	362	68	19%
Fixed ratio	362	128	35%
Fixed units	362	15	4%
Account balance starts at $30,000			
Williams fixed risk	362	119	33%
Fixed percentage	362	32	9%
Fixed volatility	362	67	19%

TABLE 8.18   Summary of strategy performances at $100,000

	Start balance	Net profits	Max $$ drawdown	Max % drawdown	Net profit/ drawdown	Trades rejected	Margin calls	Max contracts	Std. dev. profit/loss
Single contract	$20,000	$103,163	−$4,187	−9%	25	0	0	1	3.1%
Fixed risk	$20,000	$101,250	−$4,200	−5%	24	62	0	4	3.7%
Fixed capital	$20,000	$101,150	−$14,750	−22%	7	0	0	7	6.9%
Fixed ratio	$20,000	$121,213	−$5,625	−9%	22	0	0	3	4.2%
Fixed units	$20,000	$126,013	−$3,163	−6%	40	1	1	11	22.8%
Williams fixed risk	$30,000	$120,063	−$9,738	−14%	12	12	0	4	4.1%
Fixed percentage	$30,000	$102,600	−$14,163	−12%	7	1	0	15	10.3%
Fixed volatility	$30,000	$112,038	−$12,263	−13%	9	0	0	7	5.4%

highest volatility, recording a 22.8 percent standard deviation. But this volatility isn't bad when the high standard deviation is being caused by numerous higher-profit trades! In this early dash for $100,000 in profit, based on this data sample set, fixed units is the standout strategy reaching the goal first, with most profit, the lowest drawdown and highest net profit-to-drawdown ratio.

Profit Objective: $1.0 Million

Let's now assume a trader's profit objective is not to make $100,000, but to make $1,000,000. Table 8.19 shows the speed at which each strategy achieved the new higher target.

As you would expect, fixed units again was first to make $1,000,000 in profit within 25 percent of the data sample set. Table 8.20 summarizes each strategy's performance at the $1,000,000 profit mark.

Now the performance metrics are shifting. Fixed units now has the highest dollar and percentage drawdown, although it won this race as well, it did come with more pain!

Based on making a million-dollar profit, using this data sample, a trader would consider either Williams fixed risk, fixed percentage, or fixed volatility. However, if speed is of the essence, then fixed percentage would be preferred because it made its $1,000,000 within 34 percent of the data sample set, as opposed to William's fixed risk and fixed volatility, which took more than 50 percent of the trades to reach the mark.

However, as I said, there is no reason you would have to choose one strategy above the others. There is no reason you couldn't mix and match, based on your preferences given your account size. I think it would be

TABLE 8.19   Speed to make $1,000,000

	Total trades	Trade position when profit = $1.0m	
		Trade number	Trade %
Account balance starts at $20,000			
Single contract	362	NA	NA
Fixed risk	362	NA	NA
Fixed capital	362	132	36%
Fixed ratio	362	269	74%
Fixed units	362	89	25%
Account balance starts at $30,000			
Williams fixed risk	362	180	50%
Fixed percentage	362	122	34%
Fixed volatility	362	204	56%

TABLE 8.20   Summary of strategy performances at $1,000,000

	Start balance	Net profits	Max $$ drawdown	Max % drawdown	Net profit/ drawdown	Trades rejected	Margin calls	Max contracts	Std. dev. profit/loss
Single contract	$20,000	$255,100	−$13,638	−9%	19	0	0	1	2.3%
Fixed risk	$20,000	$151,538	−$4,725	−5%	32	195	0	4	2.7%
Fixed capital	$20,000	$1,075,263	−$54,275	−22%	20	0	0	61	9.6%
Fixed ratio	$20,000	$998,050	−$66,250	−9%	15	0	0	10	4.2%
Fixed units	$20,000	$1,069,613	−$105,438	−32%	10	1	4	100	14.7%
Williams fixed risk	$30,000	$1,038,713	−$85,500	−14%	12	12	0	38	6.3%
Fixed percentage	$30,000	$1,106,788	−$100,475	−19%	11	1	0	81	8.9%
Fixed volatility	$30,000	$1,040,563	−$58,850	−13%	18	0	0	27	5.2%

reasonable if traders preferred to more aggressive in the beginning, trading either fixed ratio or fixed units when they have less to lose, and then shifting to a more conservative strategy as their account builds since they will have more to lose.

No One Size Fits All

All traders are different. They have differing levels of risk tolerance and differing levels of confidence about whether their methodology's equity curve will remain stable. They have different opinions about the way individual risk and market volatility should be managed. Traders have different account sizes. Yet, despite these differences, the information provided here should be able to help you in the selection of your preferred money management strategy.

If you have a small account, you'll probably be inclined to adopt either fixed ratio or fixed units. Fixed ratio's conservative approach requires an equal profit contribution from all contracts. With fixed units it's quicker to accumulate contracts, producing more profit and allowing you to have every chance of avoiding ruin by ensuring you have at least 20 units of money to trade with as a minimum. What may be dangerous is if your expectancy turns negative and you have a long sequence of consecutive losing trades. Fixed ratio may not allow you enough opportunities to trade out of trouble. And fixed units may challenge your confidence when you've just experienced 15 straight losses and you're down to your last five units of money.

If you have a large account, you could consider Williams fixed risk, fixed percentage, or fixed volatility. Fixed percentage both will provide a lower risk of ruin, if you limit the loss of each trade to a small percentage of your account balance, and will allow you to accumulate contracts at a steady pace and earn geometric profits. In addition, fixed percentage produced the highest profits compared to Williams fixed risk and fixed volatility when the 100-contract limit was imposed, with a moderate 19 percent drawdown, and it did produce the highest net profit-to-drawdown ratio of 14.

The best way to become more familiar and comfortable with the various strategies is to test each one on your trade data set. You should examine how each strategy is sensitive to changes in their key variables. You should also test each strategy with a catastrophic loss.

Monte Carlo Simulation

The Monte Carlo simulation is another tool to help with the selection process. This technique helps add robustness to your analysis.

Although you may have developed a robust methodology with a stable equity curve, and you're comfortable with how the various strategies look on the trade history data, you cannot be sure that the trade data will repeat in the same sequence in the future. The Monte Carlo simulation allows you to road test money management strategies thoroughly. It randomly mixes the trade history data as many times as you like, recording for each sequence the key characteristics such as drawdown and the value payoff ratio (net profit to drawdown). It then examines the distribution of results calculating the mean and standard deviations. From these results you can gain further confidence that you're aware of how a strategy will fit with your methodology. But please understand that it does have limitations. It's still reliant on the same individual trade results occurring in the future, and if your equity curve remains stable, that is fine. However, if your system's results start to deteriorate, then it doesn't matter how many simulations you do, your real-time results will still be poor.

For further information on the Monte Carlo simulation you can contact me via my website www.IndexTrader.com.au.

TRADING EQUITY MOMENTUM

Although you now know how important proper money management is, you also know of its limitations. Although money management can turn a methodology with an ordinary expectancy into a money machine, it cannot turn a negative-expectancy methodology into a positive-expectancy methodology. Nor can it tell you when your methodology has fatally fallen off the rails, or when your positive expectancy has turned negative. Although money management is the number one weapon against risk of ruin, it fails to provide an early warning signal. This is where trading equity momentum comes in.

Monitoring a strategy's equity momentum will give you an early warning sign on whether your strategy's equity curve is beginning to become unstable. It will give you a heads up before your strategy stops working completely. It will allow you to step to the sidelines before the strategy's deteriorating performance removes all your risk capital.

In other words, why should you wait for your money management strategy to dictate to you when to stop trading? Shouldn't there be a smarter, earlier warning sign that can help you step to the sidelines? Running out of money seems to be a drastic course to follow, but this is money management's ultimate destination if your methodology's expectancy turns negative.

You shouldn't have to lose your financial boundary's $10,000 risk capital to know what you probably knew when you had lost $5,000. Indeed, it would be useful to have an earlier warning signal, at, say, $3,000, to make you aware that you're starting to get into trouble.

Not only should you trade a positive-expectancy methodology, you should also trade a positive equity momentum methodology, or in other words, a stable equity curve. If your equity curve, on a single-contract basis, starts to dip, you should be prepared to step aside and stop trading until positive equity momentum returns.

What I mean by this is using a stop on your methodology. Just like using stops when you trade, you should use a stop on your trading methodology. Or in other words, a system stop.

System Stop

Just as you should always trade with a stop, so should you trade with a system stop. Even though you may believe you have developed a robust positive-expectancy methodology, and you have correctly validated it using the TEST procedure, there is no guarantee your methodology's expectancy will not turn negative some time in the future. Using a system stop is an essential risk management tool.

Even though I know my strategies have an edge, there is no guarantee they will continue to have an edge into the future. I certainly have a preference that they do, and would be gobsmacked if they didn't, but I have to respect the market's maximum adversity and be prepared for the worst. Measuring equity momentum will help me determine whether my strategy's expectancy begins slipping. Using a system stop on each of my strategies will prevent me from losing the farm.

A system stop has three objectives. First, it should be able to give you a dollar value for your methodology's stop, that is, the size of your system stop. This will tell you how much money, or how much of your risk capital, you should be prepared to invest (or lose) in your methodology.

Second, it should be able to identify when your methodology's equity momentum has faltered, and notify you when to stop trading.

Third, it should be able to identify when your methodology's equity momentum has returned, and notify you when to recommence trading.

The trick is to choose an effective system stop. Just as there are a variety of different stops you can use when you trade, there are many ideas you can use for a system stop—you're only limited by your imagination. A good system stop should give your trading methodology enough space to prove itself, without giving it so much room that it will damage your risk capital.

As I have mentioned, never lose sight of the fact that if you succeed in trading, it won't be because you're a good trader; rather, it will be because you've survived, you've been a good risk manager, and a good risk manager will be prepared for the possibility his or her methodology may lose its edge at some point in the future.

Figure 8.25 shows that almost immediately after commencement of trading a new methodology, the equity curve dipped. Due to its loss of equity momentum, the financial boundary's $10,000 risk capital limit was hit, forcing an end to trading. Obviously, it would have been preferable to stop trading before the financial boundary risk capital was lost. This is where trading equity momentum comes in. A system stop would alert traders before they lost their $10,000 risk capital.

System stops are not limited to mechanical traders. Regardless of your approach to trading, whether it is mechanical or discretionary, you should

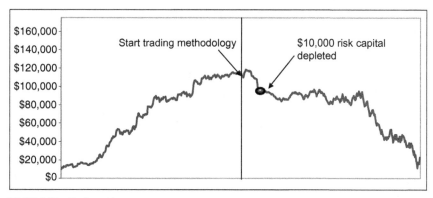

FIGURE 8.25   Trading without a system stop

design, adopt and implement a system stop. Although it is more difficult for a discretionary trader, it's still possible.

A single-contract equity curve needs to be constructed so you can overlay your system stop. It should consist of three parts:

- hypothetical trade history
- 30 emailed simulated trades (TEST) collected during your validation
- live hypothetical results.

With your live hypothetical results, ignore any slippage the market gives you in your actual trading. This is because you're more interested in your methodology's ability to maintain its edge and equity momentum, not how fast the market is trading and the resulting slippage that's been incurred. Although you'll be trading with real-time results, ignore them in favor of the hypothetical results.

Your methodology's equity curve, regardless whether you are a mechanical or discretionary trader, must be continually updated and kept "live." In addition, you must remember the equity curve is based on trading a single contract, and does not involve any money management. What you should be interested in is your methodology's raw edge, its expectancy, its continuing ability to build equity, or maintain its equity momentum, on a single-contract basis (or constant position size). This could not be seen if a money management strategy was applied.

There is no right or wrong system stop. The trick is to develop one that makes sense to you, and then stick to it. Possible ideas for a suitable system stop could include limiting your drawdown when it exceeds:

- a financial boundary's $10,000 risk capital limit
- a previous drawdown

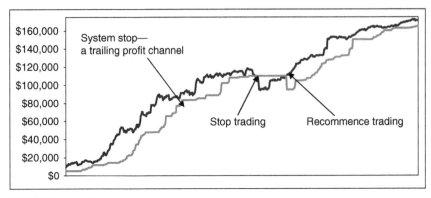

FIGURE 8.26   A profit channel system stop

- a percentage of a previous drawdown
- a swing stop below a previous equity swing low
- a moving average of your equity curve
- a channel breakout of your equity curve
- a multiple of your average monthly profit.

As you can see, there are plenty of ideas for a system stop, you're only limited by your imagination. The important point is that your system stop can measure equity momentum, particularly when it falters, and later when it returns.

In figure 8.26, I have constructed a profit channel that tracks the lowest equity curve within a 40-trade lookback period. The lowest point along the equity curve within 40 trades can provide an effective system stop. It will trail your methodology by giving it plenty of space to experience drawdowns while it continues making new equity highs.

The distance between the equity curve and the trailing profit channel represents the dollar size of your system stop. If it's too large, you can either look for an alternative system stop that is closer to your equity curve, or you could wait for the equity momentum to slow where the gap between the equity curve and system stop is small enough to commit your risk capital to. Figure 8.26 shows that if your methodology's equity curve dips below the system stop, it will signal a loss of equity momentum, and indicate you should stop trading your signals or setups. If your methodology's single-contract equity curve can recover from the loss and trade above the profit channel (system stop), it will indicate that you should recommence trading. Once this occurs, the profit channel reverts to the lowest equity in 40 trades to give your methodology space to resume its equity climb.

This is just one idea for a system stop. There are plenty of others you can look at. All it takes is a little effort and imagination. It's also important to understand that a system stop can create the same irritation that trading stops do. Too close a system stop and you'll stop trading your methodology just before it gives you the year's biggest winning trade! There are no right or wrong system stops. While there is a high probability your system stop will cause you to miss some excellent trades, it's a small price to pay to become good risk managers.

It's also important to understand that the use of a system stop is not designed to maximize profitability. Using a system stop will reduce your profitability because it will have you on the sidelines when your strategy starts to climb out of its drawdown. You will miss the early positive return to equity momentum, which will frustrate you. However, that's okay because system stops are not designed to maximize profitability. System stops are designed to preserve capital. I certainly believe the cost of missing out on some profit opportunity is well worth it to preserve your trading risk capital.

I believe that if you can combine your methodology with a system stop and a proper money management strategy, then you will have created what I call a smarter money management solution.

IN SUMMARY

This brings me to the end of the first leg of the fifth essential universal principle of successful trading—the Three Pillars of trading.

As you know, money management is a key weapon against risk of ruin. Since your objective in trading is survival you need to understand and implement proper money management. If you're unable to get a grasp on money management it's likely you'll be excluded from the 10 percent winners' circle.

Examining various money management strategies has shown how important proper money management is for both your survival and prosperity. The importance of trading equity momentum with an effective system stop has also been discussed.

The following strategies were discussed:

- fixed risk
- fixed capital
- fixed ratio
- fixed units
- Williams fixed risk
- fixed percentage
- fixed volatility.

Depending on your individual account size, risk tolerance, opinion about individual trade risk, opinion about market volatility, and aversion to ruin, one of these strategies will help you achieve proper money management. Most will force you to trade fewer contracts when you lose and more contracts when you win, that is, increase your position size when you are winning and reduce your position size when you are losing.

Traders are only limited by their imagination in designing and selecting a system stop. An effective system stop should be able to:

• provide a system stop dollar value
• identify a loss of equity momentum to stop trading
• identify a return of equity momentum to recommence trading.

Combining a system stop with an appropriate money management strategy makes for smarter money management. In the next chapter I'll take a look at the second leg of trading's Three Pillars of practical trading—methodology.

NOTES

1. Williams, Larry, *Long-term Secrets to Short-term Trading* (John Wiley, 1999).
2. Ibid., chapter 13.
3. Jones, Ryan, *The Trading Game* (John Wiley, 1999).
4. Williams, Larry, op. cit.

Methodology

Methodology represents your day-to-day combat instructions. It articulates how you'll trade for expectancy. It consists of two parts:

- setups
- trade plan.

Setups identify areas of possible future support or resistance. They identify what your preference should be—whether you should be looking to buy or sell.

Your trade plan should tell you how to take advantage of your setups. It should have clear and unambiguous instructions on how to enter, place stops, and exit.

Your methodology should be simple and logical. As I've mentioned, it should be able to pass the McDonald's test. That is, could a teenager trade your methodology? If not, it's probably too complicated, too complex, and almost guaranteed to fall apart.

Once you have designed your methodology, your next step will be to validate its expectancy using the TEST procedure. If the results are positive, with a relatively smooth equity curve in which the profits aren't reliant upon one or two extraordinary trades, you'll know you have designed a good methodology.

Your final step will be to calculate your risk of ruin. This will combine your money management strategy with your methodology. From your TEST results, you'll know your methodology's validated accuracy and average win-to-average loss payoff. Combining this with your chosen money management strategy, you'll be able to use my risk-of-ruin simulator (see appendices A and B) or a similar model to simulate and then estimate your statistical risk of ruin. If your estimated risk of ruin is 0 percent, you can be confident in your methodology. If not, it's back to the drawing board.

In this chapter, I'll be exploring a methodology's architecture. Clearly defining the process of trading will give you a solid boundary within which to work when you investigate competing theories on market behavior and various trading methodologies.

The first step in methodology is to decide which approach you should follow—discretionary or mechanical trading.

DISCRETIONARY OR MECHANICAL TRADING

Traders are generally placed into one of three groups:

- discretionary traders
- mechanical (or systematic) traders
- discretionary mechanical traders.

Discretionary traders follow a flexible trade plan. They develop a rules-based strategy that allows them a wide degree of freedom to decide their actions. They usually include a rule that says it's okay not to trade if they are confused or not confident in their setup. They are ultimately flexible on what and how they trade, and reserve the final say on whether to place a trade.

Mechanical traders follow a rigid trade plan. They develop an unyielding rules-based strategy that they can't deviate from. They have no discretion in how they trade. They will automatically and systematically trade every setup that appears. They do not think about why they trade, they only think about executing their trades. Mechanical traders have no discretion over which trades they take, they must trade every signal generated. I am a mechanical trader.

Discretionary mechanical traders are, as their name suggests, a hybrid between discretionary and mechanical traders. They develop and trade according to a very structured trade plan. However, they use their discretion over when they will follow their trade plan. And when they do decide to trade, they will follow their trade plans to the letter.

On an emotional level, the two bookends, discretionary and mechanical trading, are vastly different. Mechanical traders have no decisions to make when they trade. They update their charts, follow their rules and place a trade if they see a signal. Discretionary traders constantly have to make decisions. The more structured discretionary traders are, the fewer decisions they'll have to make. Being a discretionary trader is usually more emotionally draining than being a mechanical trader.

Most traders begin as discretionary traders, and over time, through experience and disappointment, they become more structured and simplified in their discretionary trading. A mechanical approach helps traders achieve consistency and discipline on a more balanced emotional level.

If you're new to trading, I would encourage you to consider a mechanical trading approach from the start, or a very structured and rigid discretionary trade plan. You don't have to remain a mechanical trader throughout your trading career; however, it will provide a solid foundation from which to decide the path you'll eventually follow.

Key ingredients in the successful execution of your trade plan are consistency and discipline, and a mechanical approach provides excellent training in this area. In addition, a mechanical approach is usually easier to design and initially test due to the variety of software packages available. Let's take a look at the architecture of a complete methodology.

CREATING A METHODOLOGY

Methodology refers to the mechanics of trading. At its core, trading is simply the identification of potential support and resistance levels that allow traders to:

- place precise stops that when triggered provide evidence the potential support or resistance level has failed
- enjoy profits when the potential support or resistance level holds.

It's important to remember this. Keep it simple—don't complicate what you're doing. As traders, you're simply looking to identify potential support and resistance levels. You should be aiming to enter a trade when you believe a potential support or resistance level will hold and provide you with a profit. Don't let your chosen market theory or school of analysis dominate your thinking so that you lose sight of this.

Trading Styles

As I've mentioned, there are two basic styles of trading that your methodology can adopt:

- trend trading
- countertrend trading (or swing trading).

I'd suggest you initially concentrate your energies on developing a good trend-trading methodology because it's the safest place to trade, with the trend. However, in the fullness of time and in the fullness of your success, you should also look to develop a complementary countertrend or swing trading methodology. When your trend-trading methodology begins to experience losses, and it will since markets do not trend all the time, your countertrend- or swing-trading methodology will start to enjoy good profits. Developing and trading both a trend and countertrend-trading methodology will allow you to enjoy a smoother equity curve. In addition, as your success and experience grow, you should also look to diversify your strategies further by developing both trend- and countertrend-trading methodologies across multiple time frames. Develop either shorter-term or longer-term methodologies to complement your existing strategies. The objective is to trade a diversified portfolio of trading methodologies across multiple time frames that do not duplicate but complement each other. The core of each of your methodologies will be its setup.

Setups

A setup should identify either a potential support or resistance level. A good support level will not only exist in an uptrend; it should also confirm the uptrend. A good resistance level will not only exist in a downtrend; it should also confirm the downtrend. Setups are found through market analysis. The trick is to decide which school of analysis to use to identify potential support and resistance levels. As figure 9.1 indicates, there is plenty to choose from when it comes to selecting an area of analysis to identify potential support and resistance levels.

Most traders spend most of their time wrestling with various theories on market behavior—looking for the perfect entry technique. Although this can be damaging for both their wallets and their souls, it's likely to be the most fascinating and creative experience they'll enjoy in their trading careers. It's always thrilling to search for that elusive edge. Designing your methodology is far more creative and satisfying than writing out and placing repetitive market orders when you trade.

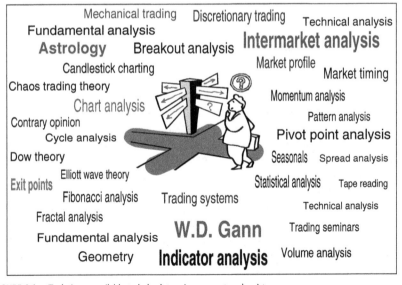

FIGURE 9.1   Techniques available to help determine support and resistance

Now I won't be spending too much time on these various competing schools of analysis because my focus is to teach you my universal principles of successful trading. Reviewing "setups" within "methodology" is just one leg of the Three Pillars, which is just one out of my six essential universal principles of successful trading. However, I will give you a brief outline of where these various schools of trading analysis sit in terms of context.

In the fullness of time, you will soon come to realize that it's not easy to discover what has an edge in identifying potential support and resistance levels. When you look at the variety of methodologies out there in the market I believe you should keep an open mind and embrace the choice you have. You should learn to ignore any prejudices you may have against certain schools of technical analysis and welcome all ideas about trading. But as I have encouraged you before, you need to reserve the right to decide whether an idea has value for you in your hands. Please always remember that just because you have either read or heard about an idea on trading, it does not make it true for you. Hearing or reading about trading techniques does not necessarily make them true. Just because I or another author may write about an idea on trading, it doesn't necessarily make it true. An idea on trading can only become true for you through your own independent validation. And this includes everything that I have written in this book. Be a sponge and soak up all the ideas you can on trading, but as you do so, please remember to remain a skeptic and be prepared to do your own work to validate the idea independently, to do the work to see whether the idea can independently provide expectancy for your trading strategy. And as you do so, it's important to keep asking yourself whether the idea will help you identify potential support and resistance levels.

Another point to keep in mind is that you will hear many voices about what works in trading. These voices range from books and DVDs to presentations and workshops. All these voices will be enthusiastic and passionate about their particular school of analysis. As you keep an open mind and listen to as many voices as you can, keep reminding yourself that it's not possible for every voice to be right about what works in trading. Someone has to be right and someone has to be wrong. Not all can be right. It will be your job to determine which voice makes the most sense to you and gives you the most value in your hands. Remember it will pay you to remain a skeptic until you can independently validate a "voice."

When searching for your preferred trading approach, it's important to remember that you should attempt to avoid becoming despondent when your chosen analysis fails to identify potential support and resistance levels, when your TEST procedure keeps coming up negative. At least you'll be able to say you've identified a school of analysis that *in your hands* doesn't provide an edge, and in trading knowing what doesn't work for you is almost as good as knowing what does!

Trading's "Pandora's Box"—Which Theory of Market Behavior to Believe?

I group the competing theories of market behavior, or the broad collection of technical analysis from which you'll choose to identify potential support and resistance levels, into three broad groups:

- the predictors
- the dreamers
- the pragmatists.

The predictors

"Predictors" include:

- astrology
- cycle analysis
- Elliott wave theory
- fractal analysis
- fundamental analysis
- geometry
- W.D. Gann.

Practitioners of these schools of analysis believe they can determine where the markets are heading and attract many followers. A central theme of these approaches is market timing, knowing when to enter and where to exit at important market turns. The two prominent theories are Elliott wave and W.D. Gann.

There are two main drawbacks to the predictors. First, looking for future turning points encourages traders to pick tops and bottoms. As I have mentioned, this is a common mistake all new traders make. Although you may not set out to do so, looking into the future and using your analysis to identify high-probability turning points encourages you to trade them. The more evidence gathered for a turning point, the more confidence you have that you're right, and therefore the more enthusiasm you'll have to take advantage of it. Before you know it, you're leaving resting orders in the market, waiting for your analysis to be proven correct.

The second drawback is that when traders begin focusing on the future, they lose sight of the present. When you're so busy looking for where the market may go, you can forget all about the trading opportunities present. As you identify a significant future date and price level, you exclude all else from your radar. This distraction will limit your trading opportunities.

The reason so many traders are attracted to the predictors is because they hold out the appealing notion that you can know the market's future direction and therefore control your own trading destiny. They project an appearance of certainty for the future. The predictors present an illusion of knowledge, which in turn presents an illusion of control. These illusions lead to a surplus of optimism and confidence.

In addition, traders can fall into what I refer to as the intellectual trap. Traders become attracted by the intellectual appeal and challenge of solving the market's puzzle, where they believe complexity is best. The predictors love complexity.

Out of Elliott wave and W.D. Gann, it's the latter that probably creates the most interest for new traders looking for an esoteric approach. Although I have not studied Gann, I am familiar with many elements of it through my study of geometry. The "mysteries" surrounding Gann attract many beginners to it. As a result of this, many trading promoters with little trading experience, but excellent marketing, selling, and presentation skills, are attracted to promoting Gann's trading techniques.

The hype surrounding Gann is usually along the lines of the following:

Learn About W.D. Gann and Market Trading

W.D. Gann was one of the greatest traders of all time. His ability to call market turns was, and still is, legendary. His profitable trades in the commodity and stock markets was an astounding 90 percent+! His trading profits are estimated to be a staggering $50 million dollars during the first half of the 20th century. Traders who have studied his techniques have found great success in markets all over the world.

Source: www.wdgann.com

Who wouldn't want to learn from the greatest trader of all time? Anyone who had an accuracy rate above 90 percent and made $50 million would have to have something of value to offer!

Unfortunately, Gann seems to be more myth than reality. Dr. Alexander Elder, a respected market participant, has examined the Gann legend in his book, *Trading for a Living.*[1] According to Elder:

Various opportunists sell "Gann course" and "Gann software." They claim that Gann was one of the best traders who ever lived, that he left a $50 million estate, and so on. I interviewed W.D. Gann's son, an analyst for a Boston bank. He told me that his famous father could not support his family by trading but earned his living by writing and selling instructional courses. When W.D. Gann died in the 1950s, his estate, including his house, was valued at slightly over $100,000. The legend of W.D. Gann, the giant of trading, is perpetuated by those who sell courses and other paraphernalia to gullible customers.

In his book, *The Right Stock at the Right Time,* Larry Williams argues further that:

> I studied the works of W.D. Gann as well as those of R.N. Elliott, several leading astrologers, and so on, which all turned out to be a waste of time. I was fortunate enough to eventually meet Gann's son, who was a broker in New York City and who explained to me that his father was simply a chartist. He asked why, if his dad was good as everyone said, the son was still "smiling and dialing, calling up customers to trade." It seemed he was somewhat disturbed by his father's press-agentry, as it had led many people to come to him seeking the holy grail. If there was one, it was never passed on to the son.
>
> At the same time I also met F.B. Thatcher, who had been Gann's promoter and advance man. He assured me in correspondence over the last five years of his life that in fact Gann was just a good promoter, not necessarily a good stock trader.

My own "Gann" experiences are similar. Since I commenced in the markets in 1983 with Bank of America, I have come across hundreds of traders, many of whom are students of Gann. Out of all the Gann traders I've met and know today, I can say that not one, let me repeat that, not one consistently makes money actively trading according to Gann. Full stop. Certainly, many Gann "analysts" can verify market turning points in hindsight with selective application of one of Gann's techniques. But that's not difficult when using both hindsight and one of Gann's many techniques—whether it be angles, degrees, vibrations, retracements, projections, anniversary dates, and points on the square of nine. If one Gann tool doesn't work, they'll usually find one that does. But to be fair, Gann is not the only school of trading that suffers from this criticism of "curve fitting." Most schools of analysis have too many degrees of freedom, where the analysts can usually come up with a different technique to justify their claims.

Now, I know one person's observations are not statistically significant, and cannot be accepted as a definitive comment on Gann. And please remember these are only my experiences. If your experience is contrary, then that's terrific, and I can only encourage you to share your personal Gann experiences with other Gann students. I know there are many who would wish to learn how you managed to unlock Gann's trading "secrets." But remember to bring along your real-time and active trading results if you do.

If you feel inclined to learn Gann and attend a Gann seminar, I can only encourage you to request a copy of the promoter's real-time trading statements. If you can see a copy of his or her real-time trading record, you should also elicit a commitment from him or her to explain each and every Gann trade to you after completion of the seminar. This is a very reasonable request since he or she is offering to teach you Gann, which he or she himself or herself trades to make his or her money (right?).

It seems that today the proponents of Gann are following in his footsteps, not necessarily being good traders and revealing "winning secrets," but continuing his good promotional work and making their money from selling courses. The overhyping of and overcharging for Gann's techniques has probably distracted people from considering those elements of Gann that are possibly worthwhile.

If Gann takes your interest, you should investigate it, or any of the other predictors, and see whether it can help you to identify potential support and resistance levels consistently. If it does, and if you can validate your method-ology's expectancy through the TEST procedure, then you should use it.

The predictors offer the most interesting analysis you'll come across, even if they may not be the most profitable. And I have to make an admission here. For the first 15 years of my trading career, I was an Elliottian, and during the latter stage of that period I overlaid geometry. I have to say that period for me was the most creative and fun time I have ever enjoyed in analyzing the markets. Nothing has come close to it. Since 1998, I have been a boring mechanical trader, and I can assure you it isn't half as interesting or fun as analyzing the markets on a multiple time frame basis across both price and time using Elliott wave and geometry. However, for me, I was unable to extract profits using Elliott wave, and I have learned from experience, that for me, boring works!

The dreamers

Dreamers are those traders who use indicators, such as, but not limited to:

- average directional index (ADX)
- directional movement index (DMI)
- envelopes
- ratio analysis
- moving average convergence/divergence (MACD)
- moving averages
- rate of price change
- relative strength indicator (RSI)
- stochastic oscillator.

I refer to these traders as dreamers because most indicators are deriv-atives of price that contain adjustable parameters. Consequently, they represent second-hand curve-fitted information. I feel traders are dream-ing if they believe they'll make money trading this type of second-hand adjustable data. While this is a generalization, and does not hold true for all indicators, most do lag the market's price action and allow too much flexibility to be relied upon to make money.

However, if an indicator does grab your attention, you should study it. As a general rule, it's better to use fewer indicators. In addition, you shouldn't let the choice of indicators overwhelm you. Indicators will either identify the:

- price
- trend
- retracement
- momentum
- sentiment
- volatility
- volume

or a combination of these. The trick is to select one indicator for each area of market structure and avoid doubling up. If a selection of indicators can help you consistently identify potential support and resistance levels and you can validate your methodology's expectancy using the TEST procedure, then you should use them.

The pragmatists

Pragmatists are those traders who use some of the following forms of analysis:

- breakout analysis
- chart analysis
- Dow theory
- intermarket analysis
- market profile
- pattern analysis
- pivot point analysis
- seasonals
- spread analysis
- statistical analysis
- tape reading
- volume analysis.

The pragmatists focus on raw price and raw volume. They're not interested in what they can't control, and have no interest in looking into the future. They prefer not to deal with substitutes such as indicators, but focus on the real thing—price.

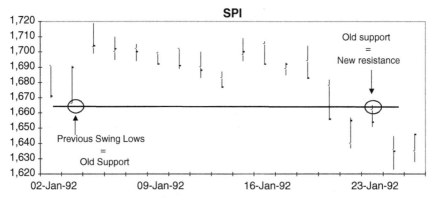

FIGURE 9.2 A simple idea for identifying support and resistance

From my experience, you'll find most successful traders within the pragmatist group. Since 1983, I've moved in and out of these various groups. I've been in the pragmatist group since 1998. Before that, however, I spent a total of 15 years with the predictors—12 years with Elliott wave, followed by three years with geometry. During that time, I would occasionally pop into the dreamers camp and become hypnotized by the dazzling array of colors on my computer screen.

At the end of the day, you have to find what works for you to identify potential support and resistance levels consistently. There are no limitations on where you can look, as long as what you use does the job and can be independently validated by you using the TEST procedure.

You should embrace the choice and enjoy your investigative journey. Figure 9.2 illustrates a simple idea for identifying potential support and resistance levels.

This figure illustrates the simple use of price and chart analysis from the pragmatist camp—a previous swing low is used to identify a potential resistance level. Often, old support levels can act as new resistance. In this example, the resistance level not only appears in a downtrend, but it also confirms the downtrend by seeing the market move lower.

Trade Plan

Your trade plan should tell you how to take advantage of your setups. It should have clear instructions on where to:

- enter a trade
- place a stop
- exit a profitable trade.

There are plenty of techniques for entering trades, placing stops, and exiting positions. There is one powerful idea I want to share with you that is more important than the best entry, stop, or exit technique, and it is overlooked by most traders. The idea is this: *an effective trade plan should support and confirm your setup.*

If your setup has found a potential support level, your trade plan should expect the market to move higher before committing you to a trade. Similarly, if you have found a potential resistance level, your trade plan should wait for lower prices before committing you to the market. That is, if you have support, your entry price should be higher. If you have resistance, your entry price should be lower. When trading, it's good practice to assume your setup is wrong until the market proves it right.

Having a trade plan that confirms your setup gives the market the respect it deserves. This is such a simple and powerful concept yet many traders fail to understand it. Setups can give you no more than an inclination of where the market may go, and they are not going to be correct all the time. A good trade plan will not follow your setups blindly. Too many traders fail to separate their setups from their trade plan, confusing technical analysis with trading. Having a trade plan wait for the market to confirm your setup is no guarantee the market will continue moving in your direction; however, it will save you from entering many marginal trades. In essence, a good trade plan should have you paying higher prices to go long and selling lower prices to go short. Figure 9.3 provides an example of this.

This chart shows the resistance level seen in figure 9.2. It shows where old support has become new resistance. In this example, there are two setups identifying potential resistance. Rather than looking to leave a resting sell price at the point of resistance, a good trade plan would wait until the market approaches its close. If the market demonstrates weakness, an effective trade

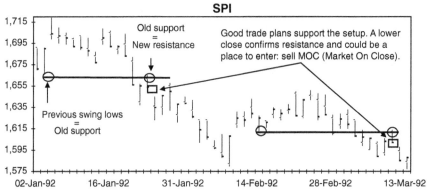

FIGURE 9.3   Support for a setup from the trade plan

plan would look to enter a trade. With the market closing lower than the previous day's close and lower than the current day's open, a good trade plan would acknowledge the weakness and look to go short, selling the market on close. In each case, the resistance levels had not only existed in a downtrend, they also confirmed the downtrend by seeing the market move lower.

Many points in market structure can be used to make your entry level confirm your setup. If your setup has identified a potential support level, your trade plan can confirm the market's strength before entering by checking whether:

- the day closed higher than its open
- the day closed higher than the previous day's close
- the day closed higher than the previous close of two, three, four, or five days
- the market rallied through the previous day's close or high
- the market rallied through the previous week's close or high
- the market rallied through the previous month's close or high.

The reverse would hold equally true for a potential resistance level. You are only limited by your imagination when it comes to determining your entry levels. For stop and exit levels, various ideas can be used, and once again you're only limited by your imagination.

Designing your methodology is often half the fun of trading. However, don't let your imagination run too wild and create complex systems. It's the simple methodologies that stand the test of time. As Tom DeMark, a well-respected market participant who has worked with market wizard Paul Tudor Jones and currently advises Steve Cohen of SAC Capital, a $16 billion investment fund, remarked in the Art Collins book *Market Beaters*:[3]

> The bottom line was, after 17 programmers and 4 or 5 years of testing, the basic 4 or 5 systems worked best.

And as Curtis Faith wrote in *Way of the Turtle*:[4]

> Keep it simple. Simple time-tested methods that are well executed will beat fancy complicated methods every time.

There are a number of general principles you can follow when designing your setups and trade plans, including:

- strive for simplicity over complexity
- ensure logic supports the methodology—don't rely on a random collection of ideas

- minimize the number of parameters with adjustable variables—this will reduce the risk of curve fitting
- use a combination of initial, breakeven and trailing stops
- use time stops where appropriate
- favor dynamic stops over fixed dollar stops
- be wary of profit targets—they generally reduce profitability
- use trailing stops as an effective way to exit profitable positions.

Urban Myth: Entries Aren't that Important

Yes, they are. If you have been involved in the markets long enough, you may have come across a belief that says entries aren't that important; exits are. Proponents will point to a chart where a market has enjoyed a strong trend, saying the entry on such a large move is irrelevant. It's the exit that is important to ensure the trader captures most of the trend. And yes, in hindsight you can understand the observation. After a huge move, the exit will be very important, and relatively more important then the entry, to ensure the trader can bank as much of the profit as possible. No one enjoys giving back profit. But that is with hindsight. The proponents are talking with the benefit of showing you a picture-perfect chart, which has already enjoyed a strong trend. When you enter a position, you have no idea whether the trade will enjoy a strong trend. So I totally disagree with their position, and when I read or hear it I automatically become suspicious about the person's trading credentials.

Entries are terribly, terribly important. They directly define your stop placement, initial risk, and potential loss. The size of your losses, compared to your wins, directly affects your expectancy! And remember, you trade for the opportunity to earn expectancy.

When you enter a trade, you have no idea whether the trade will enjoy a strong trend. When you enter a trade, you have no foresight. You have no crystal ball. You do not have the luxury of hindsight. You only have the now. And the now is all about controlling risk and trading for the opportunity to earn expectancy.

In addition, since entries define your initial risk, they also directly affect your money management strategy for position sizing. The smaller the initial stop, the larger a position size you can put on. Remember, money management is the secret to survival and big profits. Consequently, this makes your entries extremely important regardless of your time frame. And it's particularly important for long-term traders who have very low accuracy rates, meaning that once they finally snag a winning trade they need to have the largest position size on that they can afford to make up for the 67 percent of losing trades!

So in my mind I'm always suspicious of people who suggest entries are not that important, and are less important than exits. In my mind, they're all terribly important! They directly affect your initial risk, which in turn directly affects your money management's position size, which directly affects your survival and potential to earn big profits. Entries are terribly important.

Avoid the Fatal Attraction of Large Stops

The easiest technique to make a methodology seem profitable is to use large stops. Large stops will give a methodology plenty of room and time to reach its profit objective or exit point. However, in my opinion, large stops will catch up with you in time and they will hurt you.

Traders will generally keep increasing the size of their stops until their methodology produces an acceptable-looking hypothetical equity curve. They unwittingly curve fit their methodology to the historical data. By increasing the size of their stop, they manage to avoid incurring a string or series of losing trades that would render their methodology poor. They believe they have discovered the optimal stop. But all they have done is to curve fit their methodology to their data.

And invariably, due to the market's maximum adversity, when they start trading, the market will deliver a series of extraordinary losses they weren't expecting. The losses will be so large that they'll either discourage them from trading or the losses will damage their accounts beyond repair forcing them to stop trading. They will have reached their point of ruin.

In addition, large stops will hamper your money management strategy's ability to increase your position size. Stops directly define your initial risk. Your initial risk directly affects your money management strategy for position sizing. The smaller the initial stop, the larger a position size you can put on. The larger your stop, the larger your initial risk and the smaller your position's size. Remember, money management is the secret to survival and big profits.

This is terribly, terribly important. Please listen up. Hypothetically, a methodology can look good on a single-contract basis, producing a good positive expectancy. However, when you apply your preferred money management strategy, you'll invariably find your methodology's performance is hampered. Large stops drag down a money management strategy's ability to accumulate contracts or increase position size.

A methodology using smaller stops with a lower expectancy will make much more money than a methodology that uses larger stops with a higher expectancy when money management is applied. Larger stops kill money management performance. Larger stops kill big profits. If money management is the secret behind large profits, which is it, then small stops is the secret behind extraordinary profits.

Proponents of seasonal trading usually champion large stops, some ranging above 3 percent of a market's movement. Many seasonal setups require extraordinarily large stops to make the "seasonal" tendency look reliable with their high accuracy rate. But their high accuracy rate is more often than not due to the large stops employed, not the market's seasonality. Please beware of and avoid using large stops. Large stops kill.

Confirm Expectancy Through TEST

Once you have designed a setup to identify potential support and resistance levels, and developed a trade plan to confirm and take advantage of your setup, your next step is to validate your methodology's expectancy using the TEST procedure.

If your expectancy is positive and the equity curve relatively smooth without relying on one or two extraordinary trades, you can be confident you have developed a good methodology.

Your final step is to combine your preferred money management strategy with your validated methodology and calculate your risk of ruin, using the accuracy rate and average win-to-average loss payoff ratio from your TEST results. Your objective is to approach the market with a statistical 0 percent risk of ruin. Remember, if you survive, you'll succeed in trading.

Well, that's the theory. It's a good theory and it's correct according to my experience. However, what I'd like to do now is spend some time discussing the practical implications of methodology in regard to trend trading.

TREND TRADING

Although theory is good, I believe it can also help to take a look at some practical implications of methodology—especially since your methodology will underpin your expectancy, and expectancy is one of your key weapons against risk of ruin. In everything I have discussed so far, I believe that apart from actual successful trading, the greatest challenge that will face a trader is the development of a robust positive-expectancy methodology. And since your methodology is really your expectancy, just in another name, I feel it's important to spend some time in drilling down into key issues that affect methodology.

First, I'll discuss four important facts about trend trading. I'll then continue with a discussion on the core objective of any good trend-trading methodology, finding support and resistance levels. I'll then go to some length in describing why trend trading should be simple. I will then remind you about why you trade (and it's not about winning), and I'll then explore in depth the reasons so many find it so hard to trade with the trend. This will bring up key issues.

I hope this detailed discussion into the practical implications of developing a methodology will provide you with a helpful framework within which to develop your own trend-trading strategy. It will provide benchmarks against which you will be able to calibrate your ideas. In addition, I hope it will give you a real insight into why your current methodology (if you have one) is not as successful as you'd like it to be and what you can do about it.

Four Important Facts

Let's begin with four very important facts about trend trading:

- fact one: it's the safest way to trade—to trade with the trend
- fact two: trends move markets and are the basis of all profits
- fact three: it's miserable being a trend trader, you lose on 67 percent of your trades!
- fact four: there are two ways to trade with trend
  - trade breakouts
  - trade retracements.

First, trading with the trend is the safest way to trade. To do the opposite, to trade against the trend, will position you as a top and bottom picker, or swing trader. I'm not suggesting countertrend or swing trading doesn't work, because it does. Some of the biggest and most successful traders trade against the trend. It's just that it's hard to do successfully, and is inherently dangerous, since you are trading against the trend. It's not a strategy I'd recommend a struggling trader. Countertrend trading does take more knowledge and skill. Trading with the trend in my opinion is an easier mountain to climb.

Second, markets move because they trend. So trends move markets, and are therefore the basis of all profits. The longer you can hold a trend trade, the more potential you will have to earn a large profit. Day traders struggle to make large wins because they are restricted to where the market can move during a single day. Trend traders can hold trades from a couple of weeks to a couple of months to longer.

Third, the irony of trend trading is that although it's the safest way to trade, it's also one of the most miserable ways to trade. Since markets rarely trend, trend traders can usually expect to only win one-third of their trades. Consequently, they will spend on average 67 percent of their time losing! If you wish to trade with the trend, and I hope you do, you'll have to accept the fact that it will be a miserable existence. You'll be losing on 67 percent of your trades. You will not know when the profits will arrive. You will spend most of your time in drawdown. It will be painful. It will be depressing. It will be miserable. No ifs, no buts, no discussion. Trading with the trend is miserable.

However, if you can accept these first three facts then you'll be in a good position to succeed as a trend trader. If you can't, then you'll need to reassess your interest in trading. And finally. There are two basic approaches to trend trading, which both work:

- trading breakouts in the direction of the trend
  - never missing a big trend
  - using large stops
- trading retracements in the direction of the trend
  - possibility of missing big trends
  - using small stops.

Trading breakouts of higher prices or lower prices in the direction of the trend, such as the popular Turtle channel breakout strategy, is a successful strategy for trading with the trend. Breakout strategies do not wait for a retracement or pullback in an uptrend before entering the market on the long side. Nor do they wait for a relief rally or retracement in a downtrend before entering the market on the short side. They will buy much higher prices in an uptrend, and they will sell much lower prices in a downtrend. The advantage of trading breakouts is that the trader will never miss a big trend. A disadvantage is that breakout trend trading requires larger stops than retracement trend trading.

Retracement trend trading requires the market to pause and experience a pullback in an uptrend, or a relief rally in a downtrend to enter the market. A disadvantage of retracement trend trading is that sometimes strongly trending markets do not provide a retracement opportunity for a trader to enter in on. Retracement trend trading can and does miss some big trends. However, an advantage of retracement trend trading is that it does allow a trader to place much smaller initial stops.

Accordingly, since I believe your objective in trading is to survive by being a good risk manager, I will focus on retracement trend trading. It will give you smaller stops and therefore the lowest initial risk.

It's All About Support and Resistance

At its core, practical retracement trend trading is about finding areas of support to buy and finding areas of resistance to sell. It's not rocket science.

Why would you buy unless you believed the market had found support? Why would you sell unless you believed the market had hit resistance? You wouldn't on both counts. Not only is trading about identifying support and resistance levels, but it's about identifying *good* support and *good* resistance levels. A good support level will exist in, and confirm, an uptrend. A good resistance level will exist in, and confirm, a downtrend.

These definitions encapsulate the essence of successful retracement trend trading. When in an uptrend, traders should only be looking to

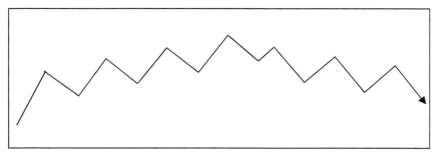

FIGURE 9.4   Nonlinearity of prices

identify good support levels for entering long trades. When in a down-trend, they should only be looking to identify areas of good resistance for entering shorts.

In addition, traders need to accept a core belief about price movements: *Prices do not move in a straight line.* They meander up and down and are not linear as shown in figure 9.4.

Prices will rotate back and forth and will not head in one direction, either up or down, in equal and discrete linear measurements. Uptrends will experience rallies and pullbacks (retracements). Downtrends will experience falling prices and relief rallies (retracements).

Markets do not head in one direction without pause. Successful retracement trend trading, as shown in figure 9.5, will see traders enter long positions after pullbacks in an uptrend and enter short positions after relief rallies in a downtrend.

An important factor in retracement trend traders' success is their patience in waiting for pullbacks and relief rallies, that is, retracements of the previous price trend. They know that in an uptrend, the market needs to come down first to go up. They know that in a downtrend the

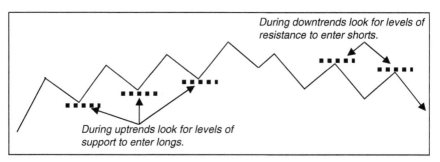

FIGURE 9.5   Retracement trend trading

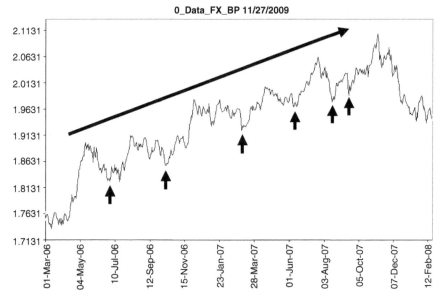

FIGURE 9.6   Areas of support in an uptrend

market needs to go up first to come down. Practical retracement trend trading is all about patience in waiting for markets to come down to areas of support in an uptrend before entering longs and waiting for relief rallies in downtrends to find areas of resistance to sell. Practical retracement trend trading is nothing more and nothing less. Please don't let anyone suggest to you that it's more then that.

As figure 9.6 shows, when a market is in an uptrend, the patient retracement trend trader will wait for prices to retrace into areas of support before looking to enter the market to catch the trend continuation. So the trick is to learn how to identify real areas of support and resistance. Now, that's the hard part! From now on, I will just refer to retracement trend trading as simply "trend trading."

Why Trend Trading Should Be Simple

Trend trading should be easy, although many do find it hard. Trend trading is so easy, or should be, that it can be broken down into three clearly defined and compatible parts:

- the philosophy
- the objective
- the execution.

Know these and you know how to trade with the trend. Easy! The philosophy believes that:

- In an uptrend prices need to come down to go up.
- In a downtrend prices need to go up to come down.

The objective is:

- If the market is in an uptrend, then the trader needs to locate a good support level to enter a long position and catch a continuation of the uptrend.
- If the market is in a downtrend, the trader needs to locate a good resistance level to enter a short position and catch a continuation of the downtrend.

The execution comprises a two step process:

- Locate a trade setup:
  - Identify the trend.
  - Wait for a retracement level.
  - Wait for a retracement pattern.
- Implement the trade plan:
  - Wait for a confirming entry signal.
  - Enter the market.
  - Place a stop.
  - Manage the trade.
  - Hopefully take profits.

Trend trading is this simple. Nothing more and nothing less. If anyone suggests otherwise, then they're pulling your leg.

Now that I have shown you how easy trend trading should be, I now want to remind you why you trade. Many people incorrectly believe the objective of trading is to pick the market direction correctly, to make money. It's not. It's actually far from it in truth. This is what I need to remind you about.

Why You Trade

It's time for me to remind you about why you trade. Now that I've shown you why trend trading should be easy, I don't want you to think you can quickly commence trading and expect to start collecting dollar notes out of thin air!

What I need to tell you is that trading with the trend doesn't necessarily mean you'll be actually trading with the trend. Although it should be your preference to trade with what you believe is the trend, for all practical purposes your trend direction could be wrong. The market's maximum adversity will make every effort to mask its true direction, and all you can hope to do is to trade in the direction you think it's going. As a result, for 67 percent of the time, you will not be making money, but you will be counting your losses after being stopped out! Remember, life as a trend trader is miserable.

So I think this is an opportune time to remind you why you trade. In my opinion you should only be trading for the opportunity to earn expectancy. You should not be trading for the gratification of making instant profit. You should not be trading to prove your market analysis correct. You should not be trading for the thrill of action. You should only be trading for the opportunity to earn expectancy, to make money over the longer term through your methodology's expectancy, not its accuracy.

Although you will be attempting to trade in the direction of the market's trend, you won't be trading to predict the market's trend. Trading with the trend is just a logical and sound proposition for trading. Trading with the trend is not the same as attempting to pick the market's trend correctly. Obviously, your preference is for the market to continue in the direction of where you *believe* the trend should be heading, but you're not banking on it. You're trading for the opportunity to earn expectancy, to make money, and you know trading with the trend is the sensible direction to trade.

Now for a sobering fact, to remind you about the misery a trend trader suffers.

Markets rarely trend. They spend most of their time range bound chopping back and forth whip-sawing trend traders. It's more ouch then ooh. What this means for trend traders is that they lose more often then they win. At best, a trend trader can only expect to win on average one-third of their trades. Life as a trend trader is miserable. However, not all is lost because their average win, because they trade in the direction of the trend, is usually much larger than their average loss. The large wins make up for the many smaller losses. So trend trading sits well with why you trade. Although it's miserable with low accuracy, it does have a positive expectancy, and makes money.

You need to remember the expectancy formula you learned earlier that is shown in figure 9.7.

As a trend trader, you have always to keep in the back of your mind that you only trade for the opportunity to earn expectancy, not to make immediate profits, not to be right. You don't trade to pick the market's

$$
\begin{array}{l}
\text{Expected} \\
\text{return per} = \left(\begin{array}{l} \text{Probability} \\ \text{of} \\ \text{winning} \end{array} \times \dfrac{\text{Average win}}{\text{Average loss}} \right) - \left(\begin{array}{l} \text{Probability} \\ \text{of} \\ \text{losing} \end{array} \times \dfrac{\text{Average loss}}{\text{Average loss}} \right) \\
\$\$
\end{array}
$$

FIGURE 9.7 The expectancy formula

Accuracy	33%
Average win	3
Average loss	1
Expectancy per dollar risked	

$E(R) = [33\% \times (3/1)] - [67\% \times (1/1)]$

$= 32\%$

FIGURE 9.8   Thirty-two percent expectancy

direction. You trade for the opportunity to earn expectancy, which can only come from executing many trades over a long period. It can only come from suffering many loses along the way. Expectancy is made up from both your winning and your losing trades. And as a trend trader, if at a minimum, you can win a one-third of your trades, and when you do, the wins on average can be three times the size of your average losses, then you can expect to earn 32 cents on every dollar you place in a trade. You can expect to earn positive expectancy. You can expect to earn 32 cents on every dollar you risk in a trade (see figure 9.8).

So as a trend trader you'll expect to make money, and 32 cents in each dollar placed in a trade is both positive and good! But this 32 cents is not really money, it's expectancy. It's taken both your wins and your loses to generate the net 32 cents you have received for every dollar you have risked in a trade. It's not immediate profit you are earning. It's expectancy that accrues over a long period that covers many executed trades with a few winners and many losses!

Now, if you're able to increase your accuracy to 50 percent, while keeping your high win-to-loss ratio, then you can expect to earn 100 cents for every dollar as shown in figure 9.9.

If you're unable to maintain your win-to-loss ratio, and see it dip to 2:1, then you can still expect to earn 50 cents for every dollar placed in a trade, as shown in figure 9.10.

Accuracy	50%
Average win	3
Average loss	1
Expectancy per dollar risked	

$E(R) = [50\% \times (3/1)] - [50\% \times (1/1)]$

$= 100\%$

FIGURE 9.9   One hundred percent expectancy

Accuracy	50%
Average win	2
Average loss	1
Expectancy per dollar risked	

$$E(R) = [50\% \times (2/1)] - [50\% \times (1/1)]$$
$$= 50\%$$

FIGURE 9.10 Fifty percent expectancy

However, if your accuracy dips to 33 percent, while your win-to-loss ratio remains at 2:1, then you can expect to start losing 1 cent for every dollar placed in a trade, as shown in figure 9.11.

The big point to remember here is that your expectancy comes from following a process. A process of applying a winning trend-trading strategy over a long period where you will execute many, many trades. And within those trades, there will be many miserable losses. And alongside those many miserable losses will be a couple of marvelously large and healthy wins, such good wins that they will pay for all the losses incurred and still have some money left over to provide you with profit. But please remember the profit is not money; it's expectancy that was generated from both the winning and losing trades.

Now for sensible trend-trading boundaries, you should always attempt to keep your accuracy and win-to-loss ratio at a minimum equal to or above 33 percent and 3:1 respectively.

And I'm sorry for being so repetitive here; however, I feel I have to drill it into you. Please let me do this one more time. You need to remember this simple objective when trend trading. You won't be trading to make immediate profit. You won't be trading to be right. You won't be trading to prove your market analysis correct. You won't be trading to pick market direction. You won't be trading for the action or thrill of being in the

Accuracy	33%
Average win	2
Average loss	1
Expectancy per dollar risked	

$$E(R) = [33\% \times (2/1)] - [67\% \times (1/1)]$$
$$= -1\%$$

FIGURE 9.11 Negative 1 percent expectancy

TABLE 9.1   Expectancy boundaries

Accuracy	Average win	Average loss	Expectancy per $1 risked
33%	3	1	32%
50%	3	1	100%
50%	2	1	50%
33%	2	1	–1%

market. You'll only be trading in what you believe is the direction of the market's trend for the opportunity to earn expectancy, which at a minimum will require you to keep your accuracy and average win-to-loss ratio above 33 percent and 3:1 respectively.

Table 9.1 summarizes the boundaries you should aspire to trade within as a trend trader.

I'm drilling this into you because it's my preference not to see you develop a satisfactory trend-trading methodology only to see you throw it away after suffering a long losing streak of losses—whether that will be 10, 20, or 30 losses. It will happen. Don't think it won't happen to you. Remember, trend trading is miserable.

It's my preference that when you're in a deep dark place that all trend traders regularly inhibit that you can remember that trend trading success-fully is all about survival, avoiding risk of ruin, and also following a good process of trading. And a big process is to earn expectancy, which will not come to you after a handful of trades. It may take you a whole year to earn your expectancy because you don't know which market will trend and you will not know when it will decide to trend. You have to think in terms of process and remember that trading is all about the active engagement with the market to enjoy the opportunities it presents to allow you to earn expectancy. Expectancy will not occur within a week, a month, or a quarter. I hope you can understand this, and remember what I have said. Please do not throw out your trend-trading strategy just because it may have failed to deliver you immediate profit after a few short months of trading. Don't be silly. Don't be stupid. Once again I apologize for banging on about this however I feel it's too important to just glance over.

I have broken down the steps necessary for successful trend trading. By doing so, I have shown you how easy it should be. I have also reminded you about why you trade, and why your minimum objective should be to achieve an accuracy rate of 33 percent while maintaining your average win to average loss ratio at 3:1. If you can do that, then you will earn 32 cents for every dollar risked in a trade. Now that I have explained why trend trading should be simple I want to explore in depth why so many traders find it so hard.

Why Most Find Trend Trading So Hard

I know, I know, I know. If trend trading is so simple, then why do so many find it so hard? Okay, I hear you. If you accept that trend trading does make money, although it loses more often then it wins, and trend trading is as simple as finding the trend, waiting for a retracement level and retracement pattern and waiting for a confirming entry signal, then why is it that so many traders still lose? Good question, and I'm glad you asked it.

You now know trend trading should be as simple as the following:

- First, locate a trade setup:
  - Identify the trend.
  - Wait for a retracement level.
  - Wait for a retracement pattern.
- And then implement a trade plan to take advantage of the setup:
  - Wait for a confirming entry signal.
  - Enter the market.
  - Place a stop.
  - Manage the trade.
  - Hopefully take profits.

Let's take a look at each step and see whether a few answers can be found. I want to restrict my review to the setup and trade plan, and not touch upon all the other reasons people fail because I've already discussed them in depth in earlier chapters. I want to see whether I can reveal some extra truths about why so many traders find it so hard to trade with the trend in terms of their methodology.

Identify the trend

If I was to ask you what the most often quoted mantra for successful trading is, what do you think you would answer? Yes, that's correct: " . . . *trade with the trend, the trend is your friend* . . . " And this is the number one execution rule for successful trend trading.

Let's now be conservative and assume that only 60 percent of all active traders have heard and understood this message (although I believe it's much higher). If this is the case, why is it that more than 90 percent of active traders still lose? Surely if most active traders know the number one execution rule for successful trading is . . . " . . . trade with the trend . . . ," why is it that so many active traders lose? Interesting, hey?

If you believe that more than 60 percent of all active traders know that they should be trading with the trend, yet more than 90 percent of all active traders fail, don't you think that sounds ironic? You know, if all traders were as smart as they would like to think they are, most traders would stop trading and return to their families and the lives they had before the markets. They would walk away from their screens because there is something very strange going on when most know to trade with the trend, yet most fail to do so. If I was as smart as I thought I was a long time ago, I would have left trading. The market has to be rigged when most know what to do, yet most fail in doing it. Well, I'm happy to admit that I'm not the sharpest tool in the shed, so I stuck with trading, but it did take me a long, long time and many bruises, frustration, disappointment, and too many losses to remember to work out where the market was rigged against me. It took me almost 15 years to work out which of the dice the market's maximum adversity was throwing my way that was loaded. Loaded against me!

Yep, right now, most traders are trading with loaded dice, tools that although they are perceived to be designed to help the trader, are actually doing the bidding of market's maximum adversity. I'm sorry to say it but most methodologies are working against the best interests of their trader.

But please let me get back on message. You know that most traders know to trade with the trend and you also know that most active traders fail. The question has to be asked, why? Now you know there are many reasons traders fail but let's restrict the discussion here to the three main pillars of successful trading.

- *Poor money management:* Most people overtrade their account, failing to use sensible money management. This contributes to a risk of ruin above 0 percent and their financial ruin.
- *Poor methodology:* Most traders do not have a stable strategy with a positive expectancy. Most have strategies with a negative expectancy, which contributes to a risk of ruin above 0 percent and their financial ruin.
- *Poor mindset:* Most traders can't follow their methodology, even if it's good. They fail to validate their methodology correctly and fail to build their confidence in their strategy. They're unable to hold the eye of the tiger. They lack confidence, focus, consistency and discipline.

Since this chapter is about methodology, please let me focus on it.

Poor Methodologies

Most people trade poor methodologies, and don't realize it. If you accept, as I do, that successful trend trading is no more and no less than simply identifying the trend and being patient enough to wait for a retracement, then trend trading can be broken down into two words: trend and retracement. I would then suggest, if this is the case, and if most traders have poor methodologies, then you would have to believe that most methodologies must be using both poor trend and poor retracement tools? Right? Or simply, garbage in garbage out.

If the core value drivers behind a successful trend-trading methodology are its trend and retracement identification tools, then you would have to accept if a methodology is poor, it's really just a reflection of its two biggest value drivers: its poor trend tool and its poor retracement tool?

Once again I'm sorry to say it, but most trend and retracement tools most traders use are poor. In my opinion, they shouldn't be using them. Because they are poor, it is very difficult for a trader to use them to identify the trend correctly. For most traders, when they believe they have identified the trend through various tools, they enter the market, only to see prices reverse! It becomes an exercise in frustration.

So this is a real quandary in technical analysis. A large proportion of technical analysis knowledge is devoted to identifying the trend because it is the number one execution rule for successful trend trading. Yet so many trend traders lose. I don't want to oversimplify it, because there are many reasons people lose, as I have already discussed. I'm suggesting another strong reason is the trend and retracement identification techniques themselves. Surely, if most trend and retracement techniques were good, wouldn't more than 10 percent of active traders win?

Poor trend tools

Probably the most popular trend tools available to traders today include the following:

- moving average indicator
- MACD (Moving Average Convergence Divergence) indicator
- ADX (Average Directional Index) indicator
- trend lines.

In my opinion, they are poor trend tools. However, before I explain why, I just need to make a couple of confessions. First, I personally think the simple moving average indicator is probably one of the best trend indicators available to traders. It does a reasonable job in identifying a trend. And second, I do personally use a moving average in my medium-term trend trading. I use a longer term 200-day simple moving average to identify what I call the dominant trend. I use it to prevent myself from placing a medium-term trend trade against what I believe is the long-term trend. However, although I do use a moving average indicator, I don't use it in my trade setup or trade plan. I only use it because I prefer not to trade against it. So I don't use a moving average to determine the trend. I don't use a moving average to identify a retracement level. I don't use a moving average to identify an entry level. I don't use a moving average to identify a stop level. I don't use a moving average to identify an exit point. No. And I should also share with you that if I removed the 200-day moving average from my mechanical models, they would actually make more money. However, when I do, the average profit per trade does decline, so it does pay for me to trade when my view of the trend is aligned with the dominant trend as measured by the 200-day moving average.

I should also say that there is nothing magical about my use of 200 days. I have always used it, and I have no idea whether it's the optimal average, nor do I care. I just use it.

So although I think the moving average is possibly one of the best indicators available for traders, and despite the fact I do personally use a 200-day simple moving average, I still believe it is a poor trend tool, and one that is not beyond criticism. I now want to take a closer look at the moving average indicator and share with you why I believe it's poor. And the same criticisms you'll hear me make can be applied to the other trend tools I've mentioned.

The moving average indicator   So let's take one of the simplest and possibly one of the most effective indicators available today, the simple moving average indicator as shown in figure 9.12. The moving average indicator has one variable. The trend interpretation will depend on the value of the variable. The indicator smooths prices, and while prices are above the moving average

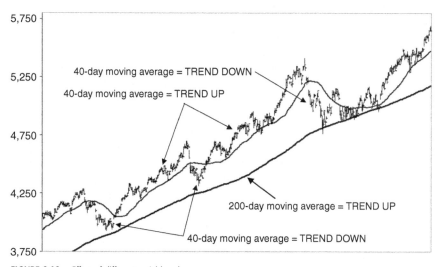

FIGURE 9.12   Effect of different variable values

the trend is considered up. When prices fall below the moving average, the trend is considered down. Alternatively, a moving average can be compared to its value the day before, and if it's rising, the trend is considered up. If the value is lower than the day before, then the trend is considered down. Very simple.

The only problem is determining the length of moving average to use, should you use 10 days, 20 days, 40 days, or 100 days?

Figure 9.12 shows two moving averages with two different values for the variable. One has a 40-day value, while the other has a 200-day value. While prices are above a moving average the trend is considered up. When prices are below a moving average, the trend is considered down. According to the 200-day moving average, the trend has been considered up for the entire period shown on the chart. According to the shorter 40-day moving average, the trend has switched back and forth as prices have flipflopped above and below the 40-day moving average. And this is the reason I believe the moving average indicator is a poor trend tool.

I could sit three identical traders down in their own soundproof booths. They could not consult with each other or hear each other. These traders could each have 20 years of trading experience behind them. They are all the same height. They all have the same color hair and the same color eyes, and carry the same passport. They have all graduated from the same university with the same master's degree. As I've said, these three traders sitting by themselves in their own soundproof booths are identical. There is nothing to distinguish among them. I could then present to them the same chart over the same period. I could then give the same single tool to help them: the moving average indicator. And I could then ask them the same question: "Today I want to trade the market I have shown you on your PC screen, could you please tell me the trend?"

Now depending on the value they place in moving average indicator I could possibly receive three different trend interpretations—one may say the trend is up, another down and another neutral—all depending on the value of the variable. But wait, I hear you say, "Yes Brent, but wouldn't it be important to tell the three traders your preferred time frame—because certainly that would be significant?"

And I'd reply by saying that trading is not a debating society. The market does not care what my time frame is. It's not sensitive to my needs. And I have asked these three identical traders all the same simple question: "Today I want to trade the market I have shown you on your PC screen, could you please tell me the trend?"

The market doesn't care what my time frame is. I don't care either. I just want to know what the trend is: up, down, or neutral? What I do with the trend for my preferred time frame is my business. I just want to know what the trend is. As I told the three traders, I want to trade the market. It's really a simple question and one not to overanalyze, discuss, dissect, debate. Please don't try to overcomplicate the issue of trading.

My valid point remains. Even if all three traders independently use a tight range for the values ranging between 18 days and 28 days, I could still possibly receive three different trend interpretations. And who is to say one trader's opinion is right or wrong? Who's to say one trader's opinion is superior to the others', and that I should listen to him or her? No one. They are all identical, so there can be no discretionary selection among them. They're all right and they're all wrong, depending on the value they placed in their moving average indicator. And who is to say using a tight range of between 18 days and 28 days is correct? Who's to say that using a range between 35 days and 45 days isn't superior? No one. There is no universal exam board that holds the correct answer, because one does not exist. The only universal master is the market itself, and through its maximum adversity, it's not going to lets its true trend intentions be known. It loves to keep all and sundry guessing.

So there is my quandary and the quandary of every trader who uses a moving average indicator: who do I believe? Which value should I use for the variable? Which value should I use in my moving average indicator? This is the big problem.

The moving average indicator has a variable. The trend interpretation will depend upon the value of the variable. The existence of the variable makes the indicator and consequently the trend interpretation subjective and therefore in my opinion too unreliable to use for its trend interpretation.

The irony   And here is the big irony very few traders get. So please listen up. The trader, you, look to this tool, the moving average indicator, for assistance in helping you interpret the trend. So you look down to this little tool and say, "Please indicator, will you help me in determining the trend?"

This little indicator, this moving average, is only too happy to oblige. So the little indicator looks up and looks you innocently in the face and says, "Yes Mr. Trader, I'm happy to help you interpret the trend. Just please give me a value for my moving average variable, and I will willingly and gladly give you exactly want you ask for . . . "

So you, the trader, enter a value for the variable and receive the corresponding trend interpretation, based on the variable's value. The moving average tool is giving you exactly what you asked for! If you placed in a low value, it will give you a short-term trend interpretation. If you enter a larger value it will give you a much longer-term trend interpretation. If you give it a middle-of-the-range value, it will give you a more medium-term interpretation. It is giving you exactly what you asked for: information you can easily see for yourself by looking at the chart. The tool is giving you nothing that you don't already know. It's giving you exactly what you asked for. It's not giving you any objective, arm's length, and independent advice.

The tool is self fulfilling, giving you a positive feedback to your input. It's putting a mirror up to your face and reflecting back the value you give it. The big irony is that you look toward this tool for assistance, but you have unwittingly and unconsciously become the tool! The moving average tool is just a poor disguise for you. You have so much influence over the interpretation it is giving you. You enter the value and it reflects back the value, although in a different guise. It's just a funny reflecting mirror, just like the ones you see at the carnivals where it distorts your image, the tool is just reflecting back your opinion on the variables value. You may not recognize the image as your own, but believe me, it's you. It's 100 percent you as you subjectively choose the value, and the tool has kindly and accurately reflected it back to you.

And the big, big irony is that you most probably are not aware of it. You're not aware that you've been effectively talking to yourself when you've been asking the moving average tool to help you interpret the trend.

In my opinion the moving average tool is too dependent on you to give you an independent interpretation of the trend. It's too dependent to be judge an effective tool for trend determination. You don't know whether the tool has been effective in determining the trend because of its particular technique, or because you were lucky in determining a good value for its variable. Where is the value in the tool? Is it in the algorithm or in the value you gave it? It's too dependent on you for the value you place on its variable. And this is why the other popular trend tools are poor as well: they all have a variable that requires subjective inputs from you. They too are just a distorted reflection of you, since you have so much influence over their individual trend interpretation. In my opinion, they are all too dependent on you for their trend interpretation to be relied upon (see table 9.2).

One reason the moving average indicator is one of the best trend tools available to a trader is its single variable. There are fewer degrees of freedom to influence its trend interpretation. There is only one variable, as opposed to the MACD and ADX, which have three! Having three gives

TABLE 9.2   Number of variables in trend tools

Trend tool	Number of variables
Moving average	1
MACD	3
ADX	3
Trend lines	2

you too many degrees of freedom to influence their trend interpretation. Having three gives you too much flexibility, too much say, too much influence, and too much wiggle room to tweak out what you want, a profitable upward sloping historical equity curve. Having one variable, let alone three, gives you too many degrees of freedom to curve fit your methodology to historical data.

Now this is why these trend tools are so poor. Different variable values will give different trend interpretations. The more variables there are, the more scope for variability in the trend interpretation. The more variability there is, the more wiggle room, and the more unreliable the trend interpretation is.

Tools with variables are too subjective. They are too flexible. They simply become electronic facsimiles of yourself. They become willing servants happily reflecting back exactly what you put in. They do not tell you anything that you don't already know. They only disguise what you have given them. They are not objective or independent enough to rely upon. They become willing collaborators in helping you to curve fit your methodology to historical data.

Key issues   And here we come to the key issues of the problem in my opinion. (And please remember everything here is just my opinion and you are welcome to differ, no worries at all. Just remember to find objective evidence to support your position.) A good trend tool should be independent of the trader. A good trend tool will be 100 percent objective, and will not rely upon any subjective interpretation or input. A good trend tool will stand on its own feet, and will not require any subjective massaging from the trader to make it work. A good trend tool will be independent of the trader. A good trend tool will be a trader-free zone, in which the trader can have no influence over its trend interpretation. Once, and only once, a trend tool can achieve these characteristics do I believe it should be consider for trend interpretation. Once it can stand free and be independent of the trader, a trend tool should then be evaluated for its own usefulness. A good independent trend tool will then either work, or it won't. It won't need any variable massaging to make it seem to work. Simple.

A trend tool that requires any input from the trader is not objective and is not independent. It should not be considered for trend interpretation. In my opinion any tool or idea that is subjective is too dangerous to use for trading. I believe any tool that is "subjective" is dangerous. I believe "subjective" can kill a trader.

Only objective and independent tools should be considered. In my opinion, anything you use to help you in your trading decisions should be able to pass the objective and independent test. If they are and they do, then they will either work or they won't. If they work with a simple objective trade plan, then you will a have tool that you can rely on.

As a trader, you know that you need assistance, so you look for tools that can help you. In the beginning of your trading careers, you believe the tools contained within your charting packages will help. However, you do not realize the flexibility of the tools is actually a handicap, not a benefit. You don't learn this until much later to your puzzlement, frustration, and cost.

For one of the best technical indicators available to traders, it's easy to understand how subjective the moving average indicator is, and how varying and unreliable the trend interpretations can be. Is it any wonder then that traders struggle with the common trend tools available to them?

These popular trend tools—the moving average, MACD and ADX indicators—all suffer from the same subjective criticism. They can give two people trading the same markets two different trend interpretations depending on the variables they use. The traditional trend line also suffers from the same criticism, when two different traders looking at the same chart can draw two different trend lines depending on the swing points they choose. Why would you use any tool that is so inconsistent with its trend interpretation? How can you objectively evaluate a trend tool for its effectiveness when its trend interpretation can differ so much between traders. These tools are like economists—they seem to be useful in explaining what has happen in the past but are useless for giving objective and effective analysis for the future.

Now these criticisms of mine don't stop with these popular trend tools; they also equally apply to the more popular retracement tools.

Poor retracement tools

Once a trend has been identified, it simply becomes a matter of patience as you wait for a retracement level to present itself. Unfortunately, traditional retracement tools suffer from the same criticism as traditional trend tools. They too have variable dependent parameters. Similar traders can reach opposite conclusions depending on the values they place on the variables, and this problem is only compounded as "subjective" retracement levels are dependent on first determining a "subjective" trend! No wonder most trend traders fail to succeed.

Some popular methods used to identify retracement levels include:

- overbought or oversold conditions
- divergence
- chart patterns
- percentage retracements.

Indicators measuring overbought and oversold conditions include the:

- ROC (rate of change) indicator
- RSI (relative strength index) indicator
- stochastic oscillator indicator.

Divergence is used to identify a loss of momentum, which can signal an imminent reversal in prices or the end of a retracement phase. Measuring divergence relies on using one of the many overbought and oversold indicators.

As do their trend cousins, these retracement measurements suffer the same variable-dependent parameter illness. Once a variable is introduced, the outcome becomes subjective and unreliable. It becomes unstable. It further disadvantages the person attempting to use them to trade with the trend. Similar to the trend dilemma, it's best to find a "fixed" retracement measurement that is beyond the reach of fiddling.

As a trader, you will want fewer subjective tools and more 100 percent objective tools to aid your trading. You will learn to take up a new mantra: " . . . no more wiggle room, no more wiggle room . . . "

You will become harsh in your review of trading tools and ideas in building a trading methodology. You will learn to squeeze out subjective and therefore unreliable tools. Once again, you can see how difficult a task it is for a trend trader to find a reliable retracement level. The popular tools have too many variables and values, making them too subjective, too unstable and too unreliable.

In table 9.3, I have summarized the number of variables that appear in a number of popular retracement tools.

Different variable values will give different retracement interpretations. The more variables there are, the more scope for variability there is in the retracement interpretation. The more variability there is, the more wiggle room and the more unreliable the retracement interpretation is.

TABLE 9.3   Variables in retracement tools

Type of tool	Retracement tool	Number of variables
Percentage retracements	Fibonacci ratios	4
	Harmonic ratios	2
	Arithmetic ratios	2
Overbought and oversold indicators	RSI	3
	Stochastic oscillator	4
Reversal chart patterns	Double bottoms/to ps	2

TABLE 9.4   Trend and retracement tools

Trend tools	Variables	Wiggle room	Retracement tools	Variables	Wiggle room
Moving average	1	Less	Fibonacci ratios	4	Extreme
MACD	3	High	RSI	3	High
ADX	3	High	Stochastics	4	Extreme
Trend lines	2	Medium	Double tops/ bottoms	3	Medium

Two negatives don't make a positive   Well, here you have two negatives. Negative trend tools and negative retracement tools. Unfortunately two negatives in trading don't make a positive, only disappointment. Table 9.4 summarizes the most popular trend and retracement tools available to the average trader.

Along with the tools, I have identified where their weakness is, their variables. The more variables a tool has, the more wiggle room or flexibility there is to massage the tool to fit your data. The more wiggle room there is, the more unreliable the interpretation is, in my opinion. In addition, these poor trend and retracement indicators, being a derivative of price, also lag price, making them slow to identify either a change in trend or completion of a retracement. Now, if these individual tools aren't bad enough individually, they become dangerously lethal when combined into a trading methodology.

Dangerously lethal   Table 9.5 summarizes some methodologies employing some of the more popular trend and retracement tools.

TABLE 9.5   Summary of methodologies and their variables

Systems	Trend and retracement		Variables	Wiggle room
System 1	Moving average		1	
	RSI		3	
		Total	4	Extreme
System 2	MACD		3	
	Stochastics		4	
		Total	7	Extreme
System 3	Moving average		1	
	ADX		3	
	Fibonacci ratios		4	
	RSI		3	
		Total	11	Extreme

Let's look at System 1, which will trade in the direction of the trend as identified by a simple moving average after a retracement measured by an RSI. The moving average on its own is generally benign because it only has one variable limiting its degrees of freedom. However, when it's combined with an RSI that has three variables, the complete methodology becomes a trading strategy containing four variables. Even a simple strategy such as this has an extreme level of flexibility and wiggle room, allowing too much influence from the trader to massage the variable values to fit the historical data. With so many variables, you couldn't expect the nice-looking equity curve to remain stable in the future.

If that simple methodology wasn't bad enough, then how about the third system? On one level, I applaud this methodology. Its conservative design requires double confirmation before finding a setup. This strategy will only trade in the direction of the trend as measured by a moving average if the trend is considered strong as measured by the ADX indicator. I like the conservatism. It will then wait patiently for a retracement that is confirmed by both a Fibonacci percentage retracement and a low RSI reading. Once again, I like the conservatism in requiring two independent retracement tools to agree. So on a conservative level, I like what the third system is attempting to do with its double confirmation. However, my fondness stops there.

What I don't like is that the combined tools produce a trading strategy that contains 11 variables! In my opinion, that's a dangerously high level. There is far too much room to fool yourself into believing you have developed a winning edge.

One school of trading believes its okay to use variables as long as the strategy continues to work across a wide range of variable values. I don't disagree, as long as there are only a few variables—say, one. With a single variable, it's easy to see whether it has value if it works across a wide range of values. However, when there is more then one variable, it isn't that easy, particularly for a strategy that contains 11 variables! As you go about fixing 10 of the variables and moving the value of the eleventh variable across a wide range, all it would be telling you is that one variable appears to provide value or support for the other 10 variables at their fixed values. However, once you change the value of one of those other 10 variables, the work you have done on the first test would no longer be relevant since its previous fixed 10 variables are no longer fixed. I'm no mathematician but when you have 11 independent variables in an equation, and that is really all a trading methodology is, an equation, I can imagine there would be an almost infinite number of possible variable combinations you would have to test, an infinite number to stress test the 11 variables thoroughly, taking them all independently through their individual degrees of freedom (range of variable values) against the other 10 variables as their values remain both fixed and variable. It's actually hurting my head just thinking about this!

My point is that it's probably impossible to correctly stress test a strategy across 11 independent but also interconnected variables. There are simply too many moving parts for you to gain any confidence that you have correctly landed upon the correct variable values.

And if you don't believe me, then just look around yourself. Almost every charting package has these popular trend and retracement tools—so everyone has access to them. They are taught in many books, and are included in many DVDs and workshops. And guess what, more than 90 percent of active traders lose and for most traders their equity curve dips as soon as they start trading their new Holy Grail trading system—and why? Because they use too many variable-dependent indicators that through tweaking individual variable values they have managed to find the correct values to produce a handsome-looking historical equity curve, which they have successfully managed to curve fit to their historical data. This will be an unstable equity curve that immediately dips the moment the person commences trading it.

These common tools, when combined into a trading strategy, become more subjective than their individual parts, becoming more flexible, more unstable, and more unreliable. And this is why most trade plans fail, they're not 100 percent objective, they're not independent of the trader.

Subjective tools

No wonder the poor trend traders, who know to trade with the trend, because the trend is their friend, fail to trade successfully with the trend when the tools that are available to them for identifying both the trend and retracement are so poor. It is no wonder they fail. It's garbage in, garbage out. What kills the trader are subjective tools.

These tools seduce the unsuspecting trader by their flexible appeal. They don't threaten a trader's fragile ego by attempting to supplant the trader's opinion. They offer comfort and cooperative existence. They offer a warm and safe union. They offer a bright future through marriage: the subjective tool with its easy flexibility together with the ever-knowing and bright trader. They offer a marriage made in heaven. And the trader falls for it lock, stock, and barrel, the whole catastrophe.

Ah, you mere mortals—to be so easily seduced by the bright lights on your trading screens. What fools you are. What ignorant and happy fools you are to be so trusting. And what a happy and ignorant fool I was for the first 15 years of my trading career to suffer the same seduction trading a subjective methodology.

So, in my opinion any tool with a variable or variables is too subjective. It becomes too flexible to rely upon. It simply becomes an electronic facsimile of yourself. It becomes a willing servant, happily reflecting back exactly what you put in. It does not tell you anything that you don't already know. It only disguises what you give it. It is not objective or independent enough to rely upon. It becomes a willing collaborator in helping you to curve fit your methodology to historical data.

Objective tools

The best you can do is to select measures of trend and retracement that have some built-in protection against fiddling by you. The best measures with built-in protection are ones without parameters or adjustable variables. The best ones are objective and independent of you. The best ones are fixed. This makes any indicator or tool with a variable a liability. Adjustable parameters produce adjustable outcomes. Adjustable outcomes are unreliable for making trading decisions.

The idea is to select objective and "fixed" measures for determining the trend direction and retracement level. There can't be any interpretation in their use. Either a 12-year-old would interpret the measure the same as you or it's thrown out. There is no wiggle room. It has to be fixed. Simple. Black and white. No shades of gray here and there. Once you're able to find such measures, the idea is to bundle them up into strategy, and apply a simple and objective trade plan. That is, when your objective setup is discovered courtesy of your objective trend and objective retracement tool, you will then apply your objective entry, stop, and exit criterion. The strategy will then either make money or it won't. You'll then need to validate its expectancy through the TEST procedure. If it makes money, then you're on your way. If not, then it's back to the drawing board.

The challenge then is to find objective measures to trade with, ones that, although not perfect, won't change through opinion; ones that can't be adjusted; ones that can't be fiddled with; ones that can be easily applied and interpreted and have a simple and objective trade plan applied to; ones that will hopefully produce a positive expectancy that can eventually be validated through the TEST procedure.

You need to use "trader-free" tools, in which the trader can have no influence over the trend or retracement interpretation, and then the tools will either work or they won't. They need to stand on their own two feet without any assistance from you through tweaking a variable here and there. Unfortunately, most indicators in my opinion are not worth your attention. You have too much influence over them through their variables. You need to create a strategy that is a "trader-free zone" where you the trader can have no influence over the equity curve.

Certainly, you will be 100 percent subjective in how you develop your strategy; you have to be. Without your subjective discretion and creative ideas, you'll have nothing. You are the creator, so you will use 100 percent of your creative and subjective thoughts to create your methodology. However, once you have created your strategy, it must become trader free. It must comprise objective tools. You cannot have any influence over its internal workings. There can't be any soft variables in your methodology, so that you can tweak a variable here and there.

You need your methodology to be independent of you. You need a methodology that does not require input from you to work. You need to receive objective evidence a strategy works, and a strategy that needs input from you is not an objective strategy, it's a subjective reflection of your own image. I hope I'm making sense here.

So far in our trend-trading journey, I have discussed the two main value drivers in trend trading—finding a trend and waiting for a retracement level. Although they possibly represent 80 percent of what a trend trader does, there are still additional steps involved in trend trading.

Remember, the execution of trend trading comprises a two-step process. First, locate a trade setup, which in turn comprises three parts:

- Identify the trend.
- Wait for a retracement level.
- Wait for a retracement pattern.

Second, implement the trade plan, which comprises five parts:

- Wait for a confirming entry signal,
- Enter the market,
- Place a stop,
- Manage the trade and (hopefully)
- Take profits.

Let's next look at waiting for a retracement pattern.

Wait for a retracement pattern

Few trend traders actually wait for a retracement pattern to occur and confirm a retracement level. Most view a retracement level, whatever it may be, as the retracement pattern. Essentially a retracement pattern represents a consolidation in price as the market pauses during either a pullback or relief rally before continuing the trend.

Retracement patterns represent congestion in price, and include traditional chart patterns such as flags, pennants, and triangles. The problem a trend trader faces is the subjective identification of a particular chart pattern.

Figure 9.13 shows a chart of gold prices.

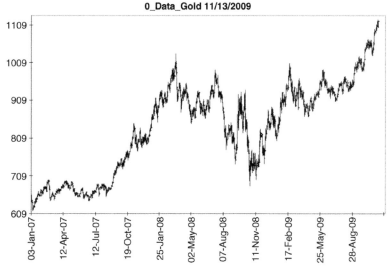

FIGURE 9.13   Daily gold chart

Chart reading is not easy. If a trader uses traditional retracement patterns within their trade setups, then they will have to use their trained eye to identify the congestion retracement patterns. This is a subjective task and in my opinion not easy. In figure 9.14, I've done my best to identify the traditional congestion chart patterns I can see.

And when I was completing this, it reminded me of the triangle puzzle you can see in figure 9.15.

Like me, you've probably seen this puzzle before. Why not try to quickly count how many triangles there are in figure 9.15 and record your answer? Now, no cheating. Do it quickly without overanalyzing it. Good.

Now solving this visualization puzzle is much like trying to identify traditional chart patterns. It's subjective. Depending on how you're feeling, you may see more or fewer triangles if you count them again.

In figure 9.16, I've shown some additional retracement patterns a friend of mine picked out for me that I missed.

And figure 9.17 shows another retracement pattern that I missed which I have just received from another friend of mine whom I also asked to take a look at this chart. Now do you see the problem with using subjective tools?

As I said, chart reading is not easy, and the market may take a few attempts before completing a pattern. In addition, patterns can have variations. For example, triangles can be symmetrical, ascending, or descending. Once again, the subjective nature of identifying retracement patterns makes them unstable and unreliable, hampering a trend trader's success.

FIGURE 9.14   Traditional chart patterns

If you don't believe me why not go back to figure 9.15 and recount the number of triangles you can see? Is the number different? Are you sure you're right? Why not try counting them again? Interesting, hey? And that puzzle is meant to be child's play. If you struggled with the triangles, what hope do you have trading real markets in real time with real money based on identifying real (but subtle) chart patterns? In my opinion, you need to find and use objective retracement patterns.

Wait for a confirming entry signal

From my experience most traders, both trend traders and swing traders, fail to wait for a confirming signal before entering a trade. If they find a setup,

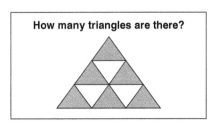

FIGURE 9.15   Triangle puzzle

FIGURE 9.16   More traditional chart patterns

FIGURE 9.17   The difficulty of identifying traditional chart patterns

they'll enter the market immediately. For example, many traders will simply buy a 50 percent retracement level. The smart traders will rely on the market first to prove their setup is correct before entering a trade by initially moving in the direction of the setup. If they required a 50 percent retracement to occur, they would first wait for it and then look to enter long if the market could then start to rally, possibly buying a breakout of the previous one, two, or three bars high. The absence of this confirming process would certainly make a trend trader's job more difficult.

Enter the market

Well this is one step every trend trader, whether successful or not, can do.

Place a stop

With so many trading books and seminars available today, I'd say that most traders would know to trade with stops. If they don't, their introduction would certainly improve their results.

Manage the trade

To my mind, managing a trade involves using a trailing stop. This involves adjusting the stop and locking in profits as a trend continues. No one likes giving back open profits.

Take profits

Obviously, not many traders do this enough to be profitable.

So What to Do?

As you can see, although a simple process, trend trading is plagued with many problems. Determining the trend, finding a retracement level and identifying a retracement pattern either relies on a variable-dependent indicator or a subjective chart interpretation. They all suffer from subjective opinion. Waiting for a confirming entry signal requires experience while entering, placing stops, managing a trade, and taking profits all require discipline and consistency.

Unfortunately, the three greatest value drivers in a trend trading plan— determining the trend, finding a retracement level, and identifying a retracement pattern are the most subjective in the whole execution process. Is it any wonder so many trend traders fail! So the question needs to be asked. What to do?

Well, in a perfect world the trend trader would only use the best trend identification and best retracement measurement tool available.

Unfortunately, the world isn't perfect, the market's maximum adversity has made sure of that.

To my knowledge, there isn't one perfect trend tool, one perfect retracement measurement, or one perfect retracement pattern that is going to strike gold each time. Trading involves probabilities, not certainties, so searching for the perfect trend and retracement tool is pointless: they don't exist. However, I believe the trader can do better in determining the trend, finding a retracement level, and identifying a retracement pattern than relying on variable dependent and subjective tools such as indicators and traditional chart patterns.

The answer is to identify and remedy the major weakness in traditional trend trading. As I've said, the common key fault shared between the three greatest value drivers is one word, *subjective*. They all rely on a subjective opinion either to nominate a variable's value or to interpret a chart pattern. I believe that if you can replace subjective with objective you will go a long way to improving a trend trader's performance. And please remember that objective does not mean perfect. There is no such thing in trading.

A trader requires independent and 100 percent objective advice on trend, retracement level, and retracement pattern interpretation. Good trend and retracement tools will not require any input from a trader to make them appear to work. Good trend and retracement tools will stand on their own feet and be judged on their own merits. They will either work or they won't. Good trend and retracement tools will work and be free from trader interference. Good trend and retracement tools have to be *independent* and *work* to be relied upon to trade.

Independence

This is the key issue that hampers most trading methodologies. They are too dependent on the trader to make them appear to work as shown in figure 9.18.

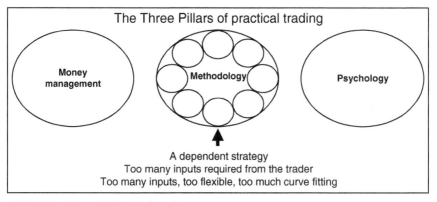

FIGURE 9.18   The unreliability of a dependent strategy

Figure 9.18 shows the three pillars of practical trading: money management, methodology, and psychology. Its also illustrates a methodology that contains multiple variable inputs that subjective trend and retracement tools require. Making the tools too dependent on the trader. They'll either require a subjective value placed on a variable or they will require a subjective interpretation of a retracement pattern. These tools simply become an extension of the trader, and therefore are the trader. And herein lies the irony. The trader is only looking at himself or herself in the mirror when they look upon these subjective tools for assistance. Traders know they need help to trade successfully. They need tools that are both objective and independent of them.

It's only when they can have no influence over the tools' interpretations can they rely on their effectiveness. If the tools, when combined with an objective trade plan, can create a positive-expectancy historical equity curve, then the traders will know they may possibly have a winning methodology. They will then be in a position to validate their strategy with the TEST procedure.

Traders need to develop a methodology that is independent of them. Certainly, the creation of their methodology will be 100 percent subjective, but once it has been developed, it has to be able to stand alone and apart from the trader for the trader to be able to rely on it. It will either work or it won't, and it won't need any massaging through malleable variables to make it appear to work. A trader will need an independent strategy, as shown in figure 9.19.

Trading is hard enough without throwing up too many balls in the air. I would rather trade with only three balls to manage, as shown in figure 9.19, remaining focused and consistent in applying sensible money management while executing my objective and independent methodology. I'd hate to have more then three balls in the air as shown in figure 9.18, where I'd also

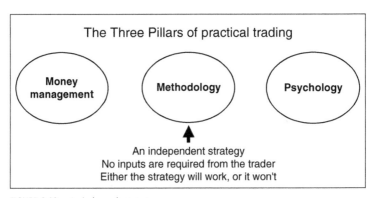

FIGURE 9.19   An independent strategy

have to worry about whether I got the variable values right. I would also be constantly worrying about whether my methodology merely represented a successful curve fit to historical data rather than an effective strategy. I'd be constantly reaching for my psychology trading pills—I'd probably be spending more time on my trading coaches' couch than at my trading desk. Give me three balls in the air any day over 10 balls! But that's me and I can only share my thoughts that come from my own experiences.

I hope this discussion has helped to give you an insight into why most methodologies fail to perform in real-time trading. I want to also let you know that, despite my zero tolerance for subjective tools, not all subjective tools are bad.

NOT ALL INDICATORS ARE BAD

I know my opinions are extreme, and that I do generally see the trading world in black and white. I simply believe trading is a numbers game. Understand the numbers, define an objective edge, trade small, trade consistently, trade patiently, and you will earn a good return on your risk capital. Fail to understand the numbers, and you'll trade with a risk of ruin above 0 percent; you'll trade with a negative expectancy; you'll overtrade your account; you'll trade impatiently; you'll trade with a nervous and hesitant disposition; and you'll fail to follow your trade plan. You will fail.

But that's me, and I know that my views on subjective tools and indicator-based methodologies do not entertain any leeway. But that's me, and you may be different; you may have a preference for indicators or other subjective tools. If that is the case I just want to let you know that not all is lost because I do know of some successful indicator-based methodologies. But what I will tell you is that they are simple methodologies, and the most successful one uses only a single indicator with one variable. It's simple as that. This strategy is profitable across a wide range of variable values. So please don't lose all heart on all indicators, because a few are good, and do have an edge. But their effectiveness is enshrined within a simple strategy.

If your preference is to consider other subjective tools or analysis for your methodology, then that is fine. There is no reason you can't entertain their use. It's just my opinion that you'll find it harder to establish a tradable edge. And at the end of the day, you can create any methodology you choose to. However, before you can consider trading it, you'll still need to validate your methodology's expectancy using the TEST procedure. It's the final gate, the final hurdle, the final arbitrator of your methodology's effectiveness.

In addition, another approach for considering subjective tools is to identify those subjective tools that traders have been using successfully for many years. Nothing beats longevity where a tool has helped a trader to extract real money out of the markets in real time and for a long time.

Another approach could be to find a software solution for a discretionary methodology—where the software program will independently provide the analysis and find the trade setups. You could even throw in an indicator-based methodology. But the trick here is not to touch the factory settings on the variables. You will have to treat them as being fixed, because the day you are tempted to tweak a variable's value here and there is the day the methodology will no longer be independent from you and objective. That will be the day it will become too subjective, too flexible, too unstable, and too unreliable to rely upon. So the idea is to accept the software or collection of indicators as they are, and keep them at arm's length from you.

As an example, traders who are interested in Elliot wave could consider a program such as Advanced GET that will independently find trade setups based on its Elliott wave interpretation of the markets. You would not alter any of the variables in the program. You would have to let it do its wave counts, and come up with its own analysis. You will then need to see whether the trade setups can be validated with the TEST procedure to deterime if the methodology can work in your hands. And it will be frustrating because Advanced GET will change its wave counts and trade setups as the market changes. But at least it will be consistently frustrating. And it will be independently frustrating. And this is the point. It will be consistent in its interpretation of market conditions. Although the approach is subjective, its delivery to you will be objective. It will be independent and consistent since you will not interfere with any of its variable settings. You'll just let the program run on the PC that sits in the corner, and let it do its own thing. You will keep it independent from yourself. Remember, no fiddling. Now, I don't know whether the trade setups it finds are good enough to trade profitably. You will need to determine that independently between yourself and your trading partner using the TEST procedure. However, what I do like about it is that it is an old program that Tom Joseph wrote between 1981 and 1986 before releasing it to the public in 1986. It's been around for a long time. I like that. And if you can leave the variables at their factory settings, and successfully validate the trade signals using the TEST procedure, then you may have yourself both a validated and objective and (since the software does the analysis independently of you) subjective (Elliott wave is subjective) trading methodology. Just an idea and food for thought.

But one word of caution. If you are lucky enough to come across a positive-expectancy methodology that contains subjective tools, and you were able to validate it with the TEST procedure, you have to understand that the subjective methodology will have less chance of remaining stable when compared to a simple 100 percent objective and independent methodology. And this is because a simple methodology has less moving parts, and therefore has fewer opportunities for things to go wrong.

And at the risk of being called a kill joy I really do need to share with you Charlie Wright's observation in Art Collins' book *Market Beaters*:[5]

> One of the interesting things that we found in our research was ultimately, indicators don't matter.

This observation comes from Charlie Wright, who runs a successful funds management business. Charlie has been involved in the markets for more than 30 years, and is a mechanical trader. Through his years of trading, research, development, and funds management, he believes indicators don't really matter. But this is only Charlie's opinion, and he is entitled to it, just like you and me, although it does come from a very experienced and successful trader. In addition, it is a generalization that can have exceptions, just as I mentioned.

BUT DON'T MARKETS CHANGE?

There is a strong school of thought in trading that believes you need flexibility in your trading methodology to adapt to changing market conditions. They say that markets change and so too should a trader's methodology change to adapt to the new conditions.

And they're correct. Markets do change, constantly and usually when you believe you have just worked them out. Markets constantly move from being range bound and choppy to expanding and trending during both bull market and bear market conditions. So markets on the surface do change. And to be fair, if markets are always changing, how can you expect a trader to use a single methodology across all market conditions? I hear that observation. I just disagree.

I believe a good methodology will work across all market conditions. I'm not suggesting a methodology should be able to make money in every market in every year. That is almost impossible. But I do believe that a well-designed simple methodology should be profitable over the long term trading many markets that exhibit all market conditions—range-bound choppy congestion trading and clean trend trading through both bull market and bear market conditions.

Who's right; who's wrong? Both and neither. Very experienced traders are able to recognize the signs, and know when to switch their strategies from bear market to bull market mode, switching from range-bound swing trading to clean retracement and breakout trend trading. But they are very experienced, and they don't get it right all the time. They are the elite, so near the real pointy end of the trading spectrum that the average trader can't see them. They're almost invisible, mythical traders. The legends.

Other more mortal traders prefer to trade one way under all conditions, trading their simple and objective robust methodology and relying upon their money management, consistency, discipline, and perseverance to succeed. Such as those who use the widely known Turtle trading strategy, which I'll be discussing shortly. For average traders, I'd suggest they consider trading one good methodology across all market conditions until they develop the necessary expertise, which is very hard to attain.

MULTIPLE METHODOLOGIES

Another approach you can consider is to develop two independent and complementary trend- and countertrend-, or swing-trading, methodologies.

Ideally, they will be both 100 percent objective and independent and work across many markets under all market conditions. They would be profitable and be able to stand alone on their own two feet. However when you combine their equity curves, you'll observe and enjoy a smoother ride in your account balance. When the trend-trading methodology hits a rough patch you would expect your countertrend methodology to be enjoying profits and vice versa.

Developing and combining complementary and independent methodologies should be your objective. Once you achieve that, you should also look to diversify your strategies further across time frames. Developing either shorter-term or longer-term trend- and countertrend-trading methodologies. This is what I do. I trade a portfolio of mechanical trend and countertrend methodologies across multiple time frames across global index and currencies markets.

Now that I have shared with you my views on why so many trend-trading methodologies fail, I want to now take a look into what I believe are the basic attributes of winning methodologies. As I mentioned, one of my objectives in this chapter is to provide you with a framework within which to develop your own trading methodology. I hope you now have an insight into why traditional trend and retracement tools have failed to help most traders. Let's now take a look at what makes a good strategy.

BASIC ATTRIBUTES OF WINNING METHODOLOGIES

Good strategies will satisfy two simple requirements, they will:

• help traders avoid fatal mistakes and
• address the basic strategy elements of successful trading

Table 9.6 summarizes the fatal mistakes most traders make.

TABLE 9.6   Fatal mistakes most traders make

Overconfident, risk too many $$ per trade
Bad losers don't cut losses
- don't use stops
- don't respect stops
- don't use small stops
- don't adjust stops.
Bad winners are too quick to take profits
- are too focused on one or two markets
- are too trusting
- are too subjective
- use too many variable dependent lagging indicators
- don't validate ideas

A good methodology will ensure traders will be conservative in their trade size, only risking a small proportion of their account on any individual trade. A good methodology will be quick to exit losing trades. It generally will use a relatively small initial stop, which will adjust and trail behind the market as positions move favorably in the trader's direction. Generally, a good methodology will be slow to exit winning trades, allowing the market to tell the methodology when to take profits. Generally good methodologies will not employ profit targets. A good methodology will generally work across a portfolio of markets. A good methodology will generally be objective, allowing anyone to trade it and enjoy the same results. Generally, a good methodology will employ few if any tools that contain subjective variables.

From my experience, these are some of the general characteristics of winning methodologies. And I say generally because there are always exceptions. But that is what they are, exceptions. I do know of successful traders who are quick to take profits. I do know of traders who use methodologies that just work in a couple of markets. I do know traders who use methodologies that use subjective tools. I do know traders who do employ profit targets. However, as I said, they are the exceptions.

Successful methodologies will also address the basic strategy elements of the universal principles of successful trading as shown in figure 9.20.

Winning approaches are not based on random ideas. They have structure, a logical belief how markets work. Retracement trend trading believes markets oscillate as they rotate through mean reversion along their trend movements. Although markets will not trend all the time, when they do, they'll impulse and pause; they'll expand and contract through retracements before expanding again as they continue in their

FIGURE 9.20   Attributes of successful trading

trend direction. Retracement trend trading believes a trader will have plenty of opportunities to catch trend-continuation movements following a retracement pullback.

As another example, Elliott wave believes market trends usually consist of five wave advancements, while retracements generally consist of three wave pullbacks. And you can see plenty of examples of this in many markets.

Winning approaches are generally simple. They're not complex. Simplicity ensures less can go wrong. Simplicity will ensure a winning approach will remain robust. Complex strategies have too many moving parts, too many balls in the air, so logically they have more chance of "dropping a ball," causing the methodology to lose its edge. More can go wrong with complex strategies.

Tom DeMark, a well-respected market analyst and trader who has worked with market wizard Paul Tudor Jones, and currently advises Steve Cohen of SAC Capital, a $16 billion investment fund, made one of the best observations I have ever read or heard. He remarked in the Art Collins' book *Market Beaters*:[6]

> . . . the bottom line was, after 17 programmers and 4 or 5 years of testing, the basic 4 or 5 systems worked best . . .

If there is anything that you can take away from my book, then you can do far worse than copying down this observation by Tom and placing it on your wall above your trading screen in a very prominent position. It's an amazing contribution that Tom has given traders, by sharing an insight into the outcome of a significant research and development project. There are not many traders like Paul Tudor Jones who can afford to employ 17 programmers over a period of four to five years of intensive market and strategy research. Not many traders at all. It's expensive enough in just employing one programmer, let alone 17 and over a four-to-five-year period. Very, very expensive.

And you and I should take note of Tom's observation. After so much time and effort, it was Tom's basic, or simple, four or five systems (strategies) that worked best. If you don't believe me, then please believe Tom, and please don't try to swim against the tide in trying to reinvent the wheel. Simple works.

And as an aside, only last night I was chatting with a friend of mine to organize a pizza catchup between our families, and as usual our conversation touched upon the markets. My friend owns and runs a successful absolute-return funds management business. His funds under management run into the hundreds of millions of dollars. We were remarking on an observation made by another trader friend of ours. And it was a simple observation about markets. And although simple it was also powerful, and we both remarked to each other how simple is one of the best-kept secrets in trading. Simple works.

Winning methodologies are both simple and objective. They don't require subjective interpretation. Ten traders following the same simple methodology should find the identical setups. It's only when a methodology is objective that it can also be measurable, having a simple trade plan applied to determine the methodology's historical expectancy, to measure all the winning and losing trades. Winning approaches will have a positive expectancy, and they will work over multiple markets.

These are key attributes of a winning methodology. They are simple and objective, allowing their expectancy to be measured. And this is what I believe you need: reliable, independent and objective evidence a methodology works! Get that and you'll be one step closer to becoming a successful trader. And I can't stress enough the importance of keeping your methodology simple.

Benefits of Keeping It Simple

Apart from developing a profitable and robust methodology, there are many additional benefits to be gained from embracing simplicity in your strategy.

Enlightenment

Developing and accepting a simple trading approach signifies that you have accepted an important reality about trading. It means you have reached that "zen" state of mind that understands there is no Holy Grail trading solution. It means you no longer feel the need to continue your never-ending search for the next best trading idea. Acceptance of simplicity gives you both enlightenment and peace of mind.

It means you now understand and accept that no one can say for certainty where a market will head in the future, and you now accept there is no benefit in attempting to do so. It means you have realized that all you can control in your trading is the adoption of a sound trading logic and good money management. It means that you now realize that you don't have to know with certainty where a market is heading to make money trading. Embracing simplicity gives you real understanding.

Simplicity of ease

There is nothing complicated with a simple methodology. There are no indicators to interpret, no angles to draw, no waves to count, no cycles to find, and no percentage retracements to calculate. Nothing. Simple is easy.

Objective

Simple makes a methodology objective. Simple means there can be nothing to fudge, to twcak, to fiddle with. Simple means you'll either see your setup or you won't. There is nothing else to interpret.

Robustness

Robustness refers to the longevity of a methodology's real-time profitability. The longer your methodology continues to add dollars to your trading account, the more robust it is. Methodologies that fail to be robust are ones that use subjective variables such as indicators. Simple methodologies usually exclude the use of variables, which helps to keep them robust. It means less can go wrong with your methodology. The less moving parts, the more robust it will be.

Emotional stability

Simple methodologies are emotionally easier to trade compared to subjective discretionary trading. Discretionary trading is much more flexible and much more dependent on the trader for making all the decisions. Whether it is identifying a setup, deciding whether to take a trade, deciding where to place the best stop, or taking profits, all the decisions depend upon the trader. For simple methodologies, traders know whether a setup exists before a market opens. They already know where they'll be entering and placing their stops if they have a trade setup. Their trading is as simple as joining dots. They know where to enter, where to place their stops, and where to take their profits. There is no decision making to do. Not having to make continuous decisions makes simple 100 percent objective trading emotionally easier.

Time management

Trading simple methodologies allows traders to achieve better time management. Because there is very little to do, traders have more free time on their hands. They don't become a slave to the market, continually searching for setups and deciding whether to trade. Simple is quick.

Irony of simplicity

I should also share with you that there is a strong irony in developing simple methodologies. Certainly, in my experience the simpler a strategy is, the more robust it is, and the more robust, the better. The irony is that usually the simpler the methodology, the rougher its equity curve. The rougher the equity curve is, the harder it is to trade!

And this is because a simpler strategy is more likely to be a real strategy. A simpler strategy will not employ variable-dependent indicators that can be used to convenient miss large losing trades or avoid a sustain adverse period of trading. It's very easy with the selection of indicators available to introduce a filter to avoid certain market conditions. It's easy to develop complex indicator-based strategies that produce smooth-looking equity curves.

So there is the irony. Simple is usually accompanied with bumpy equity curves, making trading challenging due to the very real and very normal drawdown periods that occur. So although simple is best, it's usually the hardest to trade!

Now with all my talk on what not to do and why you should embrace 100 percent objective and independent tools to create simple methodologies, I thought it was only fair that I provide you with an example of what I'm talking about, to show you a simple, 100 percent objective and independent trading methodology. A winning strategy.

EXAMPLE OF A WINNING METHODOLOGY—THE TURTLE TRADING STRATEGY

The Turtles are a famous group of traders that Richard Dennis and his partner Bill Eckhardt trained in the 1980s. They came to everyone's attention

Buy Signal	
Entry	Buy at a breakout of the highest high of the last 20 bars.
Initial Stop	Fixed volatility money management stop. Limit risk to 2% of risk capital. Volatility was defined by the 20-day ATR.
Exit	Sell at a breakout of the lowest low of the last 10 bars.
Sell Signal	
Entry	Sell at a breakout of the lowest low of the last 20 bars.
Initial Stop	Fixed volatility money management stop. Limit risk to 2% of risk capital. Volatility was defined by the 20-day ATR.
Exit	Buy at a breakout of the highest high of the last 10 bars.

FIGURE 9.21   The Turtle trading rules

in Jack D. Schwager's book *Market Wizards*.[7] Today, many Turtles continue to successfully manage money, and no doubt are still using a version of the original Turtle trading strategy they learned more than 20 years ago.

Curtis Faith, an ex-Turtle himself, summarized the strategy in his *Way of the Turtle* book.[8] It is an example of a winning methodology for trend trading using breakouts. I have summarized the basic strategy in figure 9.21.

Simple. Now there are few twists to the strategy, which you can read about in Curtis Faith's book, but for the purposes of my discussion here, the basic strategy is fine.

Now, Richard Dennis didn't develop the strategy, Richard Donchian did during the 1960s, and publicly expounded its virtues during the 1970s. It's known as the Donchian 4 Week (20 bar) Breakout Channel strategy.

This is a perfect example of a winning methodology. It has structure and a logical belief about how markets work. It believes trends begin with momentum or a movement in price. In an uptrend, it believes high prices will lead to higher prices. In a downtrend, it believes low prices will lead to lower prices. It's simple. There aren't many simpler strategies than buying the highest high and selling the lowest low. There are no variables in daily prices. No one can really influence the highest high or lowest low of the past 20 trading bars. Its objective, all traders can count to 20 and determine the highest high and lowest low. Now the "20"-day count, or "four"-week rule, is a variable, but it has remained at its "factory" settings since Richard Donchian developed the idea during the 1960s. Although both the "20"- and "10"-day counts can be considered as a variable, because they are, they have remained at their default values for more than 40 years. And the four-week rule could also be seen as a one-month rule without any variables. So in my mind the breakout entry rule is both a fixed and an objective one. However, if a trader did vary the variables' values across a wide range, I would imagine the strategy would remain profitable, since one of the twists I referred to does include a larger channel breakout. Calculating the 20-day ATR is not difficult, nor is it difficult to calculate what 2 percent of a trading account is worth. The strategy's money management stop is effective across a wide range of values for the ATR. For exiting positions, traders can identify either the highest high or lowest low of the past 10 bars. As I said, it's simple and objective, meaning it's also easy to measure for profitability and expectancy.

This strategy is one of the most successful and popular strategies for trading with the trend, and it's been around for more than 40 years, which is a very long time in trading. I love longevity. And I hope it gives you a practical insight into what a winning methodology should look like.

Now the only problem with the Turtle trading strategy, as I discussed in chapter 5, is that you have to trade it with a large account. You will need a large account for two reasons, first, for trading a large portfolio of markets and second, to handle the drawdowns. You will need a large account to be able to trade a large portfolio of markets, between 20 and 30, to make it work because markets rarely trend. And as I showed in chapter 5, although the strategy had a very profitable 2007, it did suffer a $750,000 drawdown during the year— ouch! So you also need a large account to handle the drawdowns that do occur. But as a winning strategy, it's a perfect example for my discussions here.

Well, I've covered a lot of ground on methodology. I've shared with you why I believe retracement trend trading should be easy. I've reminded you why you trade. I've discussed why I believe poor trend and retracement tools have made it hard for so many traders to trade with the trend. You know that I believe ''subjective'' and ''dependent'' are dirty words in trading. I've discussed what I believe are the basic attributes of winning methodologies, and I used the Turtle trading strategy as an example.

Before I come to the end of my discussion on methodology, I'd just like to share further examples with you: one to give you an example of what an objective trend tool should look like and the other to give you an example of why it's dangerous to use subjective retracement tools. I'll start with looking at an objective trend tool.

EXAMPLE OF AN OBJECTIVE TREND TOOL

As you know, I believe any trend tool with a variable, such as the moving average indicator, is too subjective to rely upon. I feel there are better options. An alternative could be to use price itself (much as the Turtle trading strategy does) to help determine a trend's direction.

One example of using price is to look at swing charts. Swing charts help to smooth prices. When using swing charts:

- An uptrend is defined by seeing higher swing lows. When a lower swing low occurs, the uptrend changes to a downtrend.
- A downtrend is defined by seeing lower swing highs. When a higher swing high occurs, the downtrend changes to an uptrend.

I believe using swing charts would be a better measure of trend direction then using a tool with a subjective variable. Swings are based on price. They can be based on daily, weekly, monthly, quarterly, or yearly prices. Being based on price, the swing points are 100 percent objective because no trader or institution can influence either a daily, weekly, monthly, quarterly, or yearly high or low. No one can; the markets are bigger than any individual or institution.

When swing points are created, they are 100 percent objective and 100 percent independent. No discretionary interpretation or judgment is required to interpret the trend. If the swing chart is making higher swing lows, the trend is up. If the swing chart is making lower swing highs, then the trend is down. Simple. Objective. And independent of what a trader thinks.

Depending on your preferred time frame for trend determination, you could use either a weekly (figure 9.22) or monthly (figure 9.23) swing chart to determine your trend direction.

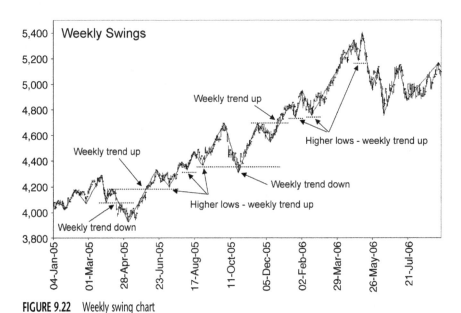

FIGURE 9.22 Weekly swing chart

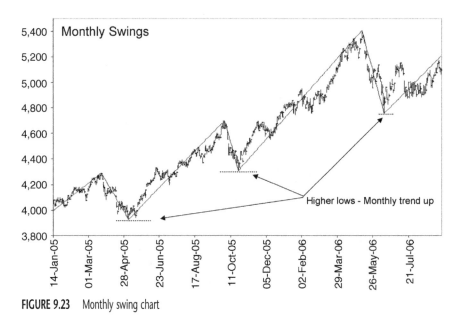

FIGURE 9.23   Monthly swing chart

Figure 9.22 shows a daily chart with a weekly swing overlaid. While weekly swings are making higher lows, the weekly trend is up. When weekly swings make lower swing highs, the weekly trend is down. Alternatively, you could consider using a monthly swing chart to determine the trend.

Figure 9.23 shows a daily chart with a monthly swing overlaid. While monthly swings are making higher lows, the monthly trend is up. While monthly swings are making lower highs, the monthly trend is down. Monthly swings can be used to determine the monthly trend, and, being longer term, can help pick up the big trades.

Using higher time frame swing charts is one example of a 100 percent objective trend tool. With this insight, I hope you can now search for other alternative trend tools that are just as 100 percent objective and independent. I now want to give you an example why it should be your preference not to use subjective retracement tools in your trend-trading methodology.

FIBONACCI: FACT OR FICTION

Percentage retracement ratios are a very popular retracement tool. The most popular, or widely known, are the Fibonacci ratios. Figure 9.24 summarizes all the recognized percentage ratios.

Now as you can see there are quite a few percentage ratios to pick from. Figure 9.25 summarizes the ratios in numerical order.

| Fibonacci ratios |
| 0.236, 0.382, 0.618, 0.786 |
| Harmonic ratios |
| 0.50, 0.707 |
| Arithmetic ratios |
| 0.333, 0.667 |
| W.D. Gann 8ths |
| 0.125, 0.250, 0.375, 0.500 |
| 0.625, 0.7500, 0.875 |

FIGURE 9.24   Popular percentage retracement ratios

Well, straight up, I hope you can see the major weakness with percentage retracements—there's so many of them! And it seems they have every decimal point covered! And they can't all be right, surely? So who's right? The Fibonacci ratios? The arithmetic ratios? The harmonic ratios or the W.D. Gann ratios?

Retracements	
0.875	W.D. Gann
0.786	Fibonacci
0.750	W.D. Gann
0.707	Harmonic
0.667	Arithmetic
0.625	W.D. Gann
0.618	Fibonacci
0.500	Harmonic
0.500	W.D. Gann
0.382	Fibonacci
0.375	W.D. Gann
0.333	Arithmetic
0.250	W.D. Gann
0.236	Fibonacci
0.125	W.D. Gann

FIGURE 9.25   Popular percentage retracement ratios in numerical order

I wish I was a skeptic when I first came to trading. If I was I would have become suspicious straight away by seeing so many ratios and reading how forthright each of the theories were about their own particular ratios. Because, certainly, they could not all be right? And if one set of ratios was correct, wouldn't that make all the other theories wrong? And if that was so—which was the Alpha Ratio, which should I pay attention to? But I wasn't.

I was an Elliott wave disciple for the first 15 years of my trading career. And when you're into Elliott wave, you're also into Fibonacci. But I couldn't seem to find the right ratio to give me either support or resistance. Since my background includes Elliott wave and Fibonacci, I'll concentrate on their ratios.

As figure 9.25 shows, the popular Fibonacci ratios include 38.2 percent, 61.8 percent, and 78.6 percent. Although not a Fibonacci ratio, the 50 percent retracement level is also accepted as important. The question is which ratio a trader would use to determine whether a retracement had found support or resistance. Would a 38.2 percent or a 50 percent retracement mark the end of a retracement? It's a difficult question to answer due to the choice of ratios to use. Unfortunately, choice makes a tool subjective.

However, "choice" is the lesser of the two problems a trader faces with Fibonacci. If a market actually finds support or resistance at a Fibonacci retracement level, a trader would be happy only to have to make a choice regarding which percentage to use. However, despite all the literature and software programs devoted to Fibonacci, it seems, certainly from my research, that the Fibonacci ratios do not have a competitive advantage over the other percentage points in identifying levels of support or resistance.

If you were to believe the Fibonacci enthusiasts, you would not only expect to see evidence of Fibonacci in nature (which you do) but also in the markets. You would expect to see the markets regularly finding support or resistance at the Fibonacci percentage retracement levels.

So I did the work, and undertook some research to determine whether Fibonacci ratios were dominant in the markets, because certainly one is led to believe it is given that so much trading literature is devoted to Fibonacci. It was an easy test to carry out, and I'll repeat it here. Essentially, all I did was to create a swing chart from my data and calculate all the percentage swings on the chart.

As shown in figure 9.26, I recorded all the percentage retracements, and I also included the percentage extensions. If Fibonacci was going to be a reliable tool for identifying support or resistance levels, then I would expect to see the 38.2 percent, 61.8 percent, 78.6 percent, and 161.8 percent ratios dominating my sample of percentage ratios. I should expect to see them being statistically significant compared to all the other ratios. I'd

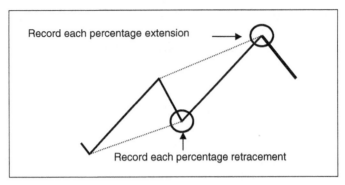

FIGURE 9.26   Measuring both percentage retracement and extension swings

expect them to appear as outliers, an abnormal amount compared to the non-Fibonacci ratios.

To ensure I was able to give Fibonacci every chance to appear in my swing collection, I also decided to create multiple time frame swing charts over multiple markets.

For each market I began with its daily data going back to 1990, as shown in figure 9.27.

From the daily data, I created a daily swing chart, as shown in figure 9.28.

FIGURE 9.27   Daily chart

FIGURE 9.28 Daily swing chart

From the daily data, I created weekly data. From the weekly data, I created a weekly swing chart, as shown in figure 9.29.

From the daily data, I created monthly data. From the monthly data, I created a monthly swing chart as shown in figure 9.30.

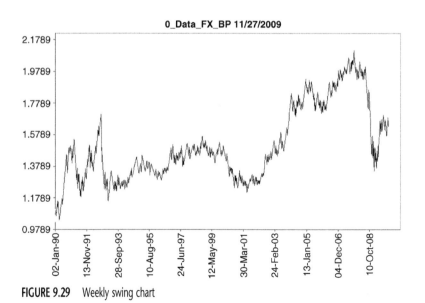

FIGURE 9.29 Weekly swing chart

FIGURE 9.30   Monthly swing chart

From the daily data, I created quarterly data. From the quarterly data I created a quarterly swing chart, as shown in figure 9.31.

And last, from the daily data, I created yearly data. From the yearly data, I created a yearly swing chart, as shown in figure 9.32. I didn't want to be accused of missing out on any significant multiple time frame swings in my investigation.

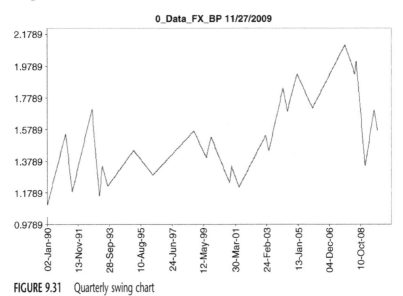

FIGURE 9.31   Quarterly swing chart

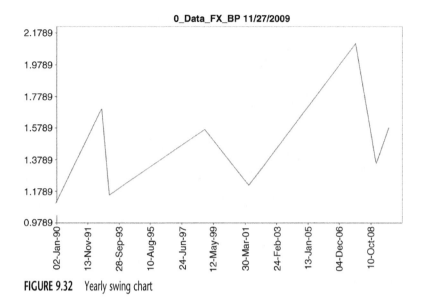

FIGURE 9.32   Yearly swing chart

Now I created all these multiple time frame swing charts over the five main currency pairs:

• euros
• British pounds
• Japanese yen
• Swiss francs
• Australian dollars

and over gold, crude oil, and the main index markets:

• SPI
• Nikkei
• Taiwan
• Hang Seng
• SiMSCI
• KLCI
• Dax
• Stoxx50
• FTSE
• Nasdaq
• SP500.

Eighteen markets all up.

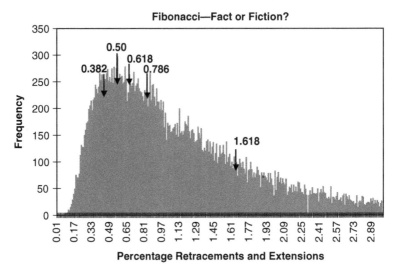

FIGURE 9.33   Histogram of percentage retracements and extensions

Out of these 18 markets and over their multiple time frame swing charts, I measured all the percentage retracement and extension swings. In total I collected and measured 36,411 swings. I then created a histogram of all 36,411 swings (hoping) to see the key Fibonacci points being the dominant percentages, being outliers. Figure 9.33 is what I saw.

Well, what a big disappointment this was to me. As you can see, none of the fabled Fibonacci ratios was a dominant percentage retracement swing or percentage extension swing.

Out of the 36,411 swings, the Fibonacci percentages occurred as shown in table 9.7.

Each of these "magical" Fibonacci ratios occurred less than 1 percent of the time! Less than 1 percent. And the extra significant 1.618 golden mean only appeared 87 times out of 36,411 swings!

And yes, you can say that markets over multiple time frames do retrace and find support and resistance at Fibonacci ratios. There are plenty of

TABLE 9.7   Occurrence of Fibonacci percentages

Fibonacci ratio (%)	Number of occurrences	Percentage of occurrences (%)
38.2	228	0.6
50.0	249	0.7
61.8	248	0.7
78.6	222	0.6
161.8	87	0.2

examples. For the 38.2 percent retracement, there were 228 examples. For the 61.8 percent retracement, there were 248 examples. And for the 78.6 percent retracement, there were 222 examples. Don't worry, there are plenty of occurrences where the market did retrace to a Fibonacci ratio. There are a lot of picture-perfect examples to fill a library of trading books on the significance of Fibonacci in the markets. You will never lack for a chart example to demonstrate the importance of a Fibonacci ratio.

However, you'll never lack for the same number of chart examples showing the importance of the percentage ratios either side of the Fibonacci ratios. As figure 9.32 shows, percentage retracements generally follow a bell curve distribution, suggesting they're normally distributed. There is nothing abnormal or special about the Fibonacci ratios.

All you can say is yes, markets do retrace and extend, but the percentage ratios seem to follow a bell curve distribution. That is, they follow a normal distribution, and there is nothing magical about any individual percentage ratio. Nothing.

Yet there is a whole industry within the trading community that keeps championing Fibonacci as a wonderful and reliable trading tool for identifying support and resistance levels! Unbelievable! Is it any wonder so many traders have failed to trade with the trend successfully, when one of the main tools for identifying retracement levels is essentially worthless?

I wish I had been skeptical when I first came across Fibonacci ratios. It took me almost 15 years before I did the work to verify their nonsignificance!

I hope this little exercise demonstrates how important it is to do the work and to verify or disprove a trading idea independently. Remember, you should welcome all trading ideas, but you should also reserve the right to determine whether an idea has value in your hands. And that will only come from your own work and effort.

And I hope this excursion into Fibonacci ratios demonstrates how it should become your preference not to rely on subjective tools, particularly ones you haven't investigated, in your trend-trading methodology.

PLACEBO TRADERS

Well, I think I have just got myself crossed off every Fibonacci traders' Christmas card list! There won't be any well wishes for me in the future, but oh well, not to worry. Maybe what I'm about to say will soften their feelings toward me.

My investigation certainly demonstrated to me that Fibonacci ratios were no more important than all the other percentage ratios. The facts spoke it loud and clear to me. However, there is a whole legion of Fibonacci fanatics out there who swear by Fibonacci, and when you throw in the Elliott wave traders, you could possibly fill up a whole continent with

Fibonacci Fans, all of them swearing by the ratios. Robert Pretcher of Elliot Wave International has possibly one of the oldest and most successful (by distribution) newsletters in the world. Who am I to say they all don't make money using Fibonacci? Because certainly you would have to imagine that at least some of them do make money trading—even though they use Fibonacci ratios to support their trade setups. So who am I to point the finger and say otherwise?

And this brings me to a very important question. If Fibonacci ratios are not statistically significant, and people swear they trade by them and make money, then are those people merely placebo traders? Are they people who successfully trade but who incorrectly base their success on a tool that has no statistical foundation? Em, interesting, hey?

So even though the ratios are not statistically golden, in the minds of the Fibonacci trader, they represent the truth about market structure, truth that gives them the confidence to engage with the market. They engage and they win. They believe their success comes from Fibonacci ratios, the Fibonacci ratios give them the confidence to trade. They trade and they win. In their mind, their success can be laid at the feet of Leonardo Fibonacci. So is Fibonacci fact, fiction, or faith?

In my mind, it's obviously faith because the statistics don't support it. But am I just arguing semantics here, while the Fibonacci trader believes it to be factual?

I call them the placebo traders: those traders whose technical indoctrination has convinced them that their particular school of technical analysis represents the truth about the markets and trading. Their indoctrination gives them the confidence to engage and trade in the markets. It gives them the faith to dive headfirst into the challenging world of trading.

And the irony here is not so much that they're unaware that Fibonacci or another subjective tool is not statistically significant; it's that they don't acknowledge the contribution of their own skills to their own success! Because the only reason they win is because they are good traders, trading small, being quick to accept losses and being slow to bank profits. The only reason they have a rising account balance is because they are straight-out good traders. Wonderful traders. Marvelous traders. Excellent traders. They may be delusional but still they know how to trade successfully.

And this brings me to another interesting question (and this may just get me back on their Christmas card list)—could I not also dare ask whether all traders aren't simply placebo traders: traders whose faith in their respective trade setups give them the faith and confidence to trade?

I'm increasingly coming to the belief that most people are not rational. Most people like to think they are when circumstances support it. But when circumstances are conspiring against them, some people become irrational, and start to look for arbitrary ways to support their decisions. It's like people having a confirmation bias. When traders are long and wrong, rather than letting themselves be stopped out, they'll move their stop and start searching the internet for information and facts to support and confirm their position. They turn a blind eye and deaf ear to any information that suggests otherwise. They're looking for confirmation that what they're doing is correct. They have a confirmation bias. Maybe all traders are the same. Traders will always have a reason to trade: a trade setup. Is the trade setup no more then a confirmation bias to trade? And if a trader is successful, then is it not because they are a good trader—being quick to take losses and slow to bank profits?

Let me start at the end. But before I continue please let me recap what I have covered. So far (I hope), I have been teaching you my universal principles of successful trading. I have started you at the beginning, from ground zero. I have taken you through five of the six universal principles, commencing with preparation. I followed it with enlightenment, and then trading style, the markets and the three pillars that I'm still in. I have covered money management, and I'm currently now with you here in methodology. Once I finish here, I'll share my thoughts on psychology, and then I'll end with the sixth and final universal principle, which involves trading, the actual doing part, the actual engagement with the market, where you'll get your hands both dirty and bloodied.

I hope to teach you the universal principles that all successful traders stand upon, regardless of the individual markets, time frames, instruments, and techniques they trade. These universal principles manifest themselves as trading profits in the trader's account. The profits come from the trader's individual trade plan. Where to enter, where to place stops, and where to exit. The reason behind their trades: their trade setups can and do vary greatly with other traders. The trade setups are what usually distinguish the difference between traders. However, the result of their trade plan is the same for all successful traders—profits in the account. The outcome is identical; there is no difference here between traders except for the size of profits. The profits are the accumulation of the universal principles of successful trading. That is what ties successful traders together, despite that they can be very different traders, that their trade setups, the reason behind their trading, can and do vary immensely. But the undeniable fact is that their successful trading results in profits. They generally use sensible money management, trading small relative to their account size; they're generally quick to take losses, and they're generally slow to bank profits; they generally trade with a definable edge; they generally execute their trade plans flawlessly. They win more then they lose. These universal principles of successful trading are undeniable. However, the reason behind their trading, their methodologies and trade setups can and do vary greatly. Generally most will trade with an objective and definable edge. And I would imagine that some don't, and yet are still successful. I'd like to spend some time addressing those traders.

My plan has been to start you from the ground up. But let me now start at the end. At time of writing, my account is up 0.5 percent for the month. Now there is only one undeniable fact for this. My total wins for the month to date have been larger than all my losses. My wins and losses, that is, my entries, stops, and exits. I have been trading profitably. That is an undeniable truth. So money in my trading account has only got there from good trading. Now the reason for my trading, my setups, I believe are supported by 100 percent objective and independent tools. That is what I like to think and that is what my models and computer programs tell me. That is what gives me the confidence to trade. My faith. My faith in my 100 percent objective and independent trade setups. My faith to trade. I have a higher account balance this month because my trade setups have given me the faith to engage with the market and my actual trading has created a net profit.

So if I go backward, I look at the new money in my trading account. I know it's only there because I have been quick to take my losses (I pride myself on being a good loser) and I'm slow to bank my profits. I have engaged and executed my trades well. The reason behind my trades has been my trade setups. They have given me the confidence to trade. Now who is to say that my objective trade setups are any better than a Fibonacci trader's subjective trade setups? If we are both profitable traders, who is to say one setup is superior to another? They have both served or achieved their purpose—in giving myself and the Fibonacci trader the confidence and faith to enter the market. Once we both enter the markets it has been our own individual trading—banking more profits than losses—that has made the money. And this is my whole point—both trade setups have achieved their purpose in creating enough confidence to warrant a trade.

Once in the market, the actual trading takes over. It's the actual trading that really counts. And if the Fibonacci trader is banking profits, then who am I to question his or her motive for trading?

I personally prefer to base my confidence to trade on quantifiable and measurable facts, not faith. And I hope you will do the same. I think you will find it easier. So I feel many traders are not as rational as they would like to think they are. And yes, I am referring to the Fibonacci traders and many of their close relatives who also base their trade setups on unquantifiable measurements, preferring unintentionally to use arbitrary ideas to support their trade setups. At the end of the day, all executed trades are a function of:

- a prejudice to either buy or sell: the trade setup
- sensible money management: ensuring the correct position size is used
- the trade plan: the rules for where to enter, place stops, and exit
- willpower: the ability to execute according to the trade plan.

A trader controls all four functions.

I'm going out on a limb here but I'd say, and I may seem to be contradicting myself given my faith in objective and independent tools, that as long as a trader's position size is not risking ruin, as long as the trader executes according to his or her trade plan, that the most important element of all trading is the trade plan, what puts money in the trading account, the entering of positions, the placement of stops and the exiting of profitable trades. The motivation behind the trade is irrelevant as long as they're good traders, being quick to take loses and being slow to bank profits. So who really cares why a trader enters a position? There are so many arguments about what works and what doesn't, and I've been guilty of participating in those. But at the end of the day, if you can be the best loser that you can be, and equally if you can be as good a winner as you are a loser, then who cares how or why you enter the market? So possibly all traders are simply placebo traders, using their individual setups to give them their faith to trade?

As I said, I personally prefer to trade with a well-defined, objective, independent, and measurable edge. However, for those of you who don't, does it really matter as long as you are a good trader? As long as you have executed 30 simulated trades according to the TEST procedure with your trading partner to validate your methodology's expectancy, who cares?

And the important point here are the 30 TEST trades. The TEST procedure will be the final arbitrator of your trading ability—whether you prefer to trade using a predefined and objectively measurable edge, or whether you prefer to trade according to a subjective edge as a placebo trader does, it may just be irrelevant as long as you pass the TEST procedure.

However, if you skip the 30 TEST trades, then you'll need to read everything that has ever been written on trading psychology to help you execute your unproven methodology. You'll need all the mental gymnastic tricks you can find basically to arm twist your conscious mind into ignoring your subconscious nemesis as you execute your unproven trade plan. Trading psychology will become the biggest hurdle for you to overcome as your subconscious mind will do everything in its power to gain domi-nance over your conscience self. It will be a battle royal that will make all the trading coaches both happy and rich.

IN SUMMARY

This brings me to the end of the second part of the Three Pillars, which is the fifth essential universal principle of successful trading. And haven't I had a lot to say? I suppose I should since I believe methodology is the second-most important element of The Three Pillars of practical trading. Methodology defines your edge, and justifies your engagement with the market. Unless you have a real methodology with a real edge, you have no business trading. So I'm glad I have spent so much time sharing my thoughts on methodology with you.

In this chapter, I explained that there were generally three approaches to trading—discretionary, mechanical, and discretionary mechanical. Most new participants commence as discretionary traders, and eventually progress toward a more structured or mechanical approach. Mechanical trading removes much of the emotional turmoil surrounding discretionary trading. Some professional traders will eventually progress to becoming discretionary mechanical traders—using their experience and discretion to choose among their very structured or mechanical trade setups. These professional traders believe they can use their years of experience to beat their mechanical strategies discretionarily.

You learned that you could trade with either a trend-trading methodology or with a countertrend-trading methodology. I explained that a complete methodology is composed of two parts:

• a setup
• a trade plan.

Your setup should only be looking for potential support and resistance levels. The various schools of technical analysis can be grouped into the predictors, the dreamers, and the pragmatists.

Trade plans should have clear rules on where to enter, where to place a stop, and where to exit a profitable trade. You learned to ignore the belief of many who say entries do not matter, because they directly affect your expectancy and position sizing. They matter. You were also encouraged to ignore the fatal attraction of large stops. They kill.

An effective trade plan should support and confirm a setup before entering a trade, and a methodology is only as good as its validation through the TEST procedure.

I explained that you need to join your preferred money management strategy with your validated methodology to calculate an estimate for your risk of ruin. You were reminded of your objective in trading—to survive financial ruin and not to trade with a risk of ruin above 0 percent.

I discussed trend trading as a sensible and preferred methodology for trading. You learned that markets trend, and that trends were the basis of all profits. You learned that life as a trend trader was miserable due to its high 67 percent loss rate. You learned that one could trade trends on either a breakout or retracement basis. You learned that retracement trend trading allowed traders to enter positions with lower risk but at the cost of sometimes missing out on a big trend. You learned breakout trend trading never missed a big trend, although it did come with a cost of usually larger stops and larger drawdowns.

I discuss the practical implications of using retracement trend trading as your methodology. You learned why retracement trend trading should be simple, and I reminded you about why you trade. You learned that retracement trend trading should not be any more difficult than simply following a step-by-step process.

You learned why I believed so many traders fail to trade with the trend even when most traders know it's the safest way to trade. You learned that the popular trend and retracement tools were ineffective due to their subjective variables and interpretation. You learned that tools with variables were too dependent on a trader, making them too flexible, too unstable, and too unreliable to base trades on. You learned that the key issues for a trader were to use tools that were both objective and independent. You learned that good trend and retracement tools either worked or they didn't. You learned that a good trading methodology had to become a trader-free zone, in which the trader could have no influence over the trend and retracement interpretation.

I discussed that not all indicators were bad. You learned that there were successful methodologies that used indicators. You learned that the most successful one only used a single indicator with a single variable that worked across a wide range of variables.

I discussed the basic attributes of successful methodologies, and you learned that the Turtle trading strategy was a good example. You learned there were many benefits to keeping a methodology simple. You learned that higher-time-frame swing charts were a good example of an objective trend tool. I shared my Fibonacci research with you to demonstrate why it's important for you to investigate subjective retracement tools independently before using them in your methodology.

I then questioned whether all traders were merely placebo traders, using the strength of their faith in their individual trade setups to engage and trade with the market. Regardless whether their setups were based upon rational objectivity or irrational subjectivity, it was a trader's faith in his or her setup that mattered. It was that faith that allowed him or her to engage in the market and have an opportunity to execute his or her good trading skills—being quick to take losses and being slow to bank profits. Traders are primarily successful because they trade well. You learned that my preference is to base my faith on fact rather then invention.

The normal progression for most people is to commence trading with a discretionary methodology. For those who persist, the majority will eventually migrate toward creating a mechanical methodology. Those who continue trading will eventually master mechanical trading and gain a competency in extracting profits from the markets. The really good traders will then shift toward becoming discretionary mechanical traders—using their years of experience (or the *art of trading* as Larry Williams calls it), to trade their very structured or mechanical setups selectively. The very elite learn how to beat their own very structured methodologies. As I said, this is the normal progression, not the absolute as there are successful traders who were always, and have remained always, discretionary traders. My advice to traders starting out is to focus first of developing a mechanical methodology. To my mind, it's the easiest trading mountain to climb.

In the next chapter, I'll conclude the Three Pillars with a discussion on psychology.

NOTES

1. Elder, Alexander, *Trading for a Living* (John Wiley, 1993).
2. Williams, Larry, *The Right Stock at the Right Time* (John Wiley, 2003).
3. Collins, Art, *Market Beaters* (Traders Press, Inc., 2004).
4. Faith, Curtis, *Way of the Turtle* (McGraw Hill, 2007).
5. Collins, Art, op. cit.
6. Ibid.
7. Schwager, Jack, *Market Wizards Wizards* (New York Institute of Finance, 1989).
8. Faith, Curtis, op. cit.

Psychology

By the end of this chapter, I will have completed my examination of the Three Pillars, the three key elements of practical trading:

- money management
- methodology
- psychology.

This will complete the fifth universal principle of successful trading. Although I rank psychology third, behind money management and methodology, it doesn't make it a poor third cousin.

Psychology is important, just not more so than being aware that every trader, including you, has a personal statistical chance of ruining their account. Psychology is important, just not more so than having the knowledge, heart, and effort to sensibly research and develop a simple and 100 percent objective and independent trading methodology. Psychology is important, just not more so than having the knowledge, heart, and effort to validate a methodology's expectancy correctly with the TEST procedure.

Psychology is important, just not more so than having the knowledge, heart, and effort to combine a methodology with sensible money management to reduce a trader's risk of ruin to 0 percent; not more so by a long shot; not more so by any sense of the imagination, in my opinion. In addition, psychology is irrelevant until you "go live" and commit real money to the markets. When you do begin trading, psychology will have a positive enabling influence.

Psychology is primarily about managing your three main emotions: hope, greed, and fear. Psychology is the glue that holds money management and methodology together. Some may point out that I've contradicted myself with this comment. However, I would argue that without money management and methodology there wouldn't be anything for psychology to glue!

Psychology is important for your survival and eventual success. However, it's all a matter of degree. If you get money management and methodology right in the first place, they'll go a long way to making both your conscious and subconscious selves feel comfortable about trading. They will start hugging. Using the TEST procedure to validate your methodology's expectancy will provide your subconscious mind with the opportunity to complete your test drive successfully, giving it more confidence. Get money management and methodology right and you will commence trading with a 0 percent risk of ruin. Do this and your subconscious mind will be a happy camper. It will be giving your conscious mind "high fives." If not, it'll do everything in its power to stop you trading. It will achieve this by increasing your anxiety and stress levels.

A good point to remember is that if you're ever feeling stressed about your trading you should stop. Listen to your subconscious mind: it's trying to tell you something that probably everyone around you knows—that you're clueless about what actually works in trading and in all probability, you're out of control!

Before I start, I just want to discuss what I feel is the consensus view about the importance of psychology in trading. And before I do, I need to confess that I'm not a psychologist. I have no formal training in it, and I have never read a book on trading psychology. I'm just giving you my opinion on this hotly discussed topic. It will be your decision whether you'll listen to me. But here I go.

THE CONSENSUS VIEW

The general belief is that you need to understand the limitations created by your subconscious mind, and you need to understand how to access your subconscious mind to unlock your potential. That is, it's all in the mind. Now I know I'll get thrown out of the educators' club for saying what I'm about to share with you because I think my thoughts on psychology have a membership of one—me!

Buy hey, aren't there always two sides to a story, and doesn't every trade in the market contain two opposite opinions, one buying and one selling? Well, I'm not buying the consensus view on psychology.

My take on it is that psychology is only important once you commence trading. I don't believe your trading success relies on understanding the limitations created by your subconscious mind. And I don't believe your success relies on you learning how to access your subconscious mind to unlock your potential. If I wasn't writing a book for public distribution, I'd probably use an expletive here. I think this talk of "limitations" and "unlocking" your potential is all silliness.

In my opinion, psychology seems to become a barrier to success when the subconscious mind is not satisfied that the trader knows what he or she is doing on the conscious level. That's it.

Most traders are clueless—despite all the courses, seminars, and workshops they've attended, despite all the books they've read, and despite all the charting programs installed on their PCs, they're still 100 percent ignorant, and their subconscious mind knows this. And this is why it will do everything in its power to stop traders entering the market. Increasing their heart rate, giving them sweaty palms, causing them heart palpitations, making them anxious. Making them stray from their trade plans.

Yet many who believe psychology should be used to beat up the subconscious mind will tell you to believe in your trade plan, stay the course, execute your trade plan—when it's plain to the subconscious mind that the trader does not have a competency in trading.

I believe that if traders adopt a sensible money management strategy and combined it with a simple and robust trading methodology that they will commence trading with a 0 percent risk of ruin. If they can achieve that, then their subconscious mind will be aware of their competency, and will remain happily in the background.

As you have learned, money management and a positive expectancy strategy are the two key weapons against risk of ruin. If a trader does the work to learn about how to reduce his or her own risk of ruin to 0 percent, and does it correctly with a simple, objective, and independent methodology, his or her subconscious mind will see him or her doing the work. It will see the person learning that trading is simply a numbers game, and it will see the person placing the odds in his or her favor. It will be more relaxed when the person starts trading. It will enable the trader to follow his or her trade plan since it knows the person has a trading edge, and is trading with a 0 percent risk of ruin. It will want the trader to make the money; it's not stupid.

So rather than tying up the subconscious mind in some sort of psychological straitjacket, I believe the trader should listen to it! And I believe if the trader can successfully get his or her risk of ruin down to 0 percent, then the subconscious mind will not place obstacles in the trader's path.

Once a trader achieves a 0 percent risk of ruin and completes the TEST procedure, everyone will be far more relaxed. The subconscious mind will enable the conscious mind to follow the trade plan. So in my opinion, I believe money management ranks above methodology, and it in turns ranks above psychology. However, once the person starts trading, psychology will be important, because it will be the glue that holds money management and methodology together. That glue is important, and it's important for a trader to be able to hold the eye of the tiger, so to speak. Anyway, that's my short take on psychology.

And before I continue, I just have one simple observation. I'd imagine that if psychology is regarded as the biggest obstacle to success, then you'd think that the people managing billions of dollars trading global markets would have to be close to suicidal due to the large amounts of money they're trading. Right? If your "head" is where it's all at—and you would have to believe it is if you believed those who think psychology is the highest mountain to climb in trading—then those large money manager traders would have to be on suicide watch—or close to being committed to an institution where everyone and including their family would forget they're there? Right? Yet those managers are normal people.

I personally know some of Australia's largest traders—trading more than a billion dollars between them. And guess what—if you passed them in the street, you wouldn't know they were trading that amount money day in, day out, night in, night out, five and half days a week across global financial markets. If you saw them walking down the street, you could easily mistake them for normal suburban professionals, not world-class super traders. You would see them for who they are, successful easy-going individuals. They're not strung out. They're not nutcases. They're not struggling to follow their trade plans. They're not locked into an arm wrestle with their subconscious minds. They're not lying down on some trading coach's lounge. They're relaxed, they're content, and they're rich, very rich. I rest my case.

Anyway, that's my thumbnail view on psychology. Let me now drill down a bit further, but not much further. As I mentioned psychology is primarily about managing your three main emotions: hope, greed, and fear.

MANAGING HOPE

Hope manifests itself when you find yourself hoping a trade will not be a loser, hoping your trade will be a winner. Hope is the lesser evil of the three psychology hurdles. I can safely say that when you find yourself hoping a trade will come good, you're almost certainly guaranteed to lose. Hope is the last feeling you have before being stopped out of a trade, and is usually magnified when the market is a few ticks away from your stop! You're hoping to earn a winner because you're sick and tired of losing. You're hoping you don't lose again, because if you do, it'll hurt the account.

Hope stems from two areas—not applying correct money management and not knowing your expectancy. Trading in the dark. The solution is to stop trading and to get your risk of ruin down to 0 percent. Using proper money management will reduce your trade size, and in turn will reduce your concerns about hurting your account. If you find you're too concerned about a trade's outcome, it's usually because you're risking too much money given your methodology's expectancy, worst drawdown, and account size. You're overtrading your account. Developing a simple, objective, and independent methodology will give you a strategy with a positive expectancy edge. Combining sensible money management with a positive-expectancy methodology will deliver you a 0 percent risk of ruin. Validating your methodology using the TEST procedure will confirm your methodology's edge. You will no longer be trading in the dark but trading with knowledge. Your subconscious mind will see you doing the work and enable your trading. You will no longer be hoping your next trade is a winner. You'll start hoping your methodology starts finding additional setups to give you more opportunities to earn expectancy. You will start focusing on the process.

Validating your expectancy with TEST will give you the confidence that you actually know what you're doing and what you should expect to earn over the longer term for every dollar you risk with your methodology. You'll stop hoping and start expecting.

MANAGING GREED

Greed manifests itself when you start wanting more. It will push your insecurity button. You'll start thinking you're missing out because you believe others are doing much better than you. You'll start wanting more money, and you'll believe more trading will give it to you. Wanting more will lead to impulse trading, which inevitably leads to a cycle of pushing marginal trades, mounting losses, and revenge trading. This cycle will continue to repeat itself at increasing frequency until you either come to your senses or your account is ruined.

Greed occurs when you're not satisfied with what you have. Greed becomes an issue when you're emotionally disoriented. Emotional disorientation results from flawed objectives and expectations. Most traders, when they begin, have an objective to achieve 100 percent accuracy. You should stop worrying about being right or wrong. They also expect to earn a 50 percent plus or 100 percent plus return on their account.

In chapter 3, I discussed the importance of achieving emotional orientation. If you can set yourself professional objectives with modest expectations, you'll go a long way to managing your greed. Accept the fact that no one can achieve on a statistically consistent basis unrealistic returns year in, year out. No one. There is no evidence that anyone can. Be content with what you have. Create modest expectations. Establish a modest return target for your risk capital, whether it be a 20 percent, 30 percent, or 40 percent return. Remember, the higher your expectations, the higher risk you'll face and the higher your probability of being ruined!

Be clear about your preferred risk capital return. You should visualize yourself at the end of a trading year looking back over the previous 12 months of trading. Visualize how good you feel about having achieved your modest return targets. Don't forget that feeling. You should be happy to stick with your modest return expectations.

MANAGING FEAR

After achieving emotional orientation to manage your greed, you'll need to learn how to manage your fear of losing, your fear of failure. Fear comes from the unknown, fear of not being in control due to the uncertainty of the future.

It's important to manage your fear because if you don't, you may not execute your trade plan correctly—failing to execute trades, moving stops, and exiting too early. You need to develop a proper mindset to keep trading your methodology regardless of your fear.

The only way you can overcome your fear of losing is to confront it. Confront your fear and take control. Remove the uncertainty of the future by creating certainty through negative expectations. Expect the worst. If you can do this, you'll never have to consider whether or not to follow one of your methodology's signals. You'll trade all the setups, inevitably lose, but benefit over the longer term from your methodology's positive expectancy. It's important to remember that although trading is relatively simple to do, it's not easy.

Fear is a personal thing—there is no "one size fits all" solution. I'll share with you how I manage my own fear, and hopefully there will be something you can gain from it.

I'm a full-time futures trader. While I've been writing this book, I've continued to trade. I trade nine global index markets and the five main currency pairs 24 hours a day, five-and-a-half days a week. A day rarely goes by without me having a trade in some market, in some part of the world, somewhere. It could be the index futures, whether it's the SPI, Nikkei, Taiwan, Hang Seng, DAX, Stoxx50, FTSE, Mini Nasdaq, or E-Mini S&P500. Right now, at time of writing, I have two orders for the Mini-Nasdaq and E-Mini SP500 for a couple of short-term countertrend trades. I'm currently long the FTSE in a medium-term trend trade that I have been holding now for two weeks. My broker is working my trailing stop. I could have had a setup in one of the five main currency pairs I trade: either the euro, British pound, Japanese yen, Swiss franc, or Australian dollar futures. But I don't today. On average, I usually execute two trades a day, and have to deal constantly with my own fear of losing. What I'm about to share with you helps me manage my fear.

Although my methodologies provide me with a long-term positive expectancy, I trade day to day with a negative short-term and negative intermediate-term expectation—I'm a pessimist when I trade.

Negative Short-term Expectation

What I mean by a negative short-term expectation is that whenever I trade, I always expect to lose. I always assume that I'm wrong, and will, without doubt, be stopped out. Consequently, when I have a setup to trade I always debit my profit and loss spreadsheet with my expected loss before the markets open. By debiting my profit and loss spreadsheet before I actually trade, I acknowledge my expected loss and I remove all emotion associated with the trade!

I find myself trading without fear! It may sound strange, but by expecting to lose every time I trade, I'm acknowledging my fear of losing. By acknowledging my fear, I conquer it, and I can trade every setup I get. By expecting to lose, I remove the uncertainty about the future. I expect to lose. I know the future. I have no fear. I find that if I expect to lose, my losses will affect me less when they occur. In addition, it helps me to become the best loser I can be, which I know makes me a long-term winner!

I encourage you to learn to welcome your losses. To expect them. By doing so, you'll remove the uncertainty about the future, allowing you to trade all your setups without fear or favor, and you'll not only reduce the sting of a loss, but you'll also become a good loser and a long-term winner!

Negative Intermediate-term Expectation

My negative expectations do not start and end with each individual trade. I expect to lose on the day a setup appears, and I also believe that I'm about to start my longest losing sequence of trades. If my previous trade was a loss, I believe that I'm in the process of trading through my worst drawdown.

I believe that my longest losing sequence and biggest continuous loss are just waiting for me around the corner. I never forget what the market's maximum adversity is capable of. I have to think this way to prepare myself for the unexpected, which means I'm continually thinking "defense, defense, defense." By confronting your fear of losing, you will overcome it!

Creating certainty through negative short-term and negative intermediate-term expectations will remove the uncertainty of the future. Create certainty, and you will remove your fear associated with trading, and you will follow your trade plan without deviation. You will become a successful trader who will not hesitate to follow his or her trade plan.

MANAGING PAIN

I want to now add my own contribution to the world of trading psychology. What amazes me is that despite the many vocal advocates for psychology being the greatest obstacle to trading success, you rarely hear any mention of the word "pain" when "hope," "fear," and "greed" are mentioned. Well, I want to correct that.

And there is nice symmetry here with me finishing the third pillar of practical trading with an all-important practical discussion on "pain." I believe that if you are unable to handle the "pain" of trading, then everything I have written on the universal principles of successful trading is irrelevant.

Although trading is relatively simple to do, it's hard, harder, and harder still to execute successfully. And it's hard, once you start practical trading, because of the pain involved that so many trading books, DVDs, seminars and workshops fail to mention.

Please let me introduce you to my painful world of active trading. You now know that the life of a trend trader is one of misery. You know that markets rarely trend, so that trend traders will usually lose on 67 percent of their trades. Trading with the trend is miserable, and so is the life of a trend trader. However, misery is not restricted to the trend trader.

The world of trading is a world of pain, and you can thank the market's maximum adversity for it. Maximum adversity will rarely allow a trader to make easy money. So here you are, and you want to trade. If you have accepted and are prepared to embrace most if not everything I have written so far, then you will be well positioned to succeed as a trader. However, there will still be one final and enormous obstacle that you will need to accommodate—the acceptance of constant pain.

So do you think you'll be able to manage the constant pain trading will immerse you in? Do you think you'll be able to handle the pain, because most can't? You see, trading well is about everything that I have mentioned so far, however for you to continue to trade well over the long term, you will also need to learn how to manage the constant pain continuous successful trading produces. Believe me, success does hurt. It's painful.

Your pain management will occur in your mind. So you'll need to push aside hope, fear, and greed in your subconscious mind to make room for "pain."

I believe that when people discuss the psychology of trading that they should not only mention the importance of managing your three main emotions of hope, greed, and fear, but they should also mention the importance of managing your psychological pain.

Now despite my best efforts in sharing with you my universal principles of successful trading, I know that for most of you, even if you agree with much that I have written, will simply ignore much of what I have offered and jump straight into trading, following your own lead, your own intuition, doing what you want to do. It's just human nature. I just hope that you remember what you have read in this book and return to it in say 12 months or whenever you feel you're really ready to not only read, but listen, absorb, comprehend, and enact what I have written. But in the beginning, you'll jump in feet first, boots and all.

From my experience, it seems to me that most people need to suffer first hand the failures of trading before they are truly ready to learn. Until they endure disappointment, they will continue to believe the marketing hype that suggests trading should be easy. Certainly trading is simple when you get down to the mechanics and execution, but it's not easy. It's hard, hard, and harder still. It's 100 percent boot camp. It's 100 percent disappointment. It's 100 percent hurt. It's 100 percent pain on so many levels.

Trading is a world of pain. When you lose money, it will hurt. When you lose money for a number of months, it will hurt. When you make money, you'll think about how much more money you could have made if you had stayed in the trade a little bit longer, just as you had thought to. When you think about the imaginary money you have left on the table, it will hurt. When you spend considerable time and energy studying a plausible theory on trading and it doesn't make you money, it will hurt. When you spend considerable money on what you think are reputable workshops, and you lose money implementing the ideas learned, it will hurt. When you spend considerable time and energy researching, developing, programming, and testing an idea, and it comes up with a negative expectancy, it will hurt.

When you and your trading partner spend considerable time and energy validating your methodology's expectancy through the TEST procedure, and it fails, it will hurt.

When you spend considerable time and energy over many years working to improve on the edge you have, and fail to improve on it, despite all the time and energy you spend, it will disappoint you and it will hurt. When you're trading with the trend and losing on 67 percent of your trades, it will hurt. When you're trading and in drawdown, which you are for most of the time, even with a higher accuracy methodology, it will hurt. And when you're out of the market looking and waiting for that next trade, the anxiety you feel about not being in the market and potentially missing out on the next big move will hurt. As I said, trading is a world of hurt and pain.

Successful traders know this from experience, and they know how to manage the pain. They know how to numb it. It'll never go away, but through experience you'll learn how to dull its incessant hum. You will need to learn how to numb the pain yourself to stay the course. The constant pain will challenge your commitment to your trade plan, your methodology. You will need to accept that you can experience a long streak of consecutive losing trades. You will need to learn how to deal with that particular pain. You will constantly be trading through drawdowns, some minor and some uncomfortably large. You will need to learn how to deal with that very particular blowtorch pain.

But inexperienced traders aren't prepared for the pain, and they believe trading and making money should be easy. They move and migrate along those lines of least resistance that suggest trading is easily achievable. If they see any suggestion of pain, they shy away, not realizing that it's the conquering of the pain that leads to continuing successful trading.

You will need to learn how to deal with your own personal pain, and no, the answer won't rely on acetaminophen. Each trader's approach will be different, depending on their own circumstances, but I'll share with you how I deal with my own pain, and hopefully you'll be able to take something away from it.

I conqueror my pain by being a systematic or mechanical trader. I conquer my pain by trading small: I don't risk a large percentage of my account on any one trade. I use sensible money management. I trade so small that the outcome of any individual trade has no interest to me. No individual outcome can affect my overall annual performance. I trade small so that when I lose it's only a nuisance; it only represents a small amount of pain. I trade simple, objective, and independent strategies that I know have a very good chance of continuing to remain robust into the future. Although it's painful to trade a rough and bumpy nonoptimized equity curve, I know I'm trading truthful market structure, structure I put to my advantage. I know that by combining my conservative money management strategy with my positive-expectancy methodologies that I'm trading with a 0 percent risk of ruin. I know my longevity in trading, although painful, will continue and remain rewarding; rewarding enough to accept the constant pain that trading presents.

Before I place my orders each day, I debit my profit and loss spreadsheet. I expect to lose, and I welcome my losses. I place all my trades with a traditional client adviser, whose brokerage firm operates a 24-hour dealing desk. As soon as I have sent all my orders in and received a confirming email, I can ignore the market for the rest of the day. I attempt to keep myself busy during the day so my mind does not drift to the market. I don't watch the market during the day. I do not leave charts up on my screens. I do not watch the market tick by tick. Ignoring the market helps me to ignore the trades I expect to lose on. Keeping myself busy distracts my mind from trading. If I can distract my mind from trading, I lessen the pain of trading. Writing a book like this is wonderful because it shuts out the market's individual tick-by-tick movements. It distracts my mind from the market. It allows me to trade almost pain free!

Being mechanical helps me to remove my emotions from trading. It allows me to treat trading like a business. It allows me to numb the pain when I lose money. It allows me to numb the pain when I see imaginary money left on the table. It allows me to numb the pain when the efforts of exhaustive research, programming, and testing result in another dead end.

And like any business that is well run, it will be profitable. It may not be a laugh a minute. It may feel like more disappointment than triumph, but at least it will be profitable, and it will reward the trader who is serious about the business of trading. And it is a business, one that needs much more work on it than it does when simply executing your trades day to day.

This is what I personally do to numb my pain. I hope it can help you to numb yours once you commence trading. And as I've said, despite my best efforts in sharing with you my universal principles of successful trading, I would not be surprised if most of you jump straight into trading, boots and all, without giving too much consideration to what I have said. It's just human nature, and you will be doing what most traders who have entered the market before you, including myself, have done in the past.

If only someone knew how to put a wise head on young shoulders—wouldn't history have been far different and wouldn't trading be an easier path to walk! So if you're starting out, I'd suggest that you prepare yourself for immediate pain. Although my thoughts on managing pain are designed for those traders who have embraced my universal principles and who are about to commence trading with 0 percent risk of ruin, I know from experience that many of you will, as I say, jump straight in feet first.

So if that's you, you'll need to erect your pain barrier immediately, not down the track when you have successfully ticked off all the necessary tasks required to implement the universal principles of successful trading. It will be defenses up immediately, and you'll experience an onslaught like you have never experienced before as the market's maximum adversity throws everything at you bar the kitchen sink. Tighten up that chinstrap and dig in. I wish you every success.

Now if you find that you are one of the impatient traders who find themselves in their foxhole under a bombardment of pain—just take a deep breath and accept that what you have done is normal. Most traders have been there, done that, including myself. Just accept it as part of the normal learning curve. And if you're impatient, please do not open a large trading account. Keep it relatively modest.

I know my universal principles of successful trading, particularly my thoughts on methodologies, are relatively simple. You should understand that it is usually only through experience and pain that a trader can come to the realization that the simple ideas work. It is only through experience and pain that a trader can appreciate and value simplicity. A beginner trader, such as yourself, through your ignorance, will not appreciate it. You're unable to comprehend that such simple ideas can work. Unfortunately most new to trading incorrectly believe that the answer to successful and profitable trading can only lie in complexity. They are naturally attracted to trading ideas that are cerebrally challenging and (more importantly to them) interesting.

I say this because despite your own honest intentions of wanting to listen and learn, you will, just like the child who can only learn by putting its finger into a candle's flame after being told not to by a parent, need to experience your own trading failure and pain first hand before you are ready really to learn. You will need to travel the well-trodden road of trading failures. It's usually only after you have traveled that road that is familiar to experienced traders that you will then be open to learning about what actually works in trading. Until you have explored and suffered first hand from the failures of traditional technical analysis, you will not be immune to its false promises. You will remain vulnerable to its lure of easy success just like the sailors in Greek mythology who are lured to their death by the Sirens' enchanting music.

It's unfortunate but there is every real chance that you will need to experience failure first hand before you can succeed. Failure will include pain. Until you can experience first hand what doesn't work, you will not be immune to empty promises that abound in trading. It's only through experience that you realize that most of what is written about trading is pure fantasy. So until you have gained enough experience in trading, you will remain susceptible to false theories on how markets work. You will remain vulnerable to being sidetracked and seduced by esoteric ideas and glittering trading screens. It's unfortunate, but there is every real chance that you will need to experience failure first hand to become immune to the many false promises that litter the trading landscape.

Once you have experienced the pain of failure, then you may be ready to embrace the universal principles of successful trading. When you are, remember this book, and put aside the time to revisit these pages and really start to listen.

Well, I hope I haven't been a total killjoy here. There is hope for everyone; it's just that the path may not be a walk in the park for most. Now, although successful trading is hard work and is accompanied by constant pain, please remember that it is also rewarding because at the end of the day you will make money. And that's not such a bad reward for all your "painful" effort.

In addition, please always keep the market's number one rule in the back of your head at all times.

MAXIMUM ADVERSITY

Maximum adversity will ensure that: "The market will do what it has to do to disappoint most traders." And you should never forget this. Maximum adversity will administer pain. Always remember maximum adversity exists. If you can remain humble, remain aware of maximum adversity and remain defensive you'll be in a good position to persevere through the pain.

If you don't remain humble, and if you don't respect what the market can do, you'll experience a very short trading career. I think Curtis Faith said it best in his book *Way of the Turtle*:[1]

> If you want to be a great trader, you must conquer your ego and develop humility. Humility allows you to accept the future as something that is unknowable. Humility will keep you from trying to make predictions. Humility will keep you from taking it personally when a trade goes against you and you exit with a loss. Humility will let you embrace trading that is based on simple concepts because you won't have a need to know secrets so that you can feel special.

And humility will allow you to accept maximum adversity exists to deliver you plenty of pain freely and willingly in its pursuit to derail you from your chosen path of becoming a successful trader.

IN SUMMARY

Psychology is the final part in the Three Pillars of practical trading, and it completes the fifth essential universal principle of successful trading. Psychology is an essential ingredient for survival and success in trading.

You have learned that I'm at odds with the majority view on psychology. You have learned that I believe money management and methodology rank above psychology. However, you also know that I believe it's very important in providing the glue that will hold your money management and methodology together. It just is not more important than money management and methodology. I have explained that I believe trading psychology is all about managing a trader's hope, greed, fear, and pain.

The correct application of money management and the correct design, development, and validation of your methodology will go a long way to easing the psychological hurdles hope presents. Developing a modest expectation will manage your greed, and if you confront your losses head-on by debiting your profit and loss spreadsheet before the markets open, you'll go a long way to managing your fear of losing.

You have learned that trading is a world full of pain, even for the elite traders who win. There is no escaping pain. I have explained how I personally manage to dull my own trading pain. You have learned that if can accept that maximum adversity exists, then you'll be well positioned and prepared to manage the pain as best you can.

To help manage these psychological hurdles, I keep the affirmations in box 10.1 above my computer screen. You may like to do the same.

This brings me to the end of trading's nuts and bolts of practical trading, the Three Pillars. The Three Pillars have shown you the operational process of trading—money management, methodology, and psychology.

In the next chapter, I'll discuss the final universal principle of successful trading—commencement of trading—where all the universal principles of successful trading I have examined come together.

Box 10.1: Affirmations

MANAGING GREED

My objective in trading is not to be right or wrong but to manage my risk capital with a modest expectation.

MANAGING FEAR

If I trade today, I'll expect to lose, and I'll expect to experience my longest losing sequence and my worst drawdown. Before I place my order, I will debit my profit and loss spreadsheet with my expected loss. I'll welcome my loss because I want to be the best loser and a long-term winner.

MANAGING HOPE

Even when I lose money today, I'll expect to have a good day, since I have followed my trade plan, which has a long-term positive expectancy.

MANAGING PAIN

As a trader I know my life will be a world of pain. When I lose, it will hurt. When I win, I'll think about the missed opportunities, and it will hurt. When I'm not in the market, I'll believe I'm missing out on the next big move, and it will hurt. When I investigate new ideas only to discover they don't work, it will hurt. I know that maximum adversity exists to fill my trading experience with disappointment and pain. I know its intentions will be to diminish my risk capital and stop me from trading. I know maximum adversity exists, and I know its potential. I will endure its pain. I will persevere. I will succeed.

NOTE

1. Faith, Curtis, *Way of the Turtle* (McGraw Hill, 2007).

CHAPTER 11

Principle Six: Trading

The sixth and final universal principle—trading, merely represents an accumulation of the previous five universal principles of successful trading.

First of all, congratulations for sticking with me and getting this far. I know what I have been sharing with you isn't particularly exciting, and no doubt reminds you more of school than the exciting world of trading. So well done on staying the course. And you will be happy to know that you're very close to the end!

Well, here you are now at the pointy end—the actual fun stuff, or perceived fun stuff, trading. When you do begin trading, you'll find it relatively straightforward and effortless. However, after the novelty has worn off, you'll probably start to find it a repetitive, boring, and painful existence. When this happens, don't be despondent, but be satisfied. You have arrived at the correct destination. You're now treating trading as a business and executing it like a job, professionally. You're no longer trading for the thrill and excitement. You're trading to make money. You're treating trading like a business, and like all jobs, there will be times (and plenty of them) that you won't like what you're doing. When you do begin to resent trading, you should feel thrilled—because you have now become indifferent to the outcome of any individual trade. It's a sign you've finally learned how to apply proper money management. You've become focused on the process of running a successful trading business, rather than the results themselves. You've now become a professional trader.

PUTTING IT ALL TOGETHER

When you commence trading, your daily routine should resemble the following sequence.

Methodology

Your first step is to identify whether a setup exists. If it does, you will determine your trade plan's entry level, stop level, and exit instructions. From your estimated entry and stop levels, you will calculate the amount of money you'll be risking on a per contract or position sizing basis.

Money management

The first survival task is to determine whether you're still within your financial boundary's risk capital limit. If your cumulative trading losses have exceeded your risk capital limit, it's time to hang up your trading boots and walk away. If not, you can continue.

The second survival task is to look at your system stop and see whether your methodology's equity momentum is positive. Remember, you need to lay your system stop over your methodology's hypothetical single-contract equity curve.

Your equity curve should consist of three parts:

• the hypothetical trade history
• 30 emailed simulated trades (TEST) collected during your validation
• live hypothetical results.

If your methodology's single-contract equity curve is above your system stop, you'll be placing an order to trade. If the single-contract equity curve is below your system stop, you won't trade. Instead, you'll continue to update your equity curve, waiting for it to move back above the system stop before you recommence trading.

If you're going to trade, your third survival task is to calculate the number of contracts, or position size, you can trade given your money management strategy and your account size. Once you have worked out your position, or trade size, you'll need to welcome your loss!

Psychology

If you're placing a trade, you should expect to lose money. As you know, the only real secret in trading is that the best loser is the long-term winner, so you should debit your profit and loss spreadsheet with your expected loss. You should then go through your positive affirmations to help manage your hope, greed, fear, and pain. Once you've accepted your loss, the next step is to place your order.

TRADING: ORDER PLACEMENT

At this stage, you should have completed your preorder placement checklist to establish the following:

- whether a setup exists
- your entry and stop levels
- your exit instructions
- the dollar risk per contract/position size
- whether you're within your financial boundary's risk capital limit
- whether your single contract equity curve is above your system stop
- what your position or trade size is.

You should then have done the following:

- debited your profit and loss spreadsheet with your expected loss
- accepted your expected loss
- gone through your positive affirmations to help manage your hope, greed, fear, and pain.

Having established and completed all of these, it's time to place an order (including both the entry and stop levels) with your client adviser. Once your adviser has acknowledged that he or she has received and understood your order, you can forget about the market. People using an electronic trading platform should take and save a screenshot of the platform's acceptance of their order.

You'll then need to wait until you hear from your adviser about whether your order was filled. If it was, you need to manage your position according to your trade plan. Once the position has been closed, update both your profit and loss spreadsheet and single-contract equity curve (ignoring slippage). When you receive your trading statement, reconcile it with your trade records. If there is a discrepancy, you should discuss it with your client adviser.

Let's now spend a little time discussing the correct way to write orders.

Orders

Although knowing how to place buy and sell orders correctly may not sound very difficult, it can be confusing at first to new traders due to the array of terminology used and the types of orders that can be placed.

If you've traded shares before, you'll be aware that there is much more to placing an order than simply giving a buy or sell instruction. With futures, spot FX, margin FX, forex, options, and CFDs, there are many types of orders and expressions used. Orders can either be given to a client adviser or entered into an online electronic trading platform. In the following examples, I'll assume I'm placing the order with a client adviser.

When placing a futures order, it's always good practice to identify the contract month you wish to trade. Although most futures trading is done in the current, or spot contract month, it's still worthwhile developing good habits now by learning to place a professional and accurate order.

Note: Margin FX, spot FX, forex, and CFDs don't expire so there is no requirement to mention "contract months." In the following order examples, I will be referring to the March FTSE futures contract. So when I refer to "1 March FTSE" I mean one March contract, not the first of March.

Straight orders

Market   A "market" order is used when you wish to enter the market immediately and you're not concerned about the price you will receive. By using a market order, you're instructing your client adviser to transact immediately, at whatever price the market is offering. If you were looking to sell the FTSE, your client adviser would hit the nearest "bid" price (the best buying price). Your order would look like this:

Sell 1 March FTSE at market.

Best   A "best" order is just like the market order; however, it allows your client adviser discretion in terms of time and price because he or she attempts to get you the best price. Your order would look like this:

Sell 1 March FTSE at best.

Limit   A "limit" order can be used when you have identified a specific price to trade at and only want to complete your transaction at that price. For example, if you wanted to buy the FTSE on a pullback (a decline) from its current rally at 6,455, say 6,445, your order would look like this:

Buy 1 March FTSE at 6,445 limit.

Stop   A "stop" order is a market order set to guard against adverse movements in a position. It is executed once certain "trigger' conditions are met. Stop orders are usually used to limit losses when trading and are often also referred to as stop losses. The level of your stop order represents the most you are willing to risk on the trade.

For example, if I'm short the FTSE at 6,425 and my trade plan tells me to exit if the FTSE trades above 6,464, I would place the following order:

Buy 1 March FTSE at 6,464 on stop.

If the FTSE continued to rally and traded at 6,464, my client adviser would buy me one FTSE contract at market. He or she would not be interested in the price they get. The focus of my client adviser is to buy me one contract.

Alternatively, traders can use stop orders to enter a position. You may have found a key support or resistance level at 6,470 and wish to go long, or buy the FTSE, if that level is traded. If so, your order would look like the following:

Buy 1 March FTSE at 6,470 on stop.

Stop limit   A "stop limit" order has two parts to it. The first part requires a condition to be triggered by the stop instruction. The second part then places a limit on the price at which the order can be executed. For example, if you want to buy the FTSE, because it is trading strongly and makes a new yearly high above 6,600, you could place the following order:

Buy 1 March FTSE at 6,600 on stop, limit 6,602.

What this means to your client adviser is that if the FTSE trades up to 6,600 you wish to buy one contract immediately, but you don't want to pay more than 6,602. In most cases, you would probably be filled at 6,600; however, if it's a key resistance level and the market is hit by huge order flows, the FTSE may skip right through 6,600.

The disadvantage of using a stop limit order is that after trading 6,600 the FTSE's next price may be 6,605, leaving you right in your market view but without a position because you placed a limit on your buy price.

Market if touched   When trading, it's not always possible for an order to be filled at a particular price due to thin volumes. For example, the market may reach your stop limit price but then immediately fall back, meaning your client adviser can't complete your order. When this occurs, you may be correct in your analysis but not have a position. To avoid this situation you can use a "market if touched" (MIT) order.

For example, if your analysis suggests the FTSE will hit heavy resistance at 6,480 and you want to sell the FTSE at that level, and you also have a strong preference to get short and not be worried about your price, you can use the MIT instruction. Your order would look like this:

Sell 1 March FTSE at 6,480 MIT.

Your client adviser will go to market to get you short once the FTSE trades 6,480.

Market on open   A "market on open" (MOO) order instructs your client adviser to transact your order at market on the market's open. For example, following some positive news overnight from the U.S., you want to enter the market on the buy side. You're not interested in what price you have to pay, only that you want to be long the FTSE as soon as the market opens, because you expect a strong rally during the day. Your order would look like this:

Buy 1 March FTSE at MOO.

Market on close   This is the opposite of the MOO order. The "market on close" (MOC) order instructs your client adviser to transact your order at market on the market's close. For example, you want to exit your position on the day's close because you're nervous about key data coming out of the U.S. Your order would look like this:

Sell 1 March FTSE at MOC.

Your client adviser would look to sell your 1 FTSE contract at market within the last minute of trading before the FTSE closes at 4.30 p.m.

Stop close only   A "stop close only" (SCO) order has two parts. The first part has a conditional level that will trigger the stop instruction, while the second part says the stop condition will only be activated on the close. For example, you're long the FTSE at 6,450 and your analysis suggests that you need a strong close to stay long, at or above 6,461. If the FTSE closes at 6,460 or lower, you don't want to be in the market. If this is the case, your order would look like this:

Sell 1 March FTSE at 6,460 SCO.

If the FTSE looks like closing at 6,460 or lower, your client adviser would have to exit your position at market on the close.

For example, if during the last minute of trading the FTSE is at 6,455, since it is below 6,460, your client adviser would sell your one FTSE contract at market.

Fill or kill   A "fill or kill" (FOK) order is a limit order that must be filled immediately or cancelled. For example, if you want to sell the FTSE if it has a weak opening, below say 6,450, your order would look like this:

> If the March FTSE opens at 6,449 or lower then Sell 1 March FTSE at market on open FOK.

If the FTSE opened at 6,449 or lower, your order would be filled; however, if the FTSE opened at 6,450 or higher, your order would be cancelled or "killed."

Fill and kill   A "fill and kill' (FAK) is an order that must be filled to the extent that is possible, and then the balance, if there is any, is cancelled. Using the previous example, if your preference is to sell five FTSE contracts when the market opened, your order would look like this:

> If the March FTSE opens at 6,449 or lower then Sell 5 September FTSE at market on open FAK.

If the FTSE opened at 6,449 or lower, such as 6,445, and only three contracts trade at the opening price before moving lower, the balance of your order that was not filled on the 6,445 open would be cancelled.

Conditional orders

Conditional orders require an event to take place before an order is triggered. The following order types are common.

Expansion order   An expansion order is used to enter a market after it has opened and after it has moved a certain distance, either up or down. It is used when traders require additional confirmation from the market (such as a rally before buying or a fall before selling) before committing to a trade. For example, you may want to sell the FTSE if it opens and then falls by 10 points. However, you don't want to sell immediately after it opens because you think it could rally. Your order would look like this:

> Sell 1 March FTSE at open −10 on stop.

Your client adviser would watch the FTSE, and if it dropped after opening by 10 points, he or she would sell you one FTSE contract at market.

If done   An "if done" instruction is conditional upon a previous instruction being triggered. Using the previous example, if the order is filled, you may want to place a stop to protect yourself, in case you are wrong.

For example, while you may be happy to remain short even if the FTSE rallies a little above your sell level, you may not be happy if the FTSE rallies 20 points against you. If your preference is to sell the FTSE if it falls 10 points after opening with a 20-point stop loss protection, you would place the following order:

Sell 1 March FTSE at open −10 on stop.

if done

Buy 1 March FTSE at open +10 on stop.

The "if done" condition would only become active if the FTSE falls 10 points, meaning your first instruction is executed. If so, your client adviser would look to buy back your short at market if the FTSE rallies and trades 10 points above the day's opening.

One cancels other   A "one cancels (the) other" (OCO) order allows traders to place two orders together, but the client adviser will execute only the order that has its attached condition triggered first.

For example, your current analysis of the FTSE suggests two interesting but conflicting scenarios. You believe that if the FTSE opens low, it will fall away immediately. However, you can see that if the FTSE opens strongly and rallies 10 points, it could increase significantly. It just depends on the FTSE's opening.

When you know your key opening levels for the FTSE and you don't want to miss either trading opportunity, what you can do is place an OCO order.

If a weak opening in your analysis is 6,420, while a strong opening is 6,460, you could place the following conditional orders:

If the March FTSE opens at 6,420 or lower then Sell 1 March FTSE at market.

OCO

If the March FTSE opens at 6,460 or higher then Buy 1 March FTSE at open +10 on stop.

Another example may involve you being long the FTSE and you want your client adviser to work both a profit target—that is, a level you believe the market will reach and where you would be happy to take your profits— and a stop loss.

For example, if you are long the FTSE at 6,450 and are happy to take profits if the FTSE can rally to 6,480, but you want to be stopped out if the market reaches 6,440, your order would look like the following:

Sell 1 March FTSE at 6,480.

OCO

Sell 1 March FTSE at 6,440 on stop.

Your client adviser would only execute the order with the condition that is triggered first. Once that happened, the other side of the order would be cancelled.

Duration of Orders

The length of time an order remains current also varies, depending on the instructions you give your client adviser.

Day only

Unless you give instructions to the contrary, all orders are day-only orders. If the order is not filled or executed by the end of day, the order expires. But it is always best to confirm this understanding with your client adviser or electronic trading platform.

Good till cancelled

A "good till cancelled" (GTC) order stays working, or alive, until it is either filled or cancelled. If you are working a stop loss order that you would prefer not to have to place each day with your client adviser, you could use the GTC instruction. If you're long and have a stop to exit the position at 6,400, you would place the following order:

Sell 1 March FTSE at 6,400 on stop—GTC.

Your client adviser would work this order until either you sold at 6,400 or you cancelled the order.

Good till date

A "good till date" (GTD) order is one that is good until the date that is specified. For example, if you wanted to leave a buy order in the market at 6,450 and you would be happy to buy the FTSE at that level for a month, you would place the following order:

Buy 1 March FTSE at 6,450 GTD 14 March 2008.

Complete Orders

When placing an entry order, either to purchase or sell the FTSE, it is good practice to place a stop loss order after an "if done" condition. Never trade without a stop.

For example, if you are looking to buy a dip in the FTSE at 6,400 and you only want to risk 20 points, your order would look like the following:

Buy 1 March FTSE at 6,400 MIT.

if done

Sell 1 March FTSE at 6,380 on stop.

Your client adviser will look to buy the FTSE at market once prices trade at 6,400. After you've entered, your client adviser will automatically look to sell your one March FTSE at market if prices fall to 6,380.

In addition, if you know your profit level, you can include it with your entry and stop loss instructions.

A Comment on Order Types

Although the order types I have discussed are common, it's always worth confirming what you mean with a new client adviser. Order types are the universal language of traders and client advisers; however, there is always a chance there could be some confusion when you begin trading with a new adviser.

Traders should also be wary of using limit orders—once again, they must focus on risk management, rather than how much money they can make trading. The greatest risk to traders is not the risk of losing a few points by going to market, on either stop or MIT orders, but the risk of missing out on a good trade by placing a limit on their entry level. It is usually a good sign when a market gives slippage, because it indicates that the supply or demand wasn't there for you, which suggests you're on the right side. Similarly, you don't want to be stuck with a losing position just because you wanted a limit price on exit.

In addition, I prefer not to use GTC orders. I like to place my orders each day, even if my profit exit and stop-loss levels never change. I do so because it's part of my risk management strategy, because it helps to ensure my order won't "fall through the cracks" at my broker. For me it's a little extra effort for sensible risk management.

Acknowledgment of Orders

Regardless how you place your order, always ensure you receive an acknowledgment from your broker, whether it's through an online electronic platform or a client adviser. Receiving an acknowledgment confirms your order will be worked. As I have mentioned, I send all my orders by email.

Remember, it's all about managing risks. I expect a return email from my client adviser acknowledging the total number of orders sent, which I usually receive by 9.00 a.m. each morning. After that, I can relax—it's my client adviser who does all the work!

Notification of trade

Once an order is executed, your client adviser will notify you of your fill (quantity and price). At the end of the day, the broker will send you a trading statement summarizing your trades, brokerage, margin movements and any open positions.

It's also worth confirming your position with your client adviser at the end of each day. Nothing will get your heart racing faster than learning of a position you thought you didn't have!

As you can see, there is much more to placing orders than simply wishing to buy or sell and with time they will become easier to understand.

Monthly Reporting

You should treat trading like a business. Each month you need to prepare a single page report for your trading partner. They will help with your discipline and consistency. You'll find it harder to stray from your trade plan when you know your trading partner is watching you.

Your report should contain a summary of your financial benchmarks, including but not limited to your:

• financial boundary risk capital limit
• modest expectations
• money management rules
• system stop
• monthly trading result
• accumulative result
• account balance.

Preparing a monthly summary of your activities will reinforce your commitment to treat trading as a business. It doesn't get much easier than that, does it?

You'll find that trading is the shortest step in your journey toward becoming a successful trader. Once you have laid the foundation during the preceding five principles, putting in the effort to succeed, you'll find trading is reasonably straightforward. It will be managing the constant pain that will be the challenge.

IN SUMMARY

This brings me to the end of the six essential universal principles of successful trading. As I said earlier, I wish this book had been written by someone else 27 years ago. It would certainly have made my personal journey a lot smoother!

I hope you now have a better understanding of what really distinguishes the winners from the losers—the awareness and acceptance of the six universal principles of successful trading:

- preparation
- enlightenment
- trading style
- markets
- the Three Pillars
- money management
- methodology
- psychology
- trading.

Regardless of the market, time frame, security, or technique the elite traders follow and use, there is no sidestepping the universal principles of successful trading. The principles are the golden thread that links the elites together and distinguishes them as being way above most traders who lose.

You now know what this golden thread is and now it's up to you to decide whether to weave it through your trade plan. I hope you do.

Figure 11.1 shows the process of trading that comprises the six universal principles of successful trading.

By learning the six universal principles of successful trading you should now be aware of the preparation that is required to place yourself in a position to survive and succeed in trading. You should also be aware of the boundaries within which to work. Staying within these boundaries will help you avoid the majority of common mistakes made by most traders and help you join the 10 percent winners' circle.

If you can accept the universal principles then you'll avoid the common mistakes most traders make, as shown in figure 11.2.

You now have the knowledge to decide whether you're prepared to move forward in your trading career. Most traders who are honest and true to themselves will realize they're not up for the effort required to succeed. They'll realize that the work required to prepare themselves for trading is too hard and that trading itself is not a shortcut to a free lunch. They'll realize their heart isn't up for the hard yards required and they will quit while they're ahead.

1. Preparation	2. Enlighten	3. Trading Style	4. Markets	5. The Three Pillars	6. Trading	
		Holy Grail				Following your trade plan - it's as easy as joining the dots!
		$$ = E (R) X O			Smarter money management	Methodology **TEST**
Maximum adversity	Emotional orientation			Liquidity	Low costs zero default risk	Psychology fear,greed,pain
			Mode:	24-Hour coverage		Volatility research
				Trend trading (15%) or swing trading (85%)		Specialization opportunities
			Avoid risk of ruin with good money management		Strive for simplicity: SUPPORT and RESISTANCE levels	Timeframes: Short or medium term
			Losing game	Random markets	Best loser wins	Risk mgt / Trading partner / Financial boundary

FIGURE 11.1 The universal principles of successful trading

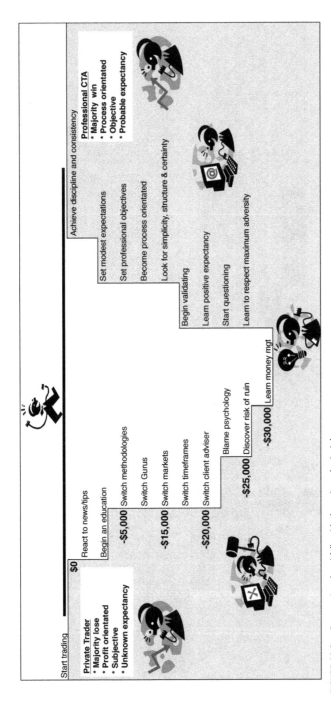

FIGURE 11.2 Overcoming the pitfalls with the universal principles

244

They are the smart ones. They'll avoid a loser's game; they'll keep their money in the bank; and they'll avoid the emotional tsunami the market's maximum adversity continually throws up against the unsuspecting and unprepared trader. They will live a relatively pain-free existence.

If you're one of those, then congratulations. You know yourself far better than 90 percent of traders who think they know themselves but only know what they want to believe. Now some of you will believe that I'm just scaremongering to keep you away from the market's honeypot of trading. Believe me there are people who think that way, because I've received plenty of emails saying as much from people who have read my first book *Trading the SPI*. That's fine if you're one of them. Just please keep my book close at hand for referral later because I have also received apologies from those same people who have learned the truth of these universal principles to the cost of their wallets, their pride, their soul, and their relationships.

For those of you with the fortitude and strength of character to succeed, then please be prepared for a ton of work and pain ahead of you. You will need to embrace these universal principles and believe in their message. You'll need them to TEST and validate your trading methodologies. You will need them to avoid your ruin point. You will need them as your reference point and compass as you navigate your way around the unforgiving trading landscape. Please do not ignore them. Please do not pay them lip service. Please embrace and implement them for your survival and trading success. To do otherwise will guarantee your trading demise.

Although this brings me to the end of my universal principles, it doesn't mean the end of giving you further insights into successful trading. In the next chapter I will be introducing you to a group of successful traders who have generously agreed to offer you one piece of advice based on their years of experience and success. Traders whom I call the Market Masters. Let's meet them.

12

Just One Piece of Advice

You're now in for a treat. So far you have heard one voice, mine. Despite how informative I may believe I sound, I'm sure you're close to having enough of me! So for relief and, more importantly, for your benefit, you are about to hear some new and rich voices on trading.

You are about to hear from a group of Market Masters, a group of successful traders who are prepared to give you one important piece of advice based on their personal experiences as successful traders. I asked each one the same question. A question I believe you would like to hear. I asked them for that one piece of advice they would like to give an aspiring trader, you.

BALANCE

The reason I have included this chapter in the book is for balance. What I have written is what I believe holds true. For me. I have written about the universal principles of successful trading. If I have been successful, then you will now have a good understanding of what I believe is important to succeed in trading. However, they are only my thoughts and words. They come from my own personal journey along the bumpy old road to trading success. They reflect my view of the trading world, what I have seen and experienced through my own eyes.

Now, earlier in the book I encouraged you to welcome all trading ideas while remaining skeptical because there is so much marketing hype surrounding trading. I encouraged you to retain the right to determine whether a trading idea has value in your hands. I'm a strong believer that despite what I may write, or what another author may write, just because it has been written does not necessarily make it true for you. It will only become true if you see it for yourself through your own effort and your own eyes.

What you have read so far in this book is merely one trader's personal opinion, mine. I naturally believe the universal principles are non-negotiable, but you'll need to investigate them for yourself to determine their worth. And if you're guarded about my universal principles, then that's fine, but my only caution to you is not to go against them deliberately. If you do, the market's maximum adversity will send an avalanche of trouble your way, guaranteed. It will be an experience you'll never forget.

But my point here is that what I have written, regardless of my beliefs, is only one person's opinion, mine. I now want to balance my lone voice with others. I want to balance my discussion on the universal principles with some practical words of wisdom. Not only do I want to balance my views, but I also want to give you the opportunity to take a privileged and private look into the minds of successful traders.

This chapter will be a real treat for you. It was certainly a treat for me in putting it together.

THE MARKET MASTERS

You are about to meet some Market Masters, successful traders who are prepared to share, to give you a leg up and inspire you along your journey by sharing with you one piece of important advice.

For these traders, I simply gave them the context of this book, its focus on those universal principles of successful trading that connects all successful traders. I gave them a draft copy of my chapter headings to paint the landscape within which their advice would sit. I then simply asked them the same question: "Given all your trading knowledge and trading experience, I'd imagine you would receive many requests for help. If you were able to give an aspiring trader one piece of advice, and one only, what would it be and why?" You are about to receive that one piece of advice.

It's not often you get the opportunity to see this closely into the minds of so many successful traders—these Market Masters. I hope you will appreciate their generosity.

So who are these Market Masters? Well, some of them will be well known to you, some slightly less so, while others will be completely new to you. However, regardless of their familiarity, they're all successful traders, and they all have some very valuable advice to give.

You will meet and learn from the current crop of championship-winning traders, the new kids on the block. You'll also meet the market legends, traders who have been actively involved in the markets for more than 40 years. Those legends have had a significant impact on the world of technical analysis, and are as active today as they were when they started. You will meet one of the largest and most active private E-Mini SP500 traders. And not only will you meet the new with the old, but you'll also meet many traders in between. Traders who are all Market Masters, traders who have all survived the Global Financial Crisis, traders who are willing to share their experiences with you.

They represent a diverse group of traders—some are discretionary, some are mechanical, some are a hybrid—discretionary mechanical traders. Some use traditional technical analysis, some exclusively follow a single market theory, some are system traders. Some are reclusive private traders, some are the biggest names in trader education. Some are the most prolific of trading authors, who apart from their trading success have that envious gift of being easy writers who can share their thoughts to the willing reader. Some run advisory services publishing successful newsletters and trading recommendations, some are money managers, managing individual accounts and large funds. Some trade shares. Some trade options. Some trade ETFs. Some trade futures. Some trade currencies. Some trade commodities. Some trade CFDs. Some trade financials. Some trade a mix. Some are day traders. Some are short-term traders. Some are medium-term traders and some are long-term traders. Some trade a combination of time frames. Some have won trading championships. Some have never appeared in public before. As I've said, they represent a diverse group of traders.

And not only diverse in terms of their approach, but also geographically diverse. Among the Market Masters, you'll meet traders from Singapore, Hong Kong, Italy, the U.K. (although currently living in Alaska), America, and Australia.

But although technically and geographically diverse, they are still all successful traders. And they're Market Masters to me because they all survived the Global Financial Crisis. They're all successful, and they all have one singularly valuable piece of advice they would like to share with you.

And as a sidebar, I hope this diversity also demonstrates to you that there is more than one way to trade the markets. You just need to find your own niche. You just need to find that one technique or combination of techniques that makes sense to you, that approach that works in your own hands that gives you your edge and allows you to trade with a validated 0 percent risk-of-ruin.

I have shared with you what I hold to be true for me, and I have neatly bundled them up into what I refer to as the universal principles. I know each and every one of these Market Masters could easily put together their own universal principles with their own emphasis here and there. And it's their emphasis that I want to share with you.

Now, these Market Masters do not have the luxury of this whole book to share all their thoughts with you. However, I wanted them to share with you their one piece of advice they hold above all else. I wanted them to share with you what their own personal "emphasis" is. I wanted to balance my thoughts by sharing with you one of their most important ones.

I personally sit at the feet of these Market Masters you are about to meet. I hope you can listen along as I ask them all the same question and hear that one singular piece of advice they would like to give you.

For each Market Master, I begin with an introduction to who they are and where they sit within the confusing world of technical analysis. I then ask them the one question and their reply follows. At the end of their advice I've recorded a contact web address you can reference if you'd like to learn more about them. You never know whose words of wisdom will help the penny drop for you, but if one or more strike a chord with you, then I'd encourage you to learn more about them and their approach to the markets.

Let me now introduce you to these Market Masters in alphabetical order:

- Ramon Barros
- Mark D. Cook
- Michael Cook
- Kevin Davey
- Tom DeMark
- Lee Gettess
- Daryl Guppy
- Richard Melki
- Geoff Morgan
- Greg Morris
- Nick Radge
- Brian Schad
- Andrea Unger
- Larry Williams
- Dar Wong.

So please pay attention and listen carefully as these Market Masters share with you and I their "one piece of advice" for trading success. Sit quietly and you may just hear that one piece of advice that will switch on your own trading lightbulb, that one piece of advice that will give you your own personal "ah-ha moment." Let's begin and remember to listen up!

RAMON BARROS

Ray Barros may possibly be the bravest trader I know. To this day, I'm still shocked at witnessing Ray teach a trading audience standard deviation. Ray was encouraging people to consider incorporating the standard deviation of their trading results into their money management strategy. To my mind, combining statistics with money management strategies presents a herculean challenge, particularly to an audience that is usually populated by people new to both the markets and trading. And like most people, I'd imagine it was an audience that would not hold particularly fond memories of learning statistics at school! Brave or foolish, Ray certainly doesn't avoid the hard tasks!

And not only is Ray brave but he may also suffer from a particular excessive compulsive behavior when it comes to trading books. You see Ray finds it very difficult not to buy a book when he's in a trading book store. And I've seen this first hand when we were both in India for a trading expo. Ray and I were both being interviewed by CNBC in a live broadcast from a Mumbai bookstore. After the interview, Ray couldn't help himself, explaining to all and sundry that he just had to buy a book before he left. And he did, two. Ray's passion and excessive compulsive acquisition of trading books makes him possibly one of the most widely read traders, with possibly one of the largest trading libraries in the world today; so well read that he has to pay warehousing fees to store his excess books!

Now, Ray's passion for trading and trading books was not allowed to blossom until later in his life. Although Ray's initial awareness of the markets came from his father, who was an active and successful trader, he was not allowed to dabble in trading. His dominant and conservative father forbid him from developing an interest in the markets. He was pushed to succeed in scholastic studies and pursue academic excellence. And like many sons with authoritative and controlling fathers, Ray wasn't able to pursue his real passion in trading until after his father had passed away.

Consequently, Ray commenced trading in 1975 at time when he was already a successful practicing lawyer. At the time, Ray was an intuitive discretionary day trader looking for opportunities that felt right. Success eluded him, and Ray decided he needed to commit himself full time to trading if he was to succeed. So in 1980 Ray left his law practice to focus 100 percent on what had become his true passion in life, despite his father's best efforts—trading. But, unfortunately, success didn't come. He failed repeatedly and suffered heavy losses.

Not to be daunted, Ray threw himself into analyzing both himself and his strategies, and success came through knowing himself better and discovering Market Profile. Peter Steidlmayer, who developed Market Profile, would become one of Ray's earliest mentors. Market Profile enabled Ray to understand better the intraday flow of market prices, and gave him his first real edge in trading. After becoming proficient with Market Profile, it didn't take long for Ray to start enjoying profitable trading. By 1986, Ray was achieving consistent success, and was developing his trading methodology beyond Market Profile.

And it wasn't long until his success became known among the banks, which placed both their funds with him to manage and their traders to learn his trading strategies. Ray became one of the first outsourced currency traders in the world and one of the few external traders used to teach institutional traders.

After his success in and enjoyment of teaching institutional traders, Ray discovered another passion—teaching others. And I think it's his love of teaching and helping others to learn correctly that have him happily and hungrily buying a couple of trading books whenever he is browsing through a trading bookstore.

And his teaching success has made Ray a sought-after and popular trading mentor, who until recently only took a limited number of five students into his 24-month mentorship program. Ray's mentoring was so popular that there was a three-year waiting list for prospective students!

I believe Ray is a deep thinker, particularly about the importance of psychology on a trader's performance. He is an advocate of neurolinguistic programming, and is a big believer in traders first fully knowing and understanding their own psychological traits before they can hope to succeed in the markets.

Today, Ray continues to trade on a discretionary basis according to his BarroMetric™ methodology. His methodology is a synthesis of Barros Swings, Ray Wave, and Market Profile. Although very structured and rule based, he does have one rule that allows him to break his rules. This allows Ray leeway for his intuition. Ray primarily uses Market-Analyst to find his BarroMetric setups, and supports it with both E-signal and Channelyse for cycle analysis. Ray prefers to trade the S&P500, the main currency pairs, gold, and 30-year bonds over a monthly time frame according to an 18-day swing. He is a stickler for record keeping, and records all the reasons behind each of his trades using Camtasia Studio. With Camtasia, Ray is able to capture both the chart image on his PC and his own voice as he dictates the reasons behind each trade. Ray will then play back the video to watch himself trade. The record keeping and video playback help Ray to reinforce his own good trading habits and to pinpoint any potential inconsistencies that may creep into his actions. This way Ray is able to mentor Ray. Smart hey!

Ray is a very familiar face in Asia due to his regular appearances on CNBC and he shares his thoughts on trend determination in his book *The Nature of Trends.*[1]

Ray's greatest passion outside trading and teaching is, yes, you guessed right, reading. Apart from trading books, you'll find Ray reading any subject from fantasy to chaos theory. And although reading is both a passion and relaxation for Ray, it's also an annoyance for his wife, who has to continually look for more space to store all his new books! Ray and his wife spend their time between Hong Kong, Singapore, and Australia. Let's now hear what Ray's one piece of advice is.

"Ray, given all your trading knowledge and trading experience, I'd imagine you would receive many requests for help. If you were able to give an aspiring trader one piece of advice, and one only, what would it be and why?"

The Hidden Principle

We all know that 80 percent to 90 percent of newbie traders fail.

The question is, why should this be so? It is not for lack of education. In the investing and trading arena, the seminar business is an ever-growing one. More importantly, great strides have been made in understanding how we can learn more effectively. Notwithstanding this, the success rate amongst traders and investors is no different to when I first started trading in the early 1970s.

We find part of the reason in the nature of trading itself. As a probability game, on any single trade, the novice trader has the same chance as winning as a seasoned professional. Often, after a series of successive wins, the novice trader mistakes good luck for skill—the market will soon set this misconception right, and the newbie loses all he made and more.

We find another part of the reason in how newbies perceive trading success is attained. They hold the false idea that all they need is a "super trading strategy," and engage in a fruitless search for the Holy Grail: that methodology that will produce unlimited wealth from a small capital base and a methodology that will have relatively few losses.

As seasoned professionals know, the methodology is but one part of the success equation:

Winning Psychology × Effective Risk Management × Written Trading Rules [with an edge].

Brent covers these traditional principles in this book.

But, in my view, there is a principle that is often overlooked and seldom talked about. This principle was in evidence in 1934 in the area of flight safety. In the winter of that year, it appeared that the most skilled pilots of the U.S. Army Air Corps were dying in crashes.

With benefit of hindsight, it is clear that the main cause of the crashes was the training program. A program that consisted of:

- the prospective student sitting in a plane where the instructor would execute a series of loops and roles. If the student did not get sick, he was admitted to ground school

- in ground school, the student being taught to fly by blackboard and some hands-on experience with an instructor
- after several weeks, student being gradually allowed to handle the controls.

The results of the training?

Fatality rates at some schools approached 25 percent.

The spectacular safety record that the aviation industry has today is due to Edward Link, who invented the Link Simulator. The simulator allowed pilots to make errors and to learn from them without risk. In short, the Link Simulator allowed pilots to practice more deeply.

This concept of "Deep Practice" was introduced by Daniel Coyle in his book *The Talent Code*. But before I go into details about the practice, let me take a moment to draw your attention to the similarities between the education traders receive and the education that pilots received back in 1934.

As traders, we tend to learn our craft by attending two-to-four-day seminars and by reading. After that, our learning is based on trial and error, with our precious capital at risk. This is similar to a trial and error learning of the 1934 pilots; the only difference is they risked their lives, and we risk our financial capital—sometimes our financial life.

Figure 12.1 explains the concept of Deep Practice.

It is my view that this concept will revolutionize trading education.

We will see seminars and tuition split into the transmission of the intellectual content followed by sessions of Deep Practice.

We see the "Deep Practice" method under the heading "Feel It." This incorporates Coyle's belief that to learn something we need to engage our reason and our emotion. In any practice session, we first set goals that are just outside our comfort zone. But to know what these goals are we first set the context (Chunk): we identify the core tenets of our learning and reduce them into their component parts.

Once we set our goals, we are ready for simulated trading practice. With the outcome in mind, we take action. At the end of the exercise, we compare the results of the action with our desired outcome—in other words, we note the gap. We then reflect and decide on actions to close the gap and take another action. We repeat this cycle until the gap closes.

This process of "error learning" exponentially reduces the amount of learning time. It's my view that, implemented properly, the Coyle model will lift the success results in trading.

Ray Barros

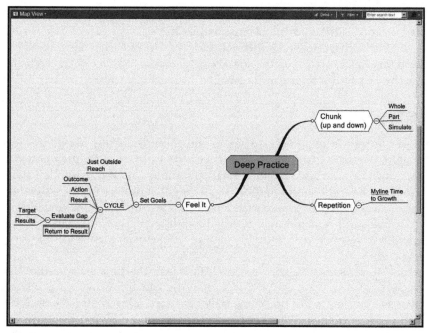

FIGURE 12.1   Deep Practice

Source: Daniel Coyle, *The Talent Code* (Bantam Dell, Random Hose 2009)

Didn't I tell you Ray was widely read and a deep thinker! You may like to take a moment to reread Ray's thoughts. And remember, if you haven't already read Daniel Coyle's book *The Talent Code*, you read about Deep Practice here first thanks to Ray! Its Ray's belief that if properly implemented Deep Practice will quicken traders along their path toward trading success. You can have all the best trading knowledge. You can have a sensible money management strategy. You can have a robust positive-expectancy trading methodology. You may even be able to hold the eye of a tiger. However without practice, practice, and more deep practice—you'll feel like you're being tossed about like a rag doll by the market's buffeting maximum adversity. You'll be so disoriented, you'll be thrown off your trade plan's course. You'll not know whether you should be buying or selling. However, with continuous proper practice, you'll be better prepared for your regular maximum adversity ambushes. You will not be swayed from your trade plan. You'll stay the course. You'll be better prepared to persevere. However, without deep practice, you'll become another market statistic. And you'll find following the TEST procedure to validate your methodology will help in your deep practice. So thanks to Ray, you now have an additional weapon to add to your trading arsenal that, to my knowledge, has never before been referred to in another trading book. You should add Ray to your Christmas card list!

If Ray's advice resonates with you and you'd like to learn more about his thoughts on trading and the markets, he can be contacted through his website at www.tradingsuccess.com.

MARK D. COOK

Mark D. Cook is an addict. He has an addiction to trading. Mark loves the markets so much that he can never keep away from them for long periods. He knows he is an addict, and will happily admit it to anyone who is willing to listen. His addiction to trading is so strong that despite his successes and the many requests for him to write a trading book, he has declined to do so. Mark just can't find the time to tear himself away from the markets long enough to put pen and thoughts to paper. Now that's what I call a strong addiction!

So I count myself lucky to have Mark take the time to entertain my request for *one piece of advice*. And I hope you can appreciate his presence here as well. There are not many traders as successful as Mark, so to have him participate in this book is a privilege for you and me.

Mark is one of the largest and most active private day traders of the E-Mini S&P500. Since the E-Mini S&P500 is one of the world's largest futures contracts that makes Mark one of the world's largest and most active private day traders!

On a busy day Mark can execute up to 40 trades.

If you, like me and many other traders, have read the Market Wizards books by Jack Schwager then you will already be familiar with Mark. Mark was the only featured S&P futures trader in *Stock Market Wizards*.[2]

Mark's story is truly inspirational. Through sheer determination and willpower, Mark was able to turn around early and repetitive setbacks, where one was of such catastrophic proportion that it nearly bankrupted him, to become one of the world's most successful day traders. Mark is living testimony to the old adage of "never give up". He is also living testimony to the power of a mother's love and confidence in a child. It was his mother's confidence in him to turn his perilous financial situation around that motivated Mark toward his eventual trading success.

If you ever feel down about your own trading, then you should remember to reread Mark's interview with Jack Schwager in *Stock Market Wizards*. It will put your own situation into perspective, and it will inspire you about what is possible if you truly wish to succeed in trading. It will also underline the importance of a good work ethic to succeed in the markets. Mark may just be the hardest-working day trader in the market. It may even help you to see the light and realize that trading is not for you if you're not prepared to put in the hard yards. Remember, if you're day trading the E-Mini SP500, then you'll probably be either trading with or against Mark. Know that Mark puts in multiple hours of preparation each morning before the market opens, and if you wish to be trading with him, rather than against him, that you'll also need to put an equal amount of effort in. If you're not prepared to work hard to succeed in day trading the E-Mini SP500, then it may be better to think of something else to do. You have to understand there are no shortcuts to successful day trading. If you think there are, then please let me remind you to reread Mark's interview.

Mark's background is farming in East Sparta, Ohio, U.S. He lives and trades from a family farmstead that has been in his family since the 1870s. Due to his success, Mark has been able to add to his family's land holdings by purchasing neighboring and local properties when they have come up for sale. Due to his conservatism, Mark is a big believer in converting good annual trading results into real arable farmland. Mark has been fortunate enough to combine both his loves—trading and farming—by using one to build the other.

However, Mark was not always so fortunate. Mark began trading in 1977 as a discretionary trader working off printed charts. His early years were filled with repeated failure. In 1982, a little success combined with greed nearly brought him unstuck when a naked call option position blew up and left him short $350,000 in his trading account. To cover the deficit in his account Mark was forced to borrow the money from both his parents and the bank. As Mark said "there is nothing more debilitating than borrowing money to put into a brokerage account to bring it up to zero."

However, that experience, combined with his mother's confidence in his ability to recover the money, was a watershed moment in Mark's career. It was his turning point. It wasn't until 1986 though before he started to experience big profitable years, and it coincided with the development of his proprietary Cook Cumulative Tick indicator, an indicator that identified overbought and oversold situations. What Mark noticed was that whenever the cumulative tick was either very negative or very positive, the market would tend to snap back. He learned that fading the extreme tick readings created profitable trading opportunities.

His Cook Cumulative Tick indicator delivered him the edge he was looking for. It became, and remains today, a big contributor to his trading success. Mark continued to trade so well that in 1987 he was able to repay the $350,000 he was forced to borrow to cover his 1982 option loss. His trading success continued, and in 1992 he won the U.S. Investing Championship with a 563 percent return. In 1993, he followed it up with a 322 percent return. Mark has been a consistently profitable trader since 1986.

Today, Mark is still a discretionary day trader, and continues to trade according to his Cook Cumulative Tick indicator. Mark monitors his indicator over multiple timeframes, and although predominately a day trader, he will place short-term three-day swing trades and longer-term trades when his indicator warrants it. Mark will hold longer-term trades until his Cook Cumulative Tick indicator neutralizes. Mark is also an avid record keeper diarizing every trade he makes. Mark is a big believer in studying and learning from his old trades.

As a trader, Mark does focus on high-accuracy strategies, and will trade any market that is sensitive to his Cook Cumulative Tick indicator. Although he is known for his E-Mini S&P500 trading, Mark will also trade options, shares, and ETFs when it's warranted.

Today, apart from trading his own money, Mark also manages money for large private accounts that are more than $1.0 million and he also manages 10 percent of the CMG Absolute Return Strategies Fund. Since early 2000s Mark has had an open invitation to any trader who would like to challenge him to a trading contest. It's a million-dollar winner-take-all challenge. And to Mark's surprise, he has never had one other trader accept his invitation! In addition, he runs a daily advisory service and when time permits Mark runs trading workshops from his farm office, where students not only learn what it takes to succeed in trading, but also get to enjoy the great home cooking of his partner, Jill!

Apart from trading, Mark enjoys speaking engagements and teaching others to trade. And although he has a passion for collecting antique tractors, it's not really enough to distract him for too long from his addiction to the markets and his burning desire always to improve, an insatiable desire that is never satisfied even when he has a million-dollar month!

Now, I hope you're ready to listen with both ears. As you know, Mark has never written a trading book, and has little free time due to his commitment to trading. So please pay special attention to what Mark has to say, and remember to keep in the back of your mind that this piece of advice comes from one of the world's largest, most active, and most successful private day traders and a market wizard!

Let me now ask Mark for his one piece of advice.

"Mark, given all your trading knowledge and trading experience, I'd imagine you would receive many requests for help. If you were able to give an aspiring trader one piece of advice, and one only, what would it be and why?"

I'd begin by telling them that success is a road paved with losing!

These words I have to offer about trading may only affect one person who reads them. However, that one person will have his or her life changed forever. Countless words of text are dedicated to making money in all aspects of investing. Almost no words are scripted to keeping the gains. The adage: "It is very easy to make money but virtually impossible to keep it" resonates in every old trader's mind.

If you are still reading this verbiage after my intro, there is hope for you. Few people understand the "art" of trading. It is not the ability to read charts, fundamental analysis, or technical analysis. It is simply knowing oneself. My 33 years of trading have taught me several truths. The most important is this absolute. You will lose money and must deal with that fact. Professional athletes accept they will be hurt. How they respond to the pain is the difference between success and failure.

I have lost millions in the investment world, but have fortunately made many more millions to the plus side. The reason is: I have accepted loss as a part of reality and rehabilitated my trading life to heal.

My first foray into trading was met by sustained losing streaks. This could not be happening to me! Then I became a mature trader and faced reality: I wasn't a victim; I had victimized myself. Inexperienced traders have not constructed a business trading plan. Experienced traders live their business plan to the letter. The pros know they need to plan for Armageddon to avoid it. The amateur never thinks about Armageddon until it is too late. The truths must be read, memorized, and assimilated into your being.

Here are the Mark D. Cook's truths that I live by:

Truth #1: I will lose money. I accept it.

I have a shutdown time when money is being lost in trading. I fervently believe in personal cycles. A person's down cycle is a vulnerable period for all life's ventures. I know my months of potential losing and guard against it; 35 percent drawdown is too much!

Truth #2: Avoid opinions. Trade the facts.

I do a daily ritual to find facts for trading. Overworking can lead to overachieving—is that bad? Once I weigh all the facts, there is no room for opinion. If it is raining, do not say the sun is shining. Live in reality, not fictitious Camelot.

Truth #3: Find the opportunities. Trade them. Do not overstay.

I am tough on myself when I lose money because I know there was an opportunity to make money that I did not find. My early years of trading and all the reading I did never mentioned finding opportunity. The market fluctuates, a fact; therefore, I must see the flows, recognize them, participate, but never overstay my welcome. Amateurs stay in trades too long! Pros get out too early; guess who makes more money?

Truth #4: Be confident. Trade to win. Don't trade to avoid losing.

Confidence and realism are blood brothers. Confidence and losing soon divorce. The game of life has a balance that maintains peace. That balance must have a defense and an offense. All of us have seen a person who just plain gives up and soon their body does also. Their offense toward life is gone; therefore, their life is also. Defense is a guard and a plan to defend against adversity while realizing it will come. A true balance is weighing all scenarios and assigning probabilities, acknowledging the probabilities, planning a course. There is a way to score! There is a way to stop the opponent from scoring. Find them both!

Amateurs look for the Holy Grail; Professionals trade by the Holy Truths!

Mark D. Cook

Well, how about that? You and many others have no doubt spent considerable time and energy searching for that universal key that would unlock the market's secrets—the unattainable Holy Grail. Instead, you should have been searching for the Holy Truths! You should have learned trading successfully was more about accepting your loses and learning how to keep your gains than making profits. So much is written about how to make money, very little is focused on how to keep what you have made. And the key is to accept losing. How much better off would you be if you had known that a lot earlier in your trading career! In addition, parts of Mark's third truth fly in the face of commonly accepted trading lore. Mark never overstays his welcome in a profitable trade. Yet traders are indoctrinated to "let profits run," not to cut profits short. Yet Mark does the complete opposite. It does make you think.

However, you must also remember that Mark is a very high-accuracy trader who can afford to take many smaller profits and the occasional larger loss. But still his words are worth their weight in gold because they don't come from a trading textbook but from the unforgiving real world of the S&P500 trading arena, where very few traders survive and succeed. As I said, his advice is worth its weight in gold and should be ringing in your ears if you're contemplating a day trading career. Well thanks to Mark, you now have his own personal Holy Truths to guide you along your trading journey. A journey that will be paved with loses, but as they say being forewarned is indeed being forearmed!

If Mark's advice resonates with you and you'd like to learn more about his thoughts on trading and the markets, he can be contacted through his website at www.markdcook.com.

A DIVERSE GROUP OF TRADERS

As I mentioned earlier, my group of Market Masters represents a diverse group of traders, some high profile, some terribly private and unknown, and some who have won trading championships. I personally believe I've been very lucky to bring together such a diverse group of successful traders. And I should say that I personally feel flattered by their generosity to contribute. Before I move on I just want to let you know that apart from Mark D. Cook, who won the U.S. Investing Championship in 1992, I also have other championship winning traders for you to meet. I have highlighted them in table 12.1. As you can see, I've been fortunate to bring together the recent winners of the Robbins World Cup Championship of Futures Trading®—Kevin Davey, Michael Cook, and Andrea Unger—an American, a British, and an Italian trader. The new young guns on the

TABLE 12.1   World Cup Championship of Futures Trading® Top Overall Performance—All Divisions

2009: Andrea Unger	115%
2008: Andrea Unger	672%
2007: Michael Cook	250%
2006: Kevin Davey	107%
2005: Ed Twardus	278%
2004: Kurt Sakaeda	929%
2003: Int'l. Capital Mngt.	88%
2002: John Holsinger	608%
2001: David Cash	53%
2000: Kurt Sakaeda	595%
1999: Chuck Hughes	315%
1998: Jason Park	99%
1997: Michelle Williams	1,000%
1996: Reinhart Rentsch	95%
1995: Dennis Minogue	219%
1994: Frank Suler	85%
1993: Richard Hedreen	173%
1992: Mike Lundgren	212%
1991: Thomas Kobara	200%
1990: Mike Lundgren	244%
1989: Mike Lundgren	176%
1988: David Kline	148%
1987: Larry Williams	11,376%
1986: Henry Thayer	231%
1985: Ralph Casazzone	1283%
1984: Ralph Casazzone	264%

Source: Robbins Trading Company http://www.robbinstrading.com/worldcup/standings.asp

street. In addition to the recent winners, I also have the most successful winner in the competition's 25-year history—Larry Williams, and through association his daughter, Michelle Williams, who at the age of 16 won the competition in 1997.

Let me now introduce you to Michael Cook, who won the competition in 2007.

MICHAEL COOK

Michael Cook is a trading champion. He won the real-money Robbins World Cup Championship of Futures Trading® in 2007 with a 250 percent return, and was runner up in 2008. One of Michael's ambitions is to win the championship three times in a row—a feat no other trader has ever achieved in the 25-year history of the competition.

Michael is a rarity among traders in that his early trading was littered with success. Unlike most students who attend university simply to study, Michael spent his time subscribing to new privatization issues. Issues he would subsequently sell on their first day of listing, and although his studies may have suffered, his finances certainly did not!

Michael is not only a rarity in that respect, but also in that he had the opportunity to learn how to trade by using other people's money. In his case, this was at Bank of America in London, where he was hired in 1997. Michael joined their emerging-markets fixed-income desk, where he was afforded the opportunity to learn about the markets and trading from seasoned institutional traders.

While at Bank America, Michael was principally a discretionary trader, trading off his multitasking Bloomberg terminals. Not only did they provide charts, analysis, and news announcements, but the terminals made great coffee coasters! Over a 10-year period, Michael was able to hone and develop his trading skills as a senior trader for various institutions, both banks and hedge funds.

In 2007, Michael left the safety of institutional trading to trade for himself full time. Michael was so successful in transitioning his institutional trading skills to his own personal account that he won the World Cup Championship of Futures Trading® with a 250 percent return. From my experience, this is an unusual occurrence because not many ex-institutional traders can successfully trade for their own personal account. The professional and emotional detachment necessary to trade successfully change when it becomes your own money. The emotional detachment evaporates as each trade's outcome has a personal impact on their own net worth. It's difficult to leave the last losing trade in the dealing room each day when that dealing room is under your own roof! So his successful transition from institutional to personal trading is another rarity for Michael.

Today, Michael is a short-to-medium-term discretionary-mechanical trader. His trades can last anywhere from a couple of days to months. Michael will trade any market where his models see an opportunity, whether it be forex, shares, options, or futures across the indices, metals, energies, or financial markets. His models use statistically based indicators to identify trading opportunities. The models attempt to identify momentum setups using groups of filters that cascade into place when certain conditions are met. His preference is to trade simple models that keep his screen relatively clutter free. His models don't use traditional overbought or oversold indicators like oscillators or stochastics. As he says, "My methods are not rocket science; they're built on just 20 or 30 lines of code." And although he is primarily a mechanical trader, he will introduce some discretion when he believes its necessary—making him the discretionary–mechanical trader he is.

For his model research, development, and testing, Michael uses a combination of Genesis and Excel, and for charting he switches between e-Signal's FutureSource and Genesis.

When not trading, you'll usually find Michael involved in a minor accident of some description somewhere. He can't explain why, but ever since moving from England to Alaska he has been alarmed at the number of times he has fallen skiing or crashing snow machines and ATVs! Michael and his wife are British, but currently live in Alaska, U.S. Let's now hear what Michael's one piece of advice is.

"Michael, given all your trading knowledge and trading experience, I'd imagine you would receive many requests for help. If you were able to give an aspiring trader one piece of advice, and one only, what would it be and why?"

For an aspiring trader, one piece of advice transcends all others. Trade smaller.

There are obviously exceptions, but in general, a new trader tends to hugely overestimate the correct size and number of positions for a given level of risk capital.

This is definitely an area where size matters—and the smaller, the better.

Most aspiring traders will have read the Market Wizard books. These books are a series of interviews with top traders who have made tens or hundreds of millions of dollars trading, in several cases billions. These traders are the equivalent of a Tiger Woods or a Roger Federer or a Pele of trading. One of the notable themes running through many of their stories is that they lost a lot of money or went broke early in their careers. This should be a salutary lesson for the man or woman in the street who is just starting out trading, these are some of the very best traders in the world, and they still nearly lost everything early on.

Those who are starting out trading have to realize that the game is tough, the competition is tough, and money made or more often lost is how the score is kept.

Trading small is less exciting than "swinging it around." But it is said that if you want loyalty—get a dog. Similarly, if you want excitement—take up sky diving. Prospective traders need to decide early on what they want from trading, and that should be to make money, not thrill seeking.

Trading small early on isn't going to make a trader profitable (that is pretty unlikely), but that should not be the aim. The aim should be staying alive long enough to be able to learn all the other lessons that will allow them to become profitable as time goes on. Then the sky is the limit.

Many of those reading this will think, "That is nothing new or original, I already know that, I have already heard that advice in some form or other a hundred times; all I ever hear about is risk management, now can you tell me what else I need to know to get rich trading . . . "

That response makes me think of a patient who goes to their physician, and asks for advice on how to lose weight. The physician explains that to lose weight the patient either has to exercise more or eat less. The patient responds, "Yes, yes, I already know that, I have already heard that advice in some form or other a hundred times, now can you tell me what else I need to know to lose weight . . . "

Ignoring this lesson is fine; no further lessons will be needed, as the aspiring trader will not be in the game long enough to need them. Trade smaller and then there is at least a chance that great things will happen!

Michael Cook

Now, can anyone see the irony here? It is an irony that underlines the strength and depth of Michael's advice. Michael, who as an ex-institutional trader would usually trade in the millions, is advising you to trade small, smaller, and smaller still. If you can listen and act according to Michael's advice, you will be one step closer to ensuring you'll commence trading with a 0 percentage risk of ruin. And as Michael says, if you can trade small it will help give you enough time to learn everything else, you'll need to succeed. Trading small will not necessarily make you profitable, but it will help ensure you survive long enough to begin benefiting from the knowledge trading small will allow you to gain. These are words from a championship-winning trader who has traded successfully at both the institutional and personal levels. It would be wise for you to pay attention to these words of advice. I hope you were listening, I certainly was.

If Michael's advice resonates with you and you'd like to learn more about his thoughts on trading and the markets, he can be contacted by email at mcook@tradingaccount.co.uk.

KEVIN DAVEY

Kevin Davey is a highly intellectual and championship-winning trader. You see Kevin has an edge most other traders don't have—an abundance of smarts. Not only is Kevin a summa cum laude graduate with a degree in aerospace engineering (who completed an internship at the U.S. space agency, NASA), he also holds an MBA. Kevin sits at the really pointy end of the smart pyramid, and makes the rest of us feel ordinary. Well, he certainly makes me feel ordinary.

Kevin is a successful short-term systematic trader, who has used his smarts to succeed. So well that in 2006 he won the Robbins World Cup Championship of Futures Trading® with a 107 percent return. And not only is Kevin a past winner, he has also been consistent, coming second in both 2005 (148 percent) and 2007 (112 percent).

Kevin is unique in my collection of traders because as far as I know he is the only one who operates fully automated mechanical trading systems in which his PC does most of the trading—executing entries, stops, and exits. He's an active trader who doesn't actively trade. He lets his computer do most of the trading. Now, that is what I call smart!

Like most traders, Kevin's earlier years were filled with disappointment. Kevin started trading in 1991, and one of his initial trading strategies was to trade a moving average crossover system. After initial losses, he decided it would be best to fade the signals and do the opposite. To his dismay, he achieved the same result, additional losses. At least his performance was consistent! After experiencing a 60 percent loss of his account, Kevin decided to quit trading, and spent the following years devouring everything he could on trading. From his efforts, Kevin was able to develop a collection of winning mechanical strategies that has allowed him to perform so well in trading championships. Kevin, despite his success, has only recently come to full-time trading when he left his job in 2008. But then developing fully automatic trading strategies didn't demand Kevin to be in front of a screen all day. He chose to leave his job to spend more time with his family and to devote even more time to studying the markets.

Today, Kevin focuses on keeping his mechanical models simple. And he believes his emphasis on their exit strategies is what gives the models their edge. He uses TradeStation software to research, develop, and back test his strategies. He also uses it for his automatic order execution. Kevin is primarily focused on short-term opportunities in which he trades multiple time frames. Some of his models will trade one-minute, 10-minute, 30-minute, and daily time frames. Some are longer term, exiting between one and five days, while his spread trades can last up to weeks or months. His main trading markets are the index futures, although he does trade at times metals, agriculturals, softs, and currency markets.

When he's not developing strategies and monitoring his automatic trading, Kevin likes to relax with his family while always keeping one eye on his favorite football teams, the Cleveland Browns and the University of Michigan Wolverines. Kevin and his family live in Ohio, U.S. Let's now hear what Kevin's one piece of advice is.

"Kevin, given all your trading knowledge and trading experience, I'd imagine you would receive many requests for help. If you were able to give an aspiring trader one piece of advice, and one only, what would it be and why?"

In nearly 20 years of trading, I've learned a lot about technical analysis, fundamental analysis, strategy programming, money management, and trading psychology. Yet even with reading countless trading books (some so complicated that even I could not even understand them), attending numerous seminars and spending countless late night coding trading ideas, I've come to realize that in trading, simplicity is best.

What do I mean by this? For me, being a successful trader means employing the principle of Occam's Razor—the simplest approach is almost always the best choice. So when developing strategies, I tend to avoid complicated theories like Elliott wave or Gann lines, preferring instead to have simple systems with very few parameters. In fact, one strategy I am trading now uses only the most recent two closing prices to determine the next trade signal. Very simple!

So what is so great about a simple strategy, compared to a complex strategy that may perform better historically? When developing a strategy, the mathematical concept of "degrees of freedom" comes into play. If you try to fit the data with too many rules, you can get a perfect fit, but you use up all the degrees of freedom. That's not good, since such a curve fit will not perform well in the future—it only performs well in the past. Simple strategies use very few degrees of freedom, and therefore have the potential to perform much better going forward.

I also employ the simplicity concept in my trading office setup. Unlike many day traders, I don't have a wall of monitors or a bank of computers. One computer, with two monitors, suits me just fine. And most of the day, I'm not even looking at current prices, since I'm busy testing new strategies on historical data. All of my systems are semi- or fully automated, which keeps things simple during the trading day.

I'll admit, sometimes I get a bit jealous of those who develop a new entry technique based on the latest advancements in quantum physics, with 10,000 lines of computer code. Or I'll get a little envious when I see a trader's office that looks like the control room for NASA, with monitors displaying dozens of price charts and indicators. One can't help but be impressed with such displays of grandeur. But, I always then take a step back and ask, "do these more complex arrangements produce better results?" The answer, at least from what I've found, is no. Simple is best, because simple works. Keep it simple.

Kevin J. Davey

Well, how about that? You have to be smart enough to know to keep it simple. The answers do not lie in complexity but in simplicity. And listen everyone. This piece of advice comes from possibly the smartest trader in this book. If anyone could develop a complex trading strategy, it would be a rocket scientist like Kevin. So Kevin is not keeping his approach simple because he's incapable of doing anything else. No. It's because he is both smart and successful enough to know one of trading's little secrets—simple works best. I hope you were listening. I certainly was.

If Kevin's advice resonates with you and you'd like to learn more about his thoughts on trading and the markets he can be contacted through his website at www.kjtradingsystems.com.

TOM DeMARK

Tom DeMark is an institutional heavyweight. He is the go-to man when some of the largest traders and investment funds need to call a friend. Tom DeMark is their brain trust, their own personal lifeline. Out of all my Market Masters, it is Tom whose trading strategies have been, and are still today, responsible for managing the largest amounts of money. Let me put it this way. Since 1997, Tom has been a special adviser to Steven Cohen at SAC Capital. Steven Cohen is a billionaire hedge fund investor and founder of SAC Capital, which he founded in 1992 with $25 million in assets under management. At the time of this writing, he manages $16 billion in assets under management, and since inception his funds have returned on average 40 percent per annum. Before working with Steven Cohen, Tom worked with the late Charlie Di Francesca—who at the time was the biggest trader on the Chicago Board of Trade. Tom is just not a heavy hitter, he is *the* heavy hitter. He has worked with some of the market's biggest names, including Paul Tudor Jones, George Soros, Michael Steinhardt, Van Hoisington, Goldman Sachs, IBM, Union Carbide, JP Morgan, Citibank, Atlantic Richfield, State of Illinois, the Tisch family, MMM, State of Illinois,

Leon Cooperman, and many other large and successful investment managers and funds.

I feel very fortunate to have such an institutional heavyweight as Tom agree to offer you one piece of advice, advice that usually comes with an institutional size consulting fee, but for you only the price of this book! And I have to thank Larry Williams again for introducing me to Tom.

Larry actually did three things for me. He first introduced me to Tom. He then encouraged Tom to consider and accept my invitation to participate in this book. And third Larry leant on Tom to hurry up his mate when I was still waiting on Tom's advice as my deadline for this book was fast approaching. I received Tom's advice within seven days of my deadline! So thank you again Larry. And as a sidebar (and it'll be interesting to see whether my comment here survives the editor's pen), all the Market Masters are good people. If they weren't, they wouldn't have gone to the trouble to help both me by contributing and you by offering their one piece of advice. And the two who have helped me the most in bringing together such a diverse and successful group of traders have been possibly the two highest-profile traders in my Market Master list—Daryl Guppy and Larry Williams. Two traders who had no reason to go out of their way to help me except for the simple fact that I asked. Neither of them are family to me, neither have any financial interest in this book, neither have a whole chapter dedicated to their individual approaches. They have simply helped me because I simply asked and that to me makes them simply very nice people—despite their high profile and time constraints. So again another big thank you to Daryl and Larry. Now back to Tom.

Tom DeMark, to my mind, is a colossus in the trading world. His original and brilliant thinking has made him one of the most sought-after and highly paid market timers in the market. Just take another look at the names above who have tapped into his thinking. Thinking that has not only seen him a highly sought-after adviser but also a successful trader in his own right.

As an elite adviser to the top traders, he may just be in a league of his own. And his very own existence and success flies in the face of the old chestnut favorite of the relative investment industry, which continually roll out their cliché across the printed media and television that " . . . It's time in the market that counts, not timing the market . . . "

Tom is Mr. Timer! Tom has spent the past 43 years researching, developing, testing, trading, and teaching his market-timing techniques to institutional traders and investors. Tom has spent more than 40 years proving it's not time in the market that counts but timing the market!

Tom started trading in 1967 as a discretionary trader using traditional chart patterns. Back then there were no PCs, no internet, no live data feeds, and no Bloomberg terminals. Tom traded off Victoria Feed commodity charts, Abe Cohen and Morgan Rogers point and figure charts, and Wyckoff charts.

After graduating from university with an MBA and having attended law school, Tom joined NNIS, a Milwaukee, Wisconsin investment company. Tom was placed in charge to determine the correct timing to initiate and liquidate investments. What he soon discovered was that it was near impossible to accumulate any meaningful positions after a market bottomed and equally difficult to liquidate significant investment holdings after a market top. Out of necessity, Tom had to develop strategies to buy into weakness, in anticipation of a market bottom, and sell into strength, in anticipation of a market top. It was due to this practical requirement for managing large sums of money that Tom was forced to think contrary to accepted market practices. Rather than avoid picking tops and bottoms, Tom was forced to anticipate them.

In 1973, Tom came across another young trader, who was as inquisitive as Tom, who was also challenging traditional trading concepts. There was a meeting of minds and spirits that saw the two young traders form a strong and lasting bond and friendship that continues to this day. These two young traders, unbeknown to them at the time, were making groundbreaking discoveries in technical analysis. One such endeavor centered around Elliott wave. Both Tom and his collaborator could easily see the existence of Elliott's defined wave structure in the market. However, what they didn't like was how subjective Elliott wave was with its flexible wave counts and recounts with waves within waves. They set out to determine whether it was possible to identify Elliot wave reversal points in a mechanical and objective manner, as opposed to Elliott's subjective and malleable five- and three-wave combinations. They wanted to develop an alternative template to explain market tops and bottoms. That endeavor saw Tom and his young friend co-develop Tom's famous TD Sequential indicator that is still used today around the world by thousands of traders across all markets and across all timeframes. Even 30 years after the objective price-based pattern was discovered by Tom and his friend, it can still be seen in the markets today. It was truly groundbreaking work these two young traders did. As you know, one was Tom DeMark, the other young trader was Larry Williams.

And it was Tom's meeting with Larry in 1973 that encouraged him to commit himself to full-time trading and the rest, as they say, is history with such a pedigree resume full of who's who in the trading and investment world.

Being a market timer makes Tom a countertrend trader. Ninety-five percent of what he does focuses on measuring price exhaustion, anticipating market tops and bottoms, or simply reversals. As you can see, Tom thinks differently about the markets. Where most look to trade with the trend, Tom looks to anticipate the end of trends. Tom is Mr. Anti-Trend.

Tom is a hard critic of general technical analysis, and personally believes it doesn't work due to it being so subjective. Although Tom agrees his work could be seen as a part of technical analysis, he doesn't see himself as a technical analyst, but rather, as you know, a market timer.

Tom believes fundamentals drive the longer-term movement of markets, but on a shorter-term basis he believes you have to time your entries and exits. And Tom believes you can do it with psychology and market-timing tools.

Tom believes in simple, nonoptimized, and objective mechanical systems, and believes they should be universal across all markets and all time frames and hold up under all bull market and bear market conditions. He doesn't believe markets change over time because markets only reflect human nature—fear and greed, which never changes. For example, Tom's TD Sequential he co-created with Larry Williams was first applied to the currency, bond, and T-bill futures during the 1970s, has generally not changed since then, and continues to work across all markets and all time frames, despite markets supposedly changing. Tom says it would take a lot to convince him that markets change.

Tom has created many market-timing models and indicators. His market-timing tools, the Tom DeMark "TD" indicators, are primarily pattern based. *His indicators are not like most indicators, which are a derivative of price.* Tom's indicators reflect 100 percent objective price patterns. They capture his particular patterns, and being an indicator they are easy to see on a screen. Many of his indicators are on the largest professional data service platforms available today—Bloomberg, Thomson, CQG, and De-Mark PRIME. Tom's indicators are now used by more than 35,000 Bloomberg traders! Tom is the heavyweight. And Tom believes in simple systems.

As you know, I believe Tom is responsible for one of the best market observations that I have read. Below is the full quote from Art Collins' *Market Beaters.*[3]

> When I was at Tudor, I created four or five systems for Paul Jones. Subsequent to creating them, they brought in guys who do optimization models, artificial intelligence, everything possible that was upper level math. The bottom line was, after 17 programmers and four or five years of testing, the basic four or five systems worked the best.

Tom was the guy who created the basic four or five systems for Paul Tudor Jones. Tom was responsible for the simple mechanical strategies that 17 programmers over four or five years could not beat, even with Paul Tudor Jones' resources behind them.

Apart from consulting, Tom continues to trade for himself using his own personal price-based indicators. Using CQG and Bloomberg, Tom's preferred time frame for trading is intraday and daily bars. He trades both shares and futures.

Tom has authored three books, *The New Science of Technical Analysis, New Market Timing Techniques*, and *DeMark on Day Trading Options*.[4] Outside trading, you'll find Tom either immersed in researching market timing or following sports, particularly basketball. And like a lot of successful and driven people Tom, to the annoyance of his family, can work too hard while maintaining his punishing and obsessive focus on global markets. Tom and his family live on the West Coast of the U.S. Let's now hear what Tom's one piece of advice is.

"Tom, given all your trading knowledge and trading experience, I'd imagine you would receive many requests for help. If you were able to give an aspiring trader one piece of advice, and one only, what would it be and why?"

Most beginning traders operate under a glaring misconception that following the market advice and the consensus outlook of most traders is the road to trading success. More than likely, this belief stems from how one is accustomed to dealing socially with others. Specifically, whereas in life compromising and siding with others is the path of least resistance, a similar approach applied to trading is often a ticket to trading disaster.

A long-held belief among traders is that the "market's trend is a trader's friend." I have added a corollary to this adage and it is: *". . . unless the trend is about to end."*

My extensive supply/demand analysis research conducted many years ago proved that markets bottom, not because of smart buyers entering the market at a perceived low, rather the low being recorded, figuratively speaking, by the last seller selling.

In fact, when premature buying does occur into a market decline, it is often due to short covering and once the buying dissipates, the decline resumes only faster due to the price vacuum caused by the premature buying.

Conversely, market tops are not formed because of astute well-informed sellers, rather they occur due to the fact that figuratively speaking, the last buyer has bought.

These observations have proven to be beneficial to the type of trading I have been associated with my entire investment career.

Specifically, for a trader managing a large fund, it is imperative that selling be done in anticipation of a market high, rather than once the high has been recorded and price is declining. So too it is more prudent to buy into weakness, rather than after a low has been recorded. This prevents dealing with price slippage and gaps and buying on the offer and selling on the bid as most trend followers are forced to do.

In other words, operating at those trend exhaustion and price inflection points can prove to be more rewarding than merely following the market's trend and the psychology of traders.

Operating against the overall commonly held market expectation is difficult at the time one may place the trade, but operating against the trend provides an advantage and opportunity for trading profits that trend followers are unable to realize, particularly were one to apply proven trading tools designed specifically to anticipate likely market trend exhaustion levels.

This anti-trend approach has proven to be more rewarding as it relates to selling than buying a market. Buying is a cumulative process. By that, I mean one may take an initial position in a market, and once the market rallies, add size. At the same time, one is more prone to seek out positive developments and recommendations, and once they are identified, one may even add to the position by purchasing on margin. Eventually, despite how much one may be enamored with a market, one's buying potential is exhausted. However, once a trader becomes negative on a market, typically an entire position is sold.

That is the reason markets typically decline three times faster than they advance. A trader can like a position in degrees and buy as price advances, but once disenchanted, all is sold.

Tom DeMark

Well, how about that? Tom believes trading with the trend may not be as friendly as you have been led to believe, particularly when it's about to end! Tom has shared with you his important observations about market tops and bottoms. Contrary to what most think, tops are not made by smart sellers, but are caused by a lack of buying. Bottoms are not made by smart buyers, but because of exhausted sellers. Understanding this has allowed Tom to become the Master Timer that he is today. And his advice to you is to question current thinking and to avoid the herd. Avoid what the majority are doing. Avoid the safety of numbers. Identify and trade trend exhaustion and price inflection points. Investigate countertrend or swing trading. They have been very profitable for him and his clients, and they can be for you too. And from Tom's experience counter- or anti-trend trading is more rewarding at market tops then bottoms, because markets decline three times faster than they advance. Tom stands alone in the world of technical analysis that trumpets trading with the trend. Like a fearless or foolish rebel, Tom stands alone in the middle of the technical analysis highway facing the traditional and majority views head on without fear or favour! And he is able to do it because he is obviously very successful at it. Tom's singularly and powerful piece of advice is to step away from the comfort of the herd's majority view on trends, and investigate strategies on how to anticipate market tops and bottoms. This is powerful advice for two reasons. First, it's opposite to what the majority think and therefore makes it controversial. This is a bold standout view. And second, it's what the Steven Cohen, Paul Tudor Jones, and George Soros-type investment and trading heavyweights pay Tom for—to identify the correct time and price to enter and exit markets before they reverse, and to do it in institutional size. Tom's advice is to focus on countertrend- or swing-trading methodologies. I hope you were listening; I know I was.

If Tom's advice resonates with you and you'd like to learn more about his thoughts on trading and the markets, he can be contacted through his websites at www.demark.com and www.marketstudies.net.

LEE GETTESS

Lee Gettess is a world-class mechanical system designer and trader. Lee has achieved an accomplishment that very few traders get to experience. To his credit, Lee is responsible for developing a mechanical trading strategy that has stood the test of time, and continues to work 21 years after it was first designed. Not many successful traders can say that. In this arena of system development Lee certainly has earned the bragging rights for system guru! Although if you know Lee then you'll know he is very self effacing and humble and not prone to brag. Proud yes, brash no.

This success of Lee's occurred in 1988, when he managed to develop his Volpat trading strategy. In addition to its continuing profitability, at time of writing, *Futures Truth*, an independent publication that monitors more then 500 trading systems, has ranked Lee's Volpat strategy in its top 10 systems. And not only was it ranked in the "top 10" for the most recent 12 months, but it was also ranked third! Third out of more than 500 trading strategies. A strategy Lee developed over 21 years ago. An extraordinary achievement.

Please let me explain what Lee has achieved. He developed an objective rule-based trading strategy according to his own theory of market behavior. Anyone following his strategy would have been profitable over the past 21 years, winning more than enough to pay for all the losses that inevitably occur and still leaving plenty over for profit. Certainly, there have been losing years. However, overall it has been shown in real time to have a stable and steadily rising equity curve. There are not many well-regarded trading theories (let alone trading strategies) that can claim the same level of success.

As I've said, very few traders can say they have achieved the same accomplishment—developing a durable trading strategy as Lee has. Certainly

Lee is not alone. Richard Donchian developed his four-week (20-bar) channel breakout system during the 1960s, which achieved "celebrity" status after Richard Dennis and Bill Eckhardt's Turtle experiment in the 1980s. There is also another trend-trading system that was developed in the mid-1980s, based on John Bollinger's Bollinger Bands. That strategy continues to make money today. And these aren't the only durable strategies out there. However, compared to the number of trading ideas that have been created over the years, durable and robust strategies that have stood the test of time for more than 21 years are very few and far between. They are as rare as hen's teeth.

Now, Lee wasn't always a trader. He began his working career mopping floors at General Motors before transitioning into computer programming. In 1985, Lee developed an interest in trading after a broker phone call suggesting easy money. After experiencing a large loss in his account, Lee threw himself into studying everything he could on technical analysis, and used his computer background to begin evaluating various market assumptions and testing ideas. And back then he didn't have the benefit of advanced trading software like traders have today, writing his own code in GWBASIC on one of the original PCs, the 88XT computer! Now, despite the absence of Pentium chips, Lee was able to develop successful pattern-based volatility breakout strategies, winning strategies that gave Lee his first edge.

Lee was doing so well in his trading that in 1987, just before the October sharemarket crash, he decided to go trading full time. Talk about perfect timing, not! Although he lost money on the day the market crashed, he didn't lose much, and survived relatively intact. Looking back, Lee does acknowledge that it was actually a good experience for him, "I saw my entire life flash in front of my eyes when the S&P crashed. It was very good for me in hindsight though because up until then I just thought trading would be easy. That slap in the face forced me to actually learn how to trade."

In 1988, Lee developed his Volpat strategy, which he later sold in 1993 for more than $675,000 to a group of professional traders that included two large public funds and one of the largest banks in North America.

Lee has been trading full time now for more than 25 years. He runs a successful advisory service, in which he personally trades every recommendation he makes. Many professional traders use Lee's advisory service to diversify the risk in their own trading. His focus today remains short term. Lee will both day trade and execute short-term trades, in which he'll hold positions for between two and four days. He continues to trade the E-Mini SP500 and U.S. 30-year T-bill futures. Lee still trades volatility breakout systems with pattern recognition, although he now combines his strategies with momentum. However, out of the three components, Lee will place a greater reliance on pattern recognition. Lee uses Genesis software for his research, development, and order generation. And although his models are systematic, he does trade them on a discretionary basis, picking and choosing which signals to trade based on his interpretation of market conditions.

When away from his screens Lee likes to relax by working out and playing golf. And to his family's annoyance Lee likes seeing the positive side of all situations regardless of how dire the circumstances are. As Lee says "I'd still rather laugh than cry. Plus, none of us is getting out of here alive, so why not have some fun while we can?" Lee and his family live in Arizona, U.S. Let's now hear what Lee's one piece of advice is.

"So Lee, given all your trading knowledge and trading experience, I'd imagine you would receive many requests for help. If you were able to give an aspiring trader one piece of advice, and one only, what would it be and why?"

I think a good trader also has to be a pessimist, at least as it relates to every individual trade. Too much positive thinking starts morphing into wishful thinking, and that is just no good for a trader. What I focus on, and what I believe every trader needs to focus on, is the risk.

I'm a very positive person. I got into trading to make money as I'm sure virtually every trader does. It is rather illogical to get into trading to lose money, isn't it? I expect to make money over time and I'm very optimistic about the long term results. Trading with the expectation and intent to make money is a given. Now that we know that . . . all I ever focus on is how much I can lose. Why? Because anyone who believes they have control over any other aspect of their trading is just kidding themselves.

We all spend hours and hours researching and analyzing price charts attempting to find what markets we should buy and what markets we should sell. But after you are done with all of the analysis and have actually put a trade on, is there anything you can do about the profit? You root for the market to go your way. You shout and curse in your own chosen language, and you question the parenthood of the market as if the market were a living being. You often even pray. But you are absolutely powerless to make the market move in your direction by any given amount. You can only hope you have done your research correctly and chosen the proper direction, but even then you have to accept that you are dealing with probabilities and not certainties. Even when you do everything right, you are going to be wrong and have to take a loss sometimes. Once you put that trade on the amount of money you are capable of making is completely out of your control.

On the other side, we do have a modicum of control over how much we lose. There are execution costs, slippage, overnight gaps, and possibly even planes crashing into buildings that can cause losses to be larger than we expect, but within reason we do have the ability to control the size of our losses. Whatever total amount of risk you decide to limit yourself to can be adhered to the vast majority of the time. Since risk is the only aspect of your trading that you actually really have any control over, it just makes sense to me that risk is what a good trader should focus on. That is what I do. That is what I suggest you do.

I want the probabilities in my favor, and I want the risk to be both quantifiable and controllable. If any of those factors are missing I would just prefer not to trade.

Lee Gettess

Well, how about that? A successful trader not talking about making profits but asking you to focus on the risk, not the reward, to become a pessimist with every trade so it concentrates your mind on how much money you can lose, to focus on what you can control, not the market's gift, but the market's curse, risk. I hope you have listened keenly to Lee's one piece of advice that he holds above all else. Longevity in trading is all about managing each and every individual trade's risk. Ignore the risk and you'll have a short career in trading. I hope you were listening, and as always I was!

If Lee's advice resonates with you and you'd like to learn more about his thoughts on trading and the markets, he can be contacted through his website at www.leegettess.com.

DARYL GUPPY

Daryl Guppy may possibly be one of the most recognizable caucasians in China's financial markets. If this is true, given China's population, he may well be one of the most recognizable people in the world. This is due to several factors. First, Daryl's wide and popular appeal in China, which is due to both the translation of many of his trading books into Mandarin, his regular commentary work in Chinese-language financial media, and his regular chart analysis work with CNBC Asia's Squawk Box; second, the Chinese love for trading; and finally, Daryl's commitment to their language. Australia not only has a Mandarin-speaking prime minister in Kevin Rudd, but it also has a Mandarin-speaking trader in Daryl Guppy! With his trademark moustache, Daryl is easily recognizable in China, and is known among Asian traders as the Chart Man.

Although Daryl does have many trading books in print, which makes him one of the leading trader educators in the world today, he doesn't see himself as only an educator. Daryl sees himself as a trader first and foremost, and producing books provides him an outlet for his passion for writing. If you have been lucky enough to have received and read one of his private journals, you will understand his enjoyment of the craft. And luckily for aspiring traders who read his books, Daryl is an easy wordsmith, making the impossible and strange appear attainable and clear.

However, there was a time when Daryl wasn't so well known, and there wasn't a published book in sight. It was back in 1989, when he started investing in shares according to Warren Buffet's value philosophy of only purchasing companies you knew and understood. Not liking the situation where he felt his financial fate was at the mercy of the company, he started to develop ideas for trading, ideas to put the control of his financial destiny back into his own hands. In time, Daryl developed a winning methodology for trading shares. On a daily basis, Daryl would create a watchlist of shares that exhibited multiple systematic trading opportunities. He would then overlay a discretionary selection criteria to determine which of those shares on the watchlist would move across to his trade list. His setups primarily revolved around high-probability chart patterns. Daryl's preferred time frame was to work off daily bars using Computrac charting software. Success didn't come immediately, but by 1993 Daryl was trading full time with both confidence and success.

News soon spread about Daryl's success and people started asking him for assistance. This interest lead to Daryl writing his first trading book, *Share Trading*, in 1996.[5] The book sold out within two weeks. Now in its 14th year of publication, this classic has enjoyed 12 print runs! Daryl was in nirvana combining his two passions, trading and writing. Since then Daryl has gone onto to publish 15 trading books in total, including translated editions, some of which have been rewritten for the China market.

Today, Daryl continues to trade much like he did when he started to enjoy success—combining a discretionary selection criteria over multiple systematic trading opportunities. He actively trades equities and associated derivatives markets including CFDs, warrants, ETFs, and indices in the Australian, Singapore, and Hong Kong markets. In addition he closely monitors China due to its ever increasing influence over world markets. He continues to focus primarily on high-probability chart patterns with some tape reading thrown in for short-term trading. Daryl is a big believer in letting market conditions direct his preferred time frame for trading. Conditions permitting, he can easily place trades lasting for as short as five minutes or for as long as a couple of weeks. He lets the market tell him the best time frame. To help him in identifying opportunities, Daryl uses a suite of charting packages that include Guppy Traders Essentials, Metastock, NextView Adviser, and Gousen for the China markets.

Daryl's contribution to trading has not been restricted to books. Over the years, he has developed several leading technical indicators that are included in MetaStock, OmniTrader, Guppy Traders Essentials, and other charting programs. He has developed a very successful trader education and training business with offices in Darwin, Singapore and Beijing. Daryl produces popular educational newsletters for the Australian, Singapore and Malaysian markets. He contributes regular material and columns to an increasing number of Chinese financial publications. He is a popular and sought-after speaker throughout Asia-Pacific, China, Europe, and North America.

When Daryl isn't trading or teaching others to trade, it can generally be assumed he is on his laptop somewhere in the world recording his thoughts to disk. And although he loves writing, it does have its drawbacks due to the prolonged periods of concentration it requires, periods of concentration his wife would prefer were better spent on household chores!

And I'm reluctant to say that Daryl and his family live in Darwin, Australia, even though they do. This is because every time I make contact with Daryl he's either in Beijing, Shanghai, Singapore, Kuala Lumpur, or some other place, but never at home!

Now, while Daryl isn't focused on the markets, catching a plane, or writing down his thoughts, please let me ask him for his one piece of advice. *"Daryl, given all your trading knowledge and trading experience, I'd imagine you would receive many requests for help. If you were able to give an aspiring trader one piece of advice, and one only, what would it be and why?"*

This seems to be a simple question, but the answer is difficult. There any many different skills required for success in the market. I remember all the books I have read and my many years of trading the market. The market behavior is very different in 2009 from the market I was trading in 1999, or in 1989. Yet there must be some common features that have not changed.

When I first started trading, I studied and learned from other master traders. Then as my skill grew, I developed my own thinking and my own approaches. I shared these in my books so others could also learn. Then I became too confident, and the market reminded me that my skill always needed to be updated to survive in developing market conditions. My single piece of advice to new traders and to traders with experience is just one word. The word is humility.

Humility means you understand and acknowledge that other people in the market know much more than you know. They understand what is happening in the business for a particular company. Other people understand what is happening in the economy, or in government. Other people have much better analysis skills, or much better information. It is not possible to personally develop this knowledge. You cannot be smarter than the market or the people in the market.

Humility means you appreciate their knowledge and you learn to follow their conclusions in the market. All of their information and analysis skill is revealed in the chart of price activity. Every day, intelligent people buy and sell in the market. You can measure their opinion by watching the price activity. This behavior develops three important basic relationships.

The first basic relationship is stable support and resistance. We show these as horizontal lines on the chart.

The second basic relationship is dynamic or developing support and resistance levels. We show these as sloping trend lines on the chart.

The third basic relationship is between traders and investors. We use the Guppy Multiple Moving Average to understand and analyze this relationship.

These are the foundations of my understanding of the market because they tell me how other people are thinking.

Humility means I accept the message created by the chart and the patterns of price behavior. Sometimes I think the market is wrong. It should not be falling. I have learned to ignore my opinion if my opinion is not confirmed by the behavior of the market price.

Humility means I listen to the chart. When you listen, you can hear money talking. So my simple one piece of advice is this. Be humble in the market, and the market will reward you.

Daryl Guppy

Humility. So simple, so subtle, and yet so powerful. This is wonderful advice because humility is usually the last emotion traders learn, to their cost. When people come to trading, it's usually with the confidence, energy, enthusiasm, and unintended arrogance that are normally associated with youth. And then it's through the market's maximum adversity that we learn to the cost of our wallets, soul, pride, and ego that we can never be more than respectful students sitting at the feet of the all-knowing and ever-changing masterful market. I hope you were listening. I certainly was. Even with all the trading acknowledge and success one can achieve, it can all go by the wayside as soon as you stop listening to what the market is telling you. Being humble will ensure that you will remain open to the market's messages, and as Daryl says, it will reward you in turn. If not, you'll be catching the high-speed express train to disappointment!

If Daryl's advice resonates with you and you'd like to learn more about his thoughts on trading and the markets, he can be contacted through his website at www.Guppytraders.com.

RICHARD MELKI

Richard Melki is a successful discretionary trader, who runs his own absolute-return fund. As a discretionary trader, Richard's style is referred to as Global Macro. This implies that Richard's mandate for trading has no boundaries. He is a free-spirited trader who can enter and exit any market at any time for any reason. If Richard believes a trade setup is developing, he'll trade it—regardless of its instrument, its market, or its geographic location.

And Richard Melki may just be one of the best discretionary traders there is. During the 2008 Global Financial Crisis, the independent research house Australian Fund Monitors ranked Richard second within his strategy category. Not bad, hey?

But then you would expect him to be good because Richard's whole career has been the markets, trading, and investing. You see, Richard is an ex-institutional proprietary trader, having spent the best part of a decade trading for merchant banks in Australia, one of them being Bankers Trust (BT), when BT was the envy of all market participants.

As a discretionary trader, Richard uses very little technical analysis or technique to support his trades. Richard relies on his own interpretation of global macroeconomic events and knowledge of market flow to support his trading decisions.

In addition, Richard Melki is also one of my oldest and best friends. We met in 1983, when we were both majoring in finance at university. I left the honors program in December 1983 to join Bank of America while Richard completed his honors degree and in 1986 joined AIDC (Australian Industry Development Corporation)—a semi-government-owned merchant bank.

As a pure discretionary trader, with no predisposition to any particular technical technique, I personally view Richard as a maverick trader who relies on his own "head" and intuition to trade. He's one of those lucky few who has the rare gift and ability to absorb many economic variables while monitoring multiple markets, and distill it all down to a clear binary decision about whether to trade. He'll then use technicals to time his entry. He is the best economic analyst I know. If you knew Richard, you'd ignore all those talking head economists you hear on the television and radio and just listen to him!

But let's start at the beginning. Richard joined AIDC as a trainee dealer in 1986. From the beginning, Richard was always a discretionary trader looking to interpret the fundamental economic landscape correctly and use technical tools to time his entries. Nothing has really changed for Richard over the past 23 years—except that he has just become better at it. Back then, Richard relied on Reuters and Telerate for his economic news and charts. By 1988, Richard was in charge of derivatives at AIDC, and had become one of its proprietary traders. His success soon became known in the markets, and it wasn't long before he was headhunted to join BT. In 1995, Richard left BT to trade for himself and pursue personal investment interests.

In 2000, he set up his own absolute-return management business to manage external funds. Richard has now been trading for more than 24 years, and it still amazes me how he can effortlessly let go of a particular market view, stop himself out, and reverse his position. When Richard is wrong, he knows it, and doesn't waste any lost pride in analyzing a particular situation incorrectly. While most of us would feel despondent about a loss, and be hard on ourselves for being wrong in our analysis, it's like water off a duck's back for Richard. He's on to the next opportunity.

Another interesting fact about Richard is that for a discretionary trader, he has a high regard for systematic or mechanical traders. And it comes from first-hand experience. Normally, discretionary traders dismiss systematic traders, believing the markets are never that simple that a mathematical algorithm, whether it be an indicator or quantitative expression, could possibly be used to extract reliable profits. They believe in the weak form of the efficient market hypothesis, which says you cannot use past price action to predict future price action. So for Richard to have a high degree of respect for systematic traders is very unusual.

But then Richard was a proprietary trader for BT during their glory days, and he has observed mechanical trading first hand. During its prosperous days, BT would group its prop traders together on one desk. Richard was one of those traders. However, not all the prop traders were the same. There was one who required constant monitoring by two young graduates, one working the day shift while the other worked the evening shift. Their jobs were to execute every order given by this unique proprietary trader that was different to Richard and the others. And this particular proprietary trader was the best-performing trader each year for the time Richard was at BT. And guess what, this proprietary trader was a PC that ran a systematic trading program—monitoring global markets 24/7, generating buy and sell orders for the young graduates to execute. For the time Richard was there at BT, a mechanical trading program was the best-performing proprietary trader at BT! And consequently Richard learned to have a high regard for mechanical trading.

And as a sidebar none of the other proprietary traders knew what the program did. It was a closely held secret within BT. However, everyone knew it was designed by the chess champion Richard Farleigh, who was highly regarded within BT. Richard Farleigh was so successful at BT that he was headhunted to run a hedge fund in Bermuda, where he later retired at the age of 34 years, and later moved to Monte Carlo. You can read more about Richard Farleigh in his book *Taming the Lion*.[6]

So Richard Melki has seen first hand how effective mechanical trading can be, and doesn't dismiss it as so many other discretionary traders do. As a discretionary trader, Richard is happy to trade over multiple time frames—from day trading to short-to-medium term. It's very rare for Richard to hang on to a long-term position. Although Richard has no boundaries on what he can trade, he does, at time of writing, have a preference for trading equity index, interest rate, commodity, and currency markets. His preferred instruments for trading are futures and options. He will also trade Australian shares if he sees an opportunity. Richard will read all economic reports, and for technicals he can use any mixture of simple trend line breaks, simple pattern recognition, divergences, and momentum change.

Outside trading, you'll find Richard with his nose in a biography, happily tuning out to the annoyance of his wife Peta. Richard has a strong faith, and is very active in his church, being a member of the board of the Antiochian Orthodox Archdiocese of Australia, New Zealand, and the Philippines. Richard and his family live in Sydney, Australia. Let's now hear what Richard's one piece of advice is.

"Richard, given all your trading knowledge and trading experience, I'd imagine you would receive many requests for help. If you were able to give an aspiring trader one piece of advice, and one only, what would it be and why?"

My name is Richard Melki and I am the CEO of the RTM Absolute Return Fund. I have been an active trader in the major asset classes since 1986, and have made money in every year of trading. In that time, I have experienced (and survived) periods of market dislocation, such as the stockmarket crash of 1987, the Asian crisis of 1997, the collapse of Long Term Capital Management in 1998, the terrorist attacks of 9/11, and the current Global Financial Crisis. In addition, I have been able to build a 20+-year career in continuous trading and not "burn out" after a few years.

Brent, your question is simple and straightforward, but the key to my trading success is based on my capital management system and trading plan and not just one thing. As a discretionary, global macro trader I am faced with a deluge of information, market observations, and technical analysis. The alignment of these variables is very much the key to my trading decision, and the execution of this decision is a function of my capital management system. In this brief comment, I'll try to give a broad outline of my strategy, rather than a single piece of advice.

Whether I am trading from a short- or long-term perspective or in equity, fixed interest or currency markets, the most important thing is to have realistic expectations, a robust capital management system, and a trading plan applicable to your time frame—don't try to achieve your objective within the first couple of months because this only increases the probability of blowing up, but rather look at each month as a stepping stone to your goal.

My trading plan is quite simple and over the years I have found that most successful traders have trading plans that are not too complex. As a discretionary trader, I am daily bombarded with loads of economic data. My trading methodology relies on forward-looking economic data and models combined with technical and market observations. Market statistics and timing also play a key role in my trading style. For example, retail sales is an important economic variable that I follow, but of equal importance to me is the ratio of inventory to sales and level of stockpiles. The manufacturing ISM index is another important economic variable, but equally important are the index subcategories such as the production and new order elements of the index. My trading methodology also incorporates market technicals, statistical and timing observations, and market mood, that is what is the market telling me. The alignment of all these variables is the key to my trading methodology.

Encompassing all my trading decisions is my capital management system. This ensures capital preservation, survival, and the efficient allocation of capital. As part of a capital management system, it is important to remind yourself continually that not every trade is a winner, in fact odds are that most trades will be losers, so the key is to manage your losses and exit your profitable trades in a way that ensures your overall expectation return is always positive. To minimize slippage when entering and exiting a trade, I only trade liquid markets and markets not subject to political manipulation (as can happen with some currencies).

Psychological toughness is important for a trader. Because losses are part of the game, it is very important to move on and not remain overly focused on losses or become obsessed with making up those losses. Remember, an opportunity presents itself nearly every day. I hope my small contribution will help your readers.

Richard Melki

Wow. That was certainly more then I expected! If your preference is to trade on a discretionary basis, then Richard has given you an invaluable look into his economic playbook, the fundamental statistics that he pays attention to. Richard has been very generous in sharing with you his trade plan, one that has allowed him to make money trading every year for the past 24 years. Richard felt he was unable to offer a single piece of advice, so he has unselfishly summarized in a nutshell what he does. And what is important for Richard is to see an alignment of his forward-looking economic variables with the market's price action. Richard always attempts to place the odds of winning on his side. He is a strong advocate of capital (money) management and for learning how to ignore the daily market noise that can distract a trader. These are wise words that come from a successful trader, who has a rare and enviable track record of 24 consecutive winning years.

Unfortunately, I can't give you a website to contact Richard, but if his thoughts have struck a chord with you then I'd suggest you photocopy his words and place them above your monitor as a constant reminder of how one discretionary trader succeeds in the market. I hope you enjoyed listening to Richard and that he has given you some invaluable insight— I know he has for me, and I've known him for 27 years!

GEOFF MORGAN

Geoff Morgan is my good friend and mentor. Geoff is responsible for placing me on the correct path toward trading success. It was Geoff who introduced to me the importance of placing the statistical odds in my favor by looking at the market in an unemotional, 100 percent objective, cold, detached, and logical manner.

At the time, I was a disciple of Elliott wave, trading the SPI. Geoff was a client adviser working for the broker I used. I had spoken to Geoff on numerous occasions over the years when I was calling up to speak with my client adviser. Although we spoke regularly, we didn't really chat about the markets.

Well, one day I was calling up for my fill on another loss, and I was once again despondent about my trading. It seemed to me that I couldn't win a trick. My client adviser was out to lunch, so Geoff picked up the phone. I asked Geoff whether he had my fill from the futures exchange, and for the first time I asked him for his opinion about where he thought the SPI was heading. Well, Geoff calmly remarked that the SPI had recorded three consecutive higher closes. He then observed, based on his knowledge of the SPI's statistical price movements, that since the SPI had reached its median move to the upside, based on its consecutive closing sequence, that he would be reluctant to buy it. He would instead be looking for opportunities to go short. The SPI stalled and saw lower prices over the following days. Well, that was my own personal enormous lightbulb moment. I thought Hollywood and Las Vegas had come together to party over my head because I felt like I was walking under a huge floodlight! From that moment, I began my transformation from being a discretionary predictor relying on my subjective interpretation of Elliott wave to a mechanical pragmatist relying on observed 100 percent objective repetitive price patterns. So I can thank Geoff for showing me the light, so to speak.

Now, most people will not have heard of Geoff Morgan because he is an exceedingly private person. He's a private trader, who trades only for himself and his family. He doesn't teach, he doesn't write books, he doesn't present at the trading expos, and he doesn't run workshops.

I was personally lucky to have met Geoff, and for Geoff to mentor me, and I'm lucky again to have him agree to participate in this book. Now, please don't be disappointed that you haven't heard of Geoff, or that, like me, he's just a private trader. You see, Geoff, as are many of the Market Masters in this book, is an original market thinker, and certainly one who has one of the most logical minds I've had the pleasure to listen to. Geoff has serious logic, serious awareness, and serious nous when it comes to the markets. And not only is he smart, he also has that unique gift of being able to explain ideas in a simple and logical manner. He's like the school teacher and university lecturer you wish you had for all your subjects. He is so good at teaching that one of my nicknames for him is the Professor, while the other is "TG"—for Trader Geoff.

Let me put it this way. I regularly have dinner with Geoff and three other full-time traders. Geoff and I are the private traders. The others run their own absolute-return funds, managing hundreds of millions of dollars of institutional and private money between them. One is Richard Melki, whom you have just met. The other two are brothers whom I invited to participate in this book because their story and success is truly inspirational. However, although flattered to be invited, they declined to be involved because their focus is the institutional market and not the private trader who may read this book.

Anyway, we regularly have dinner together, and chat about the markets. And the person who has us thinking the most and giving us more "aha" moments is, yes, you guessed right—Geoff. Geoff the Professor. He just has an amazing insight and view of the markets that come from left of field, which when he explains them sound so logical, simple, and obvious. He can sometimes make you feel lacking when it comes to the markets—but in the nicest possible way.

So although Geoff is unknown, please understand that he is a successful private trader with an enviable track record, who has an institutional-size market intellect.

Now that you have a better idea of who Geoff is, please let me fill you in on his background. Geoff's interest in risk assessment started at a very early age. From about 14 years of age, he attended the racetrack regularly, learning to play the odds and beat the bookmarkers. During the 1970s, he studied civil engineering while working part time as a cadet civil engineer. While he was studying, Geoff continued his gambling activities. By simply playing the odds, he was able to supplement his income, overall finishing ahead of the bookmakers. His winnings helped put him through university.

So from his early twenties, Geoff knew that markets—whether they were racing odds or trading—were all about identifying a statistical edge and taking an advantage of it. He was able to do this because he had a very logical and mathematical mind, one that he was using while studying civil engineering. It also saw him write an unpublished book on how to win backgammon by calculating and playing with the odds! The motivation for writing the book came after reading a book written by a world champion backgammon player. In it, he described a particular strategy as a paradox, whereas Geoff saw it immediately as an advantage based on probability. Did I tell you Geoff was smart?

After traveling overseas, rather than returning to engineering, he changed direction and enrolled in a computer analysis and programming course. He quickly landed a job as an analyst/programmer in the insurance industry.

In 1985, Geoff started his own business specializing in developing risk assessment software for the insurance industry. The business became successful, and in 1989 Geoff sold it, paid off his mortgage, and changed direction again. He completed a financial adviser's course, and became a licensed financial adviser. It also gave him the capital to pursue his interest in markets.

Unlike many new to the markets, Geoff didn't commence trading on a discretionary basis, but built probabilistic models, giving him a mechanical process for entering and exiting the market. After some initial success, Geoff soon realized there was much more to the markets than he knew. Consequently, Geoff made a decision that he needed to learn from the inside. So he commenced a relationship with an established broker that eventually saw him work alongside the adviser as a licensed futures broker. Geoff didn't see his role as a job, but as an opportunity to gain real market knowledge and real trading expertise from the inside, to observe, to listen, and to learn from both brokers and customers. Combining this practical experience with his intellectual love of numbers allowed Geoff to use his programming skills to investigate and research various trading strategies. And it didn't take long for Geoff to successfully develop volatility breakout strategies that he used to benefit both himself and his clients.

In 1995, Geoff left brokering and concentrated on trading full time. Geoff continues to trade today much as he did back in 1995, although with more discretion. Geoff trades pattern-based volatility breakouts in the direction of the medium-term trend. Geoff will day trade futures and he will trade shares short term, holding trades for between three and 10 days. For futures trading Geoff prefers trading the euro/U.S. dollar and Australian dollar/U.S. dollar currency pairs and the SPI. For share trading, at time of writing, Geoff is trading property trust and gold shares listed on the Australian Stock Exchange.

When Geoff isn't trading, he's usually doing something. He can be most annoying in that he hates to sit down and do nothing. It's difficult to relax around him. Geoff loves home renovating—yep you can take Geoff out of civil engineering, but you can't take the engineer out of Geoff. He's super competitive, loves to run, and regularly competes in the "City to Surf," an institutional Sydney 8.7-mile fun run. He loves cryptic crosswords, sudoku, and traveling. And oh, did I tell you that Geoff wrote a logic-based program to solve sudoku puzzles? And to his wife Wendy's annoyance and frustration, Geoff can be too logical, too competitive, and too singleminded at times, making him very difficult to live with! Geoff and his family live in Sydney, Australia. Let me now ask Geoff what his one piece of advice is.

"Geoff, given all your trading knowledge and trading experience, I'd imagine you would receive many requests for help. If you were able to give an aspiring trader one piece of advice, and one only, what would it be and why?"

I have been trading since 1989.

In that time, I have only had one losing year.

When Brent first asked me to contribute to this book, I was flattered.

However, the more I thought about what I was going to say the more I realized that I have a philosophical problem—I am a trader, not an educator.

Futures trading is a zero net game, that is, for me to make money somebody else must lose money. Why would I want other people to stop losing?

Geoff Morgan

Ugh? Now I have to say that wasn't the type of response I was looking for. I received Geoff's advice while I was away on holidays, and I have to say I was initially disappointed by Geoff's comment. I thought it wasn't very generous, and I didn't think it reflected Geoff's generous nature. But then we have known each other for almost 20 years now, and maybe I confused his generosity toward me as his normal generous self. Anyway, I responded to Geoff to thank him and to say that on my return, I would contact him. So I pondered on what he had to offer you. Although I was disappointed, I could also see his point. Why should he help you to reduce his prospects for profitability? Although I thought his contribution was a little slim and mean spirited, it was also the truth. Although he was being tough, he was also being both honest and fair. And as Geoff said, he's not an educator but a trader.

Anyway, on my return from holidays I called Geoff. We had a long talk. Geoff was waiting for a blast from me because he knew his contribution wasn't what I was really looking for. I agreed with Geoff that I was disappointed, but then I also observed that I understood what he was saying. However, I didn't want to let Geoff off the hook, and I wanted more from him because I knew he was special, and I knew that traders needed to know about him and his thoughts.

You see not all successful traders have a high public profile. Not all successful traders win championships. Some of the very best traders, just like Geoff, are private traders who are not in the public arena. They don't manage institutional money. They're private traders who want to remain private. So I had Geoff, and I had an opportunity to bring him out of hiding so I could let you know that not all successful traders have a high public profile. I was determined to drag him out into the light to let you know there is such a thing as a successful private trader.

So I argued my point that I wasn't asking him to be an educator, but I was asking him for one piece of advice as a trader to an aspiring trader. We battled backward and forward, each arguing our point until Geoff relented (so you have to thank me big, big time for dragging Geoff back to the table). It was when Geoff was retelling an old experience of his that I interjected and told him that aspiring traders needed to know what Geoff had just related to me. It was a powerful story relating to the time he was working as a broker. It was a story from the "inside." It was a powerful story with a powerful truth that I wanted Geoff to share with you. I think I made my point because below Geoff has kindly agreed to share it.

Initially, that was all I was going to say, but after a long talk to Brent, he convinced me that I should add a few more words.

For a five-year period from 1991 to 1995, I worked as a futures broker. Eventually, as I developed my market knowledge and trading skills, the conflict between trading and broking saw the trading win. However, it was this five-year period in which I learned the most about trading, traders, and myself.

Our small brokerage firm dealt with retail punters (clients, if you're polite), mostly one-lotters. In the five years, I literally saw hundreds come and go, and only witnessed one make money.

This sent a strong message to me: before you can start winning, you must stop losing.

This simple notion forms the basis of my trading philosophy.

Most traders, particularly trend traders, concentrate on maximizing profits. They need to do this to cover long losing runs.

But it takes a special person to be able to make rational decisions when you are on a 10-trade losing streak and down 50 percent of equity.

I take a different approach, and concentrate on minimizing losses, which avoids such psychologically difficult situations.

My only losing year came down to one trade, and I remember it vividly. It was June 1994. I had been trading bank bill spreads very successfully and, getting a bit cocky, I stepped up from trading five lots to 40 lots. I went on a family holiday to Lord Howe Island, and was out of contact with the markets for 10 days. The spreads usually move very slowly, and you cannot really use stops. While I was away, the interest rates made a drastic change and I was caught. Eventually, bill rates ended up going from 4.5 percent to 8.5 percent in six months. I learned my lesson: I overtraded, and I did not focus on minimizing my potential loss.

My parting words are: good defense wins games.

Geoff Morgan

Now that's the Geoff Morgan I was talking about. Geoff, from personal experience working as a broker to gain market knowledge and trading skills, had literally seen hundreds of retail clients come and go through his doors. And between 1991 and 1995 *he only ever saw one trader make money!*

To my knowledge, I think this honest observation from an ex-broker may just be the first one of its kind ever to appear in a trading book.

An ex-broker openly sharing his observation that over an almost five-year period that he only ever saw one client, out of literally hundreds, ever make money from trading futures!

And as a sidebar, I was one of those many clients of that brokerage firm who didn't win! And please do not quote Geoff's observation out of context to prove futures are risky. In my opinion, Geoff's comments are applicable to all active traders—regardless whether they actively trade futures, shares, options, warrants, CFDs, currencies, or whatever.

Now back to Geoff's real-life observation about small private traders—their inability to control and minimize losses. Whereas most traders focus on maximizing their wins, Geoff believes success is helped if you concentrate on minimizing your losses. And remember, expectancy is a two-part value. If you can lower and minimize your average loss, you will increase your expectancy, and remember that the reason you trade is not to make money, it's not for accuracy—but for the opportunity to earn expectancy.

So for the small private trader, Geoff's advice comes from observing hundreds of private traders come and go over a five-year period, where all but one went by the wayside due to their inability to minimize their losses, for focusing on profits, rather than focusing on minimizing potential losses. Geoff's invaluable advice is to focus on being the best loser you can be! As Geoff's parting words to you said—good defense wins games.

Now unfortunately I can't give you a contact website for Geoff. However, I do hope you appreciate his expanded one piece of advice because it comes from a trader who has experienced both sides of the fence, and from a very successful private trader who has only had one losing year in the past 21 years. And from a private trader who is admired by many much larger traders who between them manage hundreds of millions of dollars of both institutional and private funds.

GREGORY L. MORRIS

Greg Morris is a top gun, literally! Move over Tom Cruise—here comes Greg Morris, a real graduate of the Top Gun Navy Fighter Weapons School at NAS Miramar, California. There was no mincing around a movie studio here for Greg as he spent seven years during the 1970s as a Navy F-4 fighter pilot aboard the *USS Independence*. Didn't I say Greg was a top gun, literally?

After his navy career, Greg developed an interest in the markets that was eventually to replace his passion for flying. Showing the same level of focus and commitment he had to flying Greg soon became an expert market technician and successful trader.

Today, Greg is well known to the public through his best-selling book *Candlestick Charting Explained*, which was first published in 1995 and is now into its third edition. It is regarded as possibly one of the best books ever written on candlestick analysis. Greg studied the art of candlestick analysis in person while in Japan. He has also authored *The Complete Guide to Market Breadth Indicators* which presents a rich history of market internal indicators in encyclopedic format.

Greg is also well known for partnering with a legend of technical analysis, John Murphy, where they created MurphyMorris Inc., and turned it into the leading provider of web-based market analysis tools and commentary. They sold their business to StockCharts.com, Inc. in 2002.

For a some years after the sale, he continued to advise MurphyMorris Money Management's MurphyMorris ETF Fund before becoming the chief technical analyst for Stadion Money Management, Inc. (formerly PMFM, Inc.). Stadion is a large money manager, which manages more than $2 billion in funds. It was Greg who designed and developed the technical rule-based model that is used to oversee management of those funds.

Due to his high profile and success, Greg is a highly sought-after speaker, who has presented to traders throughout North and South America, Europe, and China. He has been featured in *Business Week*, and if you live in the U.S., you will regularly see Greg being asked his market views on the Fox Business, CNBC, and Bloomberg TV. Greg and his wife, Laura, live in the mountains of North Georgia, U.S.

Now, somehow I feel like I'm going to ask Greg the wrong question. I think I'd prefer to just ask him about his experiences flying an F-4 fighter plane. Hey, who hasn't dreamt about flying a fighter jet before! Oh well, maybe next time. Let me ask Greg the correct question that you would like to hear the answer for.

"Greg, given all your trading knowledge and trading experience, I'd imagine you would receive many requests for help. If you were able to give an aspiring trader one piece of advice, and one only, what would it be and why?"

This is the type of question that I could actually answer using just one word—*discipline*. Over the past 35 years, I have developed technical analysis software, written articles, two books on technical analysis, created technical indicators and trading systems, and now manage close to $2 billion in assets using a technical rules-based model. Developing a good technical model based upon sound technical principles, accompanied by a robust buy, sell, trade-up rule set is only partially responsible for consistently good money management. None of it will ever work if the user does not have the discipline to follow it.

Once you have a good technical model, you will then need a set of rules to follow for asset commitment levels (percent of available assets) based upon various readings from your model. For example, when your model is initially calling for you to invest, it is probably wise to limit your exposure until you get more evidence that the trend is going to materialize into something that is tradable. As the model improves, the buy rules will let you commit more assets. At each stage you must also know exactly at what price you will set as the stop loss—and then follow it as if your life depended on it. Never second guess a stop-loss level.

I have been on a diet most of my adult life. A few months ago, my wife and I were driving in the countryside, and stopped to get fuel for the car. It was an old service station, so I had to go inside to pay for the gas. I bought a candy bar, and was eating it when I returned to the car. My wife, knowing that I should not be eating a candy bar, said, "You just don't have any discipline." I said, "That's not true, you don't know how many of these I wanted." The point is that discipline is not something you can adjust or use partially, you either have it or you do not.

Almost any method of technical analysis will provide the discipline required to be successful, plus it will uncover and organize details about the markets that will help you build a sound set of trading rules. A model will help control impatience, and more importantly, it will keep you from deviating to another method when periods of model diversity exist. And yes, they will exist. One has to have the discipline to follow the model, and this is easier when the model was designed using logical technical measures and not things that the user does not understand fully. The discipline will help bridge the gap between analysis and action, which is the stumbling block for many. Sound discipline will help overcome those horrible human emotions of fear, greed, and hope. Discipline, discipline, discipline.

Greg Morris

Well, you read it here. Greg's solitary piece of advice to you. The one idea he holds above all else is discipline, discipline, and more discipline. And this comes from a very knowledgeable and expert exponent of technical analysis. He is the author of probably the best book ever written on candlestick analysis. He has worked closely with the grandmaster of technical analysis, John Murphy. Yet his advice does not come close to sharing one iota of a technical idea with you. His message is as powerful as it is simple. You can have all the knowledge, all the ideas on how to engage the market; however, if you don't have the discipline to follow your plan, you have nothing. Nothing, nothing, nothing. I hope you have not only read Greg's advice, but that you have also heard and felt it vibrate right down to the core of your bones. I know I did.

If Gregory's advice resonates with you and you'd like to learn more about his thoughts on trading and the markets, he can be contacted through Stadion's website at www.stadionmoney.com.

NICK RADGE

Nick Radge is possibly one of the most complete traders I know. If there is a market, an instrument, a job, or an occupation involved with the markets, then Nick has probably analyzed it, traded it, or done it. Nick has done it all. He has traded, been a broker, a fund manager, a trading educator, a trading author, a forum chat site host, and a publisher of an advisory service. The lot. Certainly from my experience I have not known another trader as complete as Nick.

Nick started trading in 1985, and since then he has traded from the trading floor of the Sydney Futures Exchange to the international desks of global investment banks in Australia, London, and Singapore. Nick has traded most global futures markets, shares in Australia, the U.S., the U.K., and Malaysia. He has run his own hedge fund, and is an ex-associate director of one of Australia's leading investment bank, Macquarie Bank. He is the vice president of the Australian Technical Analysis Association, and is the author of *Every-day Traders* and *Adaptive Analysis*.[7]

Nick's expertise lies in discretionary technical analysis (synthesizing Elliott wave with traditional chart patterns and volume analysis), trading system design and mechanical trading. Nick is also very interested in the impact of trading psychology on a trader's success.

However, as with most people, trading success did not come immediately for Nick. Although he wasn't aware of it, Nick began in the market as a mechanical trader. Back in 1985, Nick was casually walking past an adviser's desk, and saw him plotting red and blue lines on graph paper. The adviser enthusiastically told Nick that he would buy when the blue line crossed up and over the red line, and sell when it crossed down and under. Nick immediately knew he'd just been given the Holy Grail of trading right there and then. Within minutes of seeing the adviser, Nick was down the street into the local newsagent buying colored pens and graph paper. He was trading index futures within days! And to his dismay, his moving average cross system wasn't the Holy Grail he thought!

It wouldn't be for another 10 years that Nick was able to achieve consistent profitable trading. He took many detours, as many do, before he settled on trend trading as his preferred methodology. Nick really enjoys following the trend. He lives for it. Although he can place some discretionary swing trades, the core of what he does is trend following. As he says, it "is the greatest way to extract low-stress profits from the markets."

Today, Nick is a multiple time frame trend follower. Nick trades three different time frames with three different mechanical strategies. His shorter-term strategy is an adaptation of the Turtle trading strategy, which can hold trades for up to a month. His second strategy can hold positions for up to 12 months, while his third strategy can hold trades for up to a couple of years. Nick originally developed the two longer-term strategies in the late 1990s to trade commodity futures, and adapted them for shares in 2001. Nick prefers to trade shares and CFDs based off end-of-day data, although he has been known to trade currencies and futures when he sees a compelling setup. For research and developing trading strategies, Nick uses both TradeStation and Amibroker. Nick is regarded as an expert in TradeStation.

Apart from his own personal trading, Nick runs a successful advisory service. Nick is a familiar face in Australia due to his regular guest appearances on CNBC and Sky News, and is regularly interviewed in the *Australian Financial Review* for his market insights.

When not trading, Nick can usually be found with a rod in his hands at some fishing spot around Noosa. Nick loves fishing. He took it up as a relaxation outlet from the markets, and he literally became hooked! He loves it, and focuses on getting out as many times as he can during the week. And that is probably a relief for his wife because Nick can get pretty intense at times, being a perfectionist and not suffering fools too easily. But he does say he's getting better, and no doubt he can thank the poor tormented fish on Australia's eastern sideboard for that! Nick and his family live in Noosa, Australia. Let's now hear what Nick's one piece of advice is.

"Nick, given all your trading knowledge and trading experience, I'd imagine you would receive many requests for help. If you were able to give an aspiring trader one piece of advice, and one only, what would it be and why?"

Perserverance: Steady persistence in the journey of trading in spite of difficulties, obstacles, and discouragement that meets you along the way.

In today's society, it's all about the now: the latest gadget, the job promotion, the car, even ordering a meal at a restaurant.

It can't come quick enough.

Nor can trading success.

Why do so many people fail at trading? They simply don't have the perseverance or patience to allow the market to reward them. You may have the greatest strategy, the best trading plan, and fabulous money management. Yet if you don't allow these tools to work their own magic in their own time, then they are rendered useless.

This is a simple concept to grasp, but incredibly difficult to put into practice by the majority simply because one wants profit satisfaction right now.

There is an old adage embraced in the investment community: "it's time, not timing," which usually refers to the buy and hold strategy.

However, for a trader it's also a vital ingredient to success, possibly the most crucial. Regardless what kind of trading strategy you employ, the market will reward you when it's ready. It's not like your employer's pay check that comes regularly and without fail every Friday. The market will pay its dues when it's ready. All you have to do is be there when it falls due.

Think of this analogy. Do you buy a house with a three-month or six-month time horizon? For the vast majority, the answer is an unequivocal no. You take a longer-term approach of many years. During that time, you expect the value of the house to rise and fall. You readily accept that in some years the value of the house may not go up; indeed, it may even go down. This, however, is of no concern because you intimately know that over the longer term the value will rise.

So let's use this analogy in trading, specifically trend following, which, in my view, is the greatest way to extract low-stress profits from the markets. Now, I am a trend follower, specifically trading stocks on the long side. My average hold time is about 10 months. I make money from a very simple strategy of cutting losses and letting profits run. When the market is trending up, I want to be involved. When the market is trending down, I want to be in cash. It need not be any more complex than that.

Why can't everyone do it?

Because they think that each and every month must be profitable. Indeed, they demand that each and every year be profitable.

But the reality is that stock prices don't trend higher each and every year. Yes, they do trend higher during the vast majority of years, but not every year. They certainly didn't in 2008, and I was happily sitting in cash, biding my time.

The amateur trader, however, doesn't want to be in cash. He or she wants to be making money. He or she wants to be involved. He or she wants profits now.

Along comes 2009, and one of the strongest surges in stock prices for the past decade occurs.

The professional trader has cash. The professional trader has confidence. The professional trader has perseverance. The professional trader is ready with a proven strategy, and gets involved. The professional trader makes a killing in 2009.

The amateur trader, however, gave up the notion of trend following six months previously, and has tried several other strategies since, all to no avail. He or she has more than likely lost money. He or she's certainly frustrated. He or she has done a number of courses in an attempt to rectify the problem, and he or she's going around in circles.

He or she looks back on 2009 with regret. If only he or she had only had the perseverance and long-term view on how the market pays out profits.

Nick Radge

Perseverance. So, so true. I think many traders will be able to relate to Nick's advice, looking back at strategies they had discarded due to their experience of poor performance, only to revisit the strategies to see them recently hitting new equity highs. It's like swapping lines at a checkout queue to find the quickest one—only to pick the longest! As Nick advises you can have everything—a robust strategy and a sensible money management strategy, but unless you have the time, the patience, and the perseverance, you'll have nothing. You'll only have a trail of discarded strategies and mounting frustration! You have to ignore your need for instant success, instant profits, and instant satisfaction; it rarely happens in trading. Add perseverance to your trading plan, and add a word of thanks to Nick!

If Nick's advice resonates with you and you'd like to learn more about his thoughts on trading and the markets, he can be contacted through his website at www.thechartist.com.au.

BRIAN SCHAD

Brian Schad is an ex-Navy SEAL and successful trader. Brian, like most people, didn't start life as a trader. For 12 years before entering the markets Brian served as a hard-hat diver and Navy SEAL for the U.S. government. And some of his experiences can send a chill down your spine, like the time he was trapped under water with depleting oxygen while patching up the battleship *USS Iowa*. That near-death experience resulted in Brian spending eight hours in a hyperbaric chamber with a nitrogen bubble in his spine and paralysis in his arms. And who says trading is risky!

And I suppose you can take the man out of the navy, but you can't take the navy out of the man. During our discussions in putting together this section, his conversation was littered with "roger that," "over to you," "received it," and so on. It was like dealing first hand with the U.S. Navy! And I have to say, Brian was also one of the quickest traders to respond to emails and questions, which I can imagine reflects the disciple and urgency to complete tasks efficiently under pressure that he learned while in the U.S. Navy. And Brian can certainly draw parallels between the navy and trading, because both can experience random critical situations where clear decision making is required.

Brian first became interested in the markets in 1992, when he started to trade to supplement his navy income. He was primarily a discretionary trader, using traditional technical analysis to find trade setups in share options.

And unlike today where there is easy access to data through the internet Brian did have some difficulty in receiving timely data. Back then, he was receiving 10-minute delayed data through a very big satellite dish that was sitting in a spare room in his condo. The only problem was a dying cherry tree that was right outside the window. The tree was interfering with his data feed. So one night, lucky for Brian, the barren cherry tree disappeared quicker than a David Copperfield vanishing act, and hey presto he was in business!

Trading success didn't come immediately for Brian, so he threw himself into reading and researching everything he could get his hands on. One book he got his hands on was by Larry Williams. So in 1994, Brian sought him out for advice. Larry generously agreed to have coffee with Brian, and the rest, as they say, is history. Brian credits his success to Larry's teachings and mentorship. In 1996 Brian resigned as a navy instructor, and committed himself full time to the markets.

Combining Larry's teachings with his own market observations, Brian was able to successfully develop his own set of unique rules for entering and exiting the market. Between 2002 and 2005, Brian assisted Larry in publishing the *Williams Commodity Timing* newsletter, which to this day remains the second-oldest continuously published commodity newsletter in existence.

Today, Brian refers to himself as a boring supervisory trader, who overseas his own traders, who execute his orders. In addition to his own trading, Brian runs a successful advisory business. Brian prefers not to talk about his trading methodology, but he does describe it as being a "discretionary method of strategies." Brian uses Genesis software to run his strategies, looking for generally short-term trades lasting between two and four days, although he has been known to hold trades for up to three weeks when he thinks it's appropriate. Brian primarily trades futures with some options over a large diversified portfolio that covers the metal, energy, grain, interest rates, currency, and index markets.

When he's not trading Brian can be seen happily driving his family around the countryside traveling and sightseeing, although at times with a bewildered and reluctant wife beside him. But then, as Brian says, "My wife didn't grow up with her dad packing up the sedan and taking Sunday afternoon drives in the country when she was a kid. My kids see an irritated mom in the car, and a happy dad behind the wheel, and they don't know what to think!" Brian and his family live in Idaho, U.S. Let me now ask Brian that one question that I know you'd like to hear the answer to.

"Brian, given all your trading knowledge and trading experience, I'd imagine you would receive many requests for help. If you were able to give an aspiring trader one piece of advice, and one only, what would it be and why?"

Brent, what I'd like to say outright is: every new trader has the potential for trading excellence. How and when they get there, and whether they'll be capitalized enough are a completely different matter. Whether they ultimately choose to be a fundamental- or technical-based trader, with discretionary or mechanically based signals, and all the research and development and trading and evaluation involved to get where you want to be, are all the necessary steps involved that take time and money before trading excellence will be achieved.

I am from the school of thought that believes taking your time and doing it right the first time will prevent making the same mistake twice. But just how does one go about doing just that . . . ?

If I had just one bit of advice, or important insight to provide a fellow new trader coming up in the ranks, it would be this:

Strive to be able to define your trading ideas to an advanced trading software platform to back test your market convictions as early in your trading career as possible.

Other trading counterparts of mine around the world, which I'm sure you'll agree, Brent, will tell you it takes patience, self-discipline, punctuality in order placement, and so on . . . all things that are very true, but by being able to test what they feel are strong convictions about recurring market patterns and potential entry/exit signals as early in their trading career as possible will help them navigate where they want to go sooner than most—like a traveler using a GPS, rather than stopping and asking others for directions to their destination.

For me, the technology for this type of advanced trading has sure changed for the better (simpler) since purchasing "System Writer" software back in 1994. I use GenesisFT® top-of-the-line trading software (since 2000), and I don't do anything in the market these days without the ability to back test my market ideas and convictions to ultimately know my history with the markets I trade, and, more importantly, knowing my odds at any given time.

Ten years ago, I would have advised a new trader to paper trade as long as possible until he or she was absolutely convinced what they were doing felt like the right thing to carry forward. Although it would have been advice from the heart, the inherent problem with paper trading *only* is usually that it is done when a market is doing one of three things:

- trending—then there can be no wrong and off we are with real money (. . . and then unforeseen problems in #2 arise)
- nearing the end of its trend—when your paper trades are choppy leading you to scrap what could have been good trading methods
- sideways market or beginning of a new trend—same conclusion as in #2.

As you are well aware, Brent, it is at this point, or more often after a very short time of trading real money that the new traders soon fall into the 90 percent of losing traders, and soon thereafter drop out because of *not* wanting to throw in good money after bad, or continue to force trades after having developed bad habits. With paper trading, they are literally beginning from a starting point without knowing where the finish line is, and are at the mercy of fate!

With the advent of back testing paper trades, today's new traders have the uncanny ability to go back in time and inspect each one of their potentially past trades to see how they will perform in up-, down-, or sideways-trending markets. Now they will be at the starting line with a clear picture of what they will do, and how they will perform, at each and every twist, turn, and bend in the trading road ahead. Once they have the confidence, and are comfortable with what they are doing, they should just keep doing it (repeating success) and "tuning up" their method(s) every couple of years, or so.

This is absolutely the very best advice I could give readers of your book. They have the choice of making trading as easy, or as difficult, as they want it to be.

All the best for your readers' trading success,

Brian Schad

Well, I hope you were listening to Brian's advice. Don't go blind into trading. Listen to Brian's simple message—get to know what your methodology is capable of. And do it much earlier than later in your trading career. Most traders do it later, when the markets tell them what they should have known earlier: their strategy did not have a real edge. So Brian's one piece of advice is to test and get to know your trading methodology thoroughly before you commit money to the market. He is encouraging you to take advantage of the trading software that is available today to do your testing. And the earlier you can do it, the better. The implication of Brian's advice is that if you haven't already purchased appropriate software, then you should do so now. Make the investment. And you should commit yourself to learning the system's development module as quickly as you can. Pronto.

Now some of you who prefer to be discretionary traders may say this advice is not applicable to you since it's very hard to quantify what you do on a discretionary basis. What I'd say to you is that you'd be surprised what you can do with a computer.

My basic belief is this. If you can think of an idea, then you can write it down. If you can write an idea down, then you can usually program up the idea. If you can't, it's usually because you have not been articulate enough in describing your idea. As I've said, you will be surprised at what you can program up in a computer.

And please do not use the "but I'm too old to learn how to program up ideas" as an excuse! If you wish to be successful in the markets, you will have to treat it seriously, and make the necessary investment in money, time, and effort. Don't be lazy, and don't remain ignorant about your methodology's expectancy in the market. Listen to Brian. Listen to his advice, and do the work! If I had received Brian's advice in my earlier days, it would certainly have saved me a lot of money and grief! I hope you're listening to Brian; I certainly was.

If Brian's advice resonates with you and you'd like to learn more about his thoughts on trading and the markets, he can be contacted through his website at www.schadcommodity.com.

ANDREA UNGER

Andrea Unger is a championship-winning day trader. He is the back-to-back 2008 and 2009 winner of the real money Robbins World Cup Championship of Futures Trading®. If he wins it again in 2010, it will be the first time anyone has won the event three years in row in the event's 25-year history. He'll become a triple crown winner!

With a background in engineering, he has developed a specialty in designing mechanical trading strategies. So successful that in 2005 he won the European Top Trader Cup competition. He then followed it up in 2008 by winning the Robbins World Cup Championship of Futures Trading®. Andrea won it by earning a 12-month return of 672 percent!

And in 2009 he followed it up by winning again with a 115 percent return! Andrea is now the only third trader in the competition's 25-year history to win it back-to-back. Like Michael Cook one of Andrea's ambitions is to win the championship three years in a row. Will 2010 be Andrea's year to set a record in the championship's 25-year history? Only time will tell.

As I said, Andrea is a successful day trader, but as for most professional traders, life didn't begin with a computer screen, a keyboard, and a trading account. As a mechanical engineer, Andrea spent the most part of a decade in middle management for a major company in Italy. It wasn't until 1997 that Andrea developed an interest in the markets. During his initial years of trading, Andrea was primarily a discretionary trader, intuitively entering positions according to what he observed on his screen on the day.

In February 2001, Andrea discovered an inefficiency by market makers pricing covered warrants. Being a mechanical engineer and good with mathematics, he soon realized he could take advantage of the inefficiency. He was so good that within two months, he retired and commenced trading full time!

But it wasn't all plain sailing. Andrea knew the inefficiencies he was exploiting wouldn't last forever, so he set out to develop a mechanical trading system. He sought advice from the high-profile and successful Italian trader Domenico Foti, and soon became a top protégé. In time he successfully developed mechanical strategies for day trading off five-minute bars. Since then, Andrea and Domenico have become close friends, collaborating daily on trading ideas and system development.

In 2006 Andrea wrote the first Italian-language book on money management for traders called *Money Management: Methods and Applications.*

Today, Andrea continues to day trade off five-minute bar charts. He trades several mechanical systems on different markets and with different approaches. Andrea prefers to keep the mix of his strategies as diversified as possible, combining both trend and countertrend methodologies in his models. He uses both Genesis and TradeStation for researching, developing, and testing trading strategies, in addition to generating orders. He trades a mixed portfolio, containing indices, currencies, and bonds. His preferred instrument to trade is futures. Andrea runs a successful advisory service for people who wish to trade like he does.

When Andrea is not day trading, you can usually find him running through the streets training for his next half-marathon. He loves to travel, and like all Italians loves his Azzurri football team. Andrea and his family live in Ascoli, Italy. Let's now hear what Andrea's one piece of advice is for the aspiring trader, you.

"Andrea, given all your trading knowledge and trading experience, I'd imagine you would receive many requests for help. If you were able to give an aspiring trader one piece of advice, and one only, what would it be and why?"

There are several categories of traders or aspiring traders, most of them have one thing in common: they want to be right. To become a successful trader, you need to accept your mistakes, and you need to understand that not always are your beliefs right.

You need to plan your trading, and then you need to stick to the plan, and your plan must also face the possibility of failure, and act consequently.

There are many ways to trade the markets; choose a way that fits your personality, and plan your path to success. You can trade discretionary or follow trading systems, but once you decide what's your way, then go ahead and don't change your mind before your plan tells you it's time to stop.

Try to choose what's suitable for you. If you want to develop a trading system, consider your personality. Can you stand quiet in front of many losing trades in a row, but you feel bad with a big loss? Well, you need a system with a limited stop loss that is capable of catching the big moves. If this is the case, then a trend-following system is probably the one that best meets your needs. Something like a simple breakout strategy with a well-positioned stop loss, that's it. If, on the contrary, you always want to be right, and can't withstand continuous losses, then a system built with a pretty large stop may do the trick. In this case, a swing-trading system with pattern recognition is probably the best choice. You will have a very high winning percentage (if the system is well designed), having, now and then, a big loss that will not harm your personality too much.

Don't try to adapt the markets to your beliefs. You will have to figure out how the markets behave, test your ideas, and review the results. If they're not in line with your expectations, be ready to change your mind and to consider new approaches. Time spent on trying to make a poor idea work can be better spent developing new, more successful, approaches.

Always be curious and consider that markets change and that you have to discover day by day how they are doing it and what you should do to go on having the right edge.

Don't find excuses to avoid a necessary task; when you are making your plan, don't stop in front of silly obstacles. If you really want to become a trader, you need to go straight ahead.

Last but not least, never overestimate the potential of the market. Looking at charts from the past, it seems awfully easy to catch substantial gains, "if I bought here, if I sold there . . . " That's wishful thinking. The reality is different. If you happen to buy on the lows and sell on the highs, it's more due to chance than good trading. It will just be a very lucky trade. You don't have to look to pick tops and bottoms to succeed. You just need to construct a sound method of trading that complements your personality, and with it go ahead week after week, month after month, year after year.

Andrea Unger

This very sound advice comes from a back-to-back championship-winning trader. I hope you were listening. Andrea firmly believes and advises that you look to develop a trading strategy that suits your personality. Find a strategy that is compatible with you, and then stick with it. Be flexible in your beliefs about how markets work. Accept markets will change over time, and look for appropriate signals to give you clues. Be prepared to adjust your methodology as necessary. Remain inquisitive and open to new ideas about the markets. Avoid standing still. The markets aren't static, so neither should you be. Be curious, be adaptive, and be dynamic, and you will be successful. This is sound advice from a sound and very successful gold medal-winning trader. I hope you were listening to Andrea, because I certainly was!

If Andrea's advice resonates with you and you'd like to learn more about his thoughts on trading and the market, she can be contacted through the following website: www.oneyeartarget.de.

LARRY WILLIAMS

Well almost last, but definitely not least. It's kind of a nice symmetry to come toward the end of the Market Masters with the first of his kind.

As far as I know, there is no other trader like Larry Williams. You see Larry commenced following the markets in 1962, began actively trading in 1965, and has been trading full time since 1966. That's a long time. When Larry finally decides to stop sharing his ideas, I don't know who will take his place. To my knowledge there is no one following in his footsteps who has achieved what he has with his experience. I can't think of another trader. When Larry departs this stage, he will leave an incredible vacuum that I don't think any single person will be able to fill.

I say this because Larry Williams, to my mind, is possibly responsible for contributing more original and effective trading ideas than any other person. And to my mind, he is possibly responsible for launching more traders into successful money management careers than any other trader as well. Now I'm happy to be corrected, but from my own personal experience and friendships with professional money managers, I don't know of any other trader whose ideas are being used so successfully by so many traders.

Certainly, not everything Larry has ever shared has continued to work indefinitely. However, there are plenty of ideas of his that continue to work today, well after he first shared them, and I imagine they will continue to work well into the future as well.

As I've said, Larry has been trading for a long time. When you start following the markets at 19 years of age, and become an active trader by the age of 22, in a time before man landed on the moon, you'd imagine such a person would have picked up some valuable market knowledge and trading ideas along the way. Well, Larry certainly did and has. Since Larry has been following and trading the markets for the best part of half a century, you can imagine whatever I write here in a few pages will not do him justice. But let me give it a try.

In the early 1960s, Larry, as do all new traders, struggled to find his edge. Back then Larry was principally a share or stock trader who traded off both market news and views. And even when there were no news or views, he still traded and managed to find every possible way to lose money! Wishing to keep what money he had left, Larry embarked on a determined campaign to educate himself. And unlike today, there were only five or six books on trading. Larry spent many hours in libraries throughout the West Coast of America searching for trading books that were as rare as hen's teeth.

And not only was Larry handicapped by a lack of trading books, he also didn't have the luxury of using clever charting programs like we have today, maintaining hand-drawn point and figure charts. Back then, Larry focused on quick profits trading in and out of shares based on traditional chart patterns. He was making profits without setting the world on fire. It wasn't until 1967, when he met Bill Meehan, a former member of the Chicago Board of Trade, that his trading really took off. Bill explained to Larry that the big money was made by having small positions in big moves. Bill taught Larry the importance of fundamentals, and how to determine when a market was ready for a substantial up or down move. Larry was taught how the big money was made in the big moves. Once he learned that, it then became a question of timing his entries, placing his stops, and managing his exits. It took Larry almost 10 years before he finally mastered longer-term trading based on sound fundamental setups with good technically timed entries. Once Larry mastered longer-term trading, he began developing techniques for shorter-term swing trading.

An irony of Larry's trading career is that he actually benefited from the scarcity of trading books and the absence of personal computers. Back in the 1960s, Larry, through necessity, had to think for himself to nut out new edges in the market. Larry couldn't reference the latest trading book to get a new idea here and there. He couldn't program an idea and see how it looked on a chart. Although Bill Meehan gave him the big picture, Larry still had to work out his own hand-to-hand combat instructions. Just think about this for a second. There weren't multiple free internet resource sites available to reference. There was no Amazon.com to search for the latest trading title. There was no Google to shortcut answers. Larry, compared to what we have today, was literally trading in the dark! Just imagine how you would go today without the trading books you have at your fingertips; if you didn't have a personal computer and charting package; if you didn't have access to the internet; if you didn't have Excel; if you didn't have access to historical data or access to electronic data. Feel naked? Feel vulnerable? Feel a little anxious? Feel blind? Feel ignorant? Feel cast adrift? Feel in the dark? Well, that is how Larry did it. How many of us today could have accomplished what Larry did back then in the electronic stone age? Not many I suspect. But the irony is that Larry flourished by being forced to do the work. He had to learn how to improvise, investigate, and validate ideas. He was forced to become what Lee Gettess would later describe as a "tireless researcher." Those skills he was forced to develop in the 1960s are what have helped Larry to become one of the most original market thinkers and successful traders over the past half-century.

And he continues to research today, almost 50 years after he first commenced in the markets. Who would have thought a lack of trading material and services in the 1960s would have been a gift rather than a perceived handicap? Through necessity and through his curiosity and effort, Larry has learned over the years to view the markets in original and innovative ways that others have not thought of.

However, everything started for Larry in the 1960s. In 1965, he launched his *Williams Commodity Timing* newsletter. Although Larry stopped publishing it in 2008, it remains today the second-oldest continuously published commodity newsletter in the business. In 1966, he created the Williams percent R indicator, which today is a standard inclusion in most popular charting packages, 43 years after its creation. In the same year, Larry was the first to talk about pivot points in modern times when he first wrote about them in his 1969 book, *The Secret of Selecting Stocks.* Today, pivot points are very popular among newsletter services and traders. But Larry didn't invent pivot points; he learned about them from a trader called Owen Taylor, who first wrote about them during the 1920s and 1930s.

In 1970, Larry was the first to write about the Commitments of Traders (COT) report, and is generally regarded as the grandfather of COT. Since then, a whole industry has sprung up devoted to depicting and interpreting COT data. To this day, almost 40 years after Larry first wrote about the COT report, he continues to analyze it, looking for fundamental information to aid his trading. In 1974, Larry was the first to write about seasonality in commodities. Since then, another whole industry has developed around it. In 1983, Larry was the first to identify the opening price as an important reference point, and is credited with developing the volatility breakout technique. Larry was the first to write about trade day of the week and trade day of the month. Larry was the first to introduce money management techniques to private commodity trading, and he is responsible for creating many measurements for accumulation and distribution. I could go on, but space limits prevent me from mentioning every idea Larry is accredited with.

Larry is possibly best known as the all-time winner of the Robbins World Cup Championship of Futures Trading®. In 1987, Larry won the championship by trading a $10,000 account to more than $1,100,000 within 12 months, an achievement that no other trader has come close to. Larry happily admits he ran his account up to more than $2,000,000 before it dropped back to $750,000 after the October 1987 sharemarket crash. He then managed to trade it back up to more than $1,100,000 by the end of the year. As I said, to this day, no one has beaten his achievement. And then 10 years later in 1997, Larry's daughter, at the age of 16, won the same competition with a 1,000 percent return, trading according to Larry's teachings. She managed to trade her $10,000 account up to more than $100,000 by the end of the year. And no, Larry didn't find the setups and place the trades, his daughter did everything independently according to the rules Larry taught her!

Larry has taught thousands of traders all over the world. In 1982, he was the first to pioneer live trading during workshops. Since then, it has become common practice among the better workshops. But what isn't common practice today is that Larry, to my knowledge, is the only trader to have ever made more than $1.0 million trading live during a continuous series of workshops. And I can say I have personally attended two of Larry's Million Dollar Challenge Workshops and witnessed him trade live and make money during both seminars (and I along with the other attendees sharing in 20 percent of his profits). Table 12.2 summarizes his Workshop's live trading results. Amazing.

Although good friend and mentor Geoff Morgan introduced me to simple price patterns, it was Larry who opened my eyes to the wider world of pattern possibilities. I can still remember seeing Larry during my first

TABLE 12.2   Live trading results

Oct 1999	$250,000	Nov 2000	$46,481	Oct 2001	$48,225	Apr 2003	$12,046	Sep 2004	$26,023
May 2000	$302,000	Mar 2001	−$9,640	May 2002	$32,850	May 2003	−$750	Oct 2004	$92,075
May 2000	$35,000	Apr 2001	$149,000	Oct 2002	$79,825	Oct 2003	$34,600	Jun 2005	$6,000
Oct 2000	$22,637	May 2001	$23,300	Mar 2003	$35,034	Jun 2004	$34,000	Nov 2005	$34,000
								Jun 2006	$3,800
									$1,256,506

Source: Larry Williams

Million Dollar Challenge Workshop, looking at a chart and then programming up the recent sequence of daily bars into his TradeStation System Writer program, programming the relative sequence of daily highs, lows and closes. He then ran the program through the chart's historical database looking for similar pattern occurrences. He was looking to see whether the current price action was a tradable repetitive pattern. It was in that instant that I decided to write my own program, which would allow me to search for and identify high-probability repetitive patterns. This program to this day remains the custodian of the portfolio of short-term patterns I trade.

As I've said, I'm not aware of another trader who has achieved what Larry has in the markets. As a trader, Larry primarily focuses on trading futures. He trades off daily bars. He will trade any market that is set up for a rally based on his fundamental analysis. His preference is to attack those markets that are ready for substantial moves. This may mean he will not trade a particular market for a long time, but Larry isn't particularly interested in individual markets, but rather in finding markets with good fundamental setups.

Although Larry is not a mechanical trader, he is very systematic in how he approaches the markets. He looks for those markets that have most of his fundamental setup criteria in place. And I should say that when Larry talks about fundamentals, he is not referring to balance sheet or economic analysis. He is referring to the fundamental structure of a market, knowing what the participants are doing and what their likely influence will be on future price movement. One source of Larry's fundamental analysis is the COT Report. Once he identifies those markets that are fundamentally set up for a substantial move either to the upside or downside, he will then use his discretion to decide which one he will trade. Once he decides, Larry will then use his technical tools to time his entries, place his stops, and manage his exits.

Larry is also a big believer in the art of trading. He doesn't believe trading should be a "paint by the numbers business." He doesn't believe a trader should take a mechanical system and trade it for now and forever. He's not saying mechanical trading doesn't make money; he just believes a trader can do better by combining the art of trading with a systematic approach. Larry uses Genesis software to find his fundamental setups and identify his technical entry, stop, and exit levels. Larry loves Genesis so much that he wishes he had ownership in the software!

Today, Larry is still learning. He suspects he will always be learning because the markets continually change. What he trades today is not the same as what he traded in the 1960s, 1970s, 1980s, or 1990s. Today, there are different instruments and markets to trade, and the advent of electronic markets has made it totally different to the past. Nothing stands still.

Over the years, Larry has written nine books, with many being translated into 10 different languages. And for more than 40 years, Larry has been donating the royalties from his books to support a scholarship program at the University of Oregon, U.S.

When Larry isn't immersed in the markets, you will find him either studying archaeology, collecting native American art pieces, fishing, or running marathons (he has run 76 of them). However, despite these interests, according to Larry, and to his wife's annoyance, he hasn't found anything as compelling as the markets! And as a sidebar, if you ever get the chance, you should read his 1990 book, *The Mountain of Moses: The Discovery of Mount Sinai.*[8] It's a real eye opener. Larry Williams is Indiana Jones! Larry and Louise live in La Jolla, California, U.S.

What you are about to read is very special. It comes from a person who has been actively trading the markets for far longer than most other market participants. So please listen up and pay attention, Larry's advice comes from years of experience, which you can't buy. Let me now ask Larry what his one piece of advice is.

"Larry, given all your trading knowledge and trading experience, I'd imagine you would receive many requests for help. If you were able to give an aspiring trader one piece of advice, and one only, what would it be and why?"

If there was only one thing I could tell a beginning trader, it would be that this is an amazingly simple, yet complex business. There is not just one thing I could address.

If, however, I was limited to just one comment, it would be that to be successful, you have to have control.

Control is more important than the system you are trading, or the money management approach you are using. Some people confuse focus with control; there is a difference. Focus is about putting your attention on a particular thing, while control goes beyond that. Control means not only being in a high state of attention, but also following through with specific action.

Control needs to include many aspects of this trading business. You need to have total control of whatever form of money management you choose to use. In other words, it is not enough to have a money management strategy or approach to your trading. That is a bit like having snow tires for your car, but not putting them on in the winter, so you slide on the ice, totaling out your car. That is actually a good analogy, far better than I thought I could've come up with!

It is quite one thing to have an approach to money management knowing you should do such and such, that's focus, but not being in control to have application of the process is what really gets traders off track, sliding on the ice into crackups.

I'm not even certain it makes that much difference what money management strategy you might use as long as it is reasonable and not overspeculative. It is not the approach to money management, or the understanding of money management, that is going to help you, it is only the application—your control.

The same thing can be said for your trading strategy or your personal trading psychology. While everything Mom and Dad talked about living—eat correctly, exercise, don't hang out with bad people—is a truism, not everyone follows that advice.

It is much easier to talk a good fight than to fight a good fight. And trust me, in this business of trading, it is a battle. It is largely a battle of first determining a decent workable approach that really makes money trading, then a battle of the application, on a consistent basis, of that approach, the money management of that approach, and your personal persistence in following the approach and continuing to work on improving that particular strategy

While the beginner is looking for a simple answer . . . the truth is everyone is looking for such an answer. However, there are answers as such and the truth is not going to come from somebody else's answer nearly as much as from questions you ask to salt your particular issues.

Questions, not answers, make for better traders.

In almost 50 years of doing this, I have yet to have some instant insight into trading or a trade; no white light beams have shown me the way; there is not even one particular person that has given me the complete answer. You are off on the wrong foot if you're thinking there is such an answer.

This business of trading is a combination of art and science, a combination of mathematics and emotions. What works for one person may not fit comfortably for another person.

So then, the answer is not here is an indicator, here is some mathematical formula that will make money for you for the rest of your life. The answer is that this business is full of questions that you need to answer for yourself.

Without risk, there is no reward; without work, there is no reward; without dedication and perseverance, it's the same thing; there is no reward.

I wish it were not that way. I wish I could say here is the answer, the light and the truth, but that has not been my experience in trading. I do hope what I have said here will help you get on and stay on the path of profitable trading . . . that path is full of questions . . . most of which there seems to be no absolute answer. However, that does not stop me from asking them and from learning in that process and becoming just a little bit better, every day, as a professional trader.

Larry Williams

Well, how about that? There are no simple answers, only questions. And here you and I are looking for the answers! And as Larry says, seeking answers for questions without control will make it difficult for you to succeed. And not only will you need to be full of questions, you'll need to find and experience the answers for yourself. Only through personal experience will you be able to learn and achieve the necessary control required to succeed in trading. Each and every one has to travel along his or her own personal path, and if you ask enough questions along the way you may just arrive at the destination you are seeking—a sustainable and successful trading career.

I hope you were listening to Larry's advice. These are words of wisdom from a person who has been climbing the trading mountain the longest. He shares his advice from a perspective not many traders achieve. Like an enlightened person, Larry reveals there are no simple answers to the complex world of trading. Only inquisitive questions and the personal discovery of the answers. And once you have discovered the answers you'll need personal control to ensure you consistently apply those answers you have discovered that work for you.

If Larry's advice resonates with you and you'd like to learn more about his thoughts on trading and the markets, he can be contacted through his website at www.ireallytrade.com.

DAR WONG

Dar Wong is a charismatic forex trader based in Singapore. I always know when Dar is presenting at an expo because he usually has the biggest crowd of people milling around him between presentations. I only have to look around the exhibit hall and see where all the fuss is, and more times than not, it's Dar holding court to a large group of attentive traders. With a welcoming smile and confident demeanor Dar epitomizes the quintessential successful forex trader—confident, easygoing, and welcoming.

Like myself (Sydney) and Michael Cook (London), Dar commenced trading in 1989 when he joined Bank of America in Singapore. Dar joined the futures division. He worked on the floor of the Singapore International Monetary Exchange (SIMEX), where he executed customers' orders. In 1996, Dar left his then employer, Citigroup Inc., and became an individual member of the futures exchange, trading on his own account as a local trader.

As a local trader, Dar focused on day trading the Nikkei 225 futures contract. He initially traded traditional chart patterns off 30-minute bar charts. In his early days, Dar used Metastock, but soon abandoned it due to his frustration with data disparities he found in its continuous contracts. In 1998, Dar abandoned all charting packages to rely solely on Reuters and Bloomberg for their real-time live data feeds.

In 2001, in anticipation of the Singapore Exchange closing the floor and going fully electronic (which occurred in 2006), Dar left the floor to concentrate on screen trading. Like many ex-locals who leave the floor and switch to screen trading, Dar found it initially difficult to find his edge. Whereas before he had the benefit of seeing order flows on the floor, he felt detached and disconnected in his new trading office. Trading on the floor and from a screen were two completely different experiences. It took Dar nearly two years to develop his new screen-based day trading PowerWave Trading™ (PowerWave) methodology.

Today, Dar continues to day trade using multiple time frames. Using 30-minute bars to enter, place stops, and manage his exits, Dar will only trade when his PowerWave setups are synchronized and aligned with four-hour and daily bars. When his setups are synchronized and aligned across all three time frames, he'll then look for 1:3 risk–reward opportunities to trade. His PowerWave methodology is primarily price and pattern based. He looks to trade both countertrend and trend-continuation patterns. For his countertrend pattern, he looks for snapback reversal opportunities after extreme price extensions. For his trend-continuation pattern, he looks for breakout opportunities after price congestions. He is essentially an indicator-free trader, although he has been known to use a slow stochastic occasionally to measure the strength of a reversal.

Dar doesn't use any particular software to improve his PowerWave methodology except for plain candlestick charts provided by his forex service provider. Dar trades with an uncluttered screen. Dar mainly trades forex with a few indices thrown in. He prefers the euro/U.S. dollar and U.S. dollar/yen currency pairs to trade, and for indices he'll trade the Nikkei and Dow Jones index futures.

Outside trading, you'll find Dar immersed in his passion for better health. Many are usually surprised when they learn he has such a deep knowledge of and interest in better health maintenance and dietary supplements. It's no wonder he's so charismatic—he's full of all the right vitamins! Dar and his family live in Singapore. Let's now hear what Dar's one piece of advice is.

"Dar, given all your trading knowledge and trading experience, I'd imagine you would receive many requests for help. If you were able to give an aspiring trader one piece of advice, and one only, what would it be and why?"

Trading has always been a mystery to the painful losers. Winners who have found the proven strategies will simply repeat the selected trading plan respectively to technical patterns recognized each time!

Personally, I feel the concepts of trading must be correct before you could pursue this career for a lifetime. This essential comprehension is applicable on a universal basis that emphasizes low-risk exposure. Apart from trading concepts, technical strategies are just variable, and will become versatile in their parameters pursuant to the changes in fundamentals and market sentiment over years.

Before an experienced trader commences his market activities, he will definitely understand fully the leverage factor of the intended instruments followed by the trading limit permitted in his account. Generally, only part or up to one-third of the trade limit will be used for the initial trade opening. Additional usage of the trade limit will be exercised on profit pyramiding, which usually requires a short period of holding positions. In the unlikely event of making few initial losing trades, this can be well balanced by adopting a good risk–reward ratio in the trade projection that can cover the losses eventually on higher winning probability.

In tandem of a well-planned distribution of your trade margin, you have to begin searching for a set of highly proven strategies in understanding the market behavior. In a panoramic view, the various market behaviors will result in the appearance of different chart patterns and technical cycles that need to be prescribed correctly by your "diagnosis"!

On picking an entry, an experienced trader will never compromise his risk–reward ratio by less than 1:2. An ideal trade opened should give a foreview of three times in potential winnings or even more, when compared to the backend losses to be stomached.

Although the debate on risk capacity in the placement of stop loss has always been argued among many different teachings, it will depend largely on the trade tolerance of individuals versus the projected exit range, which reroute to the recognition of the market's technical appearance!

In my personal opinion, a trader has to identify himself as an intraday trader or trend (position) trader. This process of confirming your trade objectives will help your entire career in achieving your trading goals (monetary rewards) on each target periodic basis. There will be no definition of right or wrong until you can achieve consistent positive trading results.

Trading is a game of probability. There is no fixed rule on how to play it until you get it right. In summary, the winning concepts are based on the efficient management of risk in lieu of the forecast trend to be realized later. A veteran trader will always pick an entry on the proposed extreme regions of the markets or on a quick reversal for short-range profits if it is in the mid-range regions between a previous high and low already formed.

In just one sentence, what you can visualize before others could become your profits, but what you can see now would have been won by others. Yes. Visualization is the first key to your trading success!

Dar Wong

Dar firmly believes success cannot be achieved without first understanding a key concept of successful trading. That is identifying low-risk trade setups. This concept should remain constant for every trader and never change. For Dar, technical trading strategies are variable, and can and will change along with changing market conditions. However, the low-risk exposure concept can never change. Dar recommends identifying low-risk exposures that can offer a 1:3 risk reward payoff, and believes traders need to determine firmly whether their preference is for day trading or positional trading if they wish to consider a career in trading. Dar firmly believes trading is a game of probability where there are no fixed rules on how to play it until you get it right! But, unless a trader can understand success is first built upon identifying low-risk trade setups, then they'll find it difficult to succeed. For Dar it all comes back to low-risk definition and low-risk acceptance. Dar's advice to you is to focus first on the trade setup risk, and only pursue the trade if the risk is both low and accompanied by a potential reward offering a 3:1 payoff. Great advice, and I hope you were listening; I certainly was.

If Dar's advice resonates with you and you'd like to learn more about his thoughts on trading and the markets, he can be contacted through his website at www.pwforex.com.

A WEALTH OF ADVICE

Well, how about that? Did you enjoy meeting these successful traders and receiving their advice? I certainly did. In figure 12.2, I have summarized the advice you have just received from these Market Masters.

You should take the time to summarize this table, and add their advice to your trade plan. It's invaluable advice that can only come from real traders doing real battle in real markets in real time, day in and day out. It's advice that comes from a well of deep experience, great frustration, real losses, unbearable pain, and rare triumph in the unforgiving world of trading. It's not advice you can buy from your local corner store. Please take the time to write it down and pin it near your trading screens. Cast your eyes at it each day until their words let it eventually sink in.

Money Management	
Trade small.	Michael
Focus on the risk.	Lee
Methodology	
Pick a methodology that suits your personality.	Andrea
Develop a simple methodology.	Kevin
Avoid the majority, learn to anticipate reversals.	Tom
Look for alignment in setups.	Richard
Good defense wins games.	Geoff
Identify low-risk setups.	Dar
Know your methodology using software.	Brian
Psychology	
Deep practice before trading.	Ray
Expect to lose. Trade to win.	Mark
Be discipline.	Greg
Be patient.	Nick
Be humble.	Daryl
Be in control.	Larry

FIGURE 12.2   The Masters' advice

Now apart from their individual advice I hope it also underscored two important points. First, as traders they are generally all different, trading different markets, different time frames, different instruments, and different techniques. I hope this illustrates to you that there are many different ways to trade—however, please don't believe there are infinite winning strategies because there aren't. But there are enough to give you some room for choice; you just have to find them.

And second, their individual advice to you touched upon an element of the universal principles of successful trading, those principles that are common among all successful traders, despite their differences in markets, time frames, instruments, and techniques. And this is the whole point of the universal principles of successful trading. That despite how and why traders engage with the markets when they do, they all adhere to these universal key principles—trading small relative to the size of their account, focusing on risk, trading simply, trading against the majority who lose, trading with an edge, accepting losses as part of the business of trading, being disciplined, being patient, being humble, and being in control. Their individual advice emphasized the importance of the universal principles of successful trading.

And not one piece of advice touched upon an entry technique or entry idea. Although Tom DeMark did encourage you to anticipate market reversals, he was also encouraging you to challenge consensus views, to think independently. In addition, Tom was referring to market structure and didn't mention a particular technique to anticipate reversals.

This highlights the whole point. Amateur traders spend a disproportionate amount of time on finding the perfect entry technique, they just can't wait to enter the market and start trading. They don't take the time to learn and understand and implement the universal principles of successful trading. Is it any wonder so many fail in trading?

To prove my point I completed a quick search through Google using trading phrases that came into my head. Table 12.3 summarizes the Google results for each phrase. Now there isn't anything scientific about how I have gone about this. I only entered what I could think of. But look at the search phrase that has the second-highest number of hits—"trading entry." If you can accept that Google provides a reasonable reflection of people's interest on the internet, then you'd have to accept that traders do spend a disproportional amount of time on trying to find that perfect risk-free 100 percent accurate entry technique. If you are one of those traders, then I can only implore you to stop worrying about finding the perfect place to initiate a trade. There is no perfect entry technique. And more importantly, there are far more productive areas you can spend your time on, and one area I'd suggest you start with are the universal principles of successful trading.

As an aside, what is also interesting about the Market Masters' advice is how their advice is grouped under the Three Pillars of practical trading; money management, methodology, and psychology. As you know, I personally rank money management above methodology, which in turn I rank above psychology. Well, the distribution of advice you have received in figure 12.2 is certainly at odds with mine.

Out of the 15 traders, only two advised you to focus on an element of money management. Seven advised you to focus on an element of methodology, while six advised you to focus on an element of psychology.

Now I know that sampling 15 traders is not statistically significant; however, given it's rare to get this number of experienced and successful traders together I'm happy to observe the consensus view. And according to the Market Masters, methodology is ranked ahead of psychology, which in turn is ranked above my hobby horse, money management!

Now, there were no surprises for me here in psychology receiving a high score as I know that my thoughts on psychology are at odds with the majority

TABLE 12.3   Google searches

Google search phrase	Google results
Technical analysis	76,900,000
Trading entry	48,000,000
Trading markets	39,600,000
Day trading	37,900,000
Trading software	35,600,000
Trading money management	31,600,000
Trading market profile	30,600,000
Trading exit	8,050,000
Pattern trading	8,020,000
Trend trading	7,910,000
Trading indicators	6,780,000
Trading seasonals	4,530,000
Commitment of Traders report	4,160,000
Trading astrology	1,960,000
Trading stop loss	1,920,000
Trading Gann	1,850,000
Trading risk of ruin	1,540,000
Swing trading	1,080,000
Trading psychology	1,050,000
Elliott wave	956,000
Trading geometry	833,000
Trading Fibonacci	658,000
Chart patterns	614,000
Trading candle sticks	567,000
Trading multiple time frames	420,000
Turtle trading	251,000
Trading triangles	205,000

and has a membership of one—me! However, I was surprised at the lower ranking of money management. But that is the reason I wanted to invite these successful traders to offer you their advice based on their many years of experience and success. I wanted you to listen to their emphasis. I have given you my thoughts, and they have given you theirs to balance out mine. So I hope I've been successful in balancing and rounding out my universal principles with advice from these universally successful traders.

And this now brings me close to the end, and before I go, I just have a few final words to say in the next chapter.

NOTES

1. Barros, Ramon, *The Nature of Trends* (John Wiley & Sons, 2008).
2. Schwager, Jack, *Stock Market Wizards* (Harper Business, 2001).
3. Collins, Art, *Market Beaters* (Traders Press, 2004).
4. DeMark, Tom, *The New Science of Technical Analysis* (John Wiley, 1994), *New Market Timing Techniques* (John Wiley, 1997), *DeMark on Day Trading Options* (McGraw Hill, 1999).
5. Guppy, Daryl, *Share Trading* (Wrightbooks, John Wiley, 1996).
6. Farleigh, Richard, *Taming the Lion* (Wrightbooks, John Wiley, 2006).
7. Radge, Nick, *Every-day Traders* (Wrightbooks, John Wiley, 2002) and *Adaptive Analysis* (Wrightbooks, John Wiley, 2005).
8. Williams, Larry, *The Mountain of Moses: The Discovery of Mount Sinai* (Wynwood Press, 1990).

A Final Word

And this brings me to the end. There is really nothing more for me to say. I hope you like my universal principles of successful trading, and I hope you enjoyed receiving one piece of advice from the Market Masters. I hope you can take something (if not everything) from both my universal principles and the Market Masters.

I certainly believe the universal principles provide a rallying point and safe refuge for those traders who are bewildered by the cyclonic nature of changing markets and the kaleidoscope array of trading services and products available.

Because certainly today is both the best of times and the worst of times to be a private trader. It's the best of times because traders have never had it so good. There are no barriers to entry, with a multiple array of choices available just a click away. Traders have never had it so good with the availability of multiple discount brokers, electronic trading platforms, automatic trading programs, inexpensive live real-time data, charting programs, indicators, markets, time frames, instruments, fundamental and technical trading theories, trading newsletters, trading educators, trading coaches, and trading workshops to chose from. The trader today is not lacking for choice.

Institutions no longer have any competitive advantage over the private of trader. It's never been so good. It's the best of times! But it's also the worst of times. Today, more than 90 percent of all active traders continue to lose. That's bad. Nothing has changed since when I first commenced trading with Bank of America in 1983. Welcome to trading's paradox: it's both the best and the worst of times!

I hope my universal principles of successful trading can save you from the worst of times. It seems to me that the advancements in trading technology, trading services, and trading education have created so much excitement that it has distracted traders from first focusing on and understanding the universal principles. The marketing hype, the glamour, and the perception of easy money don't encourage traders to pause long enough to ponder and study the key basics of successful trading. Instead, they propel them straight into trading. And not only does the wide choice excite and propel traders toward the markets, but they also have created too much choice and too much complexity, resulting in too much confusion, too much frustration, and too much failure.

Because of this, I believe it's also the worst of times. Traders have been overloaded by the choice available, distracted by the marketing hype and promises of easy riches and have lost sight of the basics that work—the universal principles of successful trading. I hope my contribution will help ground the starry-eyed traders, to bring them back to earth with a healthy dose of reality. I hope the universal principles will make it the best of times for you.

As you now know, the markets are essentially random and maximum adversity will ensure that there are few certainties about them. One certainty I do know is that if you follow the universal principles, you will succeed, if you combine a sensible money management strategy with a simple, objective, and independent positive-expectancy methodology that has been validated using the TEST procedure, you will commence trading with a 0 percent risk of ruin. There is no better place to start trading from. If you can establish professional objectives and modest expectations, you will be emotionally oriented to follow and execute your trade plan. If you acknowledge and remain humble before the market's maximum adversity, you will be well prepared to endure and persevere through the pain it will throw your way.

You now know that trading is no panacea. You know trading is no five-star holiday. I hope you're now aware that trading will require more work than you ever thought imaginable. It's one of trading's little ironies that people can't wait to leave their day jobs and commence trading full time for themselves, but most successful traders are busier then ever, working harder than ever to continually improve. I now hope you're aware that continual successful trading over the longer term will be more about good pain management than good trading. You'll find the trading part easy. It will be managing the constant pain that will be challenging. You'll find it a relentless battle to cope with:

- the pain of losing
- the pain of resisting your strong inclination to close a winning trade to bank a profit
- the pain of leaving imaginary money on the table
- the pain of not being in the market to catch the next big move
- the pain of drawdowns
- the pain of not knowing when the winning trades will come

- the pain of believing everyone else is doing better than you
- the pain of believing everyone else is doing it easier than you
- the pain of impatience
- the pain of wanting everything now
- the pain of continuous research and development that rarely leads to a new profitable idea
- the pain of tiredness
- the pain of never having enough
- the pain of believing everyone else has a better strategy than you
- the pain of never really being satisfied with your methodology
- the pain of continually searching to improve your edge.

If you can manage the pain, then you will enjoy a successful long-term trading career. If not, you'll be destined for the sidelines.

And always be cautious if you catch yourself doing something easy in trading. Remember, it's usually the hard choices that succeed in trading. Studying, learning, and implementing the ideas in this book will be hard. Studying charts to discover repetitive patterns to trade is hard. Reading and researching market theories is hard. Learning a software program to back test strategies is hard. Coding up strategies for back testing is hard. Validating methodologies with the TEST procedure is hard. Calculating your individual risk of ruin is hard. Being quick to take losses is hard. Being slow to bank profits is hard. Trading small is trading without excitement, which is hard. Buying higher highs is hard. Selling lower lows is hard. Doing the work is hard. Defying human nature is hard. Always be wary of the easy option because it's usually the wrong option.

Like a good story, your trading career will resemble a plot with a beginning, a middle, and an end. In the beginning, you will be enthusiastic to make money, in the middle, you will embark on many adventures to secure your trading success, and in the end, you will disappointingly experience failure. However, for a privileged few, their end will just be the beginning of their own story of financial independence, trading for themselves and answering to no one. The universal principles of successful trading also have a beginning, a middle, and an end, and I hope its story will allow you to join the privileged few who succeed in trading.

And please remember, there is no rush for you to commence trading. Take your time with the universal principles. They're all about getting you back to the basics, getting back to fundamental core truths of successful trading. Take your time. No one is going to hand you a gold medal for being the first to place a trade, and while democracies and capitalism survive, there will always be a market waiting for you somewhere with plenty of setups to trade.

So be patient, develop a simple, objective, and independent methodology, validate its expectancy with the TEST procedure, marry it with an anti-Martingale money management strategy, and only when all the boxes are ticked and you have a 0 percent risk of ruin should you consider placing a trade, and not beforehand!

When you do commence trading, please concentrate on being a good loser and a good winner. Be quick to take losses, and be slow to bank profits. And remember, trading's only real secret is: the best loser is the long-term winner.

I wish you good losing.

Brent Penfold
Sydney, Australia

APPENDIX A

Risk-of-Ruin Simulator

The following risk-of-ruin simulator generated the risk-of-ruin simulations shown in appendix C and summarized in chapter 4.

With the help of good friend and fellow trader, Geoff Morgan, I wrote the following model based on our interpretation of the logic shown in appendix B of Nauzer Balsara's *Money Management Strategies for Futures Traders*.

If there are any errors in our interpretation of Balsara's logic, I'll claim them as mine. In addition, be aware that this simulator is just that, a hypothetical simulator. It will give a general impression about the benefits of having a methodology that can produce average wins larger than its average losses, not to provide absolute certainty.

I've written this simulator in Visual Basic for Applications (VBA) for Excel. If you're familiar with VBA and Excel, and have the time and inclination, you may like to write your own model similar to my simulator. Even if you're not familiar with programming you may still find that you'll be able to follow the simulator's script logic (which I have provided in appendix B) as I've tried to write it in plain English.

If you have Excel on your computer you are more than welcome to a copy of my risk-of-ruin simulator. Just contact me through my website (www. IndexTrader.com.au), mention this book and simulator, and I'll send you a copy.

SIMULATOR VARIABLES

The simulator requires you to define the two key characteristics of your methodology—accuracy rate and average win-to-average loss payoff ratio. In chapter 4 and appendix C, I used a 50 percent accuracy rate and began the simulations with a 1:1 average win-to-average loss payoff ratio.

Although the simulator will automatically calculate your expectancy, it's not necessary for simulating risk of ruin. You will also need to define the size of your trading account. I've entered $100. Note that the size of your account is immaterial as probability of ruin is affected by your accuracy rate, average win-to-average loss payoff ratio and money management strategy.

The simulator then requires you to select one of two money management strategies—fixed percentage or fixed risk. Depending on the money management strategy you select, you will need to either define the percentage of your account you would like to risk per trade or the number of units of money you want to divide your account into. In chapter 4 and appendix C, I selected the fixed dollar risk money management strategy and 20 units of money, which meant I risked $5 per trade. Anyone who is comfortable with programming can alter the simulator to include additional money management strategies.

The simulator then requires you to define your interpretation of financial ruin as a percentage of your account drawdown. In chapter 4 and appendix C, I defined financial ruin as a 50 percent account drawdown. Having defined the variables, take a look at the model's logic.

MODEL LOGIC

The simulator's logic is simple. It simulates trading according to your money management strategy and methodology. A random number generator is used to determine whether a trade is a win or a loss. If your methodology has a high accuracy rate, the simulator will generate more winners than losers; however, the random number generator will determine the sequence of wins and losses. After a trade, the model constructs a continuous equity curve measuring the depth of any drawdown. Once a drawdown from a new equity high reaches your defined level of drawdown ruin (like 50 percent), the model will stop and calculate the risk of ruin, using the following formula:

$$\text{Risk of ruin} = \frac{\text{Number of losing trades since the last equity high}}{\text{Total number of trades since the last equity high}}$$

Note that the simulator ignores all trades before the last equity high. This is because the simulator is only interested in trades between the equity high and drawdown ruin level. The simulator wants to know how long it took to reach the drawdown following an equity high as that will determine the risk of ruin.

To avoid placing the model into an infinite loop, the simulator will stop if the predefined ruin drawdown level is not reached before either the equity curve reaches $200 million or the number of trades reaches 10,000. The simulator assumes that financial ruin has been avoided if either is reached.

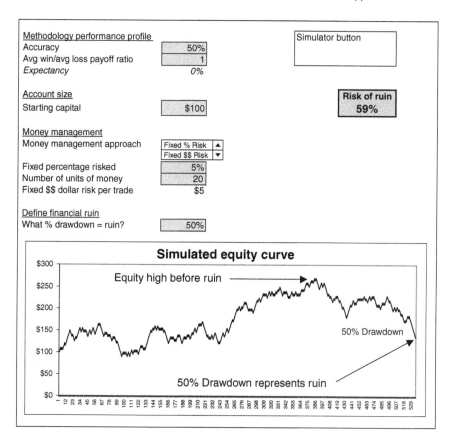

FIGURE A.1   The risk-of-ruin simulator

SIMULATOR

As you can see in figure A.1, the simulator stopped once the 50 percent drawdown was reached, and calculated a 59 percent risk of ruin. This is a very high risk of ruin and one you should prefer not to trade with because it guarantees you'll go bust.

DIY SIMULATOR

For those of you brave enough I've included my simulator's VBA for Excel programming code in appendix B.

B

Risk-of-Ruin Simulator

The following VBA for Excel script is the programming code for my risk-of-ruin simulator shown in appendix A.

If you're not familiar with VBA, don't attempt to create your own risk-of-ruin simulator. As I mentioned in appendix A, you are welcome to a copy of my simulator if you're interested in trading. If you would like to create your own simulator, you'll need to do the following before writing the VBA code.

A note of caution before I begin. I will not be defining every step that you will have to take to duplicate my simulator. I'll provide enough information to help those people familiar with VBA to create their own, but not for people new to programming because providing an introductory VBA lesson is beyond the scope of this book.

DIY VBA RISK-OF-RUIN SIMULATOR

- Open an Excel workbook and rename the first sheet "RiskOfRuin."
- In the "RiskOfRuin" spreadsheet, define the following ranges:

Range name	Position
Accuracy	C4
Payoff	C5
Start_Capital	C9
FixedPercentage	C14
Unit_of_Money	C15
Fixed_Dollar_Risk	C16
Ruin	C19
Money_Mgt_Approach	Y1
Probability	G9

- Position a list box above cell "C12", defined its input range as being "Z1: Z2" and define the link cell as "Y1."
- Enter "Fixed % Risk" in cell "Z1."
- Enter "Fixed $$ Risk" in cell "Z2."
- Go to cell "AA1" and enter random numbers in cells "AA1:AA10" to create the first hypothetical equity curve.
- Create a simple line chart, defining the input range as being the random numbers entered in "AA1:AA10" and position the chart object in the first sheet ("RiskOfRuin") above cell "A20." Resize and format the simple line chart as you see fit.
- Save the workbook as "0_Risk_of_Ruin_Simulator.xls."
- Open the VBA Editor (Alt F11) and create a new procedure called: "Simulate_Risk_of_Ruin."
- Write the following code in the new procedure.

VBA CODE FOR RISK-OF-RUIN SIMULATOR

Write the following:

Define variables

```
Const NoRecords = 10001
Dim TradeResult(NoRecords) As Long
Dim EquityCurve(NoRecords) As Long
Dim Accuracy As Variant
Dim PayOff_Ratio As Variant
Dim Money_Mgt_Approach As String
Dim Fixed_Percent_Risked As Variant
Dim Ruin_Point_Drawdown As Variant
Dim Account_Start As Variant
Dim Account_Balance As Variant
Dim Account_New_High As Variant
Dim Account_DrawDown As Variant
Dim Account_DrawDown_Percent As Variant
Dim Win_or_Loss As Variant
Dim Probility_Of_Ruin As Variant
Dim RowNumber As Variant
Dim Unit_Of_Money As Integer
Dim Fixed_Dollar_Risk As Variant
Dim Number_Of_Trades As Long
Dim Number_of_Losses_Before_Ruin As Long
Dim Number_of_Trades_Since_Account_High As Long
Dim i As Long
Dim j As Long
Dim x As Long
```

Freeze Screen

```
Application.DisplayAlerts = False
Application.ScreenUpdating = False
```

Load Variables from Spreadsheet

```
Load Accuracy Rate
  Sheets("RiskOfRuin").Select
  Range("Accuracy").Select
  Accuracy = Selection

Load the Average Win to Average Loss Payoff Ratio
  Range("Payoff").Select
  PayOff_Ratio = Selection

Load Money Management Approach
  Range("Money_Mgt_Approach").Select
  If ActiveCell = 1 Then
    Money_Mgt_Approach = "Fixed Percentage Risk Money Mgt"
  Else
    Money_Mgt_Approach = "Fixed Dollar Risk Money Mgt"
  End If

Load Starting Account Size
  Range("Start_Capital").Select
  Account_Start = Selection

Load Fixed Percentage Rate of account balance risked on each trade
  Range("FixedPercentage").Select
  Fixed_Percent_Risked = Selection

Load the percentage DrawDown rate we define ruin as
  Range("Ruin").Select
  Ruin_Point_Drawdown = Selection

Load the number of units of money we have in our account
  Range("Unit_Of_Money").Select
  Unit_Of_Money = Selection
```

Clear the Arrays

```
For i = 1 To NoRecords
  TradeResult(i) = Empty
  EquityCurve(i) = 0
Next i
```

Begin Simulating Probability of Ruin

```
Number_Of_Trades = 1
Account_Balance = Account_Start
Account_New_High = Account_Start
```

```
Account_DrawDown_Percent = 0
Number_of_Losses_Before_Ruin = 0
Fixed_Dollar_Risk = Account_Start / Unit_Of_Money

i = 1
j = 1
x = 0

Do Until Account_DrawDown_Percent >= Ruin_Point_Drawdown Or EquityCurve
(i - 1) > 200000000 Or x >= 10000
  Check For New Equity High and reset number of losing trades to zero

    If Account_Balance > Account_New_High Then
        Account_New_High = Account_Balance
        Number_of_Losses_Before_Ruin = 0
        Number_of_Trades_Since_Account_High = 0
    End If

Generate random number to see whether a trade wins or loses
    Win_or_Loss = Rnd

Check for a Win
    If Win_or_Loss >= (1 - Accuracy) Then
    We have a WIN!
      Calculate the profit
      If Money_Mgt_Approach = "Fixed Percentage Risk Money Mgt" Then
          TradeResult(j) = ((Fixed_Percent_Risked * Account_Balance)
                      * PayOff_Ratio)
      End If

    If Money_Mgt_Approach = "Fixed Dollar Risk Money Mgt" Then
        TradeResult(j) = Fixed_Dollar_Risk * PayOff_Ratio
    End If

    Add to the equity curve
    If i = 1 Then
        EquityCurve(i) = Account_Start
        i = i + 1
        EquityCurve(i) = EquityCurve(i - 1) + TradeResult(j)
    Else
        EquityCurve(i) = EquityCurve(i - 1) + TradeResult(j)
    End If

    Add to our account balance
        Account_Balance = Account_Balance + TradeResult(j)
    Else

We have a LOSS!
    Calculate the loss
    If Money_Mgt_Approach = "Fixed Percentage Risk Money Mgt" Then
        TradeResult(j) = -(Fixed_Percent_Risked * Account_Balance)
    End If
```

```
If Money_Mgt_Approach = "Fixed Dollar Risk Money Mgt" Then
    TradeResult(j) = -Fixed_Dollar_Risk
End If

Add to the equity curve
    If i = 1 Then
        EquityCurve(i) = Account_Start
        i = i + 1
        EquityCurve(i) = EquityCurve(i - 1) + TradeResult(j)
    Else
        EquityCurve(i) = EquityCurve(i - 1) + TradeResult(j)
    End If

Add to our account balance
    Account_Balance = Account_Balance + TradeResult(j)

Calculate current drawdown and percentage drawdown
    Account_DrawDown = Account_New_High - Account_Balance
    Account_DrawDown_Percent = Account_DrawDown / Account_New_High

Calculate the number of losses before ruin
    Number_of_Losses_Before_Ruin = Number_of_Losses_Before_Ruin + 1

End If
Calculate number of trades
    Number_Of_Trades = Number_Of_Trades + 1
    Number_of_Trades_Since_Account_High
    =Number_of_Trades_Since_Account_High+1

Increase counters
x = x + 1
j = j + 1
i = i + 1
Loop
```

Calculate Probability of Ruin

```
Probility_Of_Ruin=Number_of_Losses_Before_Ruin/Number_of_Trades_
Since_Account_High
```
If the Equity Curve is above $200m or we have simulated 10,000 trades then we will
```
    assume ruin has been avoided.
      If EquityCurve(i - 1) > 200000000 Or x >= 10000 Then
          Probility_Of_Ruin = 0
      End If
    Enter Probability of Ruin in Spreadsheet
          Sheets("RiskOfRuin").Select
          Range("Probability").Select
          ActiveCell = Probility_Of_Ruin
          Selection.Style = "Percent"
```

Print Equity Curve

```
Clear Previous Equity Curve
    Columns("AA:AA").Select
    Selection.Clear

Print Equity Curve in Spreadsheet - Column AA
    i = 1
Do Until i >= Number_Of_Trades + 1
    Sheets(1).Cells(i, 27).Value = EquityCurve(i)
    i = i + 1
Loop
Change Chart Range
    Range("AA1").Select
    Selection.End(xlDown).Select
    RowNumber = ActiveCell.Row
    ActiveSheet.ChartObjects("Chart 1").Activate
    ActiveChart.PlotArea.Select
    ActiveChart.SeriesCollection(1).Values =
        "=RiskOfRuin!R1C27:R" & RowNumber & "C27"
    ActiveWindow.Visible = False
    Windows("0_Risk_of_Ruin_Simulator.xls").Activate

Move cursor to the Probability of Ruin calculation
    Range("B22").Select
```

Refresh Screen

```
    Application.DisplayAlerts = True
    Application.ScreenUpdating = True
End of Simulator
End Sub
```

Return to Excel Workbook

- Return to the "RiskOfRuin" spreadsheet and add a macro button above cell "F3" and assign the macro "Simulate_Risk_of_Ruin." Label the button "Simulate Risk of Ruin."
- Save the file.
- Enter input values into the spreadsheet, hit the "Simulate Risk of Ruin" macro button and start debugging!

If you have any problems, you can contact me at my website www. IndexTrader.com.au.

Remember, your objective is to marry a proper money management strategy with a validated methodology that when combined produces a statistical 0 percent risk of ruin. Anything above 0 percent will be fatal. All the best with it.

APPENDIX C

Risk-of-Ruin Simulations

Table A3.1 summarises 30 risk-of-ruin simulations for various average win-to-average loss payoff ratios. These simulations demonstrate the effectiveness of increasing a methodology's average win-to-average loss payoff ratio to reduce the probability of financial ruin. See appendix A for the model used to create these simulations.

	Simulated Risk-of-Ruin					
	Average win to average loss payoff ratio					
	1.0	1.1	1.2	1.3	1.4	1.5
Simulation 1	66%	0%	0%	0%	0%	0%
Simulation 2	63%	0%	0%	0%	71%	0%
Simulation 3	66%	0%	0%	77%	0%	0%
Simulation 4	56%	79%	0%	68%	0%	0%
Simulation 5	54%	80%	73%	82%	0%	0%
Simulation 6	65%	0%	0%	60%	0%	0%
Simulation 7	62%	0%	63%	0%	73%	0%
Simulation 8	60%	77%	66%	0%	0%	0%
Simulation 9	68%	0%	0%	0%	0%	0%
Simulation 10	81%	0%	0%	0%	0%	0%
Simulation 11	61%	0%	82%	0%	0%	0%
Simulation 12	71%	0%	68%	0%	0%	0%
Simulation 13	70%	0%	0%	0%	0%	0%
Simulation 14	62%	0%	0%	65%	0%	0%
Simulation 15	57%	73%	0%	0%	0%	0%
Simulation 16	65%	0%	0%	0%	0%	0%
Simulation 17	85%	0%	68%	0%	0%	0%
Simulation 18	66%	0%	64%	0%	0%	0%

(continued)

Simulation 19	58%	0%	58%	0%	0%	0%
Simulation 20	65%	0%	78%	59%	0%	0%
Simulation 21	63%	0%	0%	69%	0%	0%
Simulation 22	65%	64%	0%	62%	0%	0%
Simulation 23	60%	69%	70%	0%	0%	0%
Simulation 24	68%	0%	0%	0%	0%	0%
Simulation 25	57%	0%	67%	0%	0%	0%
Simulation 26	61%	0%	74%	0%	0%	0%
Simulation 27	53%	0%	58%	0%	0%	0%
Simulation 28	69%	87%	61%	0%	0%	0%
Simulation 29	52%	0%	0%	0%	0%	0%
Simulation 30	60%	66%	0%	78%	0%	0%
Average risk of ruin	64%	20%	32%	21%	5%	0%

INDEX

www.IndexTrader.com.au

SPI • NIKKEI • TAIWAN • HANG SENG • DAX • FTSE • NASDAQ • S&P500
Euro Currency • British Pounds • Japanese Yen • Swiss Francs • Australian Dollars

Visit Brent Penfold's website to obtain more information about his products and services.

Brent is a trader first and foremost, and on his website he provides trading solutions that he personally trades with his own money, in real markets, in real time. Whether you are new to trading or a veteran, you'll find plenty of interest on IndexTrader .com.au. If your preference is to find simple mechanical trading solutions, or to discover a daily newsletter with an edge, you will not be disappointed.

On Brent's website you can obtain IndexALERT™, a daily newsletter that provides trading recommendations on global index futures, and ForexALERT™, a daily newsletter that provides trading recommendations on currency futures. Within each newsletter are specific trading recommendations, which include:

- exact entry levels
- exact stop levels
- exact exit levels
- estimated dollar risk per signal.

With IndexALERT™ and ForexALERT™ there is no ambiguity in how to execute a trade. Included with the newsletters is a complete disclosure of Brent's personal fills as he trades every recommendation in both newsletters.

Brent offers a 21-day free trial, so potential subscribers can monitor Index ALERT's™ and ForexALERT's™ performance in real time. As a special promotion for *The Universal Principles of Successful Trading* if readers enter "0% ROR" (0 per cent risk-of-ruin) when they request a trial of either IndexALERT™ or Forex ALERT™, Brent will extend the free trial offer to 28 days!